The Killing *of*
Major Denis Mahon

ALSO BY PETER DUFFY

The Bielski Brothers

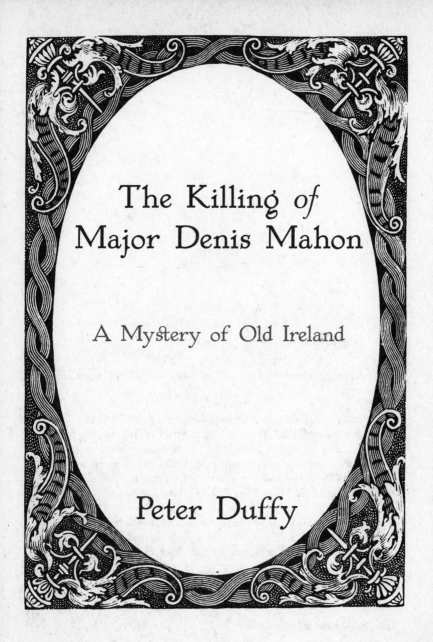

The Killing of Major Denis Mahon

A Mystery of Old Ireland

Peter Duffy

HARPER ● PERENNIAL

NEW YORK ● LONDON ● TORONTO ● SYDNEY ● NEW DELHI ● AUCKLAND

HARPER ● PERENNIAL

A hardcover edition of this book was published in 2007 by HarperCollins Publishers.

HarperCollins books may be purchased for educational, business, or sales promotional use. For information please write: Special Markets Department, HarperCollins Publishers, 10 East 53rd Street, New York, NY 10022.

FIRST HARPER PERENNIAL EDITION PUBLISHED 2008.

Designed by Mary Austin Speaker

Library of Congress Cataloging-in-Publication Data is available upon request.

ISBN 978-0-06-084051-8

08 09 10 11 12 ID/RRD 10 9 8 7 6 5 4 3 2 1

In memory of my mother

Contents

Prologue *ix*

CHAPTER 1   The Consent of Things   *1*

CHAPTER 2   Until Decisive Steps Are Taken   *25*

CHAPTER 3   In the Name of God Do Something for Us   *58*

CHAPTER 4   Good and Willing; Idle and Bad   *73*

CHAPTER 5   The Supernumerary Portion of the Inhabitants   *91*

CHAPTER 6   Quiet and Peaceable Possession   *109*

CHAPTER 7   Wretched, Sickly, Miserable   *123*

CHAPTER 8   Upon Their Devoted Heads Let the Result Lye   *136*

CHAPTER 9   That Flame Which Now Rages   *150*

CHAPTER 10   Guilty of the Blood of the Murdered Major Mahon   *164*

CHAPTER 11   Decided Measures   *183*

CHAPTER 12   *Summum Jus, Summa Injuria*   *204*

CHAPTER 13   So Injudicious a Course   *225*

CHAPTER 14   Conspire, Confederate, and Agree Together   *237*

CHAPTER 15   It Has Been Indeed, Really Proved   *263*

CHAPTER 16   This Melancholy Exhibition of Human Suffering   *282*

Epilogue   *295*

Notes   *313*

Acknowledgments   *343*

Index   *345*

Prologue

IN THE EARLY EVENING of November 2, 1847, an Anglo-Irish landlord from County Roscommon was driving a horse-drawn carriage through his property when a single gunshot was fired from a ditch on the right side of the road. With lead balls and slugs piercing his torso, Major Denis Mahon fell backward, his hat tumbling from his head. His lifeless body came to rest in the arms of the coachman, Martin Flanagan, who had yielded his place to his employer at the beginning of the trip. The Catholic doctor sitting to Major Mahon's left caught one of the balls in his arm, but he was well enough to grab the reins and steady the shocked horses. In the next instant, Dr. Terence Shanley noticed a second shooter to the left of the vehicle. The man aimed his gun and pulled the trigger. The weapon misfired. The two nearly indistinct conspirators then dashed into the darkness.

The crime occurred at a turning point in one of the great tragedies of all time. It had been precisely two years since the *Phytophthora infestans* water mold first attacked the Irish potato plant,
decimating the supply of a foodstuff that almost exclusively kept
the rural population from perishing each year. By the time of the
murder, the wealthiest and most powerful nation on the planet,
which had responded to the crisis with a series of bureaucratically
intricate relief plans of mixed utility, was in the process of severely
contracting its involvement in an aid effort that required expansion.
It was among the most disastrous decisions in the history of modern governance. The British Parliament was hoping that landlords
would shoulder the entire burden, but many landed proprietors like
Major Mahon had already given up on the poor of their estates.
While he had initially reacted to the blight with a degree of charitable concern that was universal in Britain and the rest of the world—
he served as chairman of a local relief committee; he distributed
Indian meal to his poor; he resisted what he called the "extremity"
of evictions; he paid for the passage of one thousand poor tenants
to America—since the summer he had heeded the insistent advice
of his chief lieutenant, a land agent named John Ross Mahon, who
was of no relation. The landlord had approved the removal of an
additional two thousand tenants by either offering them a pound or
two to go quietly or by sending the sheriff to evict them from their
miserable cottages. At the time of the assassination, the Mahon
estate in Strokestown had dislodged roughly three thousand of its
twelve thousand tenants. The plan was to remove an additional six
thousand starving people over the coming months, completing the
process of reforming an overpopulated property that had been mismanaged for decades.

The protest of one gunshot could not halt the march of catastrophe brought about by a brutal amalgamation of natural and
human forces. Mass death was now descending on Ireland, eventually accounting for a loss of life that would far exceed the totals,
in ratio and in actual numbers, from the African famines of recent

decades. An entire segment of peasant society was disappearing from the countryside. Tiny settlements of subsistence farmers that clung to ways of administration indigenous to an older Ireland were being swept from the earth, replaced by the pastures needed to graze sheep and cattle in the more modern economy of a new Ireland. Many survivors from these lands were joining a mass exodus of Irish men and women for far-off places, a flood that would last for more than a century and a half and turn parts of countries like the United States into hybrid versions of hazily remembered communities back home. As a spray of fire ended the life of Major Denis Mahon in the miserable days of Black '47, the future of tens of millions of people was being determined.

Even 160 years after its occurrence, the Great Irish Famine of 1845–1850 continues to be a controversial episode with varying interpretations. To many of Irish and (particularly) Irish-American descent, it has been seen as the most lethal act of savagery in the long and unjust dominion over Ireland by its more powerful neighbor. Through emotive stories told of grain shipments traveling out of the famished country, cruel evictions occurring with the aid of uniformed officers, relief initiatives being suddenly halted, and disease-ridden "coffin ships" pulling into foreign ports, generations were taught that the British were deliberate murderers unambiguously intent on the elimination of a race of people they despised. But this view was not shared by everyone, particularly the careful Irish academic establishment, which was apt to exonerate misguided but essentially well meaning British officials of purposefully causing a million deaths, instead viewing the devastation as the result of Ireland's poverty, social inequity, and agricultural backwardness. In recent years a consensus of a new generation of scholars has placed greater emphasis on the government's willful failures while at the same time acknowledging the array of factors that led to the loss of life, taking portions from both schools of thought. Yet no expert on the Famine is willing to go so far as accuse the Whig government of Lord John Russell of the crime of genocide, a charge leveled by such diverse commentators as the left-wing singer Sinéad O'Connor and the right-wing former governor of New York, George Pataki. Indeed, it is usually *Irish* writers and professors who offer their voices in opposition to such views, a signal that any extreme conclusions about the event must be made with considerable deliberation.

Unlike many national tragedies experienced by dominated peoples, then, the story of the Famine remains a matter of contention lacking a settled-upon story line even within the community of descendants. The same uncertainly surrounds the death of Major Mahon, which, with the conversion of the landlord's house into Ireland's national Famine Museum in 1994, has emerged as a representative event from the time. A prominent scholar of Ireland's past, Oliver MacDonagh, aptly summed up the case by describing it as "disputed." While some regard Major Mahon as a pitiless evictor of starving widows and children who deserved what was coming to him—the position, as it happens, taken by the British prime minister in the weeks after the shooting—others saw him as a sympathetic figure much beloved of his tenants. In fact, this is the folkloric determination of the Strokestown community and the longtime contention of the Mahon family, both of whom had to live with one another for more than a century after the Famine. This tradition alleges that the land agent (or consultant) John Ross Mahon was the intended target of the killers, the true villain of the piece. But another interpretation of equal significance says that the murderers were vengeful tenants who not only intended to kill Major Mahon but were inspired to do so by a ferocious denunciation delivered by the local priest, Father Michael McDermott, on the day previous to the act. Pope Pius IX himself was told this story during a series of meetings with a British envoy that autumn and winter. (A related tale in the folklore alleges that supernatural forces killed the landlord after he made the mistake of quarreling with the priest.) The other predominant analysis charges that the killers were members of a secret society of agrarian bandits known as the

Molly Maguires, a band of criminals with a system of oaths and disguises who would have needed no particular motivation to lash out. It isn't surprising that some merely throw up their hands and noted, as a Strokestown storyteller did in the 1930s, that "no reason for the dastardly crime was ever discovered."

The Mahon case is one of the great mysteries of Irish history, not only because it remains an unsatisfactorily explained crime with widely diverse readings. No, it is significant because its narrative contains *the* story of the Famine—the successive failures of the staple food crop, the government relief efforts (which were intended to be carried out in significant measure by local figures of authority), the harsh clearances of those unable to pay rent, and the harrowing journeys aboard emigrant ships. In conducting a full examination of the most celebrated death of the era, it is therefore necessary to tell the entire contentious tale of the Great Hunger itself. The author's intention in writing this book is to arrive at sound judgment about the latter by coming to the truth about the former.

CHAPTER I

The Consent of Things

Periculum fortitudini evasi.
Fortitude has preserved me from danger.
—MAHON FAMILY MOTTO

THE VERY NAME STROKESTOWN commemorates conflict. It is an anglicization of Ballynamully, which is derived from the Gaelic Irish language phrase meaning "the mouth of the ford of the strokes." Upon such a location on the town's river, warfare—strokes of battle—flared between rival groups of native clansmen, who, however, were reputed to use sticks to attack each other rather than more lethal weapons. Legend tells us that the Maol Mitchell, or Mulmitchell, family was the ruling authority over the vicinity from "the dawn of civilization," according to local historian Walter Jones. The Mulmitchells' principal rivals were the famed O'Conor clan, the high kings of Connacht. If the rivalry between the O'Conors and the Mulmitchells did not give the town its name, it lived up to it. Jones writes that the battles between the two families extended for generations.

The fights continued through the centuries when English rule, first introduced by the Anglo-Norman invasion in the twelfth century, was reducing the power and influence of the Gaelic chieftains throughout Ireland. Jones reports that in the fifteenth century the O'Conors finally succeeded in defeating the Mulmitchells. After twenty years in exile in County Clare, the Mulmitchells commenced a campaign to dislodge the O'Conors from their former home. Forming an alliance with the followers of Maguire, the King of Fermanagh, the Mulmitchells' army marched upon their old castle, "breathing a vengeance deadly," according to a poem commemorating the event. The O'Conors learned of the impending strike and fled to a nearby fortification. Unaware of the deceit, the Mulmitchells and their allies torched the landmark with "a sheet of fire, like an Indian's pyre."

> The Castle of O'Conor,
> The chief of endless fame,
> Soon hid its head
> In mantle red
> Of fierce and rushing flame.

But the chief of endless fame had left his infant son behind. The poem describes how the crowd watching the progress of the blaze heard the screams of the youngster "over the crackling din." A giant by the name of O'Murray was moved by the cries.

> There was a warlike giant
> Among the listening throng,
> He gazed with face defiant
> On the flames so bright and strong;
> Then rushed into the castle,
> And up the rocky stair;
> But alas! Alas!—
> He could not pass

To the burning infant there.
The walls were tottering under.
The flames were whirling around,
The walls went down in thunder,
And dashed him to the ground
Up in the burning chamber
For ever died that scream,
And the fire sprang out–
With a wilder shout,
A fiercer, ghastlier gleam.

The fire raged out of control, spreading throughout the countryside—"it glared o'er hill and hollow"—until, exhausted by its exertions, it "sank in gloom, with a whirling boom, and all was dark again."

By the sixteenth century, the castle's surroundings were occupied by an amalgam of descendants of native clans of old (the O'Conors and others) and of the Anglo-Normans (the Dillons and others), who, now referred to as the Old English, had long ago adopted the language, customs, and religion of the natives. Later that century, the Gaelic and Old English populations of Ireland, both Catholic, joined together against a new generation of invaders, the aggressive New English, Protestant colonizers of the Elizabethan age. But the carnage that occurred the following century, bringing additional victories for the great power to the east, signaled the final end of the rule of the Gaelic chiefs. In 1641 the native Irish and Old English led a bloody rising against the New English and Protestant establishment, the battles beginning in Ulster and spreading in a destructive wake southward. In 1649 Oliver Cromwell, whose Parliamentary forces had defeated the armies of King Charles I during the concurrent English Civil War, arrived in Ireland to aid his coreligionists—the Irish factions pledged loyalty to the king rather than the ferociously anti-Catholic Cromwell—and crush the resistance. His campaign of slaughter, which he led for just nine months before turning over control and returning home, would live forever in Irish infamy, an emblem of sectarian and national hatred. His forces achieved victory at Galway in May 1652.

The environs of County Roscommon, in the lush inland sector known as the Irish Midlands, were "pacified" in part by the Cromwellian forces led by Sir Charles Coote, who was implicated in atrocities against Catholic forces and cursed by his opponents as a "thrice-cruel butcher and human bloodsucker." Like Cromwellian soldiers throughout Ireland, Coote's men were rewarded for their success in battle with extensive tracts of land taken from "non-innocent" Catholics, an efficient way to ensure that military vic-

tory would take on the cast of permanence. One officer in Coote's army helped organize the distribution of the land in the vicinity of Ballynamully and throughout County Roscommon, emerging in the process as a prominent man of the new establishment. Nicholas Mahon was not a member of an English or Scottish family like many of his fellow servicemen, but was of impeccably Irish blood, a descendant of the ancient princes of Munster, according to family lore. He was probably a recent convert from Catholicism to Protestantism, and may have originally been a supporter of King Charles I, jumping sides when he saw that Cromwell was headed for victory. Scholar Susan Hood, who has studied the area's deeds from the 1650s, believes that Mahon, though recorded as the principal man of standing in an area not far from Ballynamully, was "not necessarily a landowner" in the years immediately following the conquest, meaning that he had not received a land grant. At least not yet.

In 1660 the monarchy was restored to power, and Mahon, like many of his station, duly changed his allegiances and pledged loyalty to Charles II. His position in society was preserved; indeed, it was enhanced. He enthusiastically took to cementing the king's rule in the region, serving as a collector of taxes and as the high sheriff of County Roscommon in 1663 and 1665, the very symbol of law and order during an uncertain time. He also assumed the task of hunting down rebels who persisted in opposing the new administration, including a band of prominent Irish Catholics led by a defiant figure named Dualtagh (or Dudley) Costello. His group had fled to Europe during the Cromwellian incursions and had returned to reclaim their lands following the Restoration of the Crown—as promised by the monarch. But it emerged that only the most noble and prominent Catholic families would regain any portion of their property. Certainly not the likes of Costello and his men. They remained enemies.

In a declaration written in March 1666, the Costello rebels proclaimed that they were "innocent Catholic subjects . . . kept out of our estates and abridged of our due liberties but for our being Papists."

They added, "We therefore do, in the name of Jesus Christ under whose banner we resolve to live and die, unanimously declare that the Pope's Holiness is Supreme Head of Christ's Church militant on earth, and that with our swords drawn will stand against and oppose such as believe the contrary and do so unjustly rob us of our due liberties of conscience and right." In a subsequent letter, Costello described the fact that he had been designated a traitor without being questioned or summoned as "so base a practice" that "a man of honor would die sooner" than act in such a way. Costello's war ended in the spring of 1667, when Nicholas Mahon himself succeeded in killing him, proving that he was a hands-on conqueror. He "robbed and skulled" the rebel, in the evocative description of a superior's report, in a battle near a river during which three of Costello's men were also killed.

All this devotion to the king came with a significant reward, as Mahon surely anticipated. He received his land grant, which included thousands of acres spread throughout County Roscommon in a patchwork of tracts occupied by a native population of agricultural farmers and laborers who spoke a different tongue— "our people," as the last descendant of Nicholas Mahon to live on the property called them in 1982. These peasants had suffered considerably during the warfare and confiscation of the previous decades, a time when a significant portion of Ireland's population, along with much of its farmland and industrial capacity, was decimated. As a consequence of their marginal status, the people of Mahon's new property depended increasingly on the nutrient-rich potato, which was able to be grown on small plots of inhospitable land in poor weather, providing enough sustenance (with a bit of buttermilk) to feed an entire family for the year. Disdained by the rest of European society as a lowly nightshade of no aesthetic worth—it didn't have the majestic qualities of grain, which miraculously transformed into bread—the potato was the perfect foodstuff for the circumstances of the Irish peasant. It seemed to offer, in the phrase of its great chronicler, Redcliffe Salaman, protection from "the vagaries of nature and the malignity of man."

The centerpiece of the family's sprawling new possessions was to be the Mahon residence. With several years of surveying the county behind him, Mahon knew exactly where he wanted to construct his family home: the site of the ruins of Ballynamully Castle. As befitting a military man who wasn't certain that his victory was complete, Mahon constructed an edifice that had more in common with his warrior past than his descendants' more restful future. He erected a fortresslike "bawn" that encircled a courtyard and residence with high walls, while at the same time, according to family tradition, he began construction on a larger house using the remnants of the castle's wall as a foundation.

But he was interested in more than a comfortable home. He set out to build a town, a planned development, that would lie to the west of the bawn, in an area that apparently did not contain much of a settlement in the years after Mahon's arrival. His creation would be a center of agricultural commerce from which he and his heirs would profit, a place through which all the commercial activity of the region, *his* region, would flow. In 1671 he received a royal patent permitting a weekly market and two annual fairs "to the intent that the ... inhabitants might have a free commerce and traffick amongst themselves and with others, by buying and exchanging commodities and merchandise," it reads. Further, "all issues, tolls, customs, profits" from this economic activity would be earmarked for the Mahon family. Over the final decade of Nicholas Mahon's life, the fledgling community grew to include a few buildings, an Anglican Church of Ireland school and parish, and three or four mills on the town's river, a principal industry.

Nicholas Mahon's transformation into a Protestant pillar of English rule, a landed gentleman with his own provincial seat, was nearly complete. He and his family had been elevated in the years after the Restoration of the king into the ranks of the few thousand families who owned most of Ireland and effectively served as its rulers for generations to come—the Protestant "Ascendancy." Still, a persis-

tent remnant of his past remained unchanged by his new prominence: the Catholicism of his wife, the former Magdalene French.
She declined to convert, even turning the ruins of a twelfth-century
chapel near the bawn into a working house of worship. For several
years Catholic clergy celebrated Mass within its ancient walls. This
link to the past was severed when Mrs. Mahon died. The children
would be raised "in the fear of God and in the Protestant religion,"
in the words of Nicholas's will, and the little outpost of Catholicism
within sight of the Mahon home fell into disrepair. But local people
kept its memory alive. The story goes that when the family tried to
dismantle the chapel many years later, "a mysterious voice called on
the workmen to return every stone to its original position," according to a storyteller. "Promptly the order was obeyed and for years
the building remained untouched by the vandal's hand."

Nicholas Mahon's children were born after he had already been
recognized as a "principal man of standing" in County Roscommon. His eldest son and heir, John, was just seventeen years old
when the patriarch died in 1680, never knowing anything of life
before Strokestown, as it was now being called, was his family's
possession. His path had already been established to mirror his
father's: By age twenty-three he was the high sheriff of Roscommon, regarded as a man "of very good repute and descended from
a loyal father." He opposed, probably without much consideration,
the ascension of James II, a Catholic, to the English throne in
1685, since the prospect of a king friendly to Catholic interests
jeopardized all the Protestant gains of the previous decades. He
certainly favored James's usurpation by the Calvinist William III
(William of Orange), and lent his steadfast support to the followers of William in the war against James's Jacobite, Catholic
soldiers that commenced in Ireland in 1689. The ferocious warfare between the Jacobites and the Williamites continued until
1691—"King Billy" himself commanded the victorious forces
against James and his men at the never-forgotten Battle of the

Boyne in July 1690—when the Treaty of Limerick cemented English Protestant control over Irish life.

John Mahon veered from his father's ways, although not significantly, by inaugurating a new family tradition: serving in the unrepresentative Irish Parliament. He was elected to a County Roscommon seat by the handful of male landholders, nearly all Protestant, who cast ballots in a county that was 90 percent Catholic. (Catholics would officially lose the right to vote in 1728.) He proved himself a strong supporter of His Majesty, joining in a legislative initiative to protect King William from an assassination plot, and an opponent of Catholic resurgence, participating in a (failed) campaign charging a high official with showing favoritism toward "papists." Far more significant, Mahon was present during the passage of the discriminatory Penal Laws, the ultimate attempt to wipe out the Catholic Church, which had been established in the island by St. Patrick in the fifth century. (Also targeted, although to a lesser extent, were Protestant "dissenters" of Presbyterian and other denominations). Scholars note that the enactments were haphazardly enforced and often ignored in a land where Catholics were already unable to mount a serious challenge to the Protestant order. Over time, with the restrictions relaxing in the 1720s, the Catholic Church emerged from the shadows and a dynamic Catholic middle class flourished. Nonetheless, many of the laws were shockingly extreme.

Catholics were prohibited from voting, practicing law, serving in the army or navy, or sitting in Parliament. Catholic children were forbidden from traveling abroad for schooling, and Catholics and Protestants were banned from marrying each other. Catholic nobles, the few still around, were forced to give up their guns, swords, and any horses worth more than 5 pounds. According to a 1697 law, members of the Catholic hierarchy (bishops and archbishops) and religious orders (monks and friars) were banished from the kingdom under the threat of imprisonment. Parish priests were allowed to remain and officiate at Mass, but only if they registered with the authorities. In 1704, in a major blow to those attempting to hold on to their property, Catholics were forbidden from owning land, from holding a lease exceeding thirty-one years, from inheriting land from a Protestant, and from bequeathing property to a single heir, instead forced to divide it among all their sons.

The Church struggled to cope with the laws in the early years. While the authorities never attempted a formal campaign to end public worship, which continued on a discreet basis, they did much to make life difficult for clergymen. In 1709 the bishop of the Diocese of Elphin, whose territory included Mahon's lands, wrote a breathless letter to his superiors in Rome that sounded like a desperate plea from a hunted man. "I have visited and consoled not alone my diocesan priests, but many others almost fed up and disgusted with life, harassed not alone in temporal matters, but, which is worse, in spiritual matters and in conscience," wrote Bishop Ambrose Mac Dermott, who noted that he was hiding in a hovel on a mountain. "Unheard of and horrible things, false accusations, sly suggestions and craftiness evermore resorted to in order to completely uproot our holy religion." He complained of his uncomfortable living circumstances, describing how he had to pay a messenger to travel a mile and a half to bring him water and how he couldn't afford to secure the services of a horse or a servant. "Milk is available, but no beer," he wrote. "A little light beer would be a gift!"

The bishop was distressed by a law that passed earlier that year, John Mahon's final one in Parliament. It required parish priests to go beyond simply declaring their "allegiance," a previous requirement, and forced them to take an oath of "renunciation," which, among other things, compelled them to repudiate transubstantiation, a core belief of Roman Catholicism. It was a horrifying thought for many. "I have used all possible means, explaining the gravity of the sin, the penalty for perjury on the one hand and on the other hand the denial of the faith inherent in said oath," the bishop wrote. "I fear that unless God prevents it, the Catholic religion will be totally destroyed. The few missionaries who are here are doing a lot of good but they will be forced to leave if things don't change, because they cannot live. I know for certain that they cannot spend two nights in one place (on my arrival I too was unable to spend two nights in the same place), each one fearing the rigor of the law."

Two years later a County Roscommon magistrate reported that he had "secured and delivered into the gaoler's custody" priests of several parishes on Mahon's lands, apparently for refusing to comply with the 1709 law. The group included men who were close to Nicholas Mahon's late wife. Father Thady McGreal of Lisanuffy parish, one of those jailed, was granted 20 shillings in her will. Father Terence Rory of the Kilglass parish, also named in her will, was exempted from the prison cell "by reason of his infirmities," the magistrate, John Kelly, wrote, and because "he gave sufficient security for his good behavior." A subsequent letter that same month noted, "We know of no priests in the County Roscommon who have taken the oath, though they were summoned, but we will use our utmost endeavors to put in execution against them." Only thirty-three priests, out of more than a thousand registered with the authorities, took the oath of renunciation in Ireland.

If these years would be remembered with sorrow or anger or equanimity by subsequent generations of Catholics, they would be recalled more fondly by the Mahon family. John oversaw the completion of a two-story block structure of classical design, located adjacent to the bawn, that his father had first started building thirty years earlier. (A stone on which the date 1696 was written was placed on the structure, and according to an "unbroken family tradition," the date refers to the year it was completed rather than when construction began.) He also began designing extensive formal gardens on the far side of the bawn from the new home, a place where the family would cultivate fruits and vegetables and enjoy leisurely strolls on pleasant summer afternoons.

But John Mahon's successful stewardship was interrupted by his early death in 1708 at age forty-six. He appears to have fallen ill in the early 1700s, serving on only two parliamentary committees in 1703 and 1705. His eldest son and heir, Nicholas, was just a schoolboy at the time, presenting the family its first succession crisis. The court-supervised trustees of the property—John's wife and two brothers—did have difficulty renewing leases, but the estate sustained itself until young Nicholas Mahon came of age in 1721 and set about restoring order. His time, however, was short. In 1734 he died at age thirty-four, possibly from the smallpox that took the life of his young wife the previous year. Without a ready male heir, his younger brother, Thomas, thirty-three, assumed the responsibilities. It was a fortuitous happenstance. For Thomas would evolve into the most influential Mahon outside of the founding patriarch to serve as the family's chief, which he did for nearly fifty years until his death in 1782.

In short, it was Thomas Mahon who created modern Strokestown. His portrait, which shows him as a bewigged eighteenth-century man of standing, occupied a prominent spot in the Mahon home for decades, a silent reminder of the achievements of his era. It was he who would guide the family through the height of its history, a time of comfort and prosperity when the looming tragedies of the future were far from vision. Like many of his class, he aspired to more than just wealth. He had lofty ideas touched by a spirit of grandiosity. He wanted to make his mark.

He began his tenure hewing closely to the example of his forebears. He married a young woman from a prominent family of the Anglo-Irish aristocracy, reaping the benefits of his father-in-law's (vast) wealth and political connections. He took up the almost hereditary post of high sheriff for County Roscommon and secured himself a seat in the Irish Parliament, although, uncharacteristically for the family, he needed two chances to win election. And he set out to enhance the profitability of his family's holdings, the ultimate goal of every Mahon.

He established two additional fair days in town, to add to the two instituted by his grandfather, and built a new market house to accommodate the expected increase in activity. He worked to enhance the town's principal industries of brewing—it had three breweries at one point—linen production, and milling, aiding their growth by offering generous leases of long duration and other incentives to the men who operated the businesses. And he guided the output of his farmlands in the production of the raw products needed for these industries. Through his work in Parliament, where he served nearly continuously for decades, he proved adept at bringing improvement projects to his home region, including initiatives to upgrade navigation on the Shannon River, modernize roads throughout the county, and construct a courthouse in Roscommon town.

Within thirty years of first taking over, Thomas had turned Strokestown into a successful regional market town, helped by an Irish economy that was thriving on its agricultural exports to England and elsewhere in Europe. The Mahons' town was one of the most productive suppliers of bleached cloth in the west of Ireland and enjoyed a reputation for the high quality of its product. The family was taking in three times the amount of rental money it had collected forty years earlier, and a Dublin writer visited to gaze upon what he called the "fine improvements in Stroakstown [sic]." Thomas Mahon, the writer commented, "gives employment to a great number of people . . . and withholds no encouragement from such as build good houses . . . or extend its linen manufacture." It was all evidence that he was a responsible resident landlord, rather than the loathed "absentee" of Irish folklore.

By the 1770s Thomas unveiled the two great achievements of his life. The first was the town's most distinctive feature, mentioned by every travel writer from then to today: its 147-foot-wide main street. Ostensibly created to accommodate the increased traffic of market days, the thoroughfare reputedly had a much more grandiose inspiration: Thomas patterned it after the Ringstrasse in Vienna, the celebrated boulevard of the great European capital. Beginning from the site of a Church of Ireland structure (built in the 1750s) on the west end of town, the artery proceeded down the slope through the heart of the community and terminated abruptly at the gated entrance of the Mahon family property. Thomas wasn't interested in a narrow provincial lane in the mold of every other town in Ireland. He wanted something with magnificence.

The second was on the other side of the gate: the rebuilt family home. It took three decades and two hundred workmen for construction to be completed on what the local people came to call the Bawn House or the White House. "There were six teams of master masons, each team consisting of ten men, some of whom heaved the stone into shape in [nearby] Slieve Bawn [mountain], some doing the designs on the stone, some laying the stone and so on," wrote a descendant of one of the workers in the early twentieth century. "Apart from these 60 skilled artisans, there were twelve joiners, carpenters, wood carvers and numerous apprentices, who (the latter) were chiefly employed in sharpening tools such as chisels, saws and the mixing of the lime sand mortar. It took three days to mix the mortar in its dry state and then it was screened before it was wetted. Bullocks and mules helped in the mixing of the dry mortar."

The house was constructed in the coolly formal neo-Palladianism of prominent Anglo-Irish structures like the Parliament House in Dublin. Mahon lore has it that famed Huguenot architect Richard Castle, who designed many of the great Irish mansions of this era, drew up the plans for the residence, but that assertion has been challenged by the family's most dogged chronicler, Susan Hood. The façade of the main, blocklike structure was outfitted with an Ionic portico and a balustraded cornice, recalling the classical grandiloquence that inspired Italian architect Andrea Palladio. The interior was unremarkable, featuring a dining room, parlor, drawing room, and library on the first floor, and a procession of undifferentiated bedrooms on the second. (A third floor was added later.) Emerging from the exterior of the main structure were two advancing wings, creating a partial courtyard around the front entrance, a feature that was typical of Irish Palladianism. The north wing, a long, narrow pavilion, housed the kitchen, equipped with a balcony that allowed the Mahon family to speak to the staff without actually having to set foot on the kitchen floor, and the servants' quarters, which accommodated twenty workers during these years. The south wing, a mirror image of the north, contained storage areas for coaches and produce and also a large "equine cathedral," as it was known by the family, with Tuscan columns and vaulted ceilings for the horses.

This Big House, as residences of the landed gentry were known in Irish popular culture, exuded the stolid classicism of the architecture then in vogue among the Ascendancy. But it was far less grand than some prominent Castle-built homes like Powerscourt in County Wicklow (with its sixty-eight rooms) or Carton in County Kildare. In truth, Strokestown House's majesty was a bit of an illusion, as Hood has pointed out. The advancing wings, to which additional storage facilities were attached, provided the structure with the bulk of its imposing stature, and without them the Mahon home would be nothing more than a respectable home for an "independent country gentleman," as Thomas was regarded by his parliamentary peers.

Indeed, when Arthur Young, the English travel writer and agriculturalist, arrived upon this setting in August 1776, he paid little attention to the new edifice. Instead he directed his acute gaze upon the fastidiously tended gardens and woods that Mahon had been cultivating for the past thirty years in the parklike area—the demesne—immediately surrounding the home. He marveled at the trees—"oak, English and French elm, beech, maple, spruce, Scotch and silver fir, larch, and etc."—with their "bright and beautiful" bark. He noted that "every tree gives the strongest signs of agreeing perfectly with the soil," and described how the nearby hedgerows were "planted with uncommon attention" by Mahon himself. Surveying the entire property, he wrote that the woods—"the finest woods I ever saw" of that age—and the hedgerows "take the appearance of uniting into one great range of plantations, spreading on each side of the house.

"It is one of the strongest instances of a fine shade being speedily formed in the midst of a bleak country that I have any where met with, being a perfect contrast to all the neighborhood," he gushed.

This bleak country, which Young first visited twenty years earlier, was something else entirely. Surveying the agricultural land that was used to graze cows and sheep—thus creating the flattened, charmless pastures known as "sheepwalks"—and to till potatoes, flax, barley, oats, and wheat, Young pronounced the scene "dreary." He also looked upon the people who worked the lands, sparing few superlatives in his description. While they were "better fed than 20 years ago, and better clothed," they were "not more industrious, or better housed." "They live on potatoes and milk, and butter," he wrote. "Scarce any but what keeps a cow or two. They are not allowed to keep pigs in general, but many will a tolerable quantity of poultry. . . . The men dig turf, and plant potatoes, and work for their landlord, and the women pay the rent by spinning."

The small farmers and laborers inspected by Young lived within the boundaries of the townland, a kind of settlement measurement that is unique to Ireland. Often consisting of a few hundred acres, the townland did not possess the institutions of civil and commercial society that had been established in Strokestown following Nicholas Mahon's arrival. Instead it was a world of small mud- and stone-walled cabins housing often related inhabitants. It might boast a modest and illegal (until 1782) "hedge" school for its army of barefoot children and perhaps a makeshift chapel, where an esteemed priest might come to celebrate Mass. A mystery to the landlord, who rarely ventured within its confines, the pre-Famine townland was a place of deep history and long tradition, the repository of the stories and myths and songs of a proud people. Even the most quotidian of townland landmarks could sprout the kinds of tales that survived centuries. The well in the townland of Kildalogue, just north of the Strokestown limits, was said to hold a giant eel, and generations of children trembled to hear the story of its fearsome powers.

Young recorded how some of the townlands within the Mahon estate had not yet been overthrown by the new "superstructure of law, measurement, and currency," in the words of scholar Robert Scally, introduced by the current rulers of Ireland. In particular, Young saw how collectives of peasants held the land in "rundale," a distinctly Irish brand of land distribution. Members of the rundale clachan met periodically to allot bits of land they leased in common from the landlord, each receiving an assortment of noncontiguous sections of varying quality that in the end resulted in everyone getting a roughly equitable plot. On the gale days in May and November, when the rent was due, the elder of the community would collect the funds and hand over a lump sum to the landlord. "Upon 2 or 300 acres, there will be 10 to 15 families," wrote Young, making up the typical rundale farm in the Strokestown area. It was a complex system of management that helps explains why the Irish people became such gifted navigators of political institutions. But it was also a structure that fomented internecine feuds. The nature of the allotments impelled every family to anxiously monitor the size of its neighbors' plots, creating an atmosphere where accusations of cheating and theft were forever being aired. While many Irish landlords had been successful in ending the practice, preferring a more modern and efficient method of land allocation, the Mahons didn't halt it. Young noted that it wasn't "thought here a bad system."

The whole of Strokestown's farmland was cheerless to Young, but it was clear that the problems of the coming decades were still largely disguised from his eye. The population was "upon the increase, but not much," and the potato, so vital to the survival of the Mahon tenantry, only suffered from "rot" during the occasional wet year, "but it is not at all common." He noticed that many of the sizable farms had been subdivided since his last trip, and that middlemen and larger farmers, who operated independently of the rundale system, were taking advantage of the reasonable rents Mahon offered to sublet parcels out to the smaller farmers and laborers. "Much land let to those who do not occupy

it, but who re-let it to others at an advanced rent," he wrote without elaboration.

Young preferred a view of the Strokestown area that avoided the
particulars. Ascending the perch of a nearby hill, he looked down
upon the vista stretching before him and declared it a "very noble"
sight. It was a phrase that Thomas Mahon surely appreciated.

By now the family was secure in its position as one of the leading
houses of Ireland. Its sons and daughters had married into other
respectable families, connecting the Mahons with the most important networks of wealth and influence in the British Isles. It had
relations in important positions in the military, the government,
and the Church of Ireland. The family elders could justly boast that
they had created a successful market town from what less than a
hundred years earlier had been a largely unpopulated area near the
site of a ruined castle. The Mahon family was at its height, as was
the Protestant Ascendancy to which it belonged.

During the period of Arthur Young's visit, Thomas was concluding a lifetime of service to the Irish House of Commons, where
he showed himself more or less loyal to a succession of ruling governments. On the great questions of the day, he stood up for positions that look in hindsight to be less than progressive. He opposed
the "Patriot" movement led by the eloquent Henry Grattan that
sought to distance the Irish Parliament's control from London and
advocated something approaching Irish independence, although it
was a brand of Irish nationalism that didn't threaten the entrench-
ment of the dominant Protestants. Thomas was also hostile to
relaxation of the disabilities against Catholics, which were beginning to be repealed, at English urging, by the final decade of his
life. Described as "against Popery" on an opposition list, he voted
against even minor measures to ease the Penal Laws. If the quality of his service wasn't remarkable, the length of it was. When he
died in 1782, Thomas had been in Parliament for forty-two years
and was the holder of the title "Father of the House," bestowed on

the member who had served longest. It was a seat he feared little of losing by his final years. In one of his last elections in 1776, he only needed to convince his kin of his worth. The Parliamentary List credited his 510 votes, the most of three candidates, to the number of his relations "residing in this county and marrying through one another" that offered their support.

It was soon apparent that Thomas's heir, Maurice, forty-three, would be presiding over a different era at Strokestown. As was custom, he took his father's place in the Irish Parliament, but lost it at the next election, the victim of a changing political climate. Maurice followed his father's example, coming out against the Patriot movement, which had successfully secured "legislative independence" in 1782, giving the Irish Parliament the right to make laws without the traditional checks of British oversight. Although Westminster retained much control over Irish affairs, it was seen as a great victory for the prospect of Irish Protestant nationhood, and a surge of pride swept through the country. He also opposed Catholic relief, including the 1782 act that succeeded in ending most restrictions on the ability of Catholics to hold property. While the tide of gentry opinion was divided on Catholic matters, it ran strongly in support of Patriot initiatives, and Maurice came in a distant third among three candidates. He tallied only 267 votes. It would seem even his relatives were turning against him.

The evidence shows that Maurice, looking for his own brand of splendor, responded to this defeat by seeking a greater prize than service in the Irish Parliament. He began writing letters to luminaries expressing his wish to be elevated into the ranks of nobility, hoping to be the first Mahon to truly be a lord over the land. Without initial success in convincing the authorities of his regal qualities, he contented himself with merely acting like a lord. He sank a new pond in the family's front yard, a mammoth project that required the diverting of a river, to improve the view from the dining room. He employed a landscape specialist to further cultivate the demesne woods and gardens that Arthur Young had been so impressed with just a few years earlier. He built an imposing, forty-foot-high Gothic Revival gate to separate the family property from the town of Strokestown, and purchased a town house in an upscale neighborhood in Dublin.

In the Mahon way, the new landlord sought to improve Strokestown's commercial fortunes, which, by the 1790s, even he realized would require the goodwill of the newly empowered, though hardly formidable, Catholic majority. With the passage of the 1793 law allowing Catholics who held at least 40 shillings' worth of land to vote—they still couldn't serve in Parliament or hold significant public office—Maurice understood that it would be foolish to refuse to come to terms with the changing ways. And it didn't require much effort on his part to liberalize the family's relationship with the Church's local representatives, who, if they were anything like their peers elsewhere, had so few funds that they sometimes used chalices made of tin. In 1795 Maurice offered a plot of land within the town limits for the construction of a Catholic church, providing a generous lease of 999 years for a location on Elphin Street and assisting in the process of putting a structure on the site. He conducted respectful negotiations, by all surviving accounts, with Father James Kelly, pastor of the Strokestown parish, the territory of which encompassed the ancient parishes of Bumlin and Kiltrustan in the town of Strokestown and to its northeast. There was no hint of the discord that had characterized the contacts between the men holding the equivalent positions earlier in the century. The letters Father Kelly exchanged with Maurice Mahon regarding the new church—a thatched cabin with mud walls—show a man appreciative of the landlord's gesture and uninterested in open conflict. In April 1795 the priest wrote to Maurice that he was "perfectly sensitive of the compliment you have paid to me" in allowing the new church to be placed within Strokestown, and he expressed his hope, "please God," that the traveling landlord would return soon to the area.

It was apparent that Maurice was interested in conciliating

Catholics for the purposes of enhancing his political power. He began offering plots of farmland worth precisely 40 shillings, roughly an acre, to Catholic tenants, thus creating a dutiful cadre of voters who would use their newfound right to follow the dictates of their bene-factor and, ideally, their priest. The expanding number of 40-shilling freeholders, few of whom yet voted in significant numbers, did not lead to another Mahon in Parliament. Not immediately, anyway. But it did mean that the estate was growing more crowded with small-holders and their families.

Throughout the 1790s Ireland was inching toward another violent conflict. The decade saw the rise of the Society of the United Irish-men, led by Theobald Wolfe Tone, a Dublin Protestant. Inspired by the American and French revolutions, the group decried the con-trol of Ireland "by Englishmen and the Servants of Englishmen" and sought a peaceful reform of governance that included "Irish-men of every religious persuasion." The Strokestown area witnessed the emergence of the Defenders, a secret society of rural Catholics allied with the United Irishmen but more committed to perpetrating crude violence against those with landed interests than in promot-ing a program of political ideals. During a meeting in Roscom-mon town in 1795, a number of important landholders, worried that their cattle would be "houghed [their leg tendons slashed] and killed" by the group, agreed to lower rents and increase wages. Like many concerned landlords throughout Ireland, Maurice Mahon organized a local militia of Protestants, his own brand of defend-ers, to protect the community from such disorder. Many members of these yeomanry units would join the Orange Lodges spring-ing up to defend Protestant interests, pledging, according to the Orangemen's oath, to "support and defend" the king "so long as he may support the Protestant Ascendancy." But stray acts of violence continued—fomented, according to a Strokestown gentleman's let-ter to the authorities, by "papist country schoolmasters"—until a large contingent of British troops arrived in the county and carted off as many as a thousand suspects, ending local agrarian unrest for several years.

The United Irishmen were not so easily suppressed. Formally allied with the French, who were at war with England, the organization went underground and began advocating a republican revolution. In December 1796 an attempted French invasion by sea was scuttled by severe weather and poor planning. Then, in the spring of 1798, a disorganized series of uprisings were launched in several sectors of Ireland, although Strokestown seems to have remained quiet. It perhaps isn't a surprise that a member of the Mahon family was in the middle of the action. On the evening of May 24, the day after the uprising began, Maurice's eldest son, Thomas, thirty-two, commanding officer of the British Army's Ninth Light Dragoons, directed the brutal suppression of a rebel force in County Carlow. After being tipped off by an informer, Lieutenant-Colonel Mahon's force of 450 men sprang a surprise attack on an insurgent force in Carlow town, killing many and driving the stunned survivors to seek refuge in a row of nearby homes.

"Then followed a horrible finale," reads the account in a regimental history. "The flimsy constructions into which they had fled caught fire or were set fire to; all those who tried to emerge were shot down, and those who remained inside were suffocated or burned to death. For several days afterward, it is said, gobbets of roasted human flesh kept falling down from the ruined chimneys of the burned houses."

The British Army and loyalist forces—the yeomanry units and the Orange Order—succeeded in defeating the rebels during battles that were marked by long-remembered brutality on both sides. Lieutenant-Colonel Mahon's regiment killed two hundred rebels in the Carlow battle and executed another two hundred who had been taken prisoner. Though praised for its successful defense of the town, Lieutenant-Colonel Mahon's command was admonished for executing a loyalist who had been accused of failing to warn the British of rebel plans. "How he could have done so, with the rebel host all around his house, is not easy to see," argued the regimental history. "His trial was, in fact, a grave miscarriage of justice." One of the most horrific episodes in Irish history, the rebellion of 1798 was effectively quashed in a month, with skirmishes (including with a small French invasion force) continuing for another few months.

In the aftermath of the uprising, the British government, in search of greater stability and control, pushed for the dissolution of the Irish Parliament and advocated a greater union between the two countries that would establish the United Kingdom of Great Britain and Ireland. The Catholic Church and much of its flock supported the measure, believing that the Protestant Ascendancy would be diminished in the larger aggregation and, as the government tacitly promised, that the proposed Act of Union would eventually bring "emancipation," the right of Catholics to serve in Parliament and other public offices. Many members of the Ascendancy, jealous of their Parliament and its powers, were opposed to the Union, and a bill introduced into the body in 1799 to effect the change was narrowly defeated. But the government was committed to securing the votes, using threats, intimidation, and bribes in the form of peerages to gain support. "You are not going to bribe me!" shouted the fourth Earl of Powerscourt when a government official appeared at the door of his County Wicklow home. Now sixty-one, Maurice Mahon had spent nearly twenty years angling to be named a peer. He was willing to be bribed.

Without his family occupying its customary seat in Parliament, however, Maurice's support for the Act of Union was largely meaningless. So he nominated his war-hero son for the job, successfully using his influence (with Catholics and others) to secure his victory in the 1799 elections. In January 1800 Thomas Mahon, thirty-three, was sworn into Parliament, where it was believed he would, like all his ancestors, "yield to the consent of things." But it soon became clear to Thomas that his constituents in County Roscommon were so strongly opposed to the Union that he was unable to follow his father's dictates. Under pressure to change his position, he refused to attend to the proceedings in the House.

Maurice scrambled to rectify the embarrassment. He purchased, at great expense, a County Kilkenny seat in the House—held by the ailing Sir Hercules Langrishe—for his second son, Stephen, thirty-two, who was also an ambitious officer in the British Army. Stephen Mahon served just long enough in the body—four months, from April to August 1800—to do this duty and cast a vote in favor of the legislation that established the Act of Union. The Parliament was dissolved, and Irish electoral representation, much reduced, was transferred to the British Parliament in London. The Mahon family had fulfilled its promise to the government, which offered a reward in the form of a peerage. Maurice Mahon was now the first Baron Lord Hartland.

CHAPTER 2

Until Decisive Steps Are Taken

❦

> *As long as the rent is paid we have no power to remove a tenant.*
> —JOHN MAHON, MAJOR MAHON'S
> BROTHER, BEFORE THE DEVON
> COMMISSION, JULY 22, 1844

THE HONOR REPRESENTED THE culmination of the family's efforts to elevate itself into the highest posts of national power and influence, a process that began with the patriarch Nicholas Mahon's ardent allegiances to English hegemony 150 years earlier. But no amount of influence, political or otherwise, could change the increasingly strained state of the agricultural lands as they existed at the turn of the nineteenth century.

The population had risen sharply over the previous decades, and the tenantry was thus compelled to occupy smaller plots on an ever more subdivided estate, a process that made it harder for the poorest among them to rise above a cycle of subsistence poverty. Nearly all these tenants relied to an extraordinary extent on the potato, with the average male consuming more than ten pounds of it a day by the middle of the century. The hardy tuber had long enabled the Irish pauper to survive conditions that might not otherwise sustain him. But the nation's leaders increasingly regarded it as a principal cause of Ireland's problems. Since it didn't require much labor to cultivate, the plant was seen as promoting indolence and fecklessness in the peasantry. Since it didn't require much acreage to support a family, it was widely credited with encouraging Irish paupers to marry earlier than they would have if they had to build a stake in a larger, grain-producing plot. The potato system was viewed as preventing Ireland from establishing the kind of modern economy that would be necessary to pull itself out of a spiral of poverty.

Compounding the predicament was a complex estate hierarchy whose very structure encouraged, or at least did not halt, the process of subdivision that followed from a system of potato dependence. Overlapping layers of tenants and undertenants were renting out plots—or elders of rundale collectives were granting bits of property—in response to the increasing numbers seeking land. These actors were motivated by many factors—communal tradition, familial obligation, a desire for profits, or, until the recent repeal of Penal Law limitations on the size of Catholic landholding, legal requirement. It created a world of tenants and subtenants where the definition of who was a landlord and who was a tenant was always fluid. At its most basic level, the system was glaringly unjust. The subtenants with the least means were squeezed by a succession of rent increases and forced to pay the highest sums for the smallest portions of land.

It was an arrangement that existed some distance from the immediate concerns of a long succession of Mahon landlords, who contented themselves with the higher matters of a nobleman's life. Instead, responsibility for much of the division and distribution of the land rested with other figures in the estate society.

The estate was populated by a small class of middlemen and large farmers who leased from thirty to several hundred acres of the several-thousand-acre estate at close to market rate under long-term leases. Both Protestant and Catholic, these figures were sometimes proprietors of large grazing farms who sublet portions not needed for the pasture of their sheep and cattle, or at other times acted as pure middlemen whose sole focus was letting all or most of their holdings. They resided in houses with slate roofs, ate a varied diet that included meat, and wore stylish clothes that were sometimes imported. They might possess a few horses, use the latest in farming technology (like iron plows), and hire workmen during the harvest time. Sometimes called "squireens," or little squires, they were seen in Irish lore as aspiring to the society of the landed gentry. In the manner of aspirants, they were regarded instead as "puny lords and servile imitators" who displayed a greater harshness toward the peasantry than the landlord himself. In her 1800 novel *Castle Rackrent*, Maria Edgeworth wrote that middlemen "grind the faces of the poor." Recent scholarship has drawn a more equivocal portrait of these individuals, showing that some improved their properties and showed concern for their subtenants. But it is indisputable that they were the engines behind much estate subdivision. Locked into decades-long lease agreements—set by landlords hoping to encourage industry and initiative—many were only too eager to parcel out plots for a bit of profit.

But the middleman's power was not unlimited. For one, many properties on the Mahon estate continued to operate under the rundale system. For another, the society of nonrundale subletters that existed under the landlord and his middlemen was also full of its own manner of landlords, who were engaged in their own brand of lessor and lessee relationships. Among the better-off of townland subtenants were middling farmers who practiced tillage farming of wheat, oats, and barley on farms of up to thirty acres, sometimes with the assistance of a horse or mule, and occasionally with the help of seasonal workers. Below them were small farmers who held from two to ten acres of land, which they tilled largely for subsistence—that is, to grow potatoes. They earned rent money by working as laborers for bigger farmers, selling the few cows or pigs in their possession, or hawking illegal homemade alcohol called "poteen," created from the resourceful potato. They were able to easily procure vital fuel needed to heat their cabins by spading turf out of the extensive peat bogs that filled the area. This class of farmer included the individual (or joint) tenants making up the rundale villages who occupied tracts of comparable size and supported themselves in a similar fashion.

The lower levels of estate society were composed of struggling laborers forever on the edge of destitution. Making up slightly more than a majority of the estate population, these paupers rarely handled money, instead swapping their labor for food or rent. The better positioned among them were the sizable class of "cottiers"—a group that included 40-shilling freeholders—so named because of the flimsy cabins or cottages where they resided. They were often given access to the land under a system of cottier tenure, which permitted them to receive the home and an accompanying plot of less than two acres from big or middling farmers in exchange for agreeing to work in the fields for a set number of days. Easy to build and easy to tear down, these cottages typically featured a large pot to boil potatoes, a rickety table, a few broken stools, and the straw mattresses upon which the family slept, often with their pig, a staple of cottier existence.

Occupying the lowest tier below the cottiers were landless laborers, described in later years by a government commission as "the most wretched amongst the many wretched classes in Ireland." They squatted on the edge of the estate, struggling to find employment, and often traveled to England during harvest times in search of work (which earned them the name "spalpeens"). Rarely employed for more than two hundred days a year, this class often took to begging in Strokestown, particularly during the lean, near-famine period that occurred every summer before the harvest. Without any land to grow potatoes to sustain themselves, they were forced to enter into competitive bidding for plots ready for planting, in what was known as a "conacre auction." They invariably paid grossly inflated rates for the right to use bits of land that literally meant the difference between living and dying. The farmer who refused to lower conacre rents or declined to offer plots altogether knew he was putting himself at risk of attack from desperate indigents.

By 1809, nine years after Maurice Mahon had become Lord
Hartland, and twenty-seven years after he had become landlord,
the Mahon tenants were in such a state of poverty that the estate's
management was denounced by at least one outside observer. In
June of that year the English writer Edward Wakefield paid calls
on the estates of several Roscommon gentlemen, each representing families that had ruled the county since the time of Cromwell:
the Croftons, the Frenchs, the Sandfords, and the Mahons. But it
was the Mahon estate among them that inspired a genuinely violent reaction in the writer. "I . . . found everywhere, cabins of the
most wretched aspect, infamous stone roads, very minute divisions
of land, and what usually follows it, a superabundant but miserable
population," he wrote. "The picture which I here saw will not be
easily effaced from my remembrance."

Unlike Arthur Young forty years earlier, Wakefield did not spare
any kind words for the beauty of the demesne or the quality of local
products. Instead he depicted a property that even decades before the
Famine seemed poised on the brink of disaster. "I had no letter of
introduction to the noble lord, nor to any of his agents," Wakefield
wrote, "but I must confess, that to have learnt the system pursued in
the agricultural economy of this property, would have afforded me
a useful lesson in order to recommend an opposite system, *for I do
not recollect to have travelled so many miles through any estate in Ireland
which presented such a scene of desolation*; and nothing astonished me
so much as the multitude of poverty-struck inhabitants, from whom
I could learn very little more than that the estate belonged to 'My
Lord,' whom they loaded with imprecations." (Italics added.)

The poor of Lord Hartland's town expressed themselves with more
than just verbal declamations in the years surrounding Wakefield's
visit. Residing within some of those "most wretched" cabins were
members of a new secret society with its own brand of oaths and
threatening letters, and unafraid to use violence against those bearing down upon the destitute. They were part of a long tradition of

rural paupers, or a minority of them, forming themselves into shadowy groups, often with picturesque names, to avenge the wrongs committed against the struggling tenant. By the early nineteenth century these groups were collectively referred to as "Whiteboys," because of the white sheets they wore over their clothing during nighttime incursions, and were the inspiration for a long list of "Whiteboy" or "coercion" acts in Parliament designed to curtail their growth. But their growth was hard to curtail, especially during tough economic times that put stress upon the precarious land system.

The group that showed itself in Strokestown was called the "Threshers," also prominent in counties Sligo, Leitrim, and Longford. It was formed to protest the "Established" Church of Ireland's galling practice of extracting tithes from the rural (Catholic) populace, sometimes by taking a portion of a peasant's potatoes in lieu of cash. In addition to targeting Protestant clergy, the Threshers also went after Catholic priests for charging inflated rates to perform baptisms, marriages, and last rites, the revered sacraments of the Church. From Lord Hartland's comfortable chair in the Big House, this appeared to be a principal complaint of the "Thrashers," as he called them. In an 1808 letter to one of his sons, he attributed unrest in the townlands to "a quarrell between the priests and their flocks viz christenings, marriages and for which they have lately considerably raised their fees." Indeed, secret societies like the Threshers that professed to represent the downtrodden were perhaps the most ecumenical group in Irish society, largely because everyone was treading on the peasants. Not only Protestant landlords, middlemen, ministers, and magistrates for the obvious reasons, but also Catholic middlemen and farmers, who set rents for regular and conacre plots; merchants, who charged money for food and drink; and priests, who were dependent on dues. The more comfortable classes of Strokestown society, Catholics and Protestants, then found themselves on the same side of the fight, although not exactly allies.

The secret society's profile increased in the winter of 1808—a Thresher was accused of shooting the daughter of a member of the yeomanry, among other acts—and Lord Hartland sent out his local militia to attempt to quell the disturbances. The trouble continued over the next few years. Reports were made of large groups of Threshers appearing in public in a show of strength, and of local men, Catholics and Protestants both, being forced to take the Threshers' oath under threat of violence. Other accounts told of how shopkeepers were forced to swear that they would keep prices at a reasonable level and how farmers found their sheep killed when they took land at a high rent, thus inflating the rates paid by those lower in the agrarian hierarchy. A Roscommon newspaper described how a priest was assaulted by two men for preaching against the prevalence of "outrages." The Protestant bishop in Elphin spoke of how he warded off—on horseback—a contingent of Whiteboys who descended on his land to destroy his stacks of turf. The secret society's deeds were sometimes followed by the ritualistic lighting of celebratory bonfires, which shone from the hills in a powerful display of seeming communal solidarity.

By 1813 the group's behavior, hardly quelled, so concerned Strokestown authorities that they were alerting Dublin Castle, the headquarters of British rule in Ireland, to the need for a contingent of national troops. As might be expected, the officials penned letters that highlighted the most explicitly anti-Protestant aspects of the Threshers' campaign. But one tactic that was described by these writers involved striking at the livelihood of Protestant merchants—whom the group seemed to universally regard as Orangemen, whether they were members of an Orange Lodge or not—by punishing those *Catholics* who associated with them. A sign posted in Strokestown, penned by "John the Tresher [sic] from Castlebar," warned that "no persons whatever are to buy any commodity from any of the villainous crew in this town calling themselves Orangemen." The punishment to violators was severe. One writer described how three men were "carded," or raked with a razor-sharp card used to shear wool from sheep, for violating a Thresher order against consorting with "heriticks." Only a few strokes could tear away enough skin to expose bone. Another testimony told how one man was carded for the sin of purchasing shoes from a Protestant.

Incidents of this sort petrified the local Protestant establishment, which like its leaders in Dublin and London was prone to the not-irrational, but not always founded, fear that a rise in rural crime was the first signal of a violent overthrow of the established order. A Strokestown magistrate wrote to the Irish executive in Dublin Castle about his concerns that the Thresher incidents were a prelude to systematic violence on a grand scale—"the most dreadful massacre of Protestants," as he described it. (Lord Hartland himself thought the fear overblown. "He does not care for what any other suffers," one local Protestant complained. "He thinks that, while he dare not meddle with these murderers, he will be safe.") Tensions heightened to such a point that all the female Protestants in town were herded into a shelter one evening to protect them from a suspected attack. The anxieties led to the arrival of troops, which arrested suspects and conducted trials. The punishment, intended for public edification as much as pure retribution, was administered out in the open: The guilty men were whipped in front of the crowds that gathered in Strokestown on market day, a prime-time viewing period.

United in the struggle against the extralegal doings of the Threshers, the Mahon family and the area's Catholic elders, particularly the formidable Father James Kelly of the Strokestown parish, were at a high point in their relationship. But other subjects united them. Lord Hartland and Father Kelly shared a commitment to keep the lord's second son, Stephen, as a member of the British House of Commons, each for his own reasons. A commanding officer in the military, Stephen was first elected to Parliament in 1806, pledging to continue his family's now steady support for Catholic betterment. He voted for several unsuccessful Catholic relief measures in opposition to a government that he supported on all other matters—the family's finest legislative hour, whatever the motivation. On this point, he received the firm backing of Father Kelly, who used his influence with his voting parishioners to help keep the landlord's son in power through several elections. (Lord Hartland contributed funds to church coffers to further inspire the cleric's support.) Naturally, the aging lord was less interested in Catholic liberation than in having his son pursue other objectives. In a telling sign of his priorities, he enlisted Stephen in a futile effort to have him moved up the next step on the peerage ladder, which would give him the title of viscount. Lord Hartland even urged his son to withhold all support for the government, on every matter that came up for discussion, until his request for elevation had been granted.

But perhaps the moment that represented the height of the alliance between the family landlord and the town priest happened after Father Kelly passed away in 1818. The Catholic bishop of Elphin appointed Father William Dolan to replace him as pastor, a decision that angered parishioners who wanted Father Kelly's nephew to fill the post. "The bishop would not yield," wrote a magistrate. "The people became violent—obstructed Mr. Dolan, and even threatened his life." In an extraordinary move, several members of the local Protestant elite intervened, demanding that the Catholic masses "support the existing laws of the country" and allow Father Dolan his rightful place in the pulpit. The Protestant bishop himself visited the more established parishioners and, after taking down their names, instructed them that "peace and good order should be preserved," and that he would hold them "answerable for any violation of the laws of the parish of Strokestown." Lord Hartland's Protestant establishment was thus protecting the right of a Catholic pastor to wield authority over a congregation that represented more than 90 percent of the local population. In all outward appearances, the two pillars of Strokestown society—its spiritual leader and its temporal ruler—were now firm allies, joined together by a common concern for the preservation of public calm.

* * *

While the elderly Lord Hartland was dreaming of further royal honors, the financial matters of his estate were growing ever more dire. The noble lord had long made it a practice of spending considerable amounts of money, more than the family bank account would cover, in a disastrous preoccupation that would be his most lasting legacy to his heirs. Although he used funds to expand Strokestown's commercial capacity—building a sessions and market house, among other projects—he often allocated money for purposes with much less potential for payoff. In the manner of his class, he ensured that the estate and other family properties were maintained in a grand style and that several supine relatives were able to live in luxury (though he was often required to do so under legal obligations from various ancestors' wills). But it was the purchase of land that put the family under the greatest financial stress. He bought large tracts from several indebted landowners, often with borrowed funds, enough to markedly increase the size of an estate that, if Wakefield is to be believed, was already rife with mismanagement. But Lord Hartland did not see the acquisitions as a burdensome part of his family's legacy, even telling his children in his will, quoting "the Great" Lord Burleigh, "that a man that sells an acre of his estate loses an ounce of his credit."

The Mahons' fiscal standing was also hurt by factors not of their doing. The economy in Ireland was in the midst of a major slump in the wake of the end of Britain's long conflict with France in 1815. A decrease in the demand for the country's agricultural products overseas led to price decreases in the market in Strokestown, which led to a decline in wages and jobs throughout the region. The linen, milling, and brewing industries, which were central to the town's economy, suffered setbacks, forcing more people into an already overburdened agricultural existence. Those subsistence farmers and laborers, so lately prone to anger, were further hurt by crop failures caused by poor weather in 1817–1818 and 1821–1822, two of the periodic episodes of distress that hit the area. A local physician, echoing a phrase that would be repeated decades later, wrote how "famine and pestilence stalked the land" during the 1817–1818 crisis, although the mortality figures were miniscule in comparison with the great tragedy in the future.

In 1819, after thirty-seven years as landlord, Lord Hartland died at the age eighty-one, bringing his first son and heir back to the Irish countryside to assume responsibility. Thomas, who had successfully defended Carlow against rebel attack during the 1798 Uprising, was in the midst of a respected military career that led him, among other missions, to direct troops in Britain's bizarre attempt to capture Spanish colonies in South America. The short campaign ended with the army's humiliating defeat at Buenos Aires, where Lieutenant-Colonel Mahon, blameless in the folly, commanded a rearguard force of eighteen hundred men. Looking over the ledgers, the now second Baron Lord Hartland, saw that the estate income was "totally inadequate to discharge the said debts incurred" by his father. The remark was a significant admission that the family's stewardship of its assets required radical reorganization. But the second Lord Hartland did not dedicate himself to fixing the problem he had identified.

Perhaps that is a good thing. Other landlords in Roscommon, similarly hard hit by fiscal troubles, worked to solve the dilemma in a way that added to the rural anger directed toward them. In the months and years to come, they would evict paupers and farmers, "consolidating" small patches into large, more profitable grazing farms. But the Mahons do not appear to have initiated what was becoming known as the "clearance system," opting instead to retain the small tenants who provided them with rent and political clout. The area around Strokestown continued to predominate with tillage plots—the "very minute divisions of land" that Wakefield had decried.

Instead, the new lord dedicated himself to the singular pastime of spending money, striving to fulfill the family's longtime need to show off its wealth. A new Church of Ireland structure was built in town in the years immediately after his ascension, the Mahon family crest depicted in one of the stained glass windows. A prestigious English architect was hired to make ornate improvements to Strokestown House, remaining on the payroll for nine years. All this work was done while the second Lord Hartland resided for much of the year in a lavish home at No. 40 Grosvenor Place in London. The day-to-day control of estate affairs had been handed over to a local land agent. Twenty-five years before the Famine, the Mahon landlord was not only a debtor who was falling deeper into debt, but he was also an absentee who was content with the drift of his estate.

Another problem was looming on the horizon, one that threatened to push the estate into more instability. The Mahon line of succession that stretched all the way back to the Cromwellian conquest—from Nicholas, to John, to Nicholas, to Thomas, to Maurice, and finally to Thomas—could soon be coming to end. Neither the second Lord Hartland, who was fifty-three, nor his unmarried brother in Parliament, fifty-one, nor his youngest brother, a forty-seven-year-old clergyman, had produced any children. It was clear that vast tracts of Mahon land could soon be passed into others' hands. With this dim possibility in sight, one member of the extended relations, a cousin, soon began quietly solidifying his ties with his Strokestown kin.

Just thirty-two, Denis Mahon was the oldest son of the oldest brother of the first Lord Hartland, which placed him, technically, next in the patrilineal pecking order. But he wasn't an obvious choice for a position of such prominence. The son of Reverend Thomas Mahon and Honoria Kelly, he was raised in the parish of Annaduff in County Leitrim, where his father served as rector. Upon turning seventeen, he joined the British Army's Ninth Light Dragoons (later the Ninth Queen's Royal Lancers), where he was vastly overshadowed by his older cousin Thomas (the second Lord Hartland), who was then serving as the commanding officer of the cavalry regiment. The written accounts of the Ninth's history contain many descriptions of Thomas's endeavors; they are silent on Denis's deeds. After six years during which he purchased a promotion to captain, he was transferred to an infantry regiment, the Twenty-ninth Regiment of Foot, which afforded him the opportunity to taste martial action in England's many wars. In 1814 he participated in the final stages of the Anglo-American conflict that had erupted two years earlier. His regiment fought successful battles in the state of Maine, but was forced to give up the struggle when the Treaty of Ghent ended hostilities. He was next sent to Europe to engage in the last days of the landmark struggle with Napoleon, a prospect that he and his comrades looked forward to with anticipation. In a manner that was typical of Captain Mahon's luck, he missed one of the great clashes of world history by mere hours. His regiment, according to its historian, "arrived near enough to distinctly hear the firing, but, to the great disappointment of all ranks, too late to take part in the battle of Waterloo."

In 1822, when he was thirty-five, Denis married Henrietta Bathurst at the Church of St. Martin at Palace in Norwich, England. In a scant and uneventful early biography, it would have to be considered his most noteworthy deed yet, for reasons that had less to do with the bride than with her father. Lord Bishop Henry Bathurst, then seventy-eight, was one of the most colorful characters in the hierarchy of the Church of England. He was brilliant, personable, disorganized, charitable, informal, and utterly incorruptible. But his progressive politics, expressed without concern for the consequences to his standing, truly distinguished his lifetime. His impassioned speeches in the House of Lords turned the stomachs of his fellow bishops, all members of a Tory Party dedicated to the unassailable prerogatives of the Crown and Church. He once implored a fellow lord, during an oration on the legacy of the Penal Laws, "to show me a single country, the inhabitants of which are treated with so much harshness and injustice as the Catholic inhabitants of unhappy Ireland." His Whiggish positions were widely understood to have hindered his advancement in the church hierarchy and caused the rupture of his relationship with the king and queen, with whom he had often played whist, a favorite pastime.

Over the next decade, the good bishop would develop a close relationship with his son-in-law. In 1824, when Mahon, now a major, was freed from much of his military obligations, he, his wife, and his daughter moved in with the old man, who alternated between residences in London, Norwich, and the English countryside. The arrangement, according to a member of the Bathurst family, "proved a great source of cheerfulness and comfort to him, as well as satisfaction and pleasure to them." It is not recorded how the Mahons spent their days, but, if the stories of the lord bishop's manner are accurate, it is safe to assume that they listened to him expound on all character of subjects. "He always appeared to know at least something of the history or the character, or had some anecdote to relate, of almost every person who happened to be mentioned on his hearing," wrote one of his daughters. "No man told a story better." He was said to be able to recite long memorized passages from Sophocles and Cicero, from the great English poets, from Erasmus and Grotius. It was reputed that as a child he could repeat all of Homer's *Iliad* in the original Greek. "His mind is indeed richly stored with ancient and modern literature, and an hour of tête-à-tête conversation with him has often been to me an hour of intellectual luxury," wrote a friend. But "argument and discussion" centering on political matters most animated him. It is impossible to imagine that he and the young military officer didn't speak at length on the great issue then roiling Ireland and England: Catholic emancipation. Dr. Bathurst would have been adamant on the justice of granting Catholics the right to sit in Parliament—he had been speaking on it for close to two decades—but he would have remained cordial to his son-in-law, who would later be identified as a Tory, even if the two disagreed. "If his opponent became heated, he would increase in suavity," wrote a colleague of the bishop's style. "On one occasion when the discussion turned upon the propriety of admitting Roman Catholics to full civil and political privileges," his guest became so flustered at losing the argument that he spilled his glass of port over his shirt and waistcoat. Dr. Bathurst smiled and said with his "usual urbanity," "Come, let us go to tea."

Since the passage of the Act of Union two decades earlier, the leaders of Great Britain had struggled to maintain this last great remnant of the Penal Laws. Measure after measure introduced into Parliament seeking to chip away at the prohibition was defeated either in the House of Commons or in the House of Lords, leading the bulk of Catholic Ireland to turn against the Union. Stephen Mahon, brother to the second and current Lord Hartland, had maintained his Catholic supporters, and thus his seat in the House of Commons, under the understanding that he would support these initiatives. But by the time he left the House in 1826, ending the Mahon family's century and a half of service to the parliaments of Ireland and Great Britain, the campaign for Catholic emancipation had entered a new, more confrontational stage.

The wily Catholic lawyer Daniel O'Connell had formed the Catholic Association earlier in the decade to harness the collective power of the great mass of Ireland's Catholics "by legal and constitutional means," as he said in an open rebuke to Whiteboyism. In a brilliant piece of strategy, he offered membership in his decidedly un-secret society to anyone who could pay a penny a month of what came to be called "Catholic rent," giving even the poorest of tenants their first taste of real political engagement. He also wisely enlisted the Catholic figures most in touch with the people to serve as key lieutenants and often collectors of this rent: priests. By the time of Stephen Mahon's departure from Parliament, a large section of the Catholic population, including nearly all its bishops and priests, had joined the ranks of a secular, nonviolent movement arrayed against a major injustice of British and Protestant rule. The first Irish political machine, it would later serve as a template for the organizations run by the Irish bosses of New York, Boston, Chicago, and other American cities.

By 1828, with his goal not yet achieved, O'Connell forced the hand of the government by declaring his intention to stand for election in County Clare. When he won victory with ease, the British prime minister, the Duke of Wellington, felt he was confronted with two choices: Grant emancipation or fight civil war. Defying the wishes of the majority of his party, Wellington spent months in negotiation with the angry king (who threatened at one point to abdicate), the bishops, and his home secretary, Robert Peel, hoping to gain support for legislation he felt would avoid an outbreak of violence. O'Connell, though genuinely opposed to physical force, stoked British fears of armed insurrection, wishing to convince the government that only he was able to hold the people back. By mid-April 1829 Wellington had persuaded his government to back down in the face of O'Connell and his massive army of restless Catholics. A law was passed that allowed Catholics to occupy all but a few of the public offices in the United Kingdom.

Not everything about the victory was sweet. Parliament enacted another law that raised the 40-shilling qualification to 10 pounds, which meant that far fewer Catholics were now eligible to cast ballots. It also meant that many landlords had little incentive to retain 40-shilling freeholders, inaugurating another period of evictions on many estates. O'Connell's achievement nonetheless earned him immense popularity among the Irish Catholic people, who bestowed an exalted title upon him: the "Liberator." In the elections of 1830, when the reform-minded Whigs drove the ruling Tories from power for the first time in more than a generation, a third of Ireland's new MPs were Catholics, a proportion that would increase in subsequent elections. In County Roscommon, the Catholic victory was more convincing, and the changing era was symbolized by one of the new representatives. The O'Conor don, the patriarch of the Gaelic royal clan that occupied Ballynamully Castle in the centuries before Nicholas Mahon arrived with Oliver Cromwell, was now a member of the Imperial Parliament. The *Times of London* commented, "No combination of the great landed proprietors of Roscommon could keep" him from office.

In Strokestown, a visitor during the summer of 1830 noted that "political enmities engendered by the elections" had made the area less hospitable to the formerly unchallenged elite of the community. Isaac Weld, a Dublin Quaker, wrote that the horse races had been canceled and the public balls, "once frequent and regular," had not been held for some time. Weld visited the town's inn and spoke with a housemaid who filled his ears with tales of times past in the grand ballroom. Her "tongue, once set a-going, could not be stayed from repeating the names of all the fine people, of the beautiful young ladies, with their beautiful dresses, and the handsome young gentlemen, who, in former days, were wont to grace its walls." The housemaid gave him a tour of other spaces once used by the well-to-do revelers. "A deep drawn sigh was the only answer to my inquiry, how soon the rooms were likely to be again applied to the same purposes," he commented in *The Statistical Survey of Roscommon*, which was published in 1832.

Weld recorded how the industries that had flourished during the eighteenth-century rule of the first Thomas Mahon had largely disappeared. He noted that there were currently no breweries in town—the locals depended on cheap porter conveyed from Dublin by canal—that no mills existed "in this neighborhood," and that the quality of still-prevalent linen was "very considerably diminished of late." He was impressed with Thomas Mahon's main street "of immense breadth," but lamented that its unused sections attracted "waste," causing the town to lack "order and neatness." Even the Mahon family gardens, the result of decades of cultivation, seemed to him to be past their prime. "The gardens are extensive and in profitable order," he allowed, "but did not display many traces of modern refinements, whether in arrangement, or cultivation, or in improved glass."

By this time, the second Lord Hartland, now in his late sixties and still without an heir, had decided how he was going to remedy the looming matter of his succession. His brother Stephen, the parliamentarian, had died unmarried and childless in 1828, and his other

brother Maurice, a Cambridge-educated clergyman in his early sixties, was not only childless but also mentally ill. Once a respected
orator who held posts in the Tuam Cathedral and St. Patrick's
Cathedral in Dublin, Maurice was described by family members as
"timid and nervous," yet so prone to violent outbursts that a main
preoccupation was "to divert and comfort him." His wife and her
daughter from a previous marriage had left his side, reputedly motivated, at least in part, by the discovery of a collection of erotica in
the reverend's possession. "We shall make it a rule never to speak
of them [to him]!" wrote one relative of Maurice's wife and her
daughter. The second Lord Hartland realized that Maurice, who
would take over the bulk of the estate upon his death, was utterly
incapable of managing a job that he himself was barely interested
in. He knew that it was time to bring Major Denis Mahon to Ireland to assume a level of responsibility in estate affairs that hadn't
been shown by a family member in years.

The forty-eight-year-old, who is pictured in a portrait from this
period as a slight man with warm, even pretty, eyes, tousled dark
hair, and a flower in his lapel, arrived in the spring of 1835 with his
wife and two children, Grace and Tom. "Denis will not only derive
much benefit (in a worldly point of view) from this excursion but
also much pleasure," concluded Lord Bishop Bathurst, now ninety-
one, who remained behind in England. Upon the major's arrival,
the second Lord Hartland returned to the comfort of his home in
London, where he died six months later. Because of a stipulation
in the will, a small portion of the estate was bequeathed to a rival
cousin from other branch of the family, Marcus McClausland, who
operated an estate in County Londonderry. The larger section of
the estate passed to Maurice, now third Lord Hartland, and Major
Mahon acted quickly to solidify his control of this part of the property. With the consent of his unstable cousin's estranged wife—a
significant achievement—he brought Maurice before a governmental commission that in due course declared him a "lunatic" unable
to manage his own affairs. The declaration passed control of the

estate to the Court of Chancery, which designated Major Mahon legal guardian of the lord and, far more significantly, "heir presumptive," who would gain full control upon his cousin's death. It was an extraordinary turn of events for an unexceptional military officer whose future, but for the childlessness of three of his cousins, had promised little in the way of lordly grandeur or notoriety.

The other major post in Strokestown society gained a new occupant that same year. An experienced priest, roughly the same age as Major Mahon, was appointed to tend to the spiritual needs of the area Catholics upon the death of Father William Dolan. His name was Father Michael McDermott, and he had earned a reputation in his previous pastorates as a dedicated builder of churches, fulfilling the Irish Church's goal of solidifying its standing among the people. He was also renowned for his eagerness to defend that hard-earned standing against all challengers. The Latin-language memorial plaque that would later be placed in his Strokestown church described him not only as a *pater pauperum*—"father of the poor"—but as a *martellus haereticorum*—"hammer of the heretics." Yet his first letters to the heir presumptive, Strokestown's leading "heretic," show that he was eager to continue the firm alliance between priest and landlord that had been a feature of local life for the past four decades. In March 1836 Father McDermott praised Major Mahon for his "kindness towards myself personally" and for his "encouragement to the improvement and industrious habits of my parishioners since you came to reside amongst us." He concluded on an even more effusive note. "May God Almighty render to you the full reward of your good intentions, and grant you long life to reap the fruits of your kindly disposition in the affections of your poor tenantry! I am, dear Sir, with the highest respect and gratitude, your obedient humble servant, Michael McDermott." The relationship, it seemed, was getting off to a positive start.

But Major Mahon was not yet the landlord. In order to make even basic decisions regarding the property—whether to renew a lease or not, for example—he had to apply for permission from the courts. The painstaking process made it hard for him (and his brother, who was serving as estate receiver) to do anything of consequence regarding the administration of the property. The crisis of the family debt had only gotten worse in the sixteen years since the second Lord Hartland declared estate income "totally inadequate" to maintain the debt obligations.

During these years the Whig government, which had allied with Daniel O'Connell on matters of parliamentary and tithe reform, decided that it was time to force Major Mahon and his fellow landlords to play a greater role in alleviating poverty in Ireland. The British polity resolved to introduce a Poor Law on the island, the first effort at a social welfare system in Ireland's history. Ever since the economic downturn following the end of the war with France, the British government had appointed commission after commission to study the issue of Irish "overpopulation, pauperism, mendicancy, and destitution," suggesting ameliorative programs of public works, wasteland reclamation (to create more arable farmland), compensation for tenants' improvements (to give them a greater investment in their plots), and assisted emigration (to the colonies, *not* England). Prevalent ideas of political economy, which represented the most powerful strands of conventional wisdom, often overrode attempts to introduce plans with large governmental expenditure. As Lord Grenville said in the House of Lords, "There is no principle more firmly established in political economy than this, 'That the commerce, credit, and capital of a country should always be left to itself, to find its true level. Legislative interference always tended to obstruct or divert the current from its natural channel, and, consequently, to render the advantages of it uncertain and precarious.'" Even a famine, wrote the social theorist Thomas Malthus, was a "natural" check on rampant overpopulation, the most terrible of the "instruments employed by the Deity" to ensure a properly ordered society. It was widely believed among the ruling classes that programs of relief would demoralize the poor and prevent them from exerting the initiative that was necessary to thrive in the world. The provision of welfare assistance, then, was against "the laws of commerce, which are the laws of nature, and consequently the laws of God," wrote Edmund Burke.

But the dreadfully poor of Ireland, long oppressed by a class of landlords who were increasingly seen as lazy and immoral, could not be left to their own devices, especially with British leaders growing increasingly concerned about Irish paupers seeking assistance from the English system of relief. With bipartisan support, Parliament enacted a Poor Law in 1838, a parsimonious initiative (to modern sensibilities) that was to be mostly subsidized not by the Imperial Treasury but by Irish holders of land. The legislation established a system of workhouses providing "indoor relief" to only the most destitute—on the eve of the Famine, just one hundred thousand of the eight million people in Ireland could be accommodated within the walls of 130 workhouses. The facilities were intended to be little different from prisons. A pauper could only be permitted entry with his entire family, whose members were to be segregated according to gender and age. Once inside, every able-bodied individual was required to participate in "irksome employment." Uniforms were worn; meals were eaten in silence; infractions of the rules were severely punished. The idea was to "awaken or increase a dislike to remain in the workhouse," creating the so-called workhouse test of destitution. That is, if you were willing to submit to such a regimen, you were truly poor; if you weren't, then you couldn't be classified as needy. Administered by a local Board of Guardians made up of ex officio and elected individuals from the local community, the system was to be funded with "poor rates," or taxes levied on the property holders of the "union" where the workhouse was located, with the larger proprietors responsible for a greater share of the costs. "Irish property must pay for Irish poverty," was a popular phrase of the day.

The Poor Law, then, was about Ireland's future as much as it was about its present. The goal was to teach the Irish people—tenants and landlords alike—to use their own resourcefulness to rescue Ireland from its predicament. The landlord would be instructed that it would be better to come up with his own plan to aid his poor—by offering employment, among other ideas—than it would to pay the increased rates that would come with a full workhouse. The tenant would be taught that it was better to be employed and productive than it was to be breaking rocks in a dismal, prisonlike setting. Those "who have property in the country have a strong direct pecuniary interest in repressing the spread of pauperism, and in taking care that the poor are not improperly multiplied," wrote a political economist supportive of the law. George Nicholls, who devised the Irish Poor Law, felt that it would ease the country away from the much-condemned potato-based economy centered around small subsistence plots to an anglicized capitalist economy of grazing farms staffed by a laboring class earning a wage. But Nicholls cautioned that his Poor Law should not be "expected to work miracles." It "would not give employment or capital, but it would, I think, help the country through what may be called its transition period. . . . By 'transition period' I meant that season of change from the system of small holdings, conacre, and the subdivisions of land, which now prevails in Ireland, to the better practice of daily labor for support, which is the present condition of the English peasantry." He also felt that the Irish Poor Law, which unlike the English Poor Law didn't include a provision that offered "outdoor relief" in the form of food distributed to those who remained in their homes in times of crisis, was inadequate to cope with extraordinary destitution.

In 1841 the Tories returned to power, inaugurating a new period of political agitation in Ireland. In response to the elevation of his old nemesis Robert Peel to prime minister, Daniel O'Connell soon launched a massive campaign to repeal the Act of Union, which he hoped would resurrect an Irish Parliament (in some form) within the framework of Great Britain that would now be overwhelmingly populated with Catholic members. Unlike Catholic emancipation, Repeal was opposed by nearly every shade of British political opinion, which regarded it as the first step in the destruction of the empire. O'Connell was undeterred. He energized his coalition of middle-class and gentry Catholics, clergymen and bishops, and dues-paying peasants. His effort was aided by Protestant and Catholic intellectuals centered around the *Nation* newspaper, a collection of idealistic and forward-looking Irish writers and poets called "Young Ireland." By the summer of 1843, O'Connell was holding rallies before crowds so massive that the government feared the country was again on the brink of civil war. In August Parliament passed an arms bill, which sought to limit the number of firearms.

County Roscommon was not exempt from this phenomenon. In late August 1843 O'Connell arrived in Roscommon town to host one of these so-called monster meetings, and the local Tory landlords were aghast at the idea of it. Major Mahon's cousin (on his mother's side) and close friend, Denis H. Kelly, warned his tenants in a circular "that the present agitation must eventuate in bloodshed" and "involve in ruin those who mixed themselves up with it." To protect against the outbreak of violence, the government sent a troop of the Fourth Dragoons to supplement a large contingent of the constabulary. Held in an open field just outside the town limits, the event was attended by one nobleman, eight or nine "gentlemen possessed of property," the "customary large muster of Roman Catholic clergyman, tradesmen, and shopkeepers," and a sizable crowd of peasants, according to the careful accounting of an unfriendly correspondent from the *Times of London*. Several of the gentlemen delivered brief remarks lavishing praise on "the illustrious apostle of universal liberty," as one described him, before the great man himself, now sixty-eight, rose to address the gathering. It was a speech most of the crowd would likely remember for the rest of their lives.

The Liberator recalled the glories of an Irish past before domination by "the Saxon and stranger," and asked the "men of Roscommon" to rejoice in the "confident expectation" that "their fatherland was to be a nation again." He promised that even the oldest among them would live to see the restoration of the Irish Parliament and "catch the shout" that, reverberating throughout the island, "would greet Roscommon with the cry of 'Old Ireland and liberty.'" He then proceeded to use the kind of martial rhetoric that so worried the government and landlords, hinting at his movement's potential for destructiveness while at the same time celebrating its dedication to "virtue and goodness." Praising the efforts of Reverend Theobald Mathew, then in the midst of his famous temperance crusade, O'Connell noted that *if* he had to go to battle, he would rather have a "strong and steady" army of "virtuous teetotalers" on his side than any other army, a sentiment that inspired "long-continued cheering and waving of hats," said the *Times*. Noting the British government's fear of a civil war, he told the crowd he had informed Peel that the Irish nation would never start a conflict, but neither would it cower from one. "If there is any man here who would not fight if attacked, let him speak," he said, to more cheering.

To the establishment of County Roscommon, this was simple incitement. And when a landlord was shot on the road from Roscommon town to Strokestown a month after O'Connell's speech, Major Mahon knew whom to blame. His opinion carried considerable weight. Even though the Court of Chancery was constraining his management of the estate, he had taken up the Mahon tradition of ensuring public order, a task that had been part of the family ways since Nicholas Mahon "robbed and skulled" Dudley Costello back in 1667. In the early 1840s he served as both high sheriff of Roscommon and deputy lieutenant of the county. As such, he was a principal investigator in the shooting.

It happened on September 20, 1843, at around 11 A.M. Two assailants hiding behind a stone wall opened fire on a man named Richard Irwin as he rode alone in his horse-drawn gig in the vicinity of a settlement known as Four Mile House. With shot lodged in his head and shoulders, Irwin somehow managed to maneuver his carriage to Strokestown, four miles distant, where the local doctor, Dr. Terence Shanley, nursed him back to health. One newspaper suggested that a tenant who was behind in his rent committed the crime. Another noted that Irwin had received several warnings "to say that this would be done to him in open daylight and unfortunately they have proved to be true." A third correspondent suggested that the Roscommon police had known of the attack but did nothing to prevent it.

Major Mahon convened a meeting of magistrates in Elphin to pass a series of resolutions "to arrest the alarming spread of crime"

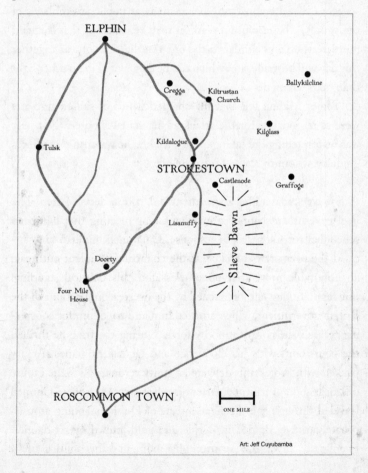

Art: Jeff Cuyubamba

in the county. The officials pledged to pay a reward to anyone who
came forward with information leading to the "discovery and conviction" of the culprits. They asked the government to institute a
dusk-till-dawn curfew on the excited peasant population. But the
most detailed and impassioned resolution expanded the scope of the
inquiry. It warned that a continued acceptance of anti-establishment
agitation would lead to what Major Mahon provocatively called a
"massacre." "Until decisive steps are taken by Government to put a
stop to the seditious publications scattered through the land, as well
as the most exciting, and, to all intents and purposes, treasonable
speeches that are constantly being made at public assemblages of
the people," the resolution read, "it may be expected that frequent
murderous attacks similar to the one that has brought us together
this day will be made, and which can be considered in no other light
than massacre in detail."

Major Mahon felt that the charged words of skilled agitators
were as responsible for the attack as the actual shooters. Not only
was he foretelling the taking of his own life, he was also providing a
guide on whom to blame for causing it.

A few weeks later the government did take a decisive step. The
Peel government banned a massive public meeting that had been
scheduled for Clontarf. In response, O'Connell blinked. He canceled the event rather than risk the chance of a violent outbreak,
an honorable move that nonetheless hurt his political standing.
His reputation would be rescued by the overreaching actions of the
British government, which arrested him and tried him for conspiring to alter the constitution by force. During the trial, he thrilled
the courtroom with his eloquence and tactical brilliance. A jury
packed with Protestants delivered a guilty verdict, which the House
of Lords soon overturned. After his release from prison, O'Connell
traveled through the thronged streets of Dublin standing atop an
ornate carriage, draped in purple and gold, pulled by six dapple-
gray horses. It was the last triumphal moment of his political life.

Peel responded to the slowing of the Repeal agitation by introducing several bills to conciliate the Catholic clergy and more moderate members of Catholic society. He offered to increase the government grant for Maynooth, the Catholic institution that educated the country's priests, in an attempt to wean the young clerics from the influence of Repeal. He sought to create nondenominational universities, complementing the national system of nondenominational elementary schools created by the Whigs in 1831, to end the people's dependence on priests for their interpretation of the world. He introduced a charitable bequests bill to make it easier for assets to be willed to the Church, addressing a long-festering Catholic grievance. While O'Connell and many of his allies were suspicious of these efforts, seeing them as little more than attempts to subjugate the Irish Church under state control, members of Young Ireland were rather supportive of the idea of creating four queen's colleges in Dublin, Cork, Galway, and Belfast, without a religious test for entry. For his part, O'Connell denounced them as "Godless Colleges."

It was another of Peel's Irish initiatives that most applies to the Strokestown story. His government established a commission chaired by Lord Devon that traveled throughout Ireland in 1843 and 1844, interviewing landlords, land agents, farmers, magistrates, clergymen, laborers, and judges about the state of relations between landlords and tenants. On Monday, July 22, 1844, John Mahon, Major Mahon's brother, appeared before the commissioners in Roscommon town. He provided the most revealing portrait of the Mahon property, as it existed on the eve of the Famine, that has survived to this day.

"What is the district with which you are acquainted?" he was asked.

"The neighborhood of Strokestown," he responded. "I am receiver upon the Hartland estate. Lord Hartland is a lunatic; and I have been appointed the receiver of the estate."

"Is that an estate of considerable extent?"

"About 6,829 Irish acres," he said. (Or about 11,000 statute or English acres.)

How long had the estate of Lord Hartland been under the courts?

"Seven years."

He added that the property had 2,097 houses with an average of five people in each house, which he calculated to mean that 10,485 people lived on the land. Only 745 tenants had leases, which meant that upward of 8,000 people were either subtenants (and sub-subtenants) or members of rundale collectives.

Mahon was asked if he had been able to "re-let" any of the lands. In other words, had he been able to clear out tillage plots and replace them with grazing farms?

"We have not in many instances," he said. But he planned to do so in May 1846, when a number of leases were set to expire.

He was asked about operating the estate under the supervision of the courts.

"[I]t is difficult to act under the court, there are so many forms, and a great deal of delay takes place."

Mahon then blamed overpopulation on the estate on his ancestors' desire for political influence and on their slack management style. "From the circumstance of the 40s [40-shilling] freeholders there was generally one member of the family in Parliament; and in order to make a number of votes it was set in very small divisions," he said. He added that his ancestors had allowed rundale collectives to flourish without check—although, according to Arthur Young's account of seventy years earlier, they had done so because it wasn't thought "a bad system."

He also blamed the trouble on the behavior of the tenants themselves.

"The early marriages in this country have been a great cause of the misery and poverty," he said. "They have no means for providing for their children but by dividing the land among them, in the proportions they give them."

Had he taken any means to rectify that subdivision?

"No," he responded. "I have not the power under the court to regulate it. As long as the rent is paid we have no power to remove a tenant."

Had many of the leases "fallen out" (or expired)?

"Yes, this last May," he said. "But I was not able to act upon them"—to conduct clearances—because of court restrictions.

"Does it frequently happen that those [rundale] companies you speak of, comprising thirty persons, hold in common?"

"Yes, which they arrange among themselves," he said. "They have a tillage ridge in one place, and pasture in another, according to the quality; and they are so tenacious of one man having a better quality than another, if one man has a better ridge than another, they will cast lots for it."

So he had no power, acting as receiver, to correct that?

"No, it has been continued long, long before I had anything to say to it," he said.

What was the state of the cultivation?

At this point, Mahon mentioned that he had some luck—after receiving permission from the courts—in clearing the land and creating "new settings," which resulted in improved cultivation. "I was anxious to enlarge their holdings and get rid of the paupers; but I had no power to give them any equivalent, except that the arrear they owed when put out was forgiven them. I was obliged to put out a good many in that way." So the court didn't constrain *all* his actions. The Mahon family "put out a good many" prior to the Famine.

He was asked if he "encouraged or assisted" the tenants "in making improvements by building and draining."

Mahon said that under the courts, "we have no power to give any encouragement to improve."

Had he applied for court approval for such a plan?

"No," he said. "I looked upon it as a matter that would require so much to be done." It *"would require so much to be done"*—Denis Mahon and his brother, then, weren't much interested in improving the living standards of their tenants.

The commissioners concluded their questioning by asking Mahon if he had any suggestions to offer.

"The only suggestion is, that it would be very beneficial if there was any mode by which these people could be provided with the means to emigrate, or some encouragement given to them to emigrate, to some other country, where they would be in a better condition; for I do not see how the principal part of the estate would be sufficient to give them relief," he responded.

"Do you think that estates, under these circumstances, might be improved by an extensive system of emigration?"

"Yes; or by any public works that would give employment to them."

"Are they well disposed to emigrate?"

"Yes; and they do themselves, whenever they can raise sufficient sums for that purpose."

Despite its measures of conciliation and coercion, the Peel government didn't end the restiveness in County Roscommon. In fact, the level of violence seemed to be increasing in 1844 and 1845. A large proportion of the trouble was tied directly to the paupers' inability to secure enough acreage to grow potatoes for survival. It stemmed from the unwillingness of farmers to offer or to lower rents for seasonal conacre plots required by those on the lowest rungs of estate society—the cottiers and landless laborers. It is an illustration of just how precarious life was that the poor were resorting to extreme acts for the right to rent properties that were typically the most expensive in the countryside.

In the period following the attempt on Richard Irwin's life, the countryside was roiled by the kind of unrest that inspired local newspapers to deliver stinging pronouncements about "the foolish and disgraceful" conduct of the poor and led local authorities to make desperate calls to Dublin Castle asking for additional troops. "This county has never been in so disturbed a state," wrote one editorialist of what was being called the "conacre movement." But this anger, for the most part, was not directed at the hard-to-reach Protestant lords of the soil, who were either absentees living in England or sheltered residents living behind the walls of the Big House. Instead it was often aimed at the large farmers and middlemen who rented large tracts from the landlords and were most responsible for transacting with the poorer segments of the population. Since many of the Roscommoners in this class were now Catholic supporters of Repeal, the unrest often pitted comfortable Catholics dedicated to moderate nationalism against poor Catholics on the verge of starvation. A Catholic farmer named John Balfe, who stood on the stage with Daniel O'Connell and seconded a motion calling for "the adoption of those measures likely to effect some amelioration in the condition of the country," was the subject of a two-year campaign of terror. In court he was described as a "cruel merciless man to his poor tenants."

Much of the trouble was blamed on a new secret society, a successor to the Threshers, a group that called itself the "Molly Maguires." No one is sure how it got such a striking name, but all the theories revolved around the identity of Ms. Maguire. She was either a poor woman evicted by a cruel landlord whom the Mollies pledged to avenge, a self-avenging angel who led the gang on horseback with guns strapped to her thighs, or the owner of a "shebeen"—illegal tavern—where the gang plotted its attacks. The Molly Maguires acted much like their predecessors, delivering intimidating missives, wearing nighttime disguises that sometimes included women's clothing, and practicing an equal-opportunity brand of grievance that targeted anyone of any class or religion who defied them. A poor laborer who dared occupy the land of someone who had recently been evicted could incur the same sort of wrath as a prosperous gentleman from the landed classes.

The gang sought to scare large farmers, who were grazing cattle and sheep on open pastures, into shrinking the size of their grasslands to accommodate an army of poor tillers of the soil, which was exactly opposite of the intentions of the landlords (who had been clearing for decades) and the government (whose Poor Law was intended to facilitate the transition from small plots to large farms). A primary tactic involved sending a team of men to dig up a farmer's pasture in the middle of the night, in effect preparing the land to be divided into tillage plots. This was often the first battle in a long war against a particular farmer during which livestock were mutilated, buildings were shot up, and employees were stalked. In the early days of the hostilities against Balfe, a gang of four men stopped him on a road near Strokestown, shot and killed his horse, and chased him into the countryside. "The [perpetrators] deliberately walked off amongst a set of Balfe's tenants, 30 or 40 of whom were within a few yards of him, and witnessed the entire transaction without rendering the slightest assistance to the landlord," wrote a correspondent for the *Dublin Evening Mail*. And these tactics were often successful. Not only did some farmers consent to offer (or lower rents for) conacre plots, but few were willing to testify in court against their antagonists. A Catholic farmer named Peter Nolan, the subject of many attacks, was castigated for his "spinelessness" by a magistrate after refusing to identify his assailants.

Both the Protestant and Catholic elites were firm in their condemnation of the rural agitators. In an open letter published in a Roscommon newspaper, a senior Repeal official described them as "miscreant traitors to Ireland" who "give strength to Ireland's enemies" and deserve "the cracking of [their] necks by the hangman in the gallows." The rural clergymen, often collectors of the Repeal "rent," were forever preaching against the impious disturbers of the peace, who responded, in one case, by destroying the pews of a church in southern County Roscommon. The Repeal officials would rather the poor blamed the landlords and not the Catholic farmers, who, an O'Connellite editorialist wrote, were "many of their best benefactors, their most charitable neighbors, and their hitherto best friends." Nonetheless, the gang seemed to have wide support for its actions in the countryside. Reports abounded of tenants standing aside while a farmer was being menaced, of juries refusing to convict men who were clearly guilty, of high-profile arrests failing to stem the tide of trouble. On a day in early 1845, some three thousand people stood on the road in front of a Strokestown farmer's property on the Mahon estate and demanded that the pasture be turned into conacre plots, according to a police report. Surely all three thousand were not oath-bound members of the Molly Maguires, and surely all were not intimated by the gang into cooperating, as was often suggested.

Indeed, one of the last major crimes of the pre-Famine era was not committed against the Protestant proprietor of Strokestown, whose actions were limited by the court system, but against the farmer just mentioned, John Dignan, and his brother. In the spring of 1845, a few weeks after the huge crowd gathered on his land, a "party of Molly Maguire's men" entered Dignan's empty house, where they stole a "gun" and a "pistol," which represented two different kinds of firearms. The four men then traveled to Dignan's brother's home, which was also empty, and began to ransack it for weapons. Informed of what was happening, the Dignan sibling returned home and plunged a knife into one of the intruders. A Molly Maguire then opened fire, shooting Dignan's brother in the head and killing him instantly.

The Mollies exited the house with their wounded comrade, but the bloodied man was left behind in a ditch. The authorities descended on the scene and took the injured man, who was expected to live, to the Strokestown bridewell. The *Dublin Evening Mail* ruefully noted that no one from among the community "would venture to identify the prisoner." The entire population of the area, the paper suggested, was complicit in the conspiracy. "Such is the state of this unfortunate country."

CHAPTER 3

In the Name of God Do Something for Us

And there shall arise after them seven years of famine; and all the plenty shall be forgotten in the land of Egypt; and the famine shall consume the land.

—GENESIS 41:30

THEN CAME THE BLIGHT.

Scientists believe the invisible menace, a funguslike water mold called *Phytophthora infestans*, began its journey in the Toluca Valley of Mexico. From there it ventured north to the United States, arriving sometime in 1843. No one knew what it was, least of all puzzled experts who put forth several off-the-mark hypotheses. But everyone saw that this was a thuggish destroyer of potato crops, a pitiless bully that gave no quarter. Traveling on the wind and thriving in wet conditions, it needed only a few days to infect a healthy field. At first, dark spots appeared on the topsides of a potato plant's leaves, which rose out of the soil on short, thin stalks. The spots then spread to blacken the entire leaf. Traveling down into the soil, the blight attacked the tuber itself. Lesions formed on the potato's body, turning it into a dark, foul-smelling, inedible mush. But in the United States the disease inspired only concern, not panic, since Americans could turn to other crops when the potato was lost.

The blight next cut a path toward a port on the Eastern Seaboard of the United States and made its way aboard a ship for Europe, surely the most noxious American traveler ever to set out for the Old World. It may have reached dry land by way of potato peelings tossed overboard from a ship in the Solent or the English Channel. In late June 1845 it revealed itself in Belgium, arriving in the Netherlands and France by mid-July, reaching northeast France, the lower Rhineland, the English countryside, and the Isle of Wight by August. It seemed only a matter of time before this "blight of unusual character," as one gardener characterized it, reached vulnerable Ireland, a nation that was now relying on the potato to an extent that may be hard for the modern mind to fully comprehend. Out of a population of 8.5 million, 3.3 million depended nearly exclusively on the vegetable for their sustenance; 4.7 million used it as a predominant item of their diet.

By September, when the potato began to be culled from the ground in earnest, reports indicated the danger had arrived. "We stop the press, with very great regret, to announce that the potato murrain has unequivocally declared itself in Ireland," wrote the *Gardeners' Chronicle*. The government asked constabulary officials to check the local crops and report back their findings. On September 26 a subinspector in Strokestown noted that "in this district a very partial failure has occurred," but added that "the injury sustained is hardly worth notice." Three weeks later, another police official in the area warned against paying too much attention to the peasants' opinions. "I have little doubt but in many instances the matter will be the subject to much exaggeration, with a hope of receiving indulgence from the landlords, in the payment of the approaching November rents," he wrote. Eleven days later the first official noted that the blight that he had first noticed one month earlier had "within the last few days . . . appeared in crops which hitherto had appeared quite sound." In the middle of November the

Roscommon Journal said that "almost" all the county's potato crop had been lost.

At this moment Major Mahon became the landlord of Strokestown. Like his arrival at the Battle of Waterloo after the guns had stilled, his entrance into the upper echelons of the Anglo-Irish aristocracy came at exactly the wrong time. The same edition of the newspaper that predicted famine carried the item that he had been waiting to read since he was named "heir presumptive" nine years earlier. His feeble cousin, the third Baron Lord Hartland, had died at the age of seventy-four. "By his death the title is extinct, and his large and extensive domains become the property of his relative Major Denis Mahon of Strokestown House," the paper wrote. The major had spent the previous few months fending off a legal challenge from his cousin Marcus McClausland, who objected to the "immense" sums that he had been spending on the house and demesne. But now, released from the constraints of court supervision and family interference, he was free to do as he wished with the property.

It was soon clear that the roughly eleven thousand residents of the Mahon property were coping with a partial failure of the potato crop, which, while representing a crisis, was not nearly as bad as the government commission appointed by Prime Minister Robert Peel had predicted. The Tory leader, who had helped coordinate relief efforts during the Irish crop failures of 1817 and 1822, knew that Ireland faced a greater risk than blight-affected but more crop-diverse England and Scotland. So with his commission warning him of a "melancholy" situation that "cannot be looked upon in other than a most serious light," a genuinely alarmed Peel announced that he wanted to repeal the Corn Laws, long-standing policies that placed price controls and other barriers on grains entering the whole of the United Kingdom. It was a radical move—his Tory Party was dominated by protectionist landowners opposed to their profits being diminished by foreign competition—that sent a rumble though the British political establishment that would be felt for decades. But Peel had come to believe that restrictive laws against food importation were sinful impediments to the natural "circulation of the Creator's bounty," as he wrote, preventing the flourishing of a free trade system that was in accord with the way the Almighty had intended humans to live. But his effort to rescind the laws, which would mean little for the most pressing needs of Ireland, was quickly bottled up in controversy. In challenging the orthodoxy of his own party and siding with the opposition, Peel found that he lacked even the support of his own cabinet on the matter.

The prime minister did initiate a policy, a temporary one, that had a more immediate effect on the Irish populace. Peel held the conventional view that an indiscriminate distribution of relief would foster dependence, lassitude, and rebellion in the Irish poor, preventing them from gaining the necessary skills to ascend out of their destitution. But because of the obvious gravity of the situation, he decided to order the purchase of 100,000 pounds' worth of Indian maize from the United States to breach the shortfall. His decision violated strict laissez-faire injunctions against undue interference in the food supply, but even the revered anti-interventionist thinker Edmund Burke, writing in his 1795 tract *Thoughts and Details on Scarcity*, understood there were exceptions to the prohibition against "meddling with the subsistence of the people." He wrote, "Nothing, certainly, can be laid down on the subject that will not admit of exceptions, many permanent, some occasional." Still, Peel was importing the foodstuffs into the country with Ireland's salvation in mind. He hoped to end the nation's unhealthy dependence on the potato and "habituate the Irish people to the consumption of a novel species of food as a substitute for their ordinary subsistence," he wrote. Secretly purchased through the firm of the Baring Bros.—so as not to affect the markets too much—the maize would be ground and distributed to depots and subdepots throughout the stricken regions, where it would be sold to paupers who earned money on public works projects. Those who were too old or too weak to work would use the country's permanent apparatus of poor relief, the dreaded workhouse.

Throughout the winter months of late 1845 and into early 1846, the government moved slowly to put the entire system in place. The delay, as most understood, would not be of major consequence. The full force of the partial loss of the potato crop wouldn't be felt until the lean summer months prior to the next harvest, when the stocks from the previous year normally ran out. The government's Indian maize was intended to supply paupers with food throughout the spring and summer. By the late summer and early fall—when it was hoped a bustling private trade in Indian maize and foreign grains would be in existence—the relief operations would come to a close.

The Molly Maguires were also expecting a good harvest in the fall of 1846. By the early months of 1846—the potato crop needed to be planted by April—the secret society was alleged to be in the midst of a campaign to intimidate farmers into renting out conacre (and other plots) at favorable rates. But there was a new desperation to the gang's tactics. One farmer in the Elphin area with only 8.5 acres of grassland left on his 150-acre expanse was warned that his cows would be fed pins if he didn't allow the remaining pasture to be let out as conacre land. Believing that the rural population was both scared of the Molly Maguires and supportive of its actions, local officials now felt that another coercion bill, long the British government's response to a spike in rural crime, would not be sufficient to improve the situation. A meeting of magistrates near Strokestown informed Dublin Castle that owing to "the dreadful state this county has been permitted to fall into," only the imposition of martial law would return tranquillity to County Roscommon.

The prime minister had received reports of this sort for months. His top officials in Ireland had been telling him the food shortage was being used as a pretext to avoid paying rents, the first step in a peasant rebellion. "We are informed from several quarters that a very bad spirit prevails—& two cases are reported this morning of priests from the altar recommending the people to make no payments—& hinting that, when the famine comes, they may help themselves, the law of nature being superior to the law of man," wrote his chief secretary. "The people begin to show symptoms of discontent which may ripen into something worse," wrote the lord lieutenant. At first Peel had resisted the idea of bringing a coercion bill before Parliament. But feeling that any regeneration effort would be unsuccessful without a requisite level of safety and security—and hoping to placate Irish landlords angry over the idea of Corn Law repeal—Peel offered the Protection of Life Bill in Parliament in February. With its most controversial provision calling for curfew violators to receive a sentence of fifteen years' transportation (or banishment), the bill would be debated for months, causing nearly as much controversy as the Corn Laws.

One figure in County Roscommon was emerging as a most vocal and uncompromising opponent of the lawbreakers. Bishop George J. P. Browne had been appointed to lead the Diocese of Elphin in 1844, after serving for thirteen years as the bishop of Galway. He had earned a reputation there as a reserved man who sought conciliation over confrontation. A contemporary described him as "a man of goodly presence, refined and most gentleman-like manners, courteous to all," whose "society was much sought after." Another praised his "suave, meek character." A mother superior noted that "Bishop Browne has love and charity enough for thousands and embraces all with genuine paternal care and apostolic affection." Daniel O'Connell himself hailed the bishop as the "Dove of Galway" and quoted Alexander Pope to describe his personality—"In wit a man/in simplicity a child." In his official portrait, the white-haired prelate in formal vestments is imbued with a patient, forgiving air, gazing as if toward an unruly yet ultimately redeemable schoolboy. At his inaugural Mass in 1831 in Galway, he appealed for unity between Catholics and Protestants—"there was scarcely a tearless eye in the chapel," wrote a newspaper—and during his welcoming dinner, representatives of both communities toasted him with "wines of the very best description." It was just this sort of conduct that his superiors hoped would improve the state of Galway, which was marred by the same kind of unrest as County Roscommon.

By many accounts, he did much to maintain calm. He told Rome in a letter that "we are all peace and tranquility at present—all thanks to the eternal God." He told a colleague that his objective was "to promote peace and harmony among our hitherto deluded peasantry and . . . to inculcate the divine precept of charity, without distinction of sect or creed." Near the end of his tenure, an ecclesiastical superior credited "the present pacific and flourishing state" of the diocese to the bishop's "conciliatory manner, wisdom, and ability." But he also was a deeply political figure whose support of Daniel O'Connell inspired the British government to regard him as an agitator. Like many Repeal bishops, he was suspicious of any British initiative, and he opposed Peel's efforts to moderate the state's relationship to the Catholic middle class. His political engagement was also unpopular with the Vatican, which forbade its clergymen from directing their parishioners' gaze away from the Gospel text. An anonymous complaint was delivered to Rome when he saluted "the people, the true source of legitimate power" at a banquet. He was as dismissive of Rome's concerns as he was of London's. Even after the pope issued a rescript in 1844 forbidding his Irish clergy from involving themselves in politics—at the request of the British government—the bishop continued to deliver toasts at Repeal dinners.

By the early months of 1846, after three years of unease in County Roscommon, Bishop Browne was using every opportunity to lambaste the secret societies. Now called the "Dove of Elphin," he had visited parishes in every corner of the diocese during the previous autumn to preside over confirmation Masses, one of the few occasions a visitor of such stature had visited remote areas.

In his sermons he pulled few punches, attacking "the irreligious, disgraceful and unfortunate conduct of those who were illegally associated or connected with any system calculated to injure their neighbors' property or life," according to a Roscommon newspaper. He also used a variety of public events to take aim at the radical Catholic and Protestant Repealers of Young Ireland, who were distancing themselves from O'Connell over his strong ties to the Catholic Church and his unwillingness to entertain the possibility of violent action. During a celebration of one of Roscommon's two MPs, Bishop Browne said he had never "associated with any party or body of men who would seek to disturb the peace of society and happiness of Ireland. I do not care by what name they might be called, whether Young Ireland or whatever else, if they wanted to attain their objects by sacrificing the peace of the country I will have nothing to do with them."

But Bishop Browne's Lenten address of March 1846, printed in all the newspapers and likely read from every pulpit, most fully laid out his views on the discontent in the countryside. Heavily leaden with scriptural quotes and high-flown liturgical-like language, the letter dealt with many doctrinal matters—it issued a dispensation from Lenten fasting requirements in light of the potato blight and warned the faithful to refrain from turning wakes into occasions of "mirth." But a large section of the text was filled with an attack on "that accursed and illegal system of Molly Maguirism, equally condemned by the law of God and the law of the land."

"We earnestly solicit and entreat, that, guided by . . . those lively convictions of the faith which we know you to possess, you would put from amongst you, as the deadliest enemies of your happiness and peace, those who would seek to connect you with secret societies or secret obligations," he wrote.

The bishop continued, "For we have heard that there are some among you who walk disorderly, working not all, but curiously meddling. Now these that are such, we denounce, and we beseech them, in the Lord Jesus Christ, that working with silence, they would eat their own bread. And if any man obey not our word by this Epistle, note that man, and do not keep company with him, that he may be ashamed; yet do not esteem him as an enemy, but admonish him as a brother. But you, my brethren, do not weary in well doing."

He took special note of how the secret societies accused the Catholic clergy of "a culpable indifference to the wants of the poor and a base subservience to the caprice of the rich." Somewhat defensively, the bishop denounced the accusations as being as "wicked as they ARE FALSE." It was the only time in the letter he ascended into capital letters for anything other than a scriptural passage. He also took care to admonish "the opulent and the wealthy to be indulgent and charitable to the poor, to sympathize with them in their wants." His primary concern, though, was in sending a message to the peasant who would seek vengeance through "illegal combinations and lawless violence."

"We are perfectly aware that the poor have many grievances to complain of, and that it is our duty to alleviate their sufferings," he wrote, in a passage that Rome would have approved of. "But it is not by violence or outrage this great end can be attained; it is by humble supplication to the Throne of Mercy, and in the midst of danger and of difficulty to place our entire confidence in the God of Justice."

Bishop Browne's life story reveals that these sentiments stemmed from a long belief in the necessity of conciliation, a steadfast faith in the political principles expressed by Daniel O'Connell, and a clear dedication to the pacific message of Jesus Christ. But he also had a more personal reason for targeting the Molly Maguires—or those involved in "Molly Maguirism," as he put it—in the spring of 1846. His father was a middleman and farmer who operated a sizable farm of some four hundred acres in County Roscommon. In fact, the now elderly Martin Browne was largest single tenant on the estate of the landlord of Strokestown, Major Denis Mahon, according to the Devon Commission testimony of Major Mahon's brother. Only about fifty acres of the property were set in tillage plots, which would have put Martin Browne, who was in his nineties, and his other son, Patrick, who ran the farm, under considerable pressure from the secret society to offer parcels to the poor. It surely didn't escape the bishop's attention that he was delivering a message to those who would strike at his own family—and, by less deliberate extension perhaps, the landlord who owned the land.

In early June the first signs of the food shortage were being recorded in Strokestown. On June 5 Father Michael McDermott, the town's parish priest, wrote a letter to the authorities noting that the market prices for potatoes and oatmeal had risen to exceptionally high levels. The priest saw evidence that this was causing restiveness. "The people wear a sullen aspect and are giving expression to their discontent in a very menacing tone—nothing is heard in the market but threats and murmurs," he wrote. With a bluntness that would characterize all his statements over the next three years, he noted that neither a relief fund nor public works initiatives had been started. "So in the name of God do something for us—have you the secretary or have you got any money to send us?" he wrote to the government. "I expect a line by the next post."

It was obvious that the parish priest wasn't aware of the relief guidelines that had been established four months earlier. A Relief Commission had been set up in Dublin to distribute the Indian maize through local committees in distressed areas, to be staffed by leading citizens. These bodies, which were vital to the smooth operation of the scheme, were instructed to raise money from local subscribers—principally the landlords, whom the government saw as "both legally and morally answerable for affording due relief to the destitute poor." The money would then be matched completely or partially with government funds, with the precise amount decided by the Relief Commission, pending the approval of the lord lieutenant, Ireland's viceroy—all under the careful guidance of Treasury officials in London (particularly the permanent assistant secretary Charles Trevelyan). The local committee would then take the lump sum and purchase the maize from the government—the same government that had contributed to that lump sum.

Only those who were too weak to work and couldn't find a place in the workhouse were to be given food "gratuitously." The rest, the "able-bodied" poor, were required to staff public works projects, enabling them to earn the wages to purchase the government maize, at market rate or just below, from the relief committees. This work-for-cash-for-Indian-meal plan was not only intended to feed the people with a "novel" species of food that would serve to replace the potato, but it was also meant to show the Irish what it was like to be wage laborers who bought their sustenance in the marketplace. Like the Irish Poor Law, then, the relief effort was intended to a foster a "transition period" from potato-dependent subsistence poverty into grain-dependent proletariat comfort.

The local committees were responsible for selecting the workers for the jobs by making up lists of each townland's residents and issuing employment tickets to those qualified for duty. The public works initiatives, which had been a part of previous government responses to food shortages, were funded with government grants with varying degrees of repayment requirements. Jobs that developed fisheries and harbors or improved landlords' estates required the local communities (that is, the landlords) to repay the full costs, while jobs constructing and repairing roads required the proprietors to repay only 50 percent of the government sum. The landlords unsurprisingly favored the more generous "half-grants," and a deluge of requests for road projects was received in Dublin.

In his response to Father McDermott, Randolph Routh, chairman of the Relief Commission, boiled the complex structure down to its essentials: The government was not willing to carry the full weight of relief. "Why is there no committee in this town, and why is there no subscription even of shillings and tenpences or of some collection at the church, something to prove the disposition of the people to make an effort in their own behalf, to which the government will so readily contribute?" he wrote. If Father McDermott was wondering why the government didn't "do something for us," Routh was asking why the residents of Strokestown didn't do something for themselves. It was, in a sentence, the essential conflict of the Famine.

One day after Father McDermott mailed the letter, however, it was reported that a relief committee met in Strokestown, with the Catholic priest among its members. Since it had raised 100 pounds from five prominent citizens—including Major Mahon—it was clear that the committee had already met on at least one occasion, probably others. But in its letter to the Relief Commission, the committee showed that it still wasn't fully aware of the relief guidelines. It said that the money had been raised for the "aged and infirm," which set off alarm bells in Dublin. The Relief Commission responded to the letter by noting that the aged and infirm— those unable to staff the public works projects—were expected to be admitted into the 900-person-capacity Roscommon workhouse, which at the time had 526 vacancies. "If the committee should find it necessary to raise a subscription for the employment of the able-bodied poor in the district, government will be prepared to add a donation when a list of the subscribers together with a certificate of the lodgment of the money has been forwarded to the commissioners," Randolph Routh wrote.

But since the public works projects had yet to be started in Strokestown, the Relief Commission's complaint was largely academic. The local committee's response does not survive, but it likely assured the commission that, yes, it was raising money for the "able-bodied poor." For within six days, on June 12, Father McDermott asked that a government depot be established in Strokestown to accommodate a supply of Indian maize. "We can afford ample storage for any quantity that may be sent here and we naturally claim the privilege of having such a depot as our town is so central and convenient to all parts of this extensive district," Father McDermott wrote. The priest again spoke of the urgency of the situation, imploring the commission to act quickly. "I can in solemn truth assure them [the commissioners] that I know several families who are contriving to make food of Bran and to go into fields to pluck wild herbs for their subsistence," he wrote. Within two weeks, on June 23, a depot was established in Strokestown, with a constabulary officer assigned to oversee the sale of meal to area relief committees.

By this time, the local committee had experienced a change in leadership. The area's principal landowner assumed the lead in coordinating a relief effort that the government saw as primarily his responsibility. At the end of June Major Mahon had been named— or named himself—chairman and treasurer of the Strokestown committee, assuming the responsibility for the bulk of its correspondence. In his first letter to the Relief Commission, he noted that the "very active" committee had raised an additional 85 pounds to relieve the "very distressed state of this town and neighborhood," which he blamed on the "very large and overgrown population of this district." He asked for "a sum of money to be placed at our disposal to enable us to carry out our laudable intentions in relieving the unparalleled distress under which we labor at present." The government responded by offering an additional 60 pounds.

The major's robust involvement on the committee can be seen in a long, pleading letter he wrote to a local gentlemen on June 28, three days after his first letter to the Relief Commission. Thomas Conry had offered a subscription to the committee but decided to rescind the money when he learned that his tenants were outside the committee's jurisdiction. At first Major Mahon played to his vanity—"consider what people will think of it, and consult any friend you like and see if you would be advised to do so," he wrote. He then suggested that even if Conry's tenants were outside the committee's boundaries, the public works projects, which the major said would be starting soon, would nonetheless "take in your people" for employment. "There are hills to be cut down, some new roads to be made," wrote the major. He noted that he was contributing funds for two road projects approved under the government's half-grant plan—including 200 pounds for a road through his estate to the Longford mail coach road. Finally, Major Mahon admitted that he wanted the man to pay his subscription "to keep myself from censure, to which I should be justly liable if, as chairman of the relief committee, I had not noticed the transaction."

The arguments were convincing, and on July 10 Major Mahon wrote a letter of thanks to Conry for changing his mind. In the course of his communication, he indicated that the Strokestown committee, like other committees in blighted areas throughout Ireland, had begun to supply Indian maize to the poor even though the public works projects had yet to be started and the workhouse was still not full. He also reported that he himself had participated in the distribution—"I was three hours yesterday . . . serving to the poor," he wrote—and that his tenants quite enjoyed the government corn. "You would be surprised how much the people like it out here," he wrote of a foodstuff dubbed by some as "Peel's Brimstone" because it caused stomach ailments and sometimes death if improperly prepared. Within weeks the major would further show his dedication to the local committee by meeting with Routh, the most influential relief official in Ireland outside of the lord lieutenant, during a visit to Dublin. In a subsequent letter to the Relief Commission, he wrote that Routh "was so kind as to say he would be most willing to afford us every assistance in his power."

By early August the relief operation in Strokestown seemed to be going as well as could be expected, although the testimony of the poor is unavailable. The surviving records show that the local committee was distributing Indian maize, while the public works projects were beginning in many areas. The committee had raised at least 315 pounds through local subscriptions and government contributions, which, with Indian meal selling for 10 pounds a ton at this point, meant that a decent amount of food would have been available for purchase. Strokestown's landlord was fulfilling his government-mandated obligation to the poor, a praiseworthy but not unusual effort for a resident landlord. (He was also doing some fishing, according to one letter.) But all was not well in his mind. For one, he claimed that a conspiracy had been hatched among some of his tenants to refuse to pay rent. "The combination not to pay rents is in existence," he wrote. "But I am determined to put down such attempt. Those that have the money, should pay. I shall not think of sparing those who want time." For another, he complained that the local representatives of the Catholic Church were not measuring up during the crisis. "I have attacked the Catholic bishop and clergy assembled here," he wrote, likely referring to a spiritual retreat that brought Bishop Browne and his diocesan clergy to Father McDermott's parish. "They have been feasting and stuffing and praying here the last weeks and I have within this half hour spoken to Bishop Browne. I got him to speak to his clergy so that I think I shall get proven them."

Feasting and stuffing and praying? While members of the Protestant Ascendancy were not known for their love of the Catholic priesthood, the charge that ministers of Christ were gorging themselves in the midst of an incipient famine was a particularly serious one. Either Major Mahon, the son of a Protestant minister and son-in-law of a lord bishop, was a bigot who deliberately misconstrued an innocuous gathering of prayerful clerics, or Strokestown's priests were blithely removed from the trials of their people. But there was another important phrase in the landlord's accusation: "I have attacked." Major Mahon wasn't afraid to begin a battle with such formidable community representatives.

CHAPTER 4

Good and Willing; Idle and Bad

I think I see a bright light shining in the distance through the dark cloud which at present hangs over Ireland. . . . God grant that we may rightly perform our part and not turn into a curse what was intended for a blessing.

—CHARLES TREVELYAN, PERMA-
NENT ASSISTANT SECRETARY TO
THE TREASURY, OCTOBER 9, 1846

A CRISIS THAT MOST regarded as temporary and conquerable was about to turn far more serious. It was soon discovered that the food shortage would not be limited to a single season. By the first week of August, reports from throughout the country were describing how the blight had appeared in the new potato crop, far earlier than it had last harvest. Correspondents told how healthy, blooming fields were being transformed into wide expanses of "putrefying vegetation" in little more than a day, an indication that this despoliation was more powerful than the last one. In a widely cited letter, Father Theobald Mathew, the famous temperance priest, wrote on August 7, "In many places the wretched people were seated on fences of their decaying gardens, wringing their hands and wailing bitterly the destruction that had left them foodless." On August 15 the *Roscommon Journal* wrote, "We have recently traveled through almost every part of this county and the complaints of everyone, from the rich grazier to the miserable peasant, is alike heartrending." While the poor of Ireland could cope with a crop failure that affected a single season's harvest, they knew that two successive seasons of rot spelled disaster. In the description of historian Peter Gray, a second failure "was outside of the bounds of Irish experience and the imagination of the government and its officials." It was typical for people of every background to speak of the now-unprecedented crisis, created by a strain of crop malady that had never been encountered before and could not be explained by science, as if it was sent by God.

As it happened, a new government in London was planning changes in the system of relief. In late June Robert Peel had finally—and barely—achieved passage of his repeal of the Corn Laws, badly fracturing his own party in the process. He next took up the Irish coercion bill that had also been the subject of heated debate. But the legislation went down to a crushing defeat not because of the merits or demerits of its provisions. Sixty-nine disaffected protectionist Tories voted against the bill to punish Peel for his treachery over the Corn Laws. With the help of the votes of Whigs, Radicals, and Repealers, Peel's ministry was toppled and Lord John Russell was elevated to prime minister over a Whig government that lacked a majority in the House of Commons. A supporter of the repeal of the Corn Laws, the diminutive Russell had loudly opposed the coercion bill, scoffing at the suggestion that the Irish poor were using the food shortage to plot a peasant rebellion, a view that wasn't universal in the party (or even his new cabinet). Like many Liberals in England, he was apt to blame Ireland's problems on her greedy landlords, whom he characterized as encouraging the growth of a poverty-stricken, potato-dependent population to fund lavish and dissolute lives in the posh parlors of distant England and elsewhere in Europe. He even suggested in the House of Commons that the increasing number of evictions were "the cause of violence and crime in Ireland."

The Repealers in Ireland were pleased. Daniel O'Connell, who had allied with the Whigs in the 1830s, had thrown his support behind the prospects of a Russell government in hopes that it would introduce "sweeping" measures for Ireland. The O'Connellite *Roscommon Journal* wrote on July 18 that it now had "strong hopes for our native land." But O'Connell's renewed alliance with the Whigs soon precipitated a formal split within his Repeal Association. Eager to expel a radical faction that might harm his standing with the Whigs and thus impair the prospects for real reform, O'Connell demanded that the Young Ireland bloc formally agree to a number of resolutions, one of which called for the total disavowal of violent actions. Even though only a small number in Young Ireland were intent on armed revolution at this point, the group refused to bow to the Liberator's demands, leading to its formal secession from the Repeal movement. At a key point in the nation's history, Ireland's nationalists were divided in two.

On August 17 Lord John Russell took to the floor of the House of Commons and declared that "the prospect of the potato crop this year is even more distressing than last year." He did not respond to this news by announcing a dramatic reconsideration of relief policy. Instead, he would allow Peel's relief schemes to be phased out as planned (and as had already been occurring) by the end of August. Following a brief period of reorganization, the Whig government's new plan would be put in place.

In County Roscommon the news didn't go over so well. When wages were lowered on a public works project outside Roscommon town in late August in an attempt to hasten its closure, an angry mob of three hundred people marched into town, surrounded the Board of Works official responsible for the change, and threatened to plunder the town. "It is my duty to state that my life was hanging on a thread, which I saw snapping at almost every moment during a considerable portion of time," the official told his superiors. "One blow, one stone thrown, or even a more malicious shout against me than usual would inevitably have proved fatal to me." Only after the official agreed to restore the wage—for one week—did the angry mob stand down. In Strokestown a group of laborers on a drainage project struck after learning that their wages were to be reduced. An anonymous letter to a newspaper described how the workers were forced to do the most grinding of labor—"drawing stones up a steep bank"—under the supervision of the most pitiless of overseers. "A more heart-rending scene of pampered official tyranny' over 'starving impotence' I never before beheld. God knows where it will end."

But a written protest lodged by some Strokestown area tenants should have been the most disquieting to Major Denis Mahon. Signed by twenty-two men from two townlands north of Strokestown, "the humble memorial" was delivered to the Strokestown Relief Committee on August 22. It described how the men had been turned away from a public works project despite possessing employment tickets issued by the committee and signed by Major Mahon. "In speaking to Mr. [Thomas] Barton [the works' overseer] he says he must break 100 men more out of the work, and thus we have no hope of relief from him. And what must we do? Our families really and truly suffering in our present and we cannot much longer withstand their cries for food. We have no food for them. Our potatoes are rotten and we have no grain—and Gentlemen—You know but very little of the state of the suffering poor." Then came an explicit threat: "Are we to resort to outrage?" Echoing the language of Bishop Browne's Lenten letter in particular and Repeal rhetoric in general, the men said that they had "peacefully and quietly conducted themselves and submitted to the will of Divine Providence," but "cannot restrain from expressing to you our feelings, and our wrongs. Gentlemen, we fear that the peace of the county will be much disturbed if relief be not immediately more extensively afforded to the suffering peasantry." In another echo of Bishop Browne's letter, they ended by noting that they were "not for joining in anything illegal or contrary to the laws of God or the land," but added, in defiance of their pastoral leader, "unless pressed to by HUNGER."

The "threats and murmurs" that Father McDermott had heard in the Strokestown marketplace two and half months earlier were now growing louder and more specific.

In fact, the fourth Earl of Bessborough, the lord lieutenant in Dublin, used his discretionary powers to halt the cessation of public works, in response to angry complaints from every segment of Irish society. Even though the Treasury felt such a move was a capitulation to "exaggerated" fears, it was in keeping with the new scheme for Irish relief. The government would not give up on Peel's work-for-cash-for-Indian-meal relief effort; it would merely reduce the Treasury's contribution for many aspects of it.

The public works would continue under a more streamlined system, but the government's purchase and resale of Indian maize would be halted (except in the most distressed districts), both recommendations of the Treasury's permanent assistant secretary Charles Trevelyan, whose power over relief had been enhanced under the new administration. Like others in elite society, Trevelyan saw the reoccurrence of the blight as an opportunity to bring permanent improvements to woeful Ireland. He was a tireless and exacting civil servant whose thinking on the crisis was animated by a rigid belief in classical laissez-faire economics and a strong evangelical Protestantism that was unashamed to speak of God's intentions. He believed that the benevolent hand of Providence had sent the food shortage to end the evil potato-based system that had caused the island to be overpopulated, indolent, poor, and violent, and that it was his job to ensure that the heavenly spirit's intentions were not thwarted by the meddling works of men. Although he was on record as unwilling to countenance actual starvation, Trevelyan was most notable for urging his officers to limit the amount of direct assistance given to the Irish poor, believing that only a stern dose of benevolent severity would wean them from their endemic lassitude. It was a position he held even when it became obvious that Ireland would be required to "pass through fearful calamities," in his description, before a meaningful transformation could be achieved.

He saw it as nothing less than his duty, ordained by the Almighty and stipulated by his service to Her Majesty's government. For his loyal service to God and country during the Famine, he would be honored with a knighthood.

The Whigs' relief scheme—embodied in a series of acts that passed Parliament without controversy—put greater faith in the powers of the free market and the coffers of Irish landlords than did the Tories' scheme. The relief committees would again be required to collect subscriptions for the purchase of Indian maize. But instead of matching or nearly matching the money raised, the Treasury would now only offer to contribute half or less than half of the amount raised, in an attempt to compel the landlords to pay a greater sum. With the government no longer in the business of purchasing or selling Indian meal (for the most part), the relief committees would be required to buy the product from private traders, many of whom had been angry over the government's entrance into the market during the Peel plan. The government would also force the landlords to pick up more of the bill for the public works projects. Instead of providing "half-grants" for some projects, the government would require the landlords to repay the Treasury advances through local taxation. And the landlords were forbidden from requesting projects to improve their estate infrastructure, as they were under Peel. The government would allow only "unproductive" works to be approved, an attempt to reduce applications and spur proprietors to start their own projects.

All other relief matters were to be handled by the workhouses, which were rapidly filling up, and a fund of 50,000 pounds made available for the hardest-hit areas.

While the Whigs' plan differed from the Tories' in some ways, the idea underpinning both was the same. The Irish poor were to be weaned from their potato dependence by being transformed into wage laborers reliant on Indian meal and other grains, products that could now be imported into the country in response to market demand without the barriers of the Corn Laws. The Irish

rich were to be forced to fulfill their responsibilities by expend-
ing resources necessary to speed their tenants' transition into this
new workforce. In his study in London, Lord John Russell hoped
that a powerful class of Catholic merchants, newly prosperous from
feeding the huge mass of wage laborers, would rise up to purchase
the land of Protestant landlords who had been made insolvent by
the demands of his relief policies. The result would be a country
that was prosperous, self-sufficient, and forever at peace with itself.
In this progressive vision, the Russell government and the potato
blight would work together to provide "justice to Ireland," one of
the Whig's longtime slogans.

The government also sought to use its powers to reform the local
relief committees, which were seen as rife with mismanagement.
With many committees accused of giving employment tickets to
those who weren't truly destitute, London decided that the committees would now merely provide lists of the poor to the officials
overseeing the public works projects. Since the government felt
the committees were too large and unwieldy, it decided to scale
back on the number of people eligible to serve on them. One provision advised that only the principal clergymen of each parish
could qualify, which permitted the exclusion of young Catholic
curates, many of whom had thrown themselves into the relief
effort. In Strokestown, Major Mahon went a step further, in clear
violation of the government's guidelines. He decided not only to
remove the Catholic curates from the new committee but also to
jettison the Catholic pastor, Father McDermott. It was another
battle in the escalating war between the two most prominent figures
in Strokestown society.

The priest, as was his wont, was not about to take the insult
without protest. On September 25 he and his two curates fired
off an angry missive to the lord lieutenant, demanding that all
three men be restored to the Strokestown committee. The memorial was written by Father McDermott and signed by each of the

priests, with Father McDermott identifying himself as the "arch-deacon of Elphin," revealing his close alliance with the bishop of Elphin, George Browne. It described how they had previously served "to the great benefit and satisfaction of the poor residing in our respective localities whose wants and individual sufferings we could easily ascertain through our constant intercourse with them." The memorial then turned into an open attack on Major Mahon. Father McDermott claimed the landlord had, "by undue influence," "usurped" the management of the relief fund, appointed "the most odious and obnoxious characters" to oversee the public works projects, and nominated intolerant bigots to the new relief committee. "This arbitrary and intolerant selection of a few adherents possessing strong party feelings is calculated to excite . . . deeprooted jealousy and suspicion . . . in the minds of a people who have already suffered too much from such undisguised bigotry," Father McDermott wrote. He then seemed to threaten the lord lieutenant himself. "If your Excellency does not forthwith issue your order . . . to reinstate us to the committee," he wrote, leaving the remainder of the line blank. In the margin of the memorial, someone, likely the lord lieutenant, wrote, "What will they do?" Undaunted, the lord lieutenant responded to the priests' memorial by saying that, according to the government rules, the curates could be excluded but the parish priest, as the principal clergyman of the town's Catholic parish, could not. Father McDermott was back on the committee.

In the weeks after the priests' letter, it became apparent that the government's relief apparatus was straining under the weight of a far greater humanitarian crisis than the previous harvest. Strokestown was one of the stricken localities exempted from the prohibition against buying and selling government maize, but only a small supply was left over from the Peel scheme, and demand far exceeded it. Relief committees from Strokestown and the small towns surrounding it wrote to the authorities begging for additional quantities of food. "The depots in Strokestown and Roscommon are inadequate to afford us any relief," wrote a member of the Tulsk

Relief Committee on October 1. By the second week of October, the Strokestown depot was empty. With other areas in western Ireland suffering similar shortages, the government sought to import additional food supplies from Europe. But poor harvests throughout the Continent limited the amount that could be purchased. In early November, Randolph Routh responded to a request from the Strokestown committee asking for grain to be sent to the local depot by noting that "due attention will be given to the acquisition ... when the supply of seed bere and rye to be imported shall arrive." At the same time, a deluge of requests for public works projects from the throughout the country—the landlords were apparently unconcerned with paying back the government advances—tangled the other aspect of the relief enterprise in bureaucracy. Many of the schemes had yet to be started by the middle of October. The *Roscommon Journal* called it an "unaccountable delay and procrastination on the part of the commissioners of the Board of Works." With food prices rising high above wage levels—speculators and "gombeenmen" (the dreaded village usurers of Irish lore) were eager to reap profits—even those lucky enough to get a job were struggling to persevere, especially with the introduction of "task work" that rewarded healthier workers with better pay and thus penalized those too debilitated to exert themselves. The *Roscommon and Leitrim Gazette* described how a man named Cunningham, who was working on a road project three miles from his home, "died of starvation." He was one of the first (and few) victims of the Famine to be named in the newspaper.

With so much of its faith placed in the restorative powers of the free market—which was the reason the Whigs came to power, after all—the Russell government (like the Peel government) resisted calls to halt grain and other food exports out of Ireland. Trevelyan believed such a "shortsighted" idea would "seriously retard the progress of general improvement." This decision has often been used as ballast for the Irish nationalist charge that the British government allowed Ireland to starve "in the midst of plenty" or instigated an "artificial" famine, statements first made in the earliest days of the Famine. The sight of crops being carted out of the starving coun- tryside would long be a fixture in the memory of the tragedy. In the 1930s the Strokestown storyteller who viewed Major Mahon's Famine actions positively said that the "wheat crop was sent to England to make flour for the tyrants." It is painful reality that a legislative action calling for the closing of the ports would have failed to garner any support in Parliament, which had just made an excruciating decision in favor of unrestrained trade. Irish merchants and farmers, who depended on exports for their livelihoods, also would have strenuously opposed such a measure. And it is clear that it would not have ended the Famine. As Cormac Ó Gráda, an Irish economic historian who has written extensively and perceptively on the era, noted, "The ensuing increased supply of food would have made only a small dent in the gap left by *Phytophthora infestans*." The potato accounted for such a large portion of the nation's food supply—some 60 percent, with poorer citizens depending on it to a degree greater than the better-off—that retaining and distributing all of the remaining foodstuffs would not have been enough. But in the autumn of 1846 a temporary grain embargo—either carried into effect forcibly by the British government or voluntarily by Irish farmers and landlords—would undoubtedly have done something to stem the misery, perhaps something significant. The repeal of the Corn Laws had not yet led to a flood of cheap grain imports into Ireland, and countless commentators recognized, as Routh did in a letter to Trevelyan, that the country "is abundantly supplied with wheat and oats."

As the crisis was growing more desperate, the number of Molly Maguire–like incidents was actually dropping off. The peas- ant revolt that the Peel government was bracing for seemed to be petering out in County Roscommon, and the conacre movement that had caused so much worry over the past two years seemed to be over. Not only did it make little sense to intimidate farm- ers into renting out (temporarily) worthless potato ground, but it was also hard to conduct any sort of covert activity in the midst of a strength-sapping famine. A judge described the county as in a "more tranquil state than twelve months ago." "The country is still, thank God, free from outrage, such as infested it last and previous winters," wrote the *Roscommon Journal* in November. A Board of Works officer stationed in the county noted the occasional "trifling" outrage, but nothing more serious. The most prevalent crime was theft of food. "The starving peasantry are however killing sheep and black cattle on the rich farmers—and we have heard of flour having been taken off various carts on the road from Clara mills to this town," wrote the *Journal*.

Bishop Browne was relieved by the news. His two major public statements in the fall of 1846 focused not on food distribution, relief committees, or public works, but on the poor's seeming reluctance to express their frustrations in the form of violence. He was eager to publicize this as evidence that the people were repudiating not only the Molly Maguires but also Young Ireland. In a September letter to O'Connell published in the local newspapers, Browne said that his recent travels around the diocese had confirmed for him that his priests and people would never be members of "a society that must expose our dear country to anarchy and revolution." And he said he had the donations to prove it. "I have a good portion of the Repeal rent collected from the priests of the diocese in the deaneries through which I have passed," the bishop wrote. "Within ten or twelve days I hope to have all received from those that did not already pay with their parishioners—when all is collected, I shall write again."

In his second public statement, an address in November at the Repeal headquarters in Dublin, the bishop credited the Church with keeping the poor from raising a hand in anger. He described how his clergymen had "some influence in endeavoring in these times to tranquilize the minds of the people—to make them patient under their severe privations—privations more intense than were ever endured by any other country in the world. And, oh God, how appalling to see our fellow creatures two or three days without food—to see them in want and misery—to see the wretched mother, with her helpless orphans, crying for bread for them.

"It demonstrates that under the canopy of Heaven there are no people to be compared to the people of Ireland for morality, religion, and piety," he said to a round of cheers. "In the midst of the most severe privations they are obedient to the laws of order, peace, and morality."

With the weather beginning to grow colder—the winter of 1846–1847 was a particularly frigid and snowy one for Ireland—Major Mahon made a personnel move that would change Strokestown's history forever.

As he prepared to leave Ireland to spend the cold months in England, the major handed considerable control over his property's affairs to a professional land agent, a man who would recommend—and often insist on—all the significant decisions made by Major Mahon during the Famine. His name was John Ross Mahon. Although he was often identified as Major Mahon's cousin, the landlord's family would always claim he was unrelated. Susan Hood seconded this assertion, writing that Ross Mahon was "a member of the Castlegar Mahons who lived at Ahasragh, County Galway, some 30 miles from Strokestown." Perhaps it's better to say that the two men were related in the sense that all Anglo-Irish gentrymen from Connaught were bounded by a shared sense of Ireland and their place in it. Just thirty-two years old, he had cofounded the Guinness Mahon land and banking agency ten years earlier with Robert R. Guinness, a grand-nephew of the founder of the famous brewery. Ross Mahon was rotund, reputedly genial, and, according to one Guinness family chronicler, fond of children. But scores of his letters in the surviving Guinness Mahon letter books reveal him to be a no-nonsense, penny-pinching, hard-bargaining advocate for his clients. Even a note to his mother among his business correspondence betrays little in the way of human affection. In Strokestown he would be forever remembered as "a very cruel man," according to a statement to the folklore commission in the 1930s.

Ross Mahon was hired at a salary of 435 pounds a year—he hoped it would be increased to 500 pounds—to "bring the estate into order," in his own blunt description. In other words, he was charged with solving the problems of overpopulation and subdivision that had been seen as the property's great flaw at least since Edward Wakefield's visit forty years earlier. In a move that revealed the depth of his immersion in the local crisis, the Dublin-based agent opened an office in Strokestown, enabling him to personally oversee the implementation of his recommendations. When he conducted an extensive survey of the property, he gained an immediate sense of the task before him. Thirty-three years later, in chillingly offhand testimony before a government commission, Ross Mahon described his thoughts upon looking over the great mass of Major Mahon's tenants. "Of course they were all absolutely starving," he said in 1880, with that casual "of course" revealing something of the barren state of his humanity. " . . . I saw the impossibility, not only of rent being paid, but of the people living."

The ambitious businessman, whose Famine-era correspondence includes many letters offering his services to prospective clients, had a simple solution: He wanted to remove two-thirds of the tenants from the property. The remaining third of the tenants, he suggested, would then expand the size of their holdings and grow the kinds of profitable grain crops that would be unhurt by any future potato blight. He believed this was the only way to propel the unprofitable estate toward solvency. In his initial recommendation to Major Mahon, the agent offered to achieve this end without the messy prospect of mass evictions, suggesting the kind of plan widely regarded as generous and humane: subsidized emigration. In Ross Mahon's mind, the solution was to spend 24,000 pounds for the passage of several thousand of his tenants to America. If adopted, it would have been one of the most extensive landlord-assisted emigration programs in the history of Ireland.

Anyone knowing the story of the Mahons' fiscal troubles would not be surprised to learn that the landlord decided the idea was too expensive. But neither was Major Mahon interested in taking the alternate route of coldly evicting the mass of excess tenants. He took this stance despite what his brother said before the Devon Commission about how the family was constrained in conducting evictions only by legal roadblocks (removed by the death of the third Lord Hartland) and by tenants who had the temerity to pay rent (ended by successive potato failures).

Instead, over the course of several letters written from England in November, December, and January, the major detailed for his land agent how he wanted the crisis on his estate managed. He spoke of reducing rents, asking Ross Mahon to make deductions on lands "that he considered as overset." In a November 21 letter Major Mahon wrote that he hoped that "such deductions" on the November 1846 rent would "be an inducement to them to pay up to November 1845. . . . The deduction on 1846 I consider an act of justice, being really the *bad* year. 1845 I consider only partially so." He sought to advance seed to "industriously inclined" tenants, enabling "the tenant in distress to crop his ground and pay for seed when he has ample means to do so." He wrote, "I shall decline in giving it until the ground is properly prepared. . . . I think you will agree with me that if we have not some fixed plan of that sort, many will get seed, but not make the proper use of it." He permitted his land agent to distrain (or seize) cattle and other goods from tenants to compel payment of rent, which was seen as a less cruel alternative to evictions. With the Russell administration now relaxing its prohibition against providing assistance for "reproductive" improvements, he decided to begin projects on his property that would benefit both him and his suffering tenants. "There are many parts of my estate that require draining and graveling and that money would be much better laid out in such works than on useless roads," he wrote to Ross Mahon on January 3, 1847. He also sought to offer private employment. He told the land agent that he wanted to begin construction on a national school—to be managed by Father McDermott—because "I consider it so desirable to let any work out that will give employment to the distressed tradesmen at this moment of such unparalleled privations as our unfortunate country has been visited with."

In acting this way, he was generally seen as a good landlord, according to the guidelines of the *Roscommon Journal*. The newspaper praised another landlord who announced that he would reduce rents in a similar fashion by calling him a "good example." Even the revolutionary nationalist John Mitchel would characterize landlords who reduced rents and distributed corn on the relief committees as devoting "themselves to the task of saving their poor people alive." But Major Mahon wasn't yet in the category of the "humane and kind-hearted," in the *Roscommon Journal*'s estimation. That honor was bestowed on a proprietor who took the step of *forgiving* "a half-year's rent and all arrears."

Indeed, Major Mahon's charity was always conditional. He continued to believe that not all his tenants were equally deserving of assistance. He saw them as existing in two categories: those who genuinely couldn't pay rent and those who refused to pay because they were involved in a conspiracy against his rule. "There are many on the estate . . . who can pay if they like," he wrote to the land agent on December 27. "Such men I am not inclined to spare. It's a bad example for others, to see men kept and encouraged that are able to pay but will not."

While Major Mahon didn't cite any evidence for this imprecise claim, he was reflecting a widespread belief in London. Charles Greville, the Whig diarist, wrote that the Irish "never were so well off on the whole as they have been in this year of famine. Nobody will pay rent, and the savings banks are overflowing." But Major Mahon's thinking was also influenced by local factors. In addition to Strokestown's long history of clandestine organizations and recent evidence of threats and murmurs, the area was in the midst of a notorious controversy that featured withholding rent as its primary act of resistance. The townland of Ballykilcline, a tract of land populated by several hundred people within the Kilglass parish, was in the twelfth year of a well-publicized rent strike against the current owner of the parcel, the British Crown. The authorities had engaged in extensive efforts to impel the tenants to give up the land, and were now preparing to remove the bulk of the townland's population by eviction and assisted emigration. The Crown's land agent described in testimony before a House of Lords select committee how the so-called rebellion, which was occurring on a piece of land that had once been part of the Mahon estate and now abutted a portion of it, "had a very bad effect on the neighboring properties."

"Has the successful resistance on the part of the Crown Tenants led to resistance on the part of other Tenants?"

"Yes, precisely," said George Knox, also a justice of the peace, who was related to Major Mahon.

Still, the Ballykilcline action, which, according to Knox, included every resident of the townland but a man named Patrick Maguire, spanned many years prior to the appearance of the blight. The rent strike on the Mahon estate revealed itself at roughly the same time as the blight arrived. How was it possible for Major Mahon to determine *why* a person wasn't paying rent in the midst of famine? Further, how do you tell the difference between a conspirator and a nonconspirator when both were subject to the same deprivations?

While Major Mahon's letters show that he believed a distinction could be made, Ross Mahon was less concerned with sorting out who was truly suffering and who was defiantly insubordinate. In his thinking, everyone—or everyone but a tiny few—was involved in the conspiracy. His 1880 testimony disclosed that he believed the tenants were both "absolutely starving" *and* immersed in an all-inclusive, Ballykilcline-like rent strike, which, he argued, was "just the description of the Strokestown estate when I took the management." In a mid-1847 letter he said a few were intimidated by the conspirators into withholding rent, but "the greater number, glad to avoid the payment of their engagements, join with alacrity in the combination." Thus, the failure to pay rent was nearly prima facie evidence of membership in the conspiracy. The blight, then, handed him the perfect opportunity to carve the estate into large farms, free from the paupers who impeded the effort. But his employer wasn't yet willing to go that far.

If Major Mahon wasn't yet prepared to engineer a large-scale clearance of his land, he was willing to allow Ross Mahon to do what he could to intimidate the recalcitrant into paying rent. In doing so, the land agent was able to lay the groundwork for his ultimate goal. He began delivering the three levels of eviction documents that were required to effect a legal removal of the paupers. The first were "notices to quit"—that is, notices giving a tenant or subtenant a set period of time, typically six months, to "deliver up . . . the quiet and peaceable possession . . . of said premises," according to the language of a notice to quit distributed by the Mahon family. The notices carried an explicit threat. "[I]n case you shall refuse or neglect to deliver up said premises, I will proceed to recover possession." An action of this sort wasn't at all unusual for an Irish landlord. The Devon Commission report noted that many landlords delivered the notices to quit each year "not with any fixed intention of proceeding upon such notices, but in order to keep up a continual power over the tenant." He also began distributing ejectment processes on all those who had already received notices to quit but had failed to deliver up peaceable possession. An ejectment process for nonpayment of rent obtained in Civil Bill court—the kind of process sought by Ross Mahon—summoned the tenant or subtenant to court to explain why he had not given up his holding as stipulated in the notice to quit. Depending on the tenant's response, the judge could then issue the third and final document: an ejectment decree (a *habere facias possessionem*, or decree for possession, or *habere* for short), which permitted the sheriff to take possession of the holding on behalf of the landlord.

Major Mahon asked Ross Mahon to only "proceed against" those tenants believed to be participating in the conspiracy. Writing from England, he told the land agent to leave the critical job of determining who was "able" to pay to his estate staff, particularly his bailiff (or driver), the hated figure responsible for going into the cabins to collect rents and otherwise serve as the townland face of the landlord. John Robinson, the Mahons' bailiff, was described in one of Ross Mahon's letters as "a very large man." The landlord believed that this show of seriousness would convince the conspirators to end their intransigence. "When they see we are determined to have the rent 'or the land,' then sooner than lose the land, they will pay," he wrote in the December 27 letter.

On January 3 he wrote, "I am quite satisfied that rents will not be paid if we give way, and I only wish to proceed against those that are known to have means to pay (at least a part) and will not do so from being joined with others in combination." Apparently referring to an attack by the local newspaper on evicting landlords, he continued, "[A]s to any remarks the *Roscommon Journal* may make, I heed them not. We are not doing any tyrannical or cruel act. And making those pay their rent or give up their land, who are known to refuse doing so from combination, is but an act of justice to those who pay and are willing to do so without putting us to trouble. I am satisfied if we allow those persons to escape paying their rent now, that we should find it impossible to get it hereafter—and where there is so much employment given, so much money raised by subscriptions for purchase of food . . . there is not a *fair* or *just* excuse for not paying part of what's due out of crop in their possession. Those who the bailiff knows to have crops and the means of paying should be the first made to pay and any of those that combination can be brought home to should be served with ejectments and got rid of without any compromise.

"[T]he object I have in view," Major Mahon concluded, "is to protect and assist the *good and willing* tenants and to get rid of the *idle and bad* ones."

CHAPTER 5

The Supernumerary Portion of the Inhabitants

*As I said before I do not think any improvement could be effected
until a clearance of tenantry is made.*
—JOHN ROSS MAHON TO MAJOR
DENIS MAHON, FEBRUARY 27, 1847

*[A]t this period of such misery and famine I should not like to put
such a number of starving creatures loose on the world without any
means whatever of feeding them.*
—MAJOR DENIS MAHON TO JOHN
ROSS MAHON, MARCH 2, 1847

BY THE END OF 1846, the disastrous folly of the state's relief effort
was becoming obvious to all. Even though the public works projects
around Strokestown were "very numerous," according to a relief committee statement, and the food depot was once again supplied with
government meal, large segments of the population were unable to
procure enough food to stay alive. Bodies were now turning up on
the roadsides and in the fields, with few families able to obtain even a
coffin for burial. Civil society started to buckle under the strain.

Many reports describe paupers appearing in droves at any institution that might aid them. The Roscommon workhouse, now
filled beyond its capacity of nine hundred, turned away helpless

people every day. On January 9, 1847, a notice was posted saying that the workhouse would no longer give small portions of bread to "disappointed applicants"—which it had done on "two occasions"—because doing so violated the 1838 Poor Law that said only inmates within the workhouse were eligible for assistance. A priest from a town near Strokestown reported that it was impossible for his people to obtain food from the Strokestown depot because of "the multitudes congregated" around the structure. The same crowds likely gathered in town for the relief committee gatherings and other public sessions, a circumstance that surely heightened the tension of the proceedings inside. A Limerick Relief Committee member told of the difficulty of conducting a mannerly proceeding with "a gloomy-looking crowd staring in through the windows with sharp, wolfish eyes." Although it was typical for such meetings to be contentious affairs, government officials were impressed with the incivility of the Strokestown gatherings. A Board of Works engineer characterized one session as full of "much argument, which is universally the case at all meetings in that town."

While the government continued to defend its policies—Lord John Russell said that undue meddling with the food supply would have meant "an end at once of all private enterprise"—it took steps to modify the scheme. It resolved to purchase more supplies of Indian maize from the United States, although it was too late in the season to make an immediate difference. It decided to resume matching (or nearly matching) subscriptions made to the local committees. It ordered a prohibition on the use of grain in distilleries and breweries. But in early January Lord John Russell realized that he needed to institute a more radical change. "The pressing matter at present is to keep the people alive," he said on January 5. He rushed legislation through Parliament that ended the work-for-cash-for-Indian-meal system in favor of a plan to provide direct relief in the form of soup, which represented a striking departure from the government's doctrinaire aversion to gratuitous aid. Officials were partly inspired by the example of the Society of Friends, the Quakers, who had opened several soup kitchens on their own initiative with impressive—and comparatively cheap—results.

The Temporary Relief Destitute Persons Act proved that the government could alter its course in the wake of an obvious policy failure. It also showed that it understood the absurdity of transforming the poor into wage laborers reliant on marketplace foods during a time of extraordinary distress. Irish regeneration would have to wait. But other aspects of the so-called Soup Kitchen Act were perfectly in keeping with the government's previous efforts. It would be a *temporary* expedient until the autumn harvest, when a new relief initiative more in line with earlier doctrinaire preoccupations would be introduced. And it would require Irish landlords to be responsible for an ever-larger proportion of expenditure. The government funds for the soup kitchen scheme would have to be repaid out of the poor rates, which were mostly the responsibility of the larger landlords. Yet the government wasn't yet ready to throw the entire load onto them. The Treasury would still be providing *advances* of loans and grants to pay for the soup kitchens.

Not coincidentally, the Whigs' soup kitchen initiative came as the world was learning the news of Ireland's calamity. Graphic accounts full of shocking details found their way into newspapers and pamphlets. The *Illustrated London News* famously wrote of the sufferings of Skibbereen, County Cork, accompanying the text with woodcut illustrations by Cork artist James Mahony that would emerge as iconic images of the Famine. Traveling writers, often clergymen and aid workers, penned descriptions that were read from pulpits and cited in appeals throughout the globe. Again the Quakers played an important role, publishing haunting essays that inspired much sympathy. "We entered a cabin," wrote William Bennett from County Cork. "Stretched in one dark corner, scarcely visible, from the smoke and rags that covered them, were three children huddled together, lying there because they were too weak to rise, pale and ghostly, their little limbs, on removing a portion of the filthy covering, perfectly emaciated, eyes sunk, voice gone, and evidently in the last stage of actual starvation." In England the response was considerable. The British Association for the Relief of Extreme Distress in the Remote Parishes of Ireland and Scotland, a philanthropic organization founded by wealthy Englishmen, was formed to collect donations, eventually gathering 500,000 pounds from everyone from the prime minister (300 pounds) to the employees of a glassmaking business in Birmingham. On January 13, 1847, Queen Victoria, who gave the single largest donation of 2,000 pounds, sent a letter to the archbishops of Canterbury and York, asking that an appeal for donations be read before the nation's congregations. Even the satirical magazine *Punch*, which was just beginning to caricature the Irish as an apelike subspecies, kicked in 50 pounds.

The donors also extended beyond the borders of the British Isles. Relief associations were formed in scores of places populated with Irish immigrants—Irish Americans donated millions of dollars and considerable amounts of foodstuffs—but many non-Irish foreigners showed an independent dedication to the relief effort. A random sampling of donors included the Freemasons of India; Pope Pius IX; the Ladies' Relief Association of Brooklyn, New York; the Shakers of New Lebanon, Pennsylvania; the citizens of hurricane-ravaged Barbados; the servants of English nobility in Florence (10 pounds); and the Choctaw Indians of Oklahoma. As in modern relief drives, it became a matter of public esteem to be seen playing a prominent role. It was reported in the Irish newspapers that the Sultan of Turkey wanted to contribute much more than his 1,000-pound donation, but was talked out of it by a British official who felt it would violate protocol to give more than the Queen herself. U.S. president James Polk faced public scorn for opposing a measure by a Kentucky senator to send $500,000 to Ireland and Scotland for famine relief. A Boston newspaper attacked him for offering up a paltry personal contribution of $50. The Irish Famine was the "first national disaster to attract sustained international sympathy on a large scale," wrote scholar Christine Kinealy.

The scale of misfortune even brought together the warring factions of Irish politics. The Repeal Association and Young Ireland discussed joining together to advocate on behalf of their people. But the rupture, which was often shockingly mean-spirited, was too great to close. Instead, some Young Irelanders formed a new organization in January, the Irish Confederation, to bring together Catholic tenants and farmers who were disaffected with the failures of the Repeal Association, and Protestant landlords who were turned off by Whigs and their burdensome relief policies. The Irish Confederation began forming Confederate clubs throughout the country to harness a revolutionary spirit, but its leaders found scant support for an organization that existed outside the mainstream of Catholic nationalism.

Unable to work with his enemies in Young Ireland, Daniel O'Connell also sought to ally with those from the landlord class. On January 14 he convened a meeting in Dublin that included prominent Irishmen of all backgrounds and persuasions, including peers, MPs, landlords, and professionals. The group issued a statement arguing that the "imperial exchequer should bear all the costs" for employment schemes, reproductive works, and compensation for evicted tenants. Following this meeting, eighty-three Irish MPs serving in both houses of Parliament agreed to act in concert to advocate such proposals. But the alliance would prove to be short-lived.

In Strokestown the local relief committee was unable to heal its divisions even for a short time. Despite funds from government, private individuals, and charitable organizations, it had a difficult time starting a soup kitchen. It was another instance of the conflict between Major Mahon and Father McDermott complicating the effort to aid the poor.

Even before the Russell administration passed the so-called Soup Kitchen Act, which would not begin offering its funding until the spring, relief officials were advising local committees to start their own kitchens. At the end of December the Strokestown

committee asked for a government contribution for a "soup shop,"
failing to mention if any money had been raised for that intention. Randolph Routh responded by repeating the message that "a
donation for that purpose cannot be recommended except in aid of
local subscriptions." On January 9 Father McDermott, who listed
himself on the letter as the committee's secretary and treasurer,
told the government that 101 pounds—including 20 pounds from
Major Mahon—had been raised for "the erection of a soup shop."
Routh responded by recommending a government payment of 101
pounds to the committee. But by mid-January the kitchen was
still unopened. When Father McDermott wrote a letter to Major
Mahon in England asking for money to purchase a boiler to cook
the soup, the landlord responded with suspicion. In a letter to John
Ross Mahon, he wondered if it might be a good idea to bypass
the committee altogether. "Will you have the kindness to inquire
into this, and ascertain if it is desirable to place our funds at the
disposal of the relief committee or open one ourselves under the
care and management of Mrs. Fallon, who . . . would be a very fit
and proper person," he wrote. Later in the letter, he conceded, "If
the plan they intend to adopt is a good one, and the soup will be
fairly and properly distributed to the poor and starving persons in
and about Strokestown, then I think one soup committee would be
sufficient." Still, the letter contained a startling allegation: Major
Mahon believed that the local committee couldn't be trusted to
"fairly and properly" distribute aid to the destitute.

It was an accusation that was often made against relief committees by the government. They were charged with offering relief—in
the form of food or spots on the public works lists—to those they
favored rather than to the truly suffering. An official in County
Roscommon complained that the relief committees "cannot be
depended on, even in recommending the poorest for employment.
It is quite distressing to see that, with the vast extent of employment provided in almost every district, the very poorest are in many
cases omitted." But a still graver accusation was being leveled at

the Strokestown committee, now chaired by George Knox, the justice of the peace and Ballykilcline land agent who was related to Major Mahon. Two Board of Works officials suggested in January and February 1847 that the relief committee was doing *nothing of consequence*. One accused the body of being "very impracticable and indolent," and suggested that it would be wise to remove all the members from their posts. Another official complained that the committee lacked even one dedicated member and that "no business is transacted." The same official wrote in a subsequent letter that the committee conducted its work "indifferently," often providing him with false information. "I cannot obtain from them anything correct," he wrote. He said that Knox had resigned his position, taking a magistrate post in County Sligo, leaving "the principal persons constituting this committee . . . the Roman Catholic clergy."

The committee's "indolence" may be attributed to the vocation of its central members. Catholic priests throughout Ireland were neglecting their paperwork to attend to the cabins and hovels where the people were dying. The *Roscommon and Leitrim Gazette* confirmed that clergymen were "day and night zealously employed ministering to the people." Three priests in the Diocese of Elphin succumbed to fever over the course of 1847. Nationwide the number was forty. They were likely as occupied blessing the dying as they were helping the living. As one of the sacraments of the Catholic Church, the administration of last rites was a vital matter for a priest entrusted to tend to the souls of his parishioners. In his 1874 history of the Famine, Canon John O'Rourke emphasized this point. "To those who are not Catholics, I may say that every priest feels bound, under the most solemn obligations, to administer the last sacraments to every individual committed to his care," he wrote.

But it remains a mystery why the committee neglected to set up a soup kitchen, as had already been done in Roscommon town and Elphin. The letters held in the National Archives from this period show that the committee continued to collect contributions throughout February and March. Donations came from Lady Hartland; John

Ross Mahon; the British Relief Association; Marcus McClausland; Mrs. Mahon; the Quakers' Central Relief Committee of Dublin; the Birmingham, England, Relief Fund; an English Catholic bishop named Right Reverend Dr. Briggs; and Bishop George Browne. By March 31 the committee reported that it had raised an additional 178 pounds, which the government agreed to match with 178 pounds. So with the 202 pounds that it had collected in January, the relief committee had raised a total of 558 pounds during the first three months of 1847. From England, Major Mahon attributed the committee's failure to open a kitchen to nothing other than its negligence. On February 26 he wrote to Ross Mahon, "I am very sorry the soup kitchen has not been finished before. I shall be glad to know what sums have been subscribed and what assistance [has been obtained] from other sources. . . . Who is the chairman of the relief committee in place of George Knox? . . . I hope some on that will take an interest in it." On March 2 he again wrote, "I received your letter this morning enclosing the list of subscriptions to our soup shop—I regret very much that the soup shop has not been opened long before this— surely the committee should not allow such a waste of time, when people around them are dying of want. A temporary kitchen even for the present moment would be desirable." And then on March 7, "I am quite surprised at the delay in opening the soup kitchen. I trust it will not be delayed much longer." Even if Major Mahon was motivated by bigoted hatred of Father McDermott and his designs, the landlord's sentiments must be seen as humanitarian in this instance.

Despite the accusations of lassitude and mismanagement, it is impossible to believe that the relief committee did not use at least some of the money to purchase food from the Strokestown depot, which, records show, was supplied in the early months of 1847 with fluctuating amounts of barley meal, Indian maize, oatmeal, and biscuit. But if so, why did the committee repeatedly *specify* that it was seeking funds for a soup kitchen? Why did it not tell the government that at least a portion of its focus was on purchasing and reselling uncooked food to the poor?

By the middle of March the government began halting the public works projects, now employing more than seven hundred thousand people throughout the country. The abrupt stoppage resulted in the fabled ("and often mythical," according to historian R. F. Foster) "famine roads" to nowhere, often pointed to as a metaphor for the failures of government policy. As in many areas in Ireland, the dismissals in Strokestown occurred before the funds had come through from the Soup Kitchen Act, promising a gap between official relief schemes that could last several weeks. The government had taken the action after hearing reports from its inspecting officers that the poor were neglecting to seed their ground for the next harvest, which would have greatly reduced the availability of food (and rent) in the fall. As a Board of Works official wrote on February 21, "Since I wrote last I have been a good deal through Roscommon, in the direction of Strokestown, Elphin, Croghan, and Boyle. The people are generally very badly off in that direction; their whole dependence appears to be 'the Public Works,' and they pay no attention to the land, although they all admit that they are alive to the necessity of putting down their crops if they are to expect anything to live on next year, but say they cannot afford to give up the pay on the works, and seem generally to have a vague expectation that the government will crop the land, or as they term it, 'give them some encouragement' to do it themselves." The government was expecting the poor to plant potatoes and "thus tend to produce food for the next harvest and procure perhaps some small wages to enable them to support their families," said Lord John Russell. But it is unclear how a large population of starving people was expected to procure seed potatoes if the potatoes from the previous harvest had all been destroyed by the blight.

The Irish nationalist press was outraged by the stoppages. As were locals around Strokestown. A memorial sent to the government by farmers on and near the Mahon estate asked that a road project that had employed hundreds be restarted. "Five hundred destitute starving families were relieved and employed on said line of road, who would be now in their graves were it not that they procured employment—and only two out of every family employed," five farmers wrote in a memorial on March 16. "That said five hundred families are now reduced to the lowest degree of poverty and starvation for want of food and employment in consequence of said line of road having been stopped." On March 26 Father McDermott wrote to Dublin pleading for assistance to tide the poor over until the money from the act enabled the committee to start a soup kitchen. He asked for an infusion of funds in recognition of "the hourly increasing difficulty and distress of our district." He noted that the "dismysal of such a large number of persons as has been ordered by the government has placed us in a situation of . . . difficulty and absolute inability to" provide assistance. This statement confirmed that the relief committee had not opened a soup kitchen with 558 pounds it had expressly collected for such a purpose over the previous three months. But the principal fact remained that further hardship was imminent. Father McDermott ended his letter by predicting that "hundreds nay thousands of lives must inevitably be sacrificed through the want of any possible means within our reach to give any further relief."

While Strokestown was edging closer to catastrophe, Major Mahon was enjoying a much higher standard of living that winter and spring. In February he took up residence at Mivart's Hotel (now Claridge's), founded thirty years earlier for the fashionable and titled world, on Upper Brook Street in Mayfair in London. In the year or two preceding his stay, the hotel was graced by the likes of the Crown Prince of Württemberg, the King of Holland, the Duke de Terceira of Portugal, Prince Waldemar of Prussia, and Ibrahim, the Pasha of Egypt. Several weeks after the landlord's arrival, the doors of the exclusive state apartments were opened to the Archduke Constantine of Russia, who was in town for Queen Victoria's birthday celebration. When the major was not installed at the hotel, he whiled away his afternoons at the United Service Club on Regent Street. Founded by officers from the Peninsular Wars, the club was a favorite of its most esteemed member, the Duke of Wellington, who could gaze upon a mammoth bust of himself in the main hall any time he liked. The club's most newsworthy event during these months happened when an elderly member who had gone blind—Lieutenant-General Sir John Wallace—asked for permission for his son, a nonmember, to accompany him to the coffee room and the library. After a careful consideration of the matter, the club's governing committee turned down the request.

Despite the opulence and exclusivity of his surroundings, Major Mahon was showing a concern for the hardship in his town in Ireland that appeared to be genuine, heartfelt, and reflective of global sentiment. In the same letters in which he complained about the unopened soup kitchen, written from Mivart's and the United Service Club in late February and early March, he formulated a new eviction policy that extended protection even to those "idle and bad" tenants involved in the alleged conspiracy against his rule. His emotions seemed to have been roused by at least two letters (now lost) he received from Father John Boyd, whose Lisanuffy parish was adjacent to Father McDermott's and contained many Mahon tenants. "I have had a letter from Mr. Boyd PP that my tenants in his parish are in a miserable state and I shall go tomorrow to the South Sea House [the headquarters of the British Relief Association] to see what I can get for them," the landlord wrote to Ross Mahon.

With words from Father Boyd and others ringing in his head, he told Ross Mahon on February 23 to spare "those who had nothing but potatoes" from evictions. "I do not think it would be fair to proceed against [them] to the extremity of 'putting them out,'" he wrote. A profound reconsideration of the estate's management—and a rare acknowledgment from an Irish landlord that evictions represented "extremity" rather than the just exercise of property rights—the injunction would safeguard nearly all the 11,958 people now living on the property, according to a new survey conducted by Ross Mahon. On March 2 he repeated the message about the evictions of potato-dependent tenants. "With regards to the *haberes* [ejectment decrees] you have got against my tenants, I should think it most advisable not to proceed on them at all, but I should like you to select a few of those that have money or have crops of corn in their haggards and proceed against them but at this period of such misery and famine I should not like to put such a number of starving creatures loose on the world without any means whatever of feeding them," he wrote. Again he was showing sympathy toward the conspirators—who, according to his January 3 letter, were the only ones he wanted targeted for eviction. But the letter also hinted that the policy wasn't inviolable. Would he support, for example, putting them "loose on the world" *with* a means of being fed? That is, if a soup kitchen were open?

To say that John Ross Mahon objected to this measured compassion would be to understate the matter. At least since the landlord's January 3 letter authorizing him to proceed against conspirators, he was serving entire townlands with the documents that would permit him to gain possession. It was a policy he saw as in keeping with his view that everyone (or nearly everyone)—since they weren't paying rent—was in the midst of Ballykilcline-like rebellion and as not contradicting Major Mahon's inexact view, stated in the December 27 letter, that "many" were involved in the plot. In a February letter to the landlord, Ross Mahon described how "the *haberes* have arrived and I have written to the sheriff to know what day" he can take "possession" of a particular farm. He also described that he had "noticed all the tenants under ejectment"—it's unclear how large this group was—"to come in and make some arrangement. Some I have already seen but with no good result." In a statement written after Major Mahon's death, Ross Mahon described his procedure explicitly. "At this time I had *haberes* in my possession, which I showed the tenants, and told them I could call on the sheriff to give me possession any day I wished, and that I could not pursue any other course, if they did not show some disposition to pay," he wrote.

Confronted with Major Mahon's statement about the "extremity" of evictions, Ross Mahon responded with exasperation. After receiving the landlord's February 23 letter speaking of "those who had nothing but potatoes," the land agent sent a note to London on February 27 in which he concluded that the excitable landlord wasn't interested in allowing him to complete the job of mass clearance. "I cannot take upon myself the responsibility of acting as I may suppose most [beneficial to] the estate because I am confident that nothing whatever can be done in the way of improvement until the land is cleared of at least two-thirds of its population," he wrote. He pointed out to the soft-headed altruist that if the "proportion of the peasantry not having any means whatever of paying rent" is "not put out," there is "no prospect" of "getting any rents for years." He described how the tenants were "not taking any steps toward preparing their land for seed."

Major Mahon responded on March 7. "I regret very much the account your letter of the 27th ultimo gives of the prospect before us as regards rents but I shall more regret that you are unwilling to remain as my agent, as I had hoped that with your experience and assistance we should have been able in the course of time to bring matters round," he wrote. After recommending that the land agent offer "reductions in the gales of rent due," he issued another directive against mass evictions. "With regard to the *haberes* I cannot bring myself to desire them to be . . . in force against all, there are some who are known to be able to pay, whom I am most anxious to proceed against. If you could get a few of those selected out and made examples of no person could complain of my doing a harsh or an unjust act," he wrote. "Altho I am aware the law admits of my taking possession, yet I would willingly in the present unfortunate state of the people, make any sacrifice sooner than put the law in force," he continued. He ended the letter on a conciliatory note, telling Ross Mahon that any tenant who exercised his legal right to challenge an ejectment process in court—thus requiring the landlord to go to the expense of a defense—deserved no "indulgence."

It was an extraordinary exchange of letters. Ross Mahon was portraying himself as a remorseless businessman who was impatient to know when the sheriff could assist evictions. "The *haberes* have arrived," he wrote expectantly. Major Mahon was presenting himself as a well-meaning landlord who was unsettled by the prospect of throwing his tenants out of their homes at such a dire time. "*I cannot bring myself* to desire [the *haberes*] to be . . . in force against all," he wrote, in the manner of someone experiencing moral crisis. (Italics added.)

But Major Mahon soon capitulated to Ross Mahon's threats, a fact that the land agent was unashamed to admit in later years. "I wrote to Major Mahon, and said I must resign the agency unless" Mahon followed his advice, Ross Mahon said in his 1880 testimony. "At the end of three days, he wrote and said he would agree to my terms." By the later half of March, Major Mahon was coming to believe that he couldn't afford *not* to introduce some kind of removal scheme. With his income from rents dwindling to nothing and his family treasury depleted by decades of profligacy (including some of his own), he was finding it hard to afford the charges spiraling upward as a result of the government's insistence that landlords shoulder such a significant financial burden for relief. The debates then raging in Parliament over what sort of government plan would replace the Soup Kitchen Act in the autumn were indicating that the bill would grow even further. In fact, the government had decided it was time to end its fiduciary role in Famine relief altogether. The entire system would be placed on the shoulders of Irish landlords, who were now being routinely vilified by all parties for luxuriating in splendor (in places like Mivart's) while their people languished in misery. The idea was to expand the provisions of the Irish Poor Law.

The existing Poor Law funded the system of workhouses by levying rates on those who held property within a particular union. Since 1843 the large landlords paid the rates for all tenants on their estates who occupied plots valued at less than 4 pounds (and half the rates for those holding more than 4 pounds), meaning the

proprietors with the more subdivided and overpopulated properties paid the highest rates. In the year and a half since the blight
arrived—and even before—landlords had been conducting evictions
to lessen their taxation charges under the 4-pound rating clause.
The new amended Poor Law would add to the poor rates by making certain categories of paupers eligible for outdoor relief in the
form of cooked or uncooked Indian meal to be distributed by the
workhouse Board of Guardians. This meant it would no longer be
always necessary for a destitute individual to be lodged within the
workhouse to receive assistance under the Poor Law. Irish landlords
not only would be responsible for paying the entire costs of this
relief endeavor, but would also be ordered under law to produce the
funds without delay. The advances of loans and grants were to end.
The government had tragically decided that Irish property would
exclusively and *immediately* pay for Irish poverty during a time of
unparalleled privation. Lord John Russell told himself that the
landed proprietors, faced with massive rate increases, would offer
widespread employment to keep their tenants off the relief rolls,
furthering the government's goal of Irish regeneration.

The Irish landlords were aghast at the idea, and their representatives in Parliament loudly fought the legislation. They felt the
entire country would be thrown upon the outdoor relief rolls, forcing *them* to seek entrance in the nearest workhouse. But over the
next few months a number of provisions would be put into the bill
to soften the blow, turning it from legislation that punished landlords into legislation that punished landlords *and* the people who
desperately needed their assistance. It did this by defining destitution much more narrowly than the Soup Kitchen Act and establishing bureaucratic procedures that delayed assistance to those who
were deemed qualified for aid. Outdoor relief would be permitted
only after a drawn-out review had determined that the workhouse
and its auxiliary structures could not hold any more people. An
order from the Poor Law commissioners would then be required
to permit outdoor relief to be distributed to the non–able-bodied

(the aged, infirm, orphans, and widows with two or more legitimate children). Another order from the commissioners would then be needed for outdoor relief to be given to the able-bodied, who would be required to work on stone-breaking crews for eight hours a day.

But the most draconian limitation was the infamous Quarter-Acre (or Gregory) Clause. It prohibited any and all relief to those who possessed more than a quarter acre of land, targeting the class of small farmers who, it was believed, were most apt to trick relief officials into providing them with help that they didn't deserve. (The government was constantly worried about being the victims of the devious Irish.) Introduced by the Irish landlord MP William Gregory, the clause was intended to ensure that only the truly destitute would seek help. A Tory representing Dublin city who would later fritter away his fortune in gambling debts, Gregory believed that "where a man held a large piece of land—half an acre, one, or two or three acres—he was no longer an object of pity." Many parliamentarians supported the clause because they believed it made sense to force small farmers to give up all but a tiny portion of their land, which would push them into wage-laboring workforce where they belonged. The Gregory Clause easily passed the House of Commons by a vote of 117 to 7.

The entire legislation would travel to passage on the strength of its most popular components, its anti-landlord animus and its elimination of state expenditure. With nothing else in the offing for Ireland, the Repeal MPs were left with no choice but to back the measure. Daniel O'Connell, who Balzac claimed had "incarnated a whole people," gave his last speech in Parliament begging for something, anything, to be done for Ireland, an ignominious end for a landmark figure. "If you do not save her she can't save herself," he said. In fact, both supporters and opponents agreed that the amended Poor Law would be painful. The Chancellor of the Exchequer, Charles Wood, believed that Ireland would have to suffer a "purgatory of misery and starvation" before it could "emerge into a state of anything approaching to quiet or prosperity."

Major Mahon responded to the prospect of ballooning poor rates by agreeing to Ross Mahon's plan to pay for the passage of his tenants to a distant land, a strategy followed by other Irish landlords like Lord Palmerston, Lord John Russell's foreign secretary, who owned property in County Sligo. Ross Mahon pointed out that it was the most economical avenue available to him. The agent calculated that it would be cheaper in the long run to pay transatlantic fare for his tenants—a one-time charge, after all—than it would be to pay the increased poor rates under the Poor Law Amendment Act for the same tenants. It was even cheaper than evictions. According to Sections 11, 12 of the amended Poor Law, any tenant who "shall have occupied some tenement" within a particular electoral division—two of which were largely within the Mahon estate—for a three-month period in the three years before applying for assistance would be eligible for indoor or outdoor relief. An emigration plan, while removing all poor rate costs, also had the advantage of being a socially acceptable to Catholic leaders on the Mahon estate. No less a representative of the people than Father Henry Brennan, whose Kilglass parish was populated by hundreds of Mahon tenants, had urged such an option in a public letter. He called for the local landlords to offer seed, enlarge holdings, and "send off to foreign countries the supernumerary portion of the inhabitants," exactly Major Mahon's strategy.

The landlord made it clear that he thought "the 'first class' for us to send is those of the poorest and worst description and who would become a charge on us for poor house, 'outdoor relief,'" a phrase of such novelty that he gave it quotation marks. But Ross Mahon knew that the plan would work only if it was "extensive"—that is, if it truly cleared the property. Yet in the few weeks after informing the land agent that he would fund an extensive plan, Major Mahon began pulling back on the scope of the undertaking, citing money problems. Once again, Ross Mahon expressed his frustration at not being allowed to fulfill his job duties, saying he could not "offer service" to the major if he wouldn't follow his recommendations. The major's response to this second, veiled threat of resignation does not survive. But Ross Mahon did not resign. Instead, as spring arrived, the two began arranging a scaled-down emigration plan, preparing to send roughly a thousand tenants to the distant shores of the place they always described in their letters as "America."

CHAPTER 6

Quiet and Peaceable Possession

THE MAHON TENANTS WOULD be joining an exodus. Since the
second appearance of the blight in the fall of 1846, crowds of paupers had been marching to the seaports looking for passage out of
their misery. Many observers described it as a desperate, even panic-
stricken, flight, which confirmed that the Irishman's long-held
reluctance to leave the cabin and townland of his birth had been
overpowered in some by the prospect of a miserable death. By early
1847 the movement of refugees was taking on mammoth proportions, even though the emigrant sailing season didn't usually begin
in earnest until the spring. In the month of January alone, some six
thousand Irish arrived in the port of Liverpool, where ships regularly left for the roughly six-week journey to North America. Many
of the distressed peasants were carriers of the epidemic diseases
that follow in the train of severe malnutrition—typhus, relapsing

fever, and dysentery—often generically known as famine fever. "Ireland is pouring into the cities, and even into the villages of this island, a fetid torrent of famine, nakedness, dirt, and fever," wrote the *Times* on April 2. "Liverpool, whose proximity to Ireland has already procured for it the unhappy distinction of being the most unhealthy town in this island, seems destined to become one mass of disease."

Some Strokestown tenants seemed to be just as eager to leave Ireland as their fellow citizens. In fact, in an indication of just how universal was the suffering, more established farmers were asking to be included in Major Mahon's emigration plan. "I have been considering over the numerous applications we have had for assistance on the score of emigration, and it strikes me that many of those applying are of the better sort of tenant, and if possible should be kept at home, but at all events if determined to go they should do so at their own expense," Major Mahon wrote to Ross Mahon on April 14. The major asked that the task of deciding who qualified as the "poorest and worst" and whose absence "would relieve the industrious tenants from having such a description on the land" be, as always, left up to the bailiff, John Robinson, and others, from the estate office. "I name this from a fear that we shall not be able to send all that apply and that in the end the worst description will be left with us," Major Mahon wrote. Of course, he decreed that conspirators be summarily excluded from such a generous scheme.

By early May the landlord and land agent were negotiating with the passenger agents who would orchestrate the journey, James and William Robinson, two figures who were spared any public opprobrium for their actions during the Mahon controversy. They operated a business under the name of J. and W. Robinson, which was located on Liverpool's bustling waterfront. A check of Liverpool directories for the years before and after 1847 reveals that the Robinsons rarely stayed for long at the same address and often changed the name of their company. In addition, each of the businesses operated by the Robinsons—the Robinson Brothers, Messrs.

Robinson and Co., and finally J. and W. Robinson—was regularly cited by the authorities for defrauding passengers in one way or another. The scholar Oliver MacDonagh has chronicled the government's efforts to punish the "infamous" Robinson Brothers during the early and middle 1830s, describing them as "indifferent to the sufferings of the penniless and ragged emigrants." In 1835 they dispatched a group of them aboard the *Henry*, which was in such a pitiful state that it foundered soon after leaving port. Following a harrowing thirty-one days in open boats with little food or water, the passengers were returned to Liverpool, where the Robinsons disclaimed any responsibility for the ship's condition and refused to refund their fares. Throughout the late 1830s and early 1840s, the doings of the Messrs. Robinson continued to reach the courts and the newspapers, most often when they were accused of overcharging emigrants.

It isn't certain how much the landlord and the land agent knew about the Robinsons' reputation—it should be noted that many Liverpool passenger agents were regarded as swindlers—but both took the matter seriously enough to travel to Liverpool to speak with the two men before striking a deal. Throughout the process, however, Major Mahon's primary concern was cost, and his decision to hire them was reached because they offered the lowest fares to the cheapest destination, Québec in British North America, from where the tenants were expected to find their own way to Irish communities in the United States. Yet his worries about expenditure didn't necessarily translate into a hazard for his tenants. On May 11 he sent a letter to Ross Mahon after reading reports about the introduction of medical inspections for Irish paupers arriving in Liverpool. "It will be necessary to lose no time in getting the first batch over in time, and I see by the papers this morning 'an order in council' respecting the strict examination of all steamers from Ireland to Liverpool to report any fever or illness on board," he wrote. "This itself will cause a few days delay there, be so kind as to make allowance for it." Then he added, "We must avoid sending any that are ill or likely to be reported as 'fever cases' when inspected at Liverpool." The major's concern was financial, but its effect was potentially humanitarian, shielding ill travelers from a journey that they might not survive.

And so the journey began. After being forgiven of all rents and arrears and in some instances selling their stock to the landlord's representatives, the few hundred emigrants who made up this first shipment journeyed into Strokestown, where they said their last farewells and were likely blessed by Father Boyd or Father McDermott. "They expressed themselves much obliged and went cheerfully," claimed Ross Mahon later that year. "[I] often heard them express their gratitude and thankfulness to their landlord for enabling them to go," wrote Thomas Morton, a Protestant middleman on the estate, the following year. In all, tenants from fourteen different townlands were bound for America, about half resident within the Lisanuffy Electoral Division and half within the Strokestown Electoral Division, the borders of each roughly corresponding with Father Boyd's Lisanuffy parish and Father McDermott's Strokestown parish. Even though Major Mahon wanted only those uninvolved in the conspiracy to be sent, more than half the families selected for the plan had been served with ejectment processes. For them, the trip could hardly be viewed as voluntary. It was either the known reality of eviction or the unknown prospect of a long ship journey to a foreign land. Of the other travelers who hadn't been served with ejectment processes—86 families (out of 217), according to Ross Mahon—it might be argued that they were more or less willing participants. But they knew that without the ability to pay rent they were sure to be targeted by subsequent eviction proceedings.

From Strokestown, the travelers made the few-day, sixty-mile trip to Dublin. Waiting for them were Ross Mahon and the bailiff John Robinson, who escorted the group aboard a packet ship for the trip across the Irish Sea to Liverpool. The tenants endured the entire voyage, which could take upward of twenty-four hours, on the deck of the vessel, where, "clothed in rags and saturated with wet," they "mixed among the cattle and besmeared with their dung," wrote a witness to a similar crossing.

The city of Liverpool must have been a startling vision for them. A young Herman Melville was transfixed by his arrival in the port eight years earlier. "[T]hese streets present a most singular spectacle, the entire population of the vicinity being seemingly turned into them," he wrote. "Hand-organs, fiddles and cymbals, plied by strolling musicians, mix with the songs of the seamen, the babble of women and children, and the groaning and whining of beggars." But the Mahon tenants were not favored guests in a port whose residents regarded the poor Irish as purveyors of death and disease. One local newspaper saw Famine refugees as introducing "fever, starvation, taxes, imprudence, and knavery, etc.," into the body politic. After presumably passing a cursory medical inspection before disembarking, the Mahon tenants were conveyed to waterfront lodging spaces that had been reserved for them by James and William Robinson. If the travelers were not already sick, it is likely that they were exposed to illness in these frightful dens. The *Times* noted three months earlier, "The filthy state in which the poor people arrive, and the shocking dark, damp, dirty places in which they herd—as many as thirty in a cellar—are the most certain constituents of malignant fever."

On May 27, after a day or two in the cellars, most of the Mahon tenants were escorted to a ship called the *Virginius* owned by H. N. Jones. Like that of many vessels making the Liverpool-Québec run, its principal mission was to transport timber from the great forests of Canada to England. Like many of his peers, the owner decided to make some extra money on the return trip by laying planks across the wide, open holds, creating temporary "'tween" decks with the bare minimum of passenger space allowed by British law. (A just-passed U.S. law required a larger allotment of room, which increased the fares to Boston and New York and forced the humblest emigrants to crowd ships bound for Canada in 1847.) Prior to boarding, the

Mahon refugees were looked over by an assistant emigration officer who pronounced them fit for travel. "The passengers . . . were, generally speaking, a less robust, as well as poorer class, than usual," the officer, T. H. Prior, wrote seven months later of the *Virginius*'s passengers, "but had no appearance of disease whatever amongst them that I am aware of, after a most minute inspection." If Mr. Prior did indeed offer a "most minute inspection," he would have been one of the few among his trade to do so. Since the port officials were paid according to the number of passengers they inspected, most did little more than glance in the direction of the Irish travelers. Yet even if the passengers were free of illness, they were dreadfully susceptible to it. A Scottish doctor, looking over a group of Irish emigrants on a Liverpool dock during the same period, felt that "no medical man of experience and reflection could fail to see plain indications of reduced stamina, and the inability to withstand the causes of diseases."

Under the power of a moderate north-northwest wind, the craft embarked at 9 A.M. on May 29, carrying 476 passengers— 397 adults and 79 children—nearly all of them former residents of the Mahon estate. After more than a year of living through one of the great calamities of European history, the tenants were bound for the New World. According to the strictures of the Imperial Passenger Act, the adults were to be provided each day with one pound of bread, flour, rice, or oatmeal (or five pounds of potatoes, considered the equivalent); three quarts of water; and a supply of cooking fuel. Smaller portions of these supplies were reserved for children below the age of fourteen and the age of seven. In addition, the tenants were in possession of what Ross Mahon would later describe as "ample rations," provided by James and William Robinson and paid for by Major Mahon, which would have put them in better stead than the average Famine voyager. Ross Mahon wrote, "Each emigrant above fourteen years age received by weekly distribution, sugar 6 lbs., tea 10 oz., coffee, rice 8 lbs., oatmeal 14 lbs., herrings one dozen, soap 1.5 lbs., vinegar 1 pint, pepper and salt, sixpenny-worth. Children under fourteen years of age received half the supply." But did James and William Robinson, men renowned for their dishonesty, provide the goods—or *all* of the goods? According to an investigation by the U.S. Senate conducted a few years later, Liverpool passenger agents were known to display a loaf of bread in their offices "to delude the poor into the belief that they will be fed at sea."

The remaining few dozen Mahon tenants who had not sailed on the *Virginius* stayed in the cellars for another three days before they were boarded onto the *Erin's Queen* along with a few hundred other Irish travelers. She set sail on June 1.

With such success sending off this first collection of tenants, Major Mahon was eager that another batch from the same electoral divisions be shuttled over to Liverpool into the waiting arms of J. and W. Robinson. So within days, the process was repeated with a similarly sized contingent traveling from Strokestown to Dublin, across the Irish Sea to Liverpool, and through medical inspection to the waterfront cellars. On June 15 most of the tenants shipped out aboard the barque *Naomi* owned by T. Froste, which carried a total of 334 passengers. The remaining few dozen Mahon tenants were sent to Québec the following day on the barque *John Munn* with emigrants from counties Louth, Fermanagh, and Cavan.

In all, Major Mahon paid for the passage of 872½ "statute" adults on the four vessels—which, since this figure counts children under the age of fourteen as half an adult, makes it difficult to calculate the precise number of travelers. But by the time the *John Munn* had sailed, the landlord had already decided that the count was too high. "I regret to say I have had some difficulty in procuring a part of this money," he wrote to Ross Mahon. His total expenditure amounted to about 3,500 pounds—far less than the 24,000 pounds that Ross Mahon had earlier calculated it would take to clear the estate of two-thirds of its tenants. "At this present rate of charges for this passage out I fear it would not be advisable to send any more just now," the landlord concluded. As in other matters, the major changed his mind. On and off over the next two months he tried to book passage for more tenants, even trekking to Liverpool to negotiate a lower rate from J. and W. Robinson. His letters speak of "a fall in the price of sending them out" and of hopes of "a reasonable offer" forthcoming from the passenger agents. But it came to nothing. Major Mahon's great charitable exertion of the Famine had come to an end.

Just then the government was instituting its most successful relief enterprise in Strokestown. Government records show that on May 24 a soup kitchen was opened with funds provided under the Soup Kitchen Act. But the surviving records are silent on whether the relief committee had succeeded in opening a soup kitchen *before* the money came through. That is, in the two months since March 26, when Father McDermott told the government that the 558 pounds the committee had collected for such a purpose in January, February, and March had already been exhausted. There is one hint. On April 2 Major Mahon wrote to Ross Mahon and asked him if he would "be so good as to name if the soup kitchen goes on well." If the landlord was suggesting that the kitchen was already open, then Father McDermott and his committee had miraculously gathered up some funds within the space of a few days and opened a much-needed facility. But if he was merely asking for the latest news about the kitchen, as seems likely, then it is probable, in the absence of any other evidence, that the Strokestown poor were left without any relief committee assistance from March 26 until May 24.

During April and May the area had been wracked by ever-mounting privations. "The inhabitants are more like the dead than the living, and if some Society does not promptly and efficiently undertake their cause it will soon be a complete charnel house," wrote the wife of the Protestant rector in Roscommon town in a letter seeking help from the Society of Friends in late April. On May 8 the *Roscommon Journal*, in a commentary headlined "Awful State of the Country," blamed London, pointing to its "apathetic"

attitude and "bad laws and misgovernment," which were causing large numbers to flee to the United States, from where they
would plot vengeance. "They have taken with them the bone and
sinew of Ireland; and not one of them ever left our shores that have
not recorded a vow in Heaven, if an opportunity ever offers, to be
avenged of those who drove them from the land of their birth—the
land of their forefathers, their dear Erin." In response to a plea from
a landlord in Strokestown—a hint that the relief committee wasn't
providing much assistance—the Quakers succeeded in delivering at
least one load of rice and biscuit to town in early May, but the new
soup kitchen proved a more significant contribution to local relief
when it opened in the third week of May.

Overseen by a newly reconstituted relief committee—
Strokestown's third—the kitchen spooned out a thin porridge of
maize, rice, and oats called "stirabout" each day to a broad range of
eligible paupers, who stood in a long line and waited for the number
on their ration ticket to be called. Although Father McDermott
was now the unchallenged leader of the committee, he had less of
a free hand in the allocation of funds: A separate finance committee was established to oversee the financial matters of all eighteen
soup kitchens in the Roscommon Union. Since the government
regulations required every able-bodied member of a recipient family to appear at the kitchen each day, the town center was continu-
ally filled with throngs from far-flung townlands, offering Father
McDermott an unobstructed view of the realities in the countryside. A fraction of these paupers were now able to receive medical assistance upon arrival in the town. In early July a temporary
fever hospital with a capacity to care for seventy-five patients was
opened with funds from another short-term piece of legislation.
Major Mahon donated land for the construction of what he called
"fever sheds," leaving it to Ross Mahon to select a suitable location
just outside town for the facility. The well-regarded local physician Dr. Terence Shanley was appointed director of the hospital.
Dr. Shanley was in the unique position of boasting both a close

friendship with Major Mahon and a prominent standing in Father
McDermott's parish.

It is true that the kitchen didn't lack for problems. The watery
nature of the soup exacerbated diarrhea, and the monotony of the
offerings gave rise to scurvy. Some regarded going to a kitchen each
day clutching a tin cup as an ignoble alternative to working for
assistance. Yet over the next few months the Strokestown facility
spooned out an average of a few thousand rations each day. The success was replicated throughout the country, where the government
proved it had the administrative capacity to provide sustenance to
more than three million people. On the Strokestown kitchen's busiest day, it was recorded that 3,159 meals were served, which, since
children under nine received less than a full ration, meant that perhaps as many as 4,000 people were fed. (According to the 1841
census, 5,410 people lived in the Strokestown Electoral Division,
the area the soup kitchen was intended to serve.) A soup kitchen
in the Lisanuffy Electoral Division, which contained a large number of Mahon tenants, fed 2,371 on its busiest day. (In 1841 it had
4,392 inhabitants.) After hundreds, perhaps thousands, of deaths
and likely an equal number of departures for new lands, the town
of Strokestown was better equipped to cope with Famine sufferers
than at any other time during the crisis. And the local relief committee headed by Father McDermott, for so long a hive of conflict
and (alleged) indolence, was at the forefront of the effort.

It was during this period that Major Mahon began permitting Ross
Mahon to begin clearances of the tenants who hadn't traveled to
America. Gone were his long-expressed worries about punishing
anyone but conspirators or being seen as perpetrating a "tyrannical
or cruel" or "a harsh or an unjust" act. Instead he took advantage
of the greatest suffering to afflict the Mahon lands since his family
took control in the late seventeenth century to begin uprooting a
mass of vulnerable tenants.

The major didn't offer an explicit explanation for his conversion to a course of action he had resisted for so long. He was surely motivated by his financial difficulties. In the words of a proprietor who was regarded as benevolent, the Marquess of Sligo, the Irish landlord was faced with the choice of "ejecting or being ejected." Lord Sligo wrote that "ejectments may not be the voluntary act of a landowner but sure consequences of laws and famine." Major Mahon was likely preoccupied with maintaining the viability of his estate because of a heightened interest in the prospects of his descendants. His daughter, Grace Catherine, had just married Henry Sandford Pakenham, the twenty-four-year-old son of the dean of St. Patrick's in Dublin, grandson of the second Baron Longford, distant relation of the Duke of Wellington, and heir to the Mount Sandford estates in counties Westmeath and Roscommon. Since Major Mahon lacked a male successor—his son had died a few years earlier at school—young Pakenham promptly received royal license to change his surname to Pakenham Mahon, securing his position as eventual inheritor of the property. Perhaps the landlord's action to begin clearances was made easier by the fact that everyone in his social class was doing much the same thing, and the soup kitchen he had been so concerned about was now in operation. Nonetheless, it is hard to imagine that Major Mahon, who had just written that he "would willingly in the present unfortunate state of the people, make any sacrifice sooner than put the law in force," did not have qualms about his decision.

The churnings of his conscience meant nothing to the targeted peasants of Strokestown. It was early in April when his talk about "those who had nothing but potatoes," broadcast to Ross Mahon in late February and March, disappeared from his letters. In the middle of April he spent three days on a cushion in the United Service Club signing and dating more than a thousand notices to quit, which would inform some five thousand occupants that they had six months to pay their rent or surrender their lands. He exhausted himself completing the notices so that Ross Mahon could serve them by May 1, enabling a new round of evictions to commence on November 1, 1847.

It appears that the first round was being executed in full force by early June. By the evidence of the few letters from the summer and fall of 1847 that survive in the family archive at Strokestown House and the National Library of Ireland, it wasn't a topic on which Major Mahon wished to dwell. On June 5, with the passengers of the *Naomi* and the *John Munn* on their way to Liverpool, Major Mahon buried a reference to evictions in a postscript to a letter to Ross Mahon. He began the P.S. by asking about the level of illness in the area. "Let me know what state the town and vicinity of Strokestown is in as regards fever." He next offered to return home, in a nod to the gravity of the situation, "if you consider it advisable for me to do so." And then, after these two sentences of seeming concern, he penned the following line: "I hope you will have the sheriff give you possession of some of those lands you have obtained *haberes* against." Since Ross Mahon had been securing *haberes* on wide tracts of the estate for months, this single, unelaborated sentence gave Ross Mahon the permission to evict perhaps a few thousand men, women, and children.

A few days later, his words of authorization were more explicit. This time he was speaking of a specific townland, Cregga, located a few miles north of Strokestown. According to Ross Mahon's calculations, a total of thirty-six families—roughly 180 people, if each family had five members (a calculation used by Ross Mahon)—had been served with ejectment processes from this locale. Fifteen of these families, about 75 people, participated in the emigration plan to America. That left twenty-one families, some 105 people, who persisted in clinging to the land. Some of these families—the "poorer class"—were offered a gratuity of a pound or two to leave quietly. In suggesting this common tactic, the land agent told Major Mahon that "it is not so charitable or liberal a plan as sending the poor creatures to America, but as there must be a stop to your expenditure I would be disposed to recommend it for the benefit of the estate." He said it would enable "them to go to work in England."

Ross Mahon later stated that he distributed 10 pounds' worth of gratuities to the residents of Cregga, which likely funded the calm removal of five families without formal eviction. That left sixteen families, or eighty people, at the mercy of the land agent and the intimidating force that backed him up. On June 11 Major Mahon instructed Ross Mahon to clear them out. "I beg to say that I should think the land of Cregga would be a good place to get out of the hands of so 'bad a lot' and such a nest of paupers." With these few words, the major revealed much about his new thinking on the situation. The line began with aristocratic insouciance—"I beg to say that I should think"—proceeded with opportunism—"a good place," as in a potentially profitable place. It ended with evidence of casual cruelty—"get out of the hands of so 'bad a lot'"—and chilling inhumanity—"such a nest of paupers." What, after all, is the practical use of retaining a *nest* of anything?

In the days to come, Ross Mahon arrived in Cregga with the sheriff, a troop of well-armed officers, and a band of ruffians known popularly as the "crowbar brigade." Upon his appearance, the tenants emerged from their huts to beg to be allowed to remain, a ritual enacted throughout Ireland. Although he was loath to negotiate any further with the tenants, Ross Mahon did allow all evictees to keep their crops, which put him and Major Mahon a class above the cruelest evictors. In his memorandum the land agent noted that he "got possession" of Cregga, a bland description for the removal of a band of starving paupers, violators of the injunction contained within the notice to quit to "deliver up . . . quiet and peaceable possession." After the sheriff's men completed the task of ensuring their removal—they were lawbreakers, after all—the crowbar brigade, composed of men hired by Ross Mahon, moved in to "tumble" the cottages. The land agent would later claim that he sometimes allowed evicted families to keep their thatched roofs, which they used to cover ditches and hollows, creating the makeshift dwellings known as "scalpeens." At other times, it would later be alleged by Father McDermott, the roofs were set on fire, which, like the bonfires lighted by the secret societies after their victories, sent a powerful message to anyone who saw the glow in the sky.

But Cregga was only a single townland. Over June and July, Ross Mahon moved from Cregga to the remaining thirteen townlands that had been partially cleared by the emigration plan, and then on to an additional three townlands. By his accounting, 191 families were removed (by formal evictions or "voluntary" surrender) from seventeen different townlands during June and July, amounting to about the same number of tenants who had participated in the emigration plan. This was still far short of the two-thirds of the twelve thousand tenants that had to be gotten rid of, according to Ross Mahon's calculations. With this in mind, the land agent wrote to Major Mahon on July 23, reminding him of the economic soundness of conducting another emigration plan. He reiterated "the impossibility of collecting poor rates or rents, or effecting any change in the condition of the people or improvement in agriculture, while the land remains in such small division in the hands of paupers, unable to support themselves, much less to till it to advantage." He repeated that it would be cheaper in the long run to send the tenants to Québec than to the pay the rates for indoor and outdoor relief under the soon-to-commence amended Poor Law. As if this weren't enough to induce Major Mahon to send his tenants to a faraway land—and the landlord was still striving to come up with a plan—Ross Mahon added that the conspiracy was growing more serious. In fact, it "is carried on with so much determination, that I am confidently informed that a considerable sum of money has been subscribed among the people in the neighborhood, for the purpose of rewarding a person hired to assassinate me, and that this plot has been got up by persons in comfortable circumstances, but who owe several years rent, and who are well-known bad characters."

CHAPTER 7

Wretched, Sickly, Miserable

~~~~~~~

BY THE TIME THE last of the Mahon tenants sailed out of the port of Liverpool, the news was spreading about the frightful conditions that existed on board the emigrant ships and in the Canadian colony where they landed. An early June letter from the archbishop of Québec, Joseph Signay, to the bishops and archbishops in Ireland was published in both Irish and English newspapers in July. It told of "transatlantic vessels . . . infected with sick and dying emigrants" and described how the quarantine station in Québec was unable to care for them all upon arrival. "Already more than a thousand human beings have been consigned to their eternal rest in the Catholic cemetery, precursors of thousands of others who will rejoin them there, if the stream of emigration from Ireland continues to flow with the same abundance," he wrote. On July 12 the Earl of Enniskillen rose in the House of Lords to ask the colonial secretary, Earl

Grey, if he had "heard of the circumstances referred to in the letter, and if so whether any steps had been taken to remedy the evil?" Grey admitted that the accounts of suffering were "too true," and he blamed fever outbreaks among shipboard Irish on the "sudden change to a more generous diet" required by government regulations. Concerns voiced by figures like Lord John Manners and Lord George Bentinck, both Tory protectionists, led the government to institute some hasty remedies—attempting to place physicians on board, increase inspecting officers at embarking ports, and charge ship owners for medical inspections.

It was all too little and too late, particularly for the Strokestown tenants. Just a single passenger from among them bequeathed to history a few-sentence account of the journey, enough to paint an awful picture of the experience. They were "packed inside of the hold of the ship," whose "unsanitary conditions . . . led to the outbreak of typhus," Thomas Quinn, who was a child of six when he boarded the *Naomi* with his parents and two brothers, Patrick, eleven, and Joseph, three, said decades later. "There was another calamity in addition to this one. We did not have enough drinking water or even food. The rations, which were already restricted, were reduced." A secondhand account of the *Naomi*'s passage confirmed Quinn's recollections. "Drinking water ran low and food was reduced to one meal a day," said Leo Tye in 1989 at age eighty-three, repeating information passed to him by his grandfather, Daniel Tighe, who was twelve years old when he made the trip. "Comfort and hygiene were nonexistent."

These details accord with the few surviving accounts of life aboard a "coffin ship" recorded by passengers traveling above the hold in the comfort of the cabin. When the Mahon tenants were still en route to Québec, Stephen De Vere had already completed his sea journey to the colony in what he described as a better than average vessel. A compassionate member of a respected Anglo-Irish family from County Limerick, he described his experience in a letter to his uncle, Lord Monteagle, a Whig landlord who funded the emigration of some of his tenants. It has become one of the most-quoted documents of the Irish Famine.

> *Before the emigrant has been a week at sea, he is an altered man. . . . How can it be otherwise? Hundreds of poor people, men, women and children, of all ages from the driveling idiot of 90 to the babe just born, huddled together, without light, without air, wallowing in filth, and breathing a fetid atmosphere, sick in body, dispirited in heart. . . . The fever patients lying between the sound in sleeping places so narrow, as almost to deny them . . . a change of position . . . by their agonized ravings disturbing those around them . . . living without food or medicine except as administered by the hand of casual charity, dying without spiritual consolation and buried in the deep without the rites of the church.*

British officials did not shrug off De Vere's words. Earl Grey even asked Lord Monteagle for permission to publish the letter. Several of De Vere's suggestions—more food, more space, more ventilation, and more medical care—would be incorporated in some form into later versions of the Passenger Act. But it would mean nothing for those embarking this year.

Around the time that De Vere arrived in Québec, a Scottish doctor landed in New York after a trip aboard an emigrant ship from Liverpool. The doctor, one of the physicians who cared for the queen, was the author of a number of medical texts, including *The Physiology of Digestion*, who "attained a celebrity rarely equaled both in Europe and America," the *Times* wrote. In late July, partially inspired by Earl Grey's supposition in the House of Lords that ship fever was caused by an *improvement* in the traveler's diet, Dr. Andrew Combe penned a long manuscript on the "nature and causes of ship fever." In his essay he described in vivid detail the conditions aboard his ship, which, since it lost only two passengers, was among the better of the year. He outlined the inadequacy of the government allowance of provisions, particularly in a season of famine when the average passenger was desperate for any scrap of food. He deplored "the impure and noxious atmosphere which the emigrants are compelled to breathe between decks," noting that "even with the utmost vigilance and care on the part of the captain to ensure cleanliness and ventilation ... the air below was so foul and offensive as to be almost intolerable to anyone unaccustomed to it." And he diagrammed how these factors caused "a moral apathy" to set in among the sufferers, causing them to be "indifferent to ordinary comforts, and indisposes them to make the slightest effort for their own wellbeing." While Dr. Combe's letter contained recommendations mirroring those of De Vere, it also came too late to make an immediate difference. It wasn't published in the *Times* until September.

A third account from another passenger from the comfortable classes—also made public after the crisis had passed—is of particular interest to those tracking the journey of the Mahon tenants. Unlike Dr. Combe and De Vere, whose generalized accounts sought to inspire government action, Robert Whyte told the tale of a particular journey made by a particular ship in *The Ocean Plague: A Voyage to Quebec in an Irish Immigrant Vessel Embracing a Quarantine at Grosse Isle in 1847, by a Cabin Passenger,* published the following year in Boston. Whyte sailed from Dublin on May 30 aboard an unnamed brig, likely the *George*, the majority of whose passengers were being transported out of Ireland by their County Meath landlord. A day earlier the *Virginius* had left Liverpool, and it happened that Whyte caught sight of the Mahon ship on June 5. "We had two ships in company with us all day; they were too distant to distinguish their names," he wrote. Three days later he was close enough to read the words on the side. "The two ships were again in sight, one was the *Tamerlane* of Aberystwyth, the other the *Virginius* of Liverpool; both fine vessels with passengers."

Like De Vere and Dr. Combe, Whyte traveled aboard one of the better vessels, although this fact does not diminish the horror of his descriptions. Within days of leaving Ireland, it was reported to the captain that a few of the 110 passengers had fallen ill. With bad food, dirty water, cramped quarters, and no medicine, the list of sick cases grew every day. The crew did what it could to help—the captain's wife, Whyte wrote, was particularly tireless in her assistance—but nothing could prevent dysentery and fever from spreading. Two weeks into the trip, some of the healthier passengers appeared on deck to demand more food, but this nascent mutiny was put down when the captain fired a single shot from his blunderbuss into the air. "If they were resolute they might easily have seized upon the provisions," Whyte wrote. "In fact, I was surprised how famished men could so patiently bear with their own and their starved children's sufferings."

By the time three weeks had passed, the sickness had spread to half the passengers and some members of the crew. Whyte watched as a man was brought on deck to breathe a little fresh air. "He was a miserable object," he wrote. "His face, being yellow and withered, was rendered ghastly by the black streak that encircled his sunken eyes." In early July deaths began to occur. "I was awakened by the noise made by the mate, who was searching for an old sail to cover the remains with," Whyte wrote after two brothers had succumbed. "In about an hour after, they were consigned to the deep, a remaining brother being the solitary mourner." A few days later this brother also died. "He was seized with dismay from the time of their death, which no doubt hurried on the malady to its fatal determination. The old sails being all used up, his remains were placed in two meal-sacks . . . He left two little orphans, one of whom—a boy, seven years of age—I noticed in the evening wearing his deceased father's coat."

On July 10, forty days after leaving Dublin, the *George* came within view of land, passing through the Cabot Strait between Nova Scotia and Newfoundland, and pushed into the gulf of St. Lawrence. At this point Whyte's attention veered from the continued sufferings in the hold and fastened upon the natural beauties of the shoreline. "No human eyes behold this region of unbroken solitude, save now and then those which can but lightly appreciate its grandeur," he wrote. With the current and the wind conspiring against the brig's progress, the trip up the St. Lawrence River was slow, giving Whyte opportunities to observe the rhythms of French Canadian life on the shore. On Sunday, July 25, he was aroused by the sound of a church bell. "Its sweet tone induced me to go on deck for a few moments where I was charmed with the appearance of the showily dressed Canadians, some standing in groups talking, others seated upon benches while *caleshes* were momentarily arriving with *habitans* from distant settlements who, after tying up their horses under a shed close by the *presbytère*, joined the chatting parties until the bell ceased, when all retired within the church." All the while, the misery continued in what Whyte called "our floating pest-house." Yet he noted that some of the passengers were beginning to improve, aided partly by the fresh river water that they were now able to drink in abundance.

Finally on July 28, sixty days after leaving Dublin, the *George* arrived at the quarantine station at Grosse Île, a small, rocky island twenty miles east of Québec City. Whyte's ship was recorded by Canadian officials as losing six passengers, although his diary makes it seem as if the number was slightly higher. Far from being shocked by the ship's condition, two Catholic priests complimented the captain on its cleanliness and told of worse ships where the "emigrants crowded together like cattle, and corpses remaining long unburied, the sailors being ill, and the passengers unwilling to touch them."

On the same day the *George*'s shadow, the *Virginius*, docked at the station after losing one-third of 476 passengers en route, making it the vessel with the highest level of in-passage mortality all season. On the following day Dr. George Mellis Douglas, the medical superintendent at Grosse Île for eleven years, boarded the *Virginius* and was stunned by what he saw. "On mustering the passengers for inspection," he wrote, "it was found that 106 were ill of fever, including nine of the crew, and the large number of 158 had died on the passage, including the first and second officers and seven of the crew, and the master and the steward were dying."

He claimed that "fever and dysentery cases came on board this vessel in Liverpool, and deaths occurred before leaving the Mersey." This statement accorded with Douglas's belief that the highest death rates were caused when passengers carried full-blown cases of illness with them into the hold. In particular, he blamed the filthy lodging houses and cellars where they huddled prior to departure for causing outbreaks. In making his declaration about the *Virginius*, Douglas was accusing the government's inspecting officer in Liverpool of failing, in violation of the law, to halt a disease- and death-ridden ship. As a result, the officer was required by his superiors to respond, and he soon made his assertion about discovering "no appearance of disease" after a "most minute inspection." The officer then asked James and William Robinson to vouch for the health of the *Virginius*'s passengers. "Upon my mentioning the subject to J. and W. Robinson, the passenger brokers, they distinctly deny the truth of the allegation as to sickness and deaths taking place on board the vessel in this port," wrote the officer, Mr. Prior. He then wrote, "As fever was very rife in Liverpool at the time, it does not appear to me very extraordinary that the *Virginius* shared the fate of other vessels similarly circumstanced as to sickness and mortality." But the implication that the *Virginius* was just another ship would not pass muster with Grosse Île's medical superintendent. To him, this was an extraordinary case, and the Mahon tenants were *not* characteristic Famine travelers. "The few that were able to come on deck were ghastly yellow-looking spectres, unshaven and hollow cheeked, and, without exception, the worst looking passengers I have ever seen; not more than six or eight were really healthy and able to exert themselves," he wrote.

Coming from Dr. Douglas, this was a considerable statement. Since Famine ships began arriving in mid-May, he had been coping with a crisis of a magnitude unprecedented in Canadian history. In a typical year, fewer than one hundred beds were required to treat sick émigrés at any one time. This year the two hundred beds that were reserved for what was expected to be a distressed season were filled within the first few days of arrivals. The doctor, a Scottish-born son of a Methodist minister, hurriedly ordered up additional facilities and requested more doctors and nurses. By May 30, makeshift tents and other structures were holding more than 1,300 patients. Another 12,175 people were waiting to be examined—and often coming down with the illnesses they had so far avoided—while confined within thirty-five ships anchored in the St. Lawrence. A captain of one of them told a Catholic priest that it would "be better to simply send a battery of artillery from Québec City to sink these ships to the bottom, than to let all these poor people suffer such a slow, agonizing death." An average of fifty people died each day, sometimes more, on the ships and in the medical tents, creating a never-ending procession of corpses to the burial ground.

To speed the flow of emigrants, in early June a government commission recommended that quarantine restrictions regarding length of detainment be relaxed, which allowed thousands of "healthy" Irish to be hurriedly placed on steamers bound for Québec City and Montréal. As Dr. Douglas predicted, this spread disease into the mainland population of Canada and points beyond, eventually claiming the mayor of Montréal, the Catholic archbishop of Toronto, and thousands of others. While the parade of ships into Grosse Île did not slow, the island did become better able to cope with the difficulties. "New hospitals were started, necessary material for the station was increased; provisions became more abundant; young doctors arrived to take care of the sick; things began to change gradually and to go less badly," wrote a French Canadian missionary. By early July an average of two thousand patients were being cared for, some in newly constructed hospital sheds, while roughly fifteen thousand passengers waited in ships for assistance or clearance. But little could be done to abate the horrors. Dr. Douglas was not only finding it difficult to enlist staff to treat the patients but he also struggled to maintain the health of those willing to work. "The accumulation of so vast a multitude of fever cases in one place generated a miasma so virulent and concentrated, that few who came within its poisonous atmosphere escaped," he wrote. Out of twenty-six medical men and attendants, only two of them—one being Dr. Douglas—did not catch an infectious disease. It was even harder to find people "to make coffins, dig graves and bury the dead," a vitally important task.

On July 11 the *Erin's Queen* became the first Mahon ship to dock at Grosse Île, arriving seventeen days before the *Virginius*. Since the ship had left Liverpool three days later than the *Virginius*—thus preceding it by nearly three weeks—it was clear that the captain, J. Davidson, had taken a different route blessed with more favorable winds. Of the *Queen*'s 517 passengers, a small minority of whom were from the Mahon estate, 45 had died during the journey, more than one a day. Nine corpses remained on board when the ship docked at quarantine, and Dr. Douglas wrote that the captain had "to bribe the seamen with a sovereign [worth 20 shillings] for each body brought out of the hold." With 130 passengers remaining ill with fever, the *Queen* was forced like every ship—twenty-one were lying at anchor on July 11—to float at anchor until help could arrive. After six days the captain fled in frustration but soon returned, "having got the better of his fears," said the *Québec Gazette*. In time, scores of sick people were taken off the vessel and admitted to the quarantine facilities on the island, while their healthy relatives were required to wait for steamer passage to nearby Québec City or more distant Montréal. If the emigrant's departure from Ireland was full of emotion—the "American wake" of lore—this moment of separation was far more frenzied and desperate. Whyte described how "the screams pierced my brain; and the excessive agony . . . rent my heart" when the ill passengers were taken off his ship. A total of seventy-one of the *Queen*'s quarantine patients would die on the island, either alone or accompanied by a family member or neighbor who was also near death.

Two days after the *Virginius* arrived on July 28, the *Naomi*, the other ship filled largely with Mahon tenants, pulled into dock. Dr. Douglas was nearly as appalled by its condition, calling it "another plague-ship." Of 334 passengers, 78 had died at sea and 100 were reported as ill. The captain, Thomas Wilson, was himself just recovering from fever. "The filth and dirt in this vessel's hold creates such an effluvium as to make it difficult to breathe," Dr. Douglas wrote. Then, two days after the *Naomi*, the final Mahon ship, the *John Munn*, arrived in Grosse Île after forty-seven days at sea with a smaller number of Strokestown residents. Although it wasn't granted a descriptive comment from the medical superintendent—a privilege bestowed on only the most awful ships—it was only slightly less horrible than the *Naomi*. Of 452 passengers, 59 had died en route and 100 were now sick.

With the temperatures reaching more than 90 degrees Fahrenheit in the shade, the three vessels remained anchored in the St. Lawrence as the medical staff struggled to reach them. The passengers, desperate for any sort of help, were now even denied the luxury of drinking river water. The Grosse Île harbor was a "floating mass of filthy straw, the refuse of foul beds, barrels containing the vilest matter, old rags, and tattered clothes," wrote Whyte, who was waiting at the same time. Over the next week and a half, the deaths continued. On the *Virginius*, nineteen succumbed; on the *Munn*, eleven; and on the *Naomi*, thirty-one. And after the sick were conveyed to the quarantine hospital on the island, still the deaths continued. Ninety more died from the *Virginius*; 117 from the *Munn*; and 87 from the *Naomi*. In fact, the miseries of the trip might be said to have increased after the ships pulled into Grosse Île, if statistics can be a measure. On each of the ships but the *Virginius*, more passengers died after reaching the station than had passed away during the entire sea passage. The *Virginius* was likely spared this fate only because its weakened travelers had already expired.

Among the four Mahon ships, it was the *Virginius* that would become renowned. Within days, Canadian newspapers were mentioning it by name as an example of the most terrible of the Grosse Île fleet. On August 14 the *Toronto Globe* quoted the Montréal Board of Health as stating, of the *Virginius* and another ship, that "the Black Hole of Calcutta was a mercy compared to the holds of these vessels," referring the infamous dungeon where more than a hundred British POWs perished from heat exhaustion in 1756. A month later the *Times* of London reprinted the article, and then, on September 17, it published a stinging commentary about the appalling conditions at sea, again mentioning the *Virginius* by name. "The worst horrors of that slave trade which is the boast or the ambition of this empire to suppress, at any cost, have been re-enacted in the flight of British subjects from their native shores," it read. The *Times's* mention of the ship guaranteed one thing: Both Major Mahon and John Ross Mahon would learn how badly their emigration plan had gone. British officials would hear of the horrors of the Mahon ships directly from Dr. George Douglas. In his summation of the unprecedented and never-repeated season for his London superiors, he singled out the *Naomi* and the *Virginius* as two of the three worst ships (out of 398) that arrived for inspection at Grosse Île all year. While the average death rate on ships from Liverpool that year was 16 percent, on these two ships it exceeded 50 percent—267 out of 476 perished from the *Virginius*, 196 out of 311 from the *Naomi*. He also singled out Major Denis Mahon for mention, the only landlord named in the lengthy missive. He wrote that the passengers of the two ships "were sent out at the expense and from the estates of . . . Major Mahon, in County Tyrone [sic], and the survivors were, without exception, the most wretched, sickly, miserable beings I ever witnessed."

By August 13 each vessel had been cleared from the quarantine station, free to travel upriver to Québec City to pick up the goods it would be carting back to England. At this point it becomes harder to track the journey of the Mahon tenants. Many who made it to Montréal and Québec City likely didn't live for even a few days. But some surely did. Research by Grosse Île scholar Marianna O'Gallagher has shown that several Strokestown orphans were placed in a local orphanage, from where they were reunited with family members or taken in by French-Canadian families. A farmer named François Colulombe adopted Daniel Tighe and his sister Catherine, who assumed a phonetic French spelling of their surname, Tye. Among this group were Thomas and Patrick Quinn, the boys who endured the journey of the *Naomi*. While in the quarantine hospital—it appears that the youngest Quinn, three-year-old Joseph, died at sea—the brothers were transferred to the care of a Catholic priest, who escorted them to the death-beds of James and Margaret Quinn. Thomas would later recall how his parents "were able to attain their final sleep in peace with God, pardoning their enemies, and carrying away their ineffable consolation of leaving their children under the protection of the French-Canadian priest."

Once discharged, six-year-old Thomas Quinn was transported to Québec City and then, with a group of twenty-five other orphans, to the small town of Nicolet on the St. Lawrence River. "I was very weak from the misery and deprivation," he recalled in 1914. "When we arrived I was put to bed, and fell into a deep sleep. When I woke up, all my compatriots had disappeared, and Christian families had adopted them. Thus, I was the last, and was adopted by Mr. George Bourque," a maintenance employee at the town's Catholic seminary. When his twelve-year-old brother, Patrick, was released from quarantine—still wearing a formal overcoat likely woven by his late mother, perhaps intended for confirmation ceremonies—he was also taken to Nicolet. "I did not even recognize him at first," recalled Thomas. "My adoptive father could not resist Patrick's legitimate wish and agreed to keep both of us. What a joy it was for the two brothers to live together."

Some Mahon tenants did make it to America. The Charitable Ladies of Québec City recorded that five Sheridan siblings from the *Naomi* "left for Lockport," in western New York state, after a few months' stay in the organization's orphanage. The logbook also noted that Mary Byrne, sixteen, "left for Baltimore to her brother," apparently in December 1847, although it seems she still hadn't arrived two months later. In February 1848 her brother, Michael Byrne of 49 Frederick Street, Baltimore, Maryland, placed an ad in an Irish-American newspaper seeking "any information" regarding his sister's whereabouts. A few years later, an ad in the same newspaper sought John Corcoran, a native of the Kilmacknanny townland in Father Boyd's Lisanuffy parish. It noted that "when he was last heard from," he was residing in the state of Rhode Island. "Any person knowing him will confer a favor by writing to his brothers, John and Patrick Gill, Altoona, Blair County, Pennsylvania." In 1851, four years after his arrival on the *Naomi*, Peter Dempsey had a man named James Washington place a heartbreaking ad in the paper seeking the location of two of his sons, John and Martin Dempsey. "Their father left them in hospital at quarantine sick—since heard they were in Buffalo and went from there to Chicago. Any information respecting them will be thankfully received by their father . . . care of Jas Washington, West Street, Cleveland, Ohio." It is with a sense of relief that one discovers that neither John nor Martin Dempsey was recorded as being buried on the sorrowful island on the St. Lawrence River.

CHAPTER 8

Upon Their Devoted Heads Let the Result Lye

Whatever I did with regard to my property I conceived rested with myself; that I would not allow him or any man to interfere with me in that respect, and desired him not to presume to meddle with my private affairs.

—Major Denis Mahon,
describing his words to Father
McDermott, August 28, 1847

While the ships were still en route to Québec, Major Mahon landed back in Ireland after eight months in England, arriving in Dublin around June 30. After a week's stay in the Irish capital, he left for a visit with his sister in County Louth. On July 6 he wrote to Ross Mahon from her home, Prospect House in Dundalk, telling him that he would be returning to Strokestown on July 12. He described a conversation he had with Lord Monteagle, the prominent Whig, about the possibility of the government funding an emigration plan, a continuing preoccupation.

By the time he reached Strokestown in the second week of July, he likely read—or was told about—the previous week's *Roscommon Journal*, which roundly attacked his eviction policy in a lead editorial. The newspaper noted that more than two thousand eviction proceedings had been initiated in Strokestown court, while failing to identify Major Mahon as the landlord responsible for most of the filings, as anyone in town would know. "About five times the number that we ever recollect to be brought into court at any time within the last twenty years," it wrote. "Our prison will be kept crowded; our poorhouse will be kept full; and our streets will be inundated by this 'Clearance System'—this new mode of depopulising," the paper continued. "Where it will end God only knows—upon their devoted heads let the result lye. A hundred times have we preached the doctrine of the ever-to-be-lamented [Thomas] Drummo[n]d [former Irish undersecretary], 'that property had its duties as well as its rights.' The Landlords appear to have totally forgotten the first part of the noble sentiment, and to carry the latter into the most rigid effect. Time will yet prove to them that 'a bold peasantry—a country's pride/if once destroyed, can never be revived.'"

Since few of his letters survive from this few-month period of the story—he was no longer writing much to his now close-at-hand land agent—it is difficult to track the landlord's activities during the first few weeks after his return. But after about a month, he provided explicit proof that he was sensing the community's wrath over his campaign of clearances. On August 12 he penned a note to Ross Mahon, who was then in the midst of a brief sojourn to Dublin. "I shall be very much obliged to you to call at Bapetts gunmakers Parliament St. and make him lend to you a small mahogany case he has of mine containing a six-barrel pistol," he wrote. "If he had it ready before you leave Dublin, perhaps you will bring it down to me." His concerns about local anger may also explain why he did not attempt during these weeks to communicate with the Strokestown Relief Committee, which was busy, it is true, conducting the considerable operations of the soup kitchen. He even skipped its July 24 meeting. These were curious moves for a man who had played such a significant early role in the body and had closely monitored its conduct (or misconduct) from London earlier in the year. Although he may have been hesitant to face the people coping with the destitution that his policies were exacerbating, he may also have felt he was doing quite enough for the soup kitchen—since he was ultimately responsible for footing most of the bill—without speaking with the members.

Then, on August 28, he made an appearance at its monthly meeting, and it soon became obvious that he had good reason to stay away. Upon his arrival he began looking over the account books, noting the fact that the committee hadn't met since July 24. "And on my asking Mr. McDermott if there had been any, or if he had called a meeting, he replied, No, and that he did not see any occasion—that things were going on regular and correct; and even added, that, had he known it was desirable, he would have done so," according to the landlord's written report, composed on the day of the meeting and made public four months later. The priest added that it was useless for the landlord to bother examining the paperwork since it would require many days of study to understand all the details. The major responded that he "had no other wish in these inquiries but to make myself acquainted with what, as a member of the committee, I ought to know.

"We then proceeded to examine the accounts and look over the vouchers, etc., etc.; and having found them correct, I expressed myself to that effect, and then proposed we should go over the lists, which we were called on to revise that day with a view to reduce the number getting relief, according to the instructions given by Major Howard," he wrote.

By any measure, this was a grave undertaking. The government was asking that the soup kitchen begin preparing for final closure in two weeks by steadily decreasing the number of paupers receiving rations. The roughly three thousand people who had been served daily by the kitchen at the height of the summer—and the thousands being served by the seventeen other soup kitchens in the Roscommon Union—were now expected to obtain harvest employment or seek relief from the Roscommon workhouse under the amended Poor Law. But, as both Father McDermott and Major Mahon surely knew, there wasn't much harvest work and the overcrowded and indebted Roscommon workhouse was neither able (because of a lack of funds) nor permitted (because government directives were required) to provide outdoor relief to either non–able-bodied or able-bodied recipients. The act of striking a pauper off the relief list, as the law required, amounted to something close to a sentence of death for the most debilitated.

Upon Major Mahon broaching the subject of the relief lists, Father McDermott began to act in a "very uncivil and uncourteous manner." Seeking to "avoid any altercations with Mr. McDermott," the landlord instead directed his questions to the committee's chief clerk, Charles Costello. He then asked a question. "Who revised those lists?" he asked Costello. The implication in his question was that the lists had already been at least partially slashed, which would have made sense. Earlier in the month the government had told the relief committees in the Roscommon Union that they could continue serving soup past August 15—when many kitchens in other parts of Ireland were scheduled to close—if they proceeded on "a very reduced scale, with respect to numbers."

"For some time I got no answer; but on pressing for one, Costello said, the committee. I asked, who were those of the committee that did so? He replied, Mr. McDermott, and that he (Costello) and the other clerks assisted him. On which Mr. McDermott rose up in a violent passion, and asked how I dared to come there to tyrannise over him? How dare I come at the eleventh hour, after leaving him to do all the work, and attack him by 'my side wind' allusions? But that he would not bear it; he had a hand to defend himself, and would do so."

If Major Mahon's account is accurate, Father McDermott was interpreting the landlord's questions not as an attack on the poor but as a criticism of his management of the relief committee. With his words about Major Mahon tyrannizing "over *him* . . . after leaving *him* to do all the work," he seemed to be engaging in what was so tragically typical during the Famine: a bureaucratic tussle. (Italics added.) But it remains unclear what about Major Mahon's question about revision of the relief lists could be interpreted as a "side wind" allusion. It is possible that the priest believed that the landlord was accusing him of reserving spots on the lists for those who were not among the most destitute, a charge often leveled against relief committee members in Ireland.

Major Mahon wondered what the priest was so upset about. "He was certainly in a violent passion, and would not listen to my repeated assurances that I had not in the slightest manner said or intended to say, anything to annoy him." Exasperated, he turned to his friend Dr. Terence Shanley, director of the temporary fever hospital, and asked him to assure the priest that "I had said nothing which Mr. McDermott ought to consider as meant towards him." Shanley did so.

But nothing could stop the priest's increasingly vitriolic attack. "He still continued to use the most abusive and insulting language that could be used by any man to a gentleman. . . . I was a 'stupid ass.' I had not common sense. He only wondered where, or if I had any schooling; for a more ignorant fellow he never met. Such an ass, that if I had had any schooling it was quite thrown away on me." The priest then sought to enlist the clerks and Dr. Shanley into his ranks. "'Here have I been for two hours trying to drive into his stupid head some information, and he is so ignorant he cannot understand it,'" he told them. What was the "information" that the priest was apparently attempting to impart to Major Mahon? The landlord does not tell us.

Major Mahon wrote that he turned again to the passive committee members to ask them to vouch for his good intentions. He then told the priest that if he had reason "to find fault with his conduct," he would "do so openly." He "defied him to state my ever having done so, as I assured him I was not afraid to tell him to his face anything that I had to complain of." In this, he was being plainly disingenuous. To take one example, Major Mahon had accused Father McDermott and other local priests of "feasting and stuffing and praying" to the face of a second party, Bishop

George Browne. It was hardly the kind of allegation either man was likely to forget.

At this point in the confrontation, according to Major Mahon, the priest escalated his attack beyond personal pique. For the first time he sought to assume the voice of the evicted tenants, launching into a denunciation of the policies that were causing so much misery in and around the town. He charged, according to the major, "that I had spent my winter in London to amuse myself, and had left my people to starve in the streets and die, without ever looking after them; that I had done nothing for them, and had no right now to come and interfere; and also he stated to me that I had not attended a committee or done anything for the poor since my return, but had amused myself burning houses and turning out the people to starve."

No matter how we judge the conduct of Major Mahon and Father McDermott during the Famine, this was an extraordinary moment in the history of the tragedy. A landlord was being confronted in public about actions that heightened the suffering of a people immersed in the struggle for survival. A representative of the masses was assailing a delegate of the dominant gentry. An O'Connellite Repealer was facing off against a Tory Unionist. To starving tenants disfigured by their agony, it surely symbolized a confrontation between good and evil, something like Christ standing before Pilate and telling him, "To this end was I born, and for this cause came I into the world, that I should bear witness unto the truth."

Major Mahon did not respond with eloquence. "That, I was obliged to assure the reverend gentleman, was not the case . . . ," he quoted himself as saying, failing to note what "that" referred to in Father McDermott's array of charges. He concluded, in a tacit acknowledgment that some of the accusations might have merit, "[A]nd whatever I did with regard to my property I conceived rested with myself; that I would not allow him or any man to interfere with me in that respect, and desired him not to presume to meddle with my private affairs." In the end, it was nobody's business but his own how he treated the thousands of people who lived on his estate.

Pronouncing himself "hurt" by the priest's tirade, Major Mahon said he "would not remain any longer, or do any act that day, after the manner in which I had been insulted by him." Walking outside the building with Dr. Shanley, Major Mahon told his friend that he would report the priest's conduct to Major Howard, letting "him know that . . . nothing had been done respecting the revision of the relief list." Since Major Mahon had sparked the argument by asking who had conducted an earlier revision of the list, this must have meant that the rolls had not been revised further. He also said he would request another meeting of the relief committee to discuss the priest's outburst. Then he asked the doctor "to keep in mind the manner in which Mr. McDermott had behaved to me that day." Dr. Shanley assured him that he would.

It's hard to imagine that the fracas was not an immediate matter of public discussion around town. On the following day, a Sunday, Father McDermott guaranteed that his words of condemnation would be given even wider broadcast. According to a letter that Major Mahon wrote to the priest, Father McDermott rose in his chapels—one on Church Street in Strokestown and one in the Kiltrustan townland just north of town—and repeated the "very unwarrantable language" from the committee meeting. "If I am rightly informed," Major Mahon wrote. In another document, later found in "Major Mahon's handwriting," the landlord recorded an informant's description of the priest's sermons in the wake of the meeting. "'There is Major Mahon absent from you all the winter. Not looking after your wants or distresses, but amusing himself, and he returns and finds his property all safe—his place unmolested; and the return he makes you is the burning and destroying of your houses, and leaving the poor to starve on the road,'" the major wrote. Then he commented, "This day I had a respectable person who said he heard, and was present in the chapel and distinctly heard, my name mentioned, and the language used." It was unsettling news to a landlord who already believed that a widespread conspiracy was targeting his estate management. In a letter to Father McDermott written on September 8, he demanded the opportunity of "replying to these very serious charges" at the next relief committee meeting. "I am determined to lay the matter before the committee on that day (or whatever day they shall meet), and submit to them how far you were warranted in making such charges against me."

The priest was not Christ-like in his September 9 response. He neither denied the charge that he was denouncing the landlord nor asserted his right to condemn injustice wherever he saw it. Instead he declared that *his* feelings had been hurt by the landlord's behavior at the committee meeting. He seemed to have attended a wholly different gathering from the one Major Mahon had described. "Until you make atonement to my feelings as a clergyman, for your insolent and personal attacks, I shall attend no meeting where you are present, either publicly or privately," he wrote. "I make this reply to convince you that I am only anxious to avoid a person whose conduct seems so extraordinary, and who seems to disregard the ordinary forms of civil society. My calling does not allow me to resent the insults I receive, and therefore common prudence, as well as religion, point out to me the necessity of withdrawing myself from the society of persons who may be inclined to offend me." Nowhere in this letter does the priest detail the character of the "insolent and personal attacks." He also does not suggest that he would end his public rebuke of the landlord's actions.

On September 12, three days after the priest mailed this letter to the landlord, the local soup kitchen ceased issuing provisions, formally ending the stormy tenure of the Strokestown Relief Committee. The kitchen had clearly proven the best and cheapest way to feed the largest amount of people. The government had advanced a total of 1,273 pounds to pay for its operation for five months. If Major Mahon had used the 3,500 pounds he spent on the emigration plan to operate a soup facility, he could have fed a sizable proportion of his tenants for more than a year.

According to the now operative amended Poor Law, the Roscommon workhouse was now the principal engine for relief in the county. Yet even the government recognized that the facility was unable to handle the task. The Roscommon Union was one of 22 (out of 130) unions in Ireland to be declared "distressed"—meaning the union's destitution exceeded the ability of the rate payers to fund it. But the Treasury wasn't willing to supply advances to the distressed unions in Ireland except in the most dire of circumstances. Instead it offered to coordinate the distribution of a mix of small grants and loans from the British Relief Association, the private relief organization that had such a successful fund-raising campaign in the early months of 1847. Still, the funding would be provided only after it had been decided that every exertion had been made to collect poor rates from the local landlords: The unions that had already been declared "distressed" would have to further prove that they were distressed. This requirement promised weeks and months of bureaucratic delay, creating another disastrous interval between relief schemes. With the overburdened workhouse unable and forbidden to distribute outdoor relief—it could barely afford to feed the paupers within its walls—nearly all the fifty thousand residents within the Roscommon Union who had received aid from eighteen soup kitchens were cut off from assistance. Instead of being replaced by the amended Poor Law, the Soup Kitchen Act was replaced with nothing.

But there was some good news. Father McDermott confirmed that in Strokestown, as elsewhere throughout Ireland, the new potato crop was healthy for the first time in three years. The *Roscommon Journal* gave the credit to "an all-bountiful Providence." As elsewhere in the nation, however, the yield was small, which meant that it would only feed some of the people for a short time. "The breadth of land sown this year is about one-third of the cultivation of 1845," Father McDermott wrote in a survey of his parish that had been requested by Bishop Browne. It was also largely a commercial crop grown by larger farmers, which meant the destitute would have to purchase potatoes at high cost in the marketplace. Father McDermott argued that if the grain crop were distributed among his parishioners, it "might support the people for about three months"—enough time, perhaps, for the Roscommon workhouse to arrange funding and receive permission to distribute outdoor relief. But the priest was not hopeful. "About five-sixths of the population are wholly destitute. Between four and five hundred died of actual starvation, and 200 more of diseases produced by the famine. Three hundred more emigrated, and fully 600 are infected by disease at the present moment. . . . Their condition is wretched; scarcely a pig or any poultry in their possession. No means devised for relief. No public works, and the [poor] rate 3s [3 shillings] to the pound [that is, high]."

"It is fearful to describe the present state of the poor or the fearful prospects of distress," Father McDermott wrote. "It is as bad as can be, and the people must die in numbers unless relieved."

During these days of hardship, Major Mahon's clearance policy—both evictions and "voluntary" surrenders—was being carried out with the same intensity as it had been in the first months of the summer. It appears that with the arrival of the harvest, Ross Mahon was inducing some tenants to leave solely by allowing them to retain their crops, which would have been more sizable than during the summer clearances. On September 14 Major Mahon wrote, "I quite agree with you that it will be very advantageous to get rid of the pauper tenant in many instances by giving the crop as you propose." On September 21 he wrote of a tenant who agreed to leave "on getting" his crop, "I should say it would be advisable to get him out as he is not at all inclined to be an 'improving tenant' and is, I fear, but badly off."

These harvest clearances were concentrated, as were the previous ones, on clearing out "the poorest and worst," but they were also bent on targeting the "better sort" of tenants. Of particular focus were five townlands just outside the Strokestown limits, a placement that made them more valuable than farther-flung townlands and meant they were occupied by more comfortable renters. When the possibility of retaking the townland of Castlenode, just southeast of Strokestown, was first mentioned to Major Mahon in June, he wrote, "I was under the impression that 'they paid rent' pretty well and were rather what we call 'snug people.'" But he was soon convinced of the advantage of clearing the land, which he conceded "will be sure to let well." According to an eviction list, 112 people were dislodged from the townland during the harvest of 1847. Ross Mahon asserted that each Castlenode family was allowed to keep its crops after surrendering the lands.

It wasn't only small, "snug" farmers who were being cast out. The middlemen and big farmers who would be expected to benefit from the conversion from tillage to grazing were also targeted for expulsion. After all, they were also dependent on the rents of starving cottiers below them in the estate hierarchy. In one instance a middleman who couldn't afford his rent asked the landlord to take back his farm. Major Mahon responded that he would only agree to the deal if the farmer, who held land in the townland of Newtown, first removed all his undertenants. "Mr. Hague forgets that for the several years those tenants did pay, that he enjoyed the profit and now that they fail he would willingly hand me over the land, the bad tenants and all ... tenants that most likely with neither pay me any rent or even acknowledge me as landlord," Major Mahon wrote. The evidence suggests that the farmer declined to conduct the evictions, forcing Ross Mahon to complete the job. According to an eviction list, the land agent cleared seventy-three people from Newtown in the fall of 1847.

The most prominent eviction proceeding on the Mahon estate during these weeks targeted the Browne family, the esteemed Catholic clan that operated the largest farm on the estate, the boyhood home of the current bishop of the Diocese of Elphin. According to a statement from early the following year, Major

Mahon asked his land agent to "take legal proceedings for the ejectment of Messrs. Browne"—Martin, the elderly father, and Patrick, the son and brother of the bishop—for the nonpayment of 400 pounds in rent. After securing an *habere*—were they, too, conspirators?—Ross Mahon arrived at the Browne's townland of Clonfad (or Cloonfad) with a contingent of police and military officers and his gang of privately hired cabin destroyers. Like so many marked for eviction, the family pleaded to be spared. "The bishop's brother expressed a hope of being able to liquidate the arrears if given time," wrote Ross Mahon. "Anxious to show every consideration to Messrs. Browne," the land agent agreed to allow them to remain. Then, according to Ross Mahon, Patrick Browne "took advantage of my having the sheriff on the land and put every tenant out who had not paid up his rent."

During the two months following the closure of the soup kitchen, the landlord and his land agent removed roughly a thousand tenants from some fifteen townlands, meaning some three thousand people had now been dislodged from the Mahon property by eviction, surrender, or emigration since the clearances began back in May. It represented less than half the number of tenants Ross Mahon had earlier estimated needed to be removed to bring the estate to order. It was evident, then, that the upheavals would continue into the winter and spring. The idea was frightful to contemplate. "My heart sickens at the sight of the multitude of wretches who swarm in these ill-fated valleys of Slievebawn without food or employment, or a prospect of either, and who have not a perch of tillage on the earth," wrote Father Boyd at the expiration of the Soup Kitchen Act. "Death by starvation stares them in the face, and they already speak the language of despair."

But the news of the sound harvest had been greeted in England as proof that the Famine was now over. Word that an increase in imports of Indian maize and other grains into Ireland had led to a drop in prices seemed to confirm the wisdom of repealing the Corn Laws. (Indeed, imports of cheap grain far surpassed grain exports in 1847 and 1848, a fact often ignored in Irish nationalist histories of the Famine that seek to highlight the export of Irish food away from Irish stomachs. The problem, of course, was that without public works projects or much private employment the Irish poor could not afford to purchase newly arrived grains, no matter how cheap.) In a country that was experiencing its own economic hardships, the populace and its representatives had lost patience with the costs of saving Ireland. As the Whig administration was forcing government expenditures for Famine relief onto the landlords, the public was decreasing the amount of money it was giving to private charities. An appeal letter written in October by Queen Victoria was far less successful than the one she sent during January at the high point of international sympathy for Ireland. With streams of famine refugees entering English cities every day, many wondered why they should contribute money to Ireland when so many Irish paupers were bound to be served by the *English* Poor Law anyway. The results from the general election dealt another blow to English sympathy for Irish suffering. Although the Repeal Association had been weakened by its early support of Russell's government, it succeeded in winning thirty-eight seats. The victory was attributed more to an outpouring of affection for Daniel O'Connell, who had died a month earlier, than to a confidence in his unimpressive successor, John O'Connell, his son. It was also credited to popular resentment of the Young Irelanders of the Irish Confederation, who were blamed for causing the Liberator's death with their intransigence. Only a single Confederation MP, William Smith O'Brien, its nominal leader, was returned to Parliament. "I see that almost all the Irish elections have gone in favor of Repeal candidates, and this just after two or three millions of Irish have been saved from famine and pestilence by money which, if the union had not existed, their own parliament would never have been able to raise," wrote Lord Palmerston, the foreign secretary, speaking of the soup kitchens. (In fact, the Repeal candidate in County Roscommon, backed by a majority of the priests, failed in his attempt to gain office. Instead two Irish Whigs—Oliver D. J. Grace, a Catholic gentleman who served on the Elphin Relief Committee, and longtime representative Fitzstephen French, a Protestant from the venerable Roscommon family—were elected to Parliament. Quietly supported by that diehard Repealer Bishop Browne, who regarded him as "illustrious," French had been a middling presence in the House of Commons during debates over the amended Poor Law. But he was on record as opposing outdoor relief in the manner of the supporters of the landlord class.)

The enduring matter of Irish violence also dampened British enthusiasm for extending sympathy to the stricken nation. While it is true that violent acts were increasing in Ireland—the number of homicides went from 170 in 1846 to 212 in 1847; the number of shots fired at persons went from 158 in 1846 to 266 in 1847—a far greater rise was recorded in nonviolent crime. The newspapers in County Roscommon were reporting far fewer of the sorts of outrages that they catalogued incessantly during the few years prior to the second appearance of the blight. Instead of mailing threatening letters, digging up pastures, or taking potshots at magistrates, agents, or farmers, most of the lawbreakers were stealing sheep and cattle to feed themselves and their families. Father Boyd argued that few were even doing that in his parish. "Whilst hundreds of our unfortunate neighbors were—as they are now—famishing around us, not a half a dozen of individuals were found to disturb the rights of property by the commission of petty larceny," he wrote. "At no period within our recollection did this district enjoy a more perfect exemption from all disturbance." Still, nearly every crime of violent intent was reported in portions of the English press as evidence of the increasing brutality of the starving Irish peasant. By October the new lord lieutenant, George William Frederick Villiers, the fourth Earl of Clarendon, was bringing up the perennial topic of coercive legislation. He told the prime minister of the necessity of "permanent severe police measures" to pacify the population.

CHAPTER 9

That Flame Which Now Rages

~~~ GOD ~~~

The tyrannous and bloody act is done,
The most arch deed of piteous massacre
That ever this land was guilty of.
— SHAKESPEARE, *Richard III*

IF ANYTHING IS CLEAR from the testimony that would later be aired, it is the simple fact that many people were hearing about the plot to kill the landlord of Strokestown in the fall of 1847. A shoemaker was told about it over drinks at Martin Kenny's public house. One of his fellow imbibers said he would "give his own two cows to anyone who would shoot Major Mahon." A man was approached by an acquaintance one evening and asked whether he would be willing to subscribe half a crown toward a fund to pay the assassin. He was told about a conversation in a room of a public house in Strokestown, during which a group of upwards of forty men openly debated the plan. According to evidence offered in court, a cast of plotters based around the settlement of Four Mile House, a part of the Mahon estate yet untouched by mass clearances, was ready to murder the landlord by early October. But on two occasions within the first week of the month, Major Mahon's carriage passed through the area, along the same stretch of road where Richard Irwin was shot four years earlier, without the disorganized gang getting off a shot. The landlord had no idea of the extent of his good fortune. The frustrated conspirators then waited a few weeks until making another attempt, according to prosecutors.

In the early part of Tuesday, November 2, the men or their sympathizers likely caught sight of Major Mahon's carriage as it made its bumpy way through Four Mile House on the way to Roscommon town. The major was traveling to a meeting of the beleaguered Roscommon Board of Guardians, the body that administered the workhouse. It would later be said that he was attending in an effort to keep the workhouse from closing and to secure funding for the temporary fever hospital in Strokestown. But Major Mahon's words would have meant only so much on this occasion. The most pressing matter on the agenda was the board's inability to collect enough poor rates from the landlords to properly fund its obligations. During the month of October, the guardians had mustered only 94 pounds from the rate payers, one of the lowest amounts gathered by any of the eighteen unions in the province of Connaught. As a result of this paltry sum, the board was now in danger of being dissolved by the government and replaced with paid "vice-guardians" who would more ruthlessly extract the rates. Three out of five of the unions in County Mayo had already suffered this fate. While it is not known what Major Mahon said during the meeting, his mission contained at least a charitable component. He attended with the fever hospital's director, Dr. Terence Shanley, perhaps the most knowledgeable and interested Strokestown resident (outside of Father McDermott) on the matter of local destitution. It is hard to imagine that Dr. Shanley would have been present for any other reason than to secure some kind of aid to his suffering patients.

At around 5 P.M., Major Mahon, Dr. Shanley, and Martin Flanagan, the coachman, boarded the open phaeton for the ten-mile ride back to Strokestown. For unexplained reasons, Major Mahon took the reins of the horses, sitting high on the right side of the vehicle next to Dr. Shanley. Flanagan sat behind and below the two in the comfortable seat designated for the esteemed gentleman who employed him. In his statement of eight days later, the doctor said the landlord soon launched into a discussion about helping the poor, "our only and entire" conversation during the journey. "'Shanley, point out to me what is best to be done, and we shall be able to keep them from destitution,'" said Major Mahon, according to Dr. Shanley. "'They shall get plenty of bread, and I think by getting on market days some cow heads and plain joints of mutton, with whatever Mrs. Mahon can send us from Strokestown House, we shall be able to support the poor at a moderate expense. You will apply to Mr. McDermott for the [soup] boiler, and we will get it erected in one of the houses on Church Street, and then appoint some respectable person to superintend it according to our directions. By giving a little of our time we shall do much good.'"

Although it is hard to determine whether Major Mahon gave this speech on this particular trip, it must be admitted that it does sound like him. The plan outlined to Dr. Shanley is similar to the one sketched to Ross Mahon in January, when Major Mahon suggested that they start a new relief committee run by "Mrs. Fallon" in place of the dreaded Father McDermott. Indeed, one can't help but notice the characteristic jab at the priest in Major Mahon's hint that he didn't qualify as a "respectable person." It was also the kind of charitable endeavor—with its suggestion of food from Mrs. Mahon and moderate expenditure—that would exist outside his obligations under the amended Poor Law. The line about "giving a little of our time" even has the ring of the landlord about it. In the summer of 1846 he described personally handing out Indian corn to his tenants—"you would be surprised how much the people like it out here," he had written. Yet it remains a fact that the landlord was speaking these lines while continuing a campaign that was contributing significantly to the distress he was pledging to alleviate. If he were truly interested in attempting to "keep them from destitution"—and these were his bold words, as recorded by Shanley—he would have halted clearances, forgiven arrears, and offered extensive employment, the kind of plan followed by the most generous of Irish landlords. In any event, it was too late.

About an hour into the trip, the phaeton veered right at Four Mile House, following the road as it turned northeast for the final leg to Strokestown. It passed near a settlement of cottages in the Doorty (or Dooherty) townland to the left, descended a hill, and traveled along a flat stretch. When the vehicle had "nearly reached the bridge of Doorty," which marked the end of the townland's boundary, a single gunshot rang out from the right side of the road, Dr. Shanley testified at the inquest two days later. Major Mahon, who was in clear view of the shooter because of his placement in the driver's seat, dropped the reins and fell backward, his hat tumbling from his head. Flanagan stood up in his seat to catch the falling major, at the same time noticing the shooter rising from behind "a ditch or gripe." Riddled up and down the right side of his midsection with balls and slugs, the landlord "expired immediately," Flanagan testified. "The deceased never spoke after he received the contents of the gun." Dr. Shanley, struck in the arm by a single "ball or slug," grabbed the reins as the horses reduced speed. Looking around, he saw "in the fields" a second figure pointing a gun toward the carriage. "The man attempted to fire, but the gun burned priming," he said. Since "it was dark," he could not "accurately describe the size or description of the man." But "the light caused by the flash of the pan" enabled Dr. Shanley to see that he was wearing a cap. In the next instant the first figure, the assassin, passed in front of the carriage carrying a gun. Flanagan didn't think he was wearing a cap but couldn't say for sure because he "could not see distinctly" in the darkness of the evening.

Within "fifty or sixty perches" of the carriage—or some three hundred yards—were three houses, according to Flanagan. He said that "when they passed there was light in the houses; the doors were open." No one came "out of the houses, nor did they take any notice of the shot being fired."

Shanley and Flanagan raced the phaeton, its hood and dashboard "perforated by slugs," the final four miles to Strokestown, where Dr. Shanley informed Thomas Blakeney, the local subinspector, of what had happened. Dr. Shanley's son, who was also a physician, performed the postmortem examination on a body that was "literally riddled," said the senior Dr. Shanley. It appears that Blakeney did not arrive at the crime scene until the following morning. By that afternoon a party of military and constabulary had detained "several persons residing in the immediate locality." They were brought to Roscommon town for questioning before a collection of county lieutenants, magistrates, and justices of the peace, nearly all landlords or big farmers with close ties (or related, in the case of D. H. Kelly, his cousin) to Major Mahon. Police released a description of "two strangers and suspicious looking characters . . . seen lurking about the spot where he was murdered and who are suspected to have been the persons who committed the act." The first man, presumably the assassin, had a "hooked long nose, black hair, no whiskers, a dark brown frieze bog coat." The other wore a blue cap over his eyes, had a "bad countenance," with whiskers "longer than common," and sported blue stockings drawn over the knees. A police inspector noted, "It is believed that they were hired for the purpose and will endeavor to make their escape to America." In his official report on November 4, Blakeney concluded that the murder occurred in the townland of Doorty "in consequence of the injured person having evicted a number of his tenants for nonpayment of rent, as supposed." According to the estate's rent books, the Mahon family had rented out eighty-four acres in Doorty to "James Hunt and co."—that is, to a rundale collective of many families represented by an elder named James Hunt—since 1808.

On the following day the authorities ended their interrogations in frustration, concluding that everyone residing in the area knew more than they were admitting. "From . . . their uniform denial of circumstances which must have been within their knowledge, we can have no doubt that an extensive and deep-laid conspiracy existed against this gentleman's life," according to the statement issued by the officials. They also asserted, in keeping with Ross Mahon's long-standing analysis of estate affairs, that the conspiracy had been ongoing for some time. "A general resistance against rents and the legal exercise of the rights of property is in existence and likely to extend and these circumstances place more than ordinary difficulties in the way of justice." The authorities argued that Major Mahon "had to deal with" tenants owing three to four years' worth of rent who were "unable to till the land, and unable and unwilling to pay anything for it." He was "thus obliged to dispossess them or abandon his property altogether." But, the authorities emphasized, the landlord was keen to mitigate the traumas of dispossession, a line of argument that would be repeated by his defenders. During evictions "no unnecessary harshness has been used, and very large sums have been expended in giving compensation and sending them to America." Further, "in proof of the benevolence of his disposition, it was his anxiety to obtain the means of keeping open the fever hospital in this town, and preventing the poorhouse in Roscommon from being closed, that brought him to that town on the morning of the day of his murder."

On November 8 John Ross Mahon made his first public statement since his employer's death, offering more details of the universality and irrationality of the insubordination. In reviewing his year as land agent, Ross Mahon emphasized the generosity of the policies adopted by Major Mahon, particularly the emigration initiative. "Emigration on an extensive scale was the principal feature of my plan," he wrote. The cost of the endeavor was 3,500 pounds, but "including rations supplied, moving, money given, loss of rent," the total sum "was not less than £6,000." The tenants chosen to travel to America, he wrote, were deeply thankful for the aid. He also described the effort to reduce rents for those who remained behind, describing how this had "no effect" in getting the vast majority to pay. A few offered payments when the sheriff appeared, "which I refused, stating that I could not retain persons as tenants who acted so very improperly." And when it came time to clear the land, no flagrant cruelties were committed. "In no case has there been any undue severity used in taking possession," he wrote; "and no fever patients were removed from their houses" until after they recovered and were given "a small pecuniary recompense." "No" ejected individual was "deprived of his crop," even though "during the past year the receipts have not amounted to half a year's rent of the estate." In one unnamed townland, "where great opposition was given to the sheriff," Ross Mahon was not dissuaded from conducting clearances. "But, in order, if possible, to carry on matters quietly," he gave "them the price of seed, and also the value of their labor, and paid them liberally for cutting and drawing home the crop." These tenants "expressed their sense of Major Mahon's kindness in strong terms, and all seemed satisfied." Yet Ross Mahon made it clear that the starving remainder on the property were still defiant. "The combination . . . against the payment of rents . . . is now as strong as ever," he wrote.

The clearest evidence of the "extensive and deep-laid" conspiracy, all agreed, was the behavior of the rural folk upon learning the news of the landlord's death. The authorities recorded in their November 5 statement that "bonfires, manifesting a very bad disposition among the peasantry of the neighborhood, have been lighted since the murders, and . . . very considerable excitement prevails." The *Roscommon and Leitrim Gazette* wrote that "within one hour after the foul deed was perpetrated the several hills were lighted by bonfires in every direction," proof that "many of the people about Strokestown were aware of the intended assassination." Blakeney concluded his November 4 report, "I think it is right to observe that . . . on last night lights were exhibited through part of the county, seemingly in exultation at this melancholy event." A Board of Works engineer, writing four days after the killing, described the scene for a superior. "As soon as it was dark . . . signal was given of the deed having been perpetrated by lighting straw upon some of the hills in the neighborhood of

Strokestown, and on the following evening, when the people were better prepared, bonfires were to be seen on the hills for many miles extent." He wrote that the "exultation of the country people at Major Mahon's death was general and undisguised."

Major Denis Mahon, who was sixty years, seven months, and twenty-one days old when he died, was laid to rest in the family vault on the grounds of Strokestown House. The chief mourners at his private service, according to the *Illustrated London News*, were the major's brother John, Dean Pakenham of St. Patrick's in Dublin, D. H. Kelly, and the landlord's son-in-law and heir, Henry Sandford Pakenham Mahon. It isn't clear whether Major Mahon's daughter, Grace Catherine, was present during the solemn rite. But according to family lore she pledged after the killing that she would never again set foot in Strokestown. It is said she died sixty-six years later on the Isle of Wight, having kept her promise.

From the moment of its occurrence, Major Mahon's death was about much more than the unfortunate demise of a prominent Roscommon landlord. In the eyes of its various interpreters, the event signified something larger about the state of Ireland at the height of a devastating crisis. To those grouped on what might be called the Irish and English left, it showed the inevitable consequences of the brutal evictions that landlords were conducting throughout the country. The *Freeman's Journal*, the Dublin-based, Repeal-supporting newspaper, largely attributed the murder to Major Mahon's "clearing away what he deemed surplus population." The paper spoke of the "murderous 'clearances,' the desolation, the leveling, and burning of villages wrought by landlords." The *Nation*, the organ of Young Ireland, headlined its article about the killing "Ejectment Murder," and added the detail that "the victim exclaimed, 'Oh, God!' and spoke no more," contradicting the coachman's inquest testimony that Major Mahon "never spoke after he received the contents of the gun." The *Morning Chronicle*, the most prominent Whig paper in London, deplored the Mahon murder as "appalling" but attacked

> *another class of Irish crimes, of which it is by no means so certain that we shall ever know either the extent to which they are committed, or the circumstances of remorseless cruelty by which they are accompanied. We speak of the slow murders done upon the smaller holders of land by regular process of law. In innumerable instances the dispossession of tenants may be effected without arresting public observation. The victims are poor and friendless. Fever perhaps completes in a few days the work of the bailiffs, and where the voice of complaint is not thus silenced, the expelled wretch wanders off in search of bread, and comes to swell the tide of misery in English cities. We hear, indeed, from time to time, specific instances of the clearance of Irish estates, but we cannot doubt that the system is going forward to a much greater extent than is publicly recorded.*

The murder brought together what might be named the Irish and English right. They believed the assassination of such an exemplary landlord revealed that the Irish peasant was beyond the reach of civilization. The *Dublin Evening Mail*, the Ascendancy mouthpiece, felt that "ejectment by a landlord no more imports *prime facie* injustice or harshness on his part than would an action upon a bill of exchange, or a book account, imply severity on the part of a merchant." Thus, Major Mahon was a paragon of magnanimity. The paper noted that even in the face of rent-withholding tenants, he had shown dedication to the poor with his costly emigration plan. Still, an ungrateful populace targeted him for elimination. "Long . . . before this occurred it was well known in the country that Major Mahon was a doomed man," it wrote. The *Times*, the unaffiliated but Tory-leaning newspaper that shaped and reflected middle-class English opinion with a circulation more than ten times that of the *Morning Chronicle*, had been critical of irresponsible landlords who had allowed Ireland to descend into ruin, calling them, among other things, "shameless and importune mendicants." But Major Mahon, "a man of high family . . . connected by intermarriages with the Duke of Wellington," was one of those who deserved respect. His murder was evidence that the Irish poor weren't interested in coexisting with a proprietor working to rescue the land from "barrenness" and "barbarism," the paper wrote on November 6. "While we urge men of patriotism and honor to reside on their properties, and be the stewards of heaven for the good of their people, hideous catastrophes drive them back to security and indifference. Who will take British capital and enterprise to Ireland with such expectations? . . . Better people a desert, or conquer a savage tribe, than dwell in a society of conspirators, who for years can gloat on their victim, and enjoy the sweet anticipation of his last mortal agony." Thus the country will remain irremediable. "Ireland will have it so. Those sons of Cain will still eschew the arts of peace, and cling to their privilege and destiny of blood. We cannot help it. We have written, and written in vain. The blunderbuss is more than a match for the pen."

It is likely that Queen Victoria learned about the murder by reading the *Times* article of the previous day, November 5—headlined "Atrocious Assassination"—a reprint of the *Dublin Evening Mail* story of two days earlier. In her diary entry on that Friday, she wrote, "A shocking murder has again taken place in Ireland . . . Major Mahon, who had entirely devoted himself to being of use to the distressed Irish, was shot when driving home in his carriage. Really they are a terrible people, & there is no civilized country anywhere, which is in such a dreadful state, & where such crimes are perpetrated! It is a constant source of anxiety & annoyance."

To those occupying the political middle ground, blame was more evenly distributed. The *Daily News*, the London paper founded less than two years earlier by a group including Charles Dickens (its first editor) to rival the *Morning Chronicle*, argued that the Irish landlord was placed in a "terrible" dilemma. "Government and the public call upon him to improve, to drain, to give extra employment on his land," it wrote. "Prudence tells him not to trust the potato crop, or feed his laborer on conacre, for such crop may fail, and then the poor-rates or the necessity of feeding the population gratuitously, will not only swallow up his rent, but the very fee of his estates. If, however, the landlord clears, giving half the laboring class the means to emigrate, and promising the other half daily wages, he is murdered because he refuses the potato and the conacre. This was the case of Major Mahon, whose inhuman murder has spread horror throughout the land."

(A week after the killing, Randolph Routh, the relief official in Dublin who had met with Major Mahon in the summer of 1846 to discuss supplying meal to Strokestown, praised the landlord to Charles Trevelyan. He wrote that "a milder and more charitable man could not be found.")

In the seat of Irish government in Dublin, Lord Clarendon was among those who were convinced that the slaying was a sign of things to come, regarding it as a clear indication that the servile insurrection he had been scanning the horizon for was at last coming into view. "I am sorry to say intelligence was this morning received of another murder, that of Major Mahon of Strokestown in the County Roscommon," he wrote to the prime minister on the day after the killing. "I am afraid that this murder may be followed by others of the same class, and that people of fortune and station will be marked for assassination." Within days he forwarded to the prime minister drafts of three bills asking for additional police powers, including a suspension of the Habeas Corpus Act. "There never was so open or so widely extended a conspiracy for shooting landlords and agents, and my fear is that this will spread (there are already symptoms of it), and that flame which now rages in certain districts will become a general conflagration," he wrote to a friend. "Between 300,000 and 400,000 stand of arms are now in possession of the people; the sale of them increases every day; every beggar walks about with his blunderbuss, and laborers go to work (if work it can be called) with as good double-barreled guns as sportsmen use. The ordinary powers of the law are not sufficient to deal with this state of things, because every man is in favor of the criminal: law and order have no friends."

Lord John Russell was unmoved by Clarendon's fulminations. He was among those who thought the landlords had brought their troubles upon themselves. He told Clarendon that he would not legislate against the Irish poor with a coercion bill without also legislating against the Irish landlord with a bill curbing evictions. "It is quite true that landlords in England would not like to be shot like hares and partridges by miscreants banded for murderous purposes; but neither does any landlord in England turn out fifty persons at once, and burn their houses over their heads, giving them no provision for the future," he wrote. "The murders are atrocious, but so are the ejectments."

The lord lieutenant responded that he was "disheartened" by Lord Russell's statement of understanding for the assassins, and once again gave air to his fears for civil order. He couldn't understand "how any government can think it expedient to leave 300,000 arms in possession of some of the most ferocious people on earth, at the commencement of a winter when there will be great poverty and little employment, when armed outrages are increasing every day, when almost every post brings an account of some fresh murder, and when the reign of terror is so complete that all those who are unable to fly from the disturbed districts must purchase their existence by the surrender of their rights." On the following day his frustration had risen to such levels that he threatened to resign. "If I do not see any reasonable ground for believing that I can perform the duties of government in maintaining the law and affording some protection to life and property, I cannot, and I am sure you will not ask me to, remain here when I feel my power of usefulness is gone," he told the prime minister.

Against his better judgment, Lord John, who was mindful that he had come to power upon the *defeat* of a coercion bill, convened a cabinet meeting on the matter. He soon discovered that his ministry was more inclined to take Lord Clarendon's position. Lord Palmerston believed that Ireland was full of "ferocious blood thirsty ruffians" who were seeking to force landlords to surrender their properties. The prime minister countered that Irish landlords, who had grown rich by pitilessly extracting rents from tenants they were now ejecting, shouldn't be protected from the "organic" consequences of their own actions. He maintained that a coercion bill would only encourage them to commit "more atrocities than before." In another cabinet meeting two days later, Russell kept up his campaign, arguing that nothing had changed about the state of violent agitation in Ireland and that a coercion bill might *foment* an agrarian insurrection. He even had one of his supporters make the case against Strokestown's landlord to the cabinet, offering evidence that he was one of those proprietors who deserved the hatred of his tenants. "Major Mahon was harsh and fearless—he had sent 900 of his tenants to America of whom 300 were lost in one of the vessels—and this was imputed to design," wrote another cabinet member in his diary, summarizing the presentation. The leader of Her Majesty's government was repeating a rumor that was finding its way around political circles in London and suggesting that Major Mahon, guilty of the willful murder of three hundred of his tenants, might just have deserved to be shot.

But the prime minister failed in his efforts to persuade his cabinet that Irish landlords weren't worthy of exceptional assistance. A majority felt that "the outrages had assumed a new form" and voted on November 19 in favor of Clarendon's bills. Lord John Russell announced that if remedial legislation protecting poor cottiers was not part of a legislative package, he would tender his resignation.

The British public was siding with Russell's cabinet. According to Charles Greville, writing in his diary on November 21, "the public voice loudly demands coercion and repression." Each of the three London newspapers mentioned above soon came to reflect this consensus. In its commentary of November 11 the *Times* slashed and hacked at the landlords—"under their careless guidance the soil of Ireland thrust forth its fresh thousands of human beings annually into most wretched existence"—but championed a bill keeping them from harm. "In Ireland, no man's life is secure, and public feeling will go with any measure that will root out the murderers from the land." The *Morning Chronicle* threw its support behind "a vigorous effort" to stem outrages but didn't forget to castigate landlords who "stripped the miserable tenantry of what famine may have left them, burned down their habitations, and cast the wretched people out upon the roads. . . . Extermination—wholesale and pitiless extermination for a whole people—would be the meaning of a coercive measure at the present time uncombined with bold and comprehensive plans for eradicating the causes which make coercion necessary." The *Daily News*, safely positioned between these two poles, felt that once the Irish peasant accustomed himself to the amended Poor Law, "agrarian outrage will receive a check that no arms bill or insurrection act ever gave it." But the paper nonetheless endorsed "some well-considered measure to remedy, or at least palliate, the evil of a state of the law so scandalous, so immoral, so barbarous, so intolerable, as never disfigured any community arrived at the same stage of general civilization."

On the other side of the Irish Sea, the petrified gentlemen of the landed classes were relieved by the news. The pro-landlord *Dublin Evening Mail* saw the public's support as a sign that "Englishmen—whether Ministers or people—are beginning to see their way into the true condition of Ireland, her evils, and their remedies. . . . Perhaps we are indebted for it to the murder of Major Mahon: and if such should have been the result, the excellent, honorable, but unfortunate gentleman has not fallen in vain—has, in fact, fallen in a cause to which he would have cheerfully sacrificed his life." So there it was: The landlord of Strokestown had been martyred for the cause of taming the restive Irish peasant.

CHAPTER 10

Guilty of the Blood of the Murdered Major Mahon

Molly never takes a mean advantage without giving due notice, and the exterminator of the tyrant Mahon will dare anything.

—THREATENING LETTER SENT
TO COUNTY SLIGO LANDLORD,
NOVEMBER 24, 1847

FROM THE FIRST DAYS of the investigation, police officials in County Roscommon understood that they had a difficult case to solve. "The lower orders exult in the murder," an internal report claimed. Despite the enticement of a handsome 200-pound reward offered by the government and an additional 800 pounds put up by the Mahon family, the authorities had little luck in breaching the wall of silence. Several individuals believed to have been "concerned" with the plot were arrested and charged with "having been in the vicinity" of the crime scene in a futile attempt to impel them to admit involvement and possibly implicate others. One suspect confined under such a charge, James Farrell, didn't survive his several-day stay in the overcrowded and fever-infested county jail. "His death was instantaneous," according to a report. "Neither clergyman nor doctor had time to be with him. From the moment he was committed until his death he appeared completely broken down in spirit, and unable to do more than move about the ward."

Even when information was obtained, it was often tainted by the desire for the reward, police concluded. Patrick Rigney, a retired army soldier, and a young man named Matthew Dunnigan were arrested on the testimony of an informant who claimed she saw them running from the spot of the murder. The two passed within a few yards of the woman, who said she heard one of them say, "He is down now not like the last time." But police dismissed her tale as improbable. "It is supposed that she thought money would be given to her, and then proceed to America where her husband is," subinspector Blakeney wrote. There were other problems with her story. The two men hadn't fled from the area, as she claimed. Blakeney determined (after visiting the scene with two magistrates) that she couldn't have viewed the events from where she said she was standing in the darkness of the early evening. "It is impossible she could observe them at such a distance at so late an hour, the distance being about four hundred yards," he wrote. And Rigney and Dunnigan were suffering from the ill effects of famine, making them incapable of committing such a crime, Blakeney implied. "Rigney is aged between sixty and seventy, feeble and emaciated, and is it appears afflicted with rupture, and Dunnigan altho young is in bad health," he wrote. While the examination of this informant's story shows the difficulties the police were encountering, it also reveals that the murder investigation was being conducted in a serious fashion in its initial stages, intent on finding the criminals who were truly involved.

Investigators also combed through several townlands looking for men who were regarded as troublemakers, although the police reports do not name them as members of a secret society. In the townland of Cullagh, a Mahon property subject to the eviction and emigration plans, they sought out five members of the Cox family who were thought to be "very intimate" with Andrew Connor of the Graffoge townland, also a Mahon property. Connor was "a well known character and leader in this locality," police said, failing to specify what sort of organization he led. Another report described Connor as "suspected to be in the confidence of the ill-disposed in this neighborhood." In the rebellious townland of Ballykilcline, police conducted "a strict and general inquiry" even though the land was not within the Mahon estate. In particular, they sought out John McGann, a twenty-four-year-old schoolmaster, a relation of the Coxes, who was thought to be "one of the party involved in the murder." But an investigator was discouraged from pursuing McGann by a local constable acquainted with his family. The constable believed McGann "would not be likely to be concerned in the fatal deed."

To add to the frustrations, the authorities were taunted with several threatening letters, sent to jittery landlords, that promised more murders. A newspaper correspondent wrote, likely in reference to the landlord's son-in-law, "As the son of Major Mahon was going to his father's funeral a man came openly to his carriage window, and handed him a notice, saying that, if he did not alter his conduct to the people, he would be murdered in the same manner as his father had been." A cousin of Major Mahon and his wife both received frightening missives in the weeks following the death. "Unless you become a better man than what you are at present to your tenants, you will share the same fate as your kinsman the demon Major Mahon did," read the letter to Marcus McClausland, who feuded with Major Mahon before the Famine. "I am to inform you that there are resolutions made in this country to take down all tyrannizing landlords. You are numbered amongst them, which I do sorely regret, unless you give a full remittance of the arrears and begin in new from the 1st of August last.... As to Ross Mahon, any part of Europe he goes he will fall if known where he is, there is a fund at present formed in this country for shooting oppressors, the subscribers chiefly American emigrants from this country." The letter to Mrs. McClausland warned that it would be "useless" for her to think that her husband was "far from the rath of this country. . . . I hope you will not suffer yourself to be a widow, the same as Mrs. Mahon. As to Ross Mahon, the cries of the starved and desolated have reached the Heavens, and, after shooting him, he is to be hanged and quartered, unless he quits Ireland." An Anglo-Irish diarist wrote that Ross Mahon had received "several" threatening letters. "At last has come a warning one signed by a 'grateful friend' telling him he is doomed—the next on the fearful list—begging him not to sit in the rooms of the ground floor, not to let anyone know when he is going out or coming in nor where he is going to, nor ever to return by the way he goes out," wrote Elizabeth Smith in her journal.

Farther-flung branches of the gang were using the Mahon murder to intimidate the landlords in their areas. "Molly Maguire wishes to let you know she still lives as the protector of the injured and the exterminator of tyranny," read a letter to a County Sligo landlord. "She is in possession of Roscommon and Leitrim and intends planting a colony in Sligo very shortly. . . . She wishes to know how you disposed of the many remittances you got from charitable institutions to feed the poor and is it by charging two shillings and six pence a perch for turnips to a starving people you intend disposing of said funds. There is another affair she is informed you busied yourself lately in but when she hears the particulars you shall hear from her again. You are . . . one of the chosen few in Sligo whose days are numbered. Molly never takes a mean advantage without giving due notice, and the exterminator of the tyrant Mahon will dare anything. By order of Molly Maguire, Headquarters, Strokestown Bawn."

On Sunday, November 28, the gravity of the threats was borne out when a Protestant parson and minor County Roscommon landlord, Reverend John Lloyd, was stopped by two men as he rode home from a church service. The first man grabbed the reins of the horses while the other fired a pistol. The shot "immediately deprived the unfortunate gentleman of life," a report said. Reverend Lloyd was a double hit for the assassins. Not only was he an evicting landlord, he was also a cleric accused of gaining Protestant converts by offering them relief assistance. Father Henry Brennan of the Kilglass parish had said that Lloyd's school was a "factory where numbers of famine Protestants are manufactured." Although historians are careful to note that the practice wasn't as prevalent as sometimes alleged, the folklore of the Famine is replete with references to those who "took the soup" or became "soupers," an imputation that would taint a family's descendants for generations.

In London, the public inquiry into the murder was focusing on a different suspect. Evidence was being collected against the alleged spiritual leader of the plot, the man who was said to have urged the deluded and easily led miscreants to fire the fatal shot.

Within days of Major Mahon's death, a story was circulating among the highest officials of the British government about the behavior of the parish priest of Strokestown in the days before the November 2 murder. On November 11, a week before Russell convened his cabinet to discuss Clarendon's legislation, Lord Palmerston wrote to a Scotch earl, Lord Minto, who was conducting a mission in Vatican City to discuss the possibility of reestablishing formal diplomatic contacts between Great Britain and the Holy See. (They had been severed in 1534.) Palmerston wanted Lord Minto to ask Pope Pius IX to "take some quiet step to get the Catholic priests to exert their spiritual influence to prevent these murders which disgust and revolt the feelings of all parties and which the priests at present do *not* discountenance but rather encourage." He then cited an example. "Major Mahon who was shot the other day was denounced by his priest at the altar the Sunday before he was murdered." Lord Palmerston believed the priest's words "made all the people in the neighborhood think the deed a holy one instead a diabolical one."

On November 18 an anonymous letter in the *Times* from "A Southern Landlord" repeated the charge for public consumption. "He was denounced by the priest on Sunday, and on the following

Monday, while returning from his charitable office in Roscommon, he was shot dead in his carriage," the letter read. More damning and specific information was provided in the November 20 edition of the *Spectator*. The magazine lauded Major Mahon as an excellent landlord who enjoyed the kind regard of his tenants. But, "however warm the gratitude of an Irish peasant may be, he owes another allegiance. In a chapel of the district this beneficent landlord was denounced as an 'exterminator,' with many harsh expressions; and the priest wound up his denunciation in these words—'He is worse than Cromwell: and yet he lives!' Coming out of that chapel, that Sunday, one of the congregation said to another—'If he lives a month after this, he is immortal!' He was shot on the Monday." (Actually, he was shot on Tuesday.)

A source for some of these details may have been Lord Clarendon, who was known to have carried on correspondences with members of the Tory press. In a November 17 letter he had passed on a version of the *Spectator*'s story to the prime minister. "Two Sundays before Major Mahon was murdered, he was denounced by name from the altar, called worse than Cromwell; 'and yet,' said the priest, 'this man lives!'" the lord lieutenant wrote. "From this very priest, however, I have seen letters for the last ten years to Major Mahon, blessing him for his kindness to the people and to himself," he continued, in an indication that Clarendon's source was either a Mahon family member or someone intimately involved with his affairs, like John Ross Mahon. The lord lieutenant then gave an unsettling reason for the priest's animosity toward the landlord. "[B]ut he (M.) last year discovered some irregularities in the management of the relief fund by the priest, who then vowed vengeance against him." Since Clarendon alleged that the confrontation occurred during 1846, he didn't appear to be suggesting that Major Mahon had accused the priest of impropriety at the explosive August 28, 1847, relief committee meeting. Of that incident, Major Mahon had written that he found the committee's financial accounts to be "correct." Father McDermott lost his temper, he wrote, when the landlord asked a question about the revision of relief lists.

By the time Parliament reconvened in late November, the matter of the denunciation was the subject of much discussion in both houses, with Sir Benjamin Hall, the Tory MP from Marylebone, reading from the *Times* letter in the Commons and wondering whether it could "be said, then, that the priests had no power in Ireland?" Without evidence to counter the charges against the anonymous priest, Irish nationalist MPs concentrated on the provoking behavior of Major Mahon himself. "What was the cause of Major Mahon being shot?" wondered Henry Grattan Jr., son of the famous Patriot leader. "He was a most excellent individual, it was stated, and he had freighted two ships in which he sent out those tenants he had cleared from his estates, to America. But one of these ships was unfortunately lost, and the survivors having some of them returned and told their sad story, nothing could persuade the people that emigration was not a plot against their lives. Added to this, it was stated that Major Mahon said he would make a sheep-walk of Strokestown. Within a fortnight afterwards he was shot." In these sentiments Grattan was seconded by Maurice O'Connell, a son of Daniel O'Connell and MP for Tralee, who repeated a slightly different rumor about one of the Mahon ships: He said the vessel returned to port after being discovered to be unseaworthy. He also wondered "whether, if the people of England had suffered the same privations, had been reduced to the same necessities, and had been exposed to the same cruelties as the people of Ireland, they would have remained quiet?"

One man who was prepared to respond to the charge of priestly misconduct was the Archbishop of Tuam, the redoubtable John MacHale. There was no more forbidding figure in the Irish Catholic firmament than the prelate known as "the Lion of the Fold of Judah." He was a fervent nationalist and a strong advocate for the Irish Gaelic language who would always remember watching as a young boy while French troops marched through a mountain pass during the 1798 rebellion. He was so suspicious of British intentions that he would rather his people forgo school altogether than attend those supported by the government. Seán O'Faoláin wrote of his "stubborn, tight mouth, and small hard, eyes" and described how his "nationalism and fervor were unsweetened by any form of liberality, whose attitude to the 'private lives' of his flock would probably have been that they had no right to such a luxury." It is not a shock that "John of Tuam," who had been attacking the government's policies in a steady stream of public letters, didn't bother to conduct an investigation before responding to the assault on the unnamed priest from his portion of western Ireland. In a November 26 letter to an English Catholic lord, he rejected such "vague charges . . . originating from the bitter calumniators of the Catholic Church, and widely circulated through those adverse organs," and instructed the lord to "read and hear of the cruelties, the ordinary and every day recurring cruelties enduring by the Irish peasantry and inflicted by those whose position and education some humanity should be expected." In a letter to Lord John Russell on November 29, he alleged that the charges were "propagated for the purpose of diverting public sympathy from the suffering people of Ireland, and of excusing ministers from the responsibility of relieving them." The public figure who had become Ireland's most influential nationalist upon the death of Daniel O'Connell had joined the fight.

On the same day as MacHale's letter to the prime minister, Sir George Grey, the home secretary, introduced the Crime and Outrage (Ireland) Bill in the House of Commons, failing to mention Strokestown's priest's alleged role during his detailed explication of the Mahon case. To the surprise and dismay of many, the legislation, which had been drafted over the previous two weeks, was less stringent than expected. Its main provisions called for additional police to be sent to disturbed districts—with all costs of the deployment charged to the local communities—and for restrictions to be placed on possession of arms in such areas. Unlike Peel's coercion bill of 1846, no curfew would be instituted. Lord Clarendon, whose more draconian ideas suspending the Habeas Corpus Act were set aside by Russell, admitted that he "did not like it very much" and thought it would "prove unsatisfactory to all parties." The Tory press was outraged. The exclusion of a component specifically punishing denouncing clerics was a particular source of pique. The *Dublin Evening Mail* felt the legislation was worthless without a clause targeting such "accessories before the fact." The omission served as a call to arms to the seventh Baron Farnham, Henry Maxwell, a County Cavan landlord who hailed from a militantly anti-Catholic family that had long sought to convert its tenants to Protestantism. (It boasted 428 converts in 1828.) On December 6 in the House of Lords, he rose to deliver the most comprehensive indictment yet against the priest of Strokestown, naming him for the first time in public as Father Michael McDermott.

Using material likely provided by Lord Clarendon's source, Lord Farnham read from friendly letters sent by Father McDermott to Major Mahon prior to the Famine. In one, the priest spoke of "your kindness towards myself personally, and your encouragement to the improvement and industrious habits of my parishioners." In the other, he wrote, "I always use my utmost exertions to promote peace among the people; and, above all, respect and punctuality to their landlords and proprietors of the soil." Lord Farnham then repeated the words of denunciations that Father McDermott had allegedly delivered in the autumn of 1847 as documented "in the handwriting of Major Mahon himself," he said. According to Major Mahon's testimony, coming as if from beyond the grave, Father McDermott had sermonized that "he returns and finds his whole property all safe—his place unmolested; and the return he makes you is the burning and destroying of houses, and leaving the poor to starve." Lord Farnham then asked the House, "And what was the character of the man who was so inhumanly murdered?" The peer read aloud from Dr. Shanley's description of Major Mahon's impassioned call to "keep them from destitution" during his final carriage ride through his property. Finally, Lord

Farnham said that "the expressions used by Priest McDermott, in denouncing Major Mahon from the altar, on the 31st of October, were—'Major Mahon is worse than Cromwell, and yet he lives.' A respectable person coming out of the chapel remarked, 'If the major lives a month after this he is immortal.'"

For these assertions about the Sunday, October 31 sermon, he did not cite a source. But it deserves notice that the unconfirmed denunciation about Cromwell bears some similarity in form to the better-documented denunciation "in the handwriting of Major Mahon himself." In both statements, Father McDermott expressed indignation that Major Mahon, despite "being worse than Cromwell" and "burning and destroying of houses," should remain unpunished for his crimes. The difference is only in the implied degree of punishment. In the first example, he still "lives," and thus deserved death. In the second, his property remains "unmolested," and thus merited, it seemed, some level of sabotage.

Lord Farnham then turned to his fellow lords and asked if evidence of such conduct did not render the priest "amenable to punishment"? If not, he wondered whether "it be the intention of the government, to amend and strengthen the law, in this respect?"

The Whig leader in the House of Lords, the Marquess of Lansdowne, assured Lord Farnham that "the authors of such outrages" could be brought to justice under the law as it currently existed. But he noted the difficulty of procuring enough evidence to actually secure a conviction against a priest. Lord Lansdowne's statement outraged another member of the body, Lord Stanley, who owned extensive estates in County Tipperary. The former Tory frontbencher and future prime minister wondered what more was needed to be known about the behavior of Father McDermott, who was "legally, as well as he was—I have no hesitation in saying, if the facts were so—morally in the sight of man, guilty of the blood of the murdered Major Mahon." At the end of Lord Stanley's thunderous demand for a prosecution—if the current law was inadequate, he asserted, then it was time for the government to alter it—the House of Lords filled with shouts and cheers of "Hear! Hear!"

Unknown to Lords Farnham and Stanley, the Whig government was having some success in its alternate effort to punish the Strokestown priest. In the week before the debate in the House of Lords, Lord Minto, the British envoy in the Eternal City, was ushered into the presence of the Holy Father, where he asked for ecclesiastical legislation, as it were, to keep Father McDermott and other likeminded priests in proper order. During the November 30 meeting, Lord Minto described to the pope how "the people were incited to disaffection and turbulence and crime by inflammatory addresses in their Chapels, where it happened, as in the case of Major Mahon, that the denunciation of an individual from the Altar was the immediate prelude to his murder." The pontiff affectionately known by Italians as "Pio Nono," then in the second year of his thirty-one-year reign, asked to be provided with some proof to buttress the claims. He then assured Lord Minto "not only of his readiness, but of his great desire to do whatever might be in his power to apply a remedy to such disorders," wrote Minto to Lord Palmerston.

At this point in the debate, those seeking to use the Mahon case to defend the distressed Irish poor and highlight the cruelty of clearances suffered further setbacks in the battle for public advantage. Henry Grattan Jr., faced rebuke for charging in the House of Commons that Major Mahon "said that he would make Strokestown a sheep-walk," a line that indeed doesn't sound like him. D. H. Kelly published a letter to Grattan in the newspapers saying that "such language is completely out of character with the gentleman-like demeanor and benevolent heart of my lamented relative; and I firmly believe that no such statement was ever made by him. It is to be hoped you will not emulate your assassin friends and stab in the dark." Kelly called "the son of the patriot Grattan" an "apologist for the Thugs of Roscommon," who had been "made the cat's paw of the base malignity of those who, not content with depriving an honorable man of his existence, seek to go beyond the grave to wound his reputation." Within days Grattan announced his support for the coercion bill, saying he "would have no parley with assassins."

After reading Kelly's statement, John Ross Mahon prepared a letter for the *Times* that addressed the charge that had been a central plank of the public case against Major Mahon. "Mr. D. H. Kelly having refuted Mr. Henry Grattan's assertions in the House of Commons respecting the late Major Mahon, I now beg to refute the other, by informing you that no ship with emigrants from his estate foundered," he wrote. But the land agent decided against mailing the letter, understanding that it would be foolhardy to defend an emigration plan that had led to hundreds of deaths. As he told Kelly, "Upon consideration I thought it more advisable not to send it, as very many died of fever and I was afraid of getting into any newspaper warfare."

But on December 9 the persistent rumor—in his speech introducing the coercion bill, Sir George Grey had said that a Mahon vessel had sunk, arguing that the unfortunate occurrence couldn't be blamed on the landlord—was discredited via another route. In private conversation, Oliver D. J. Grace, the newly elected Whig MP from Roscommon, had provided evidence to Maurice O'Connell that the story the Repeal MP had told about one of the Mahon ships returning to port was false. Grace asked him to withdraw it during open debate. When O'Connell failed to do so, Grace took the floor and demanded that he clear "the memory of the murdered man from any stain." Humiliatingly, O'Connell asked for the indulgence of the House. He said that it had "escaped his memory" in the "heat of the debate" to withdraw his allegation, an explanation that was greeted with mocking cries of "Oh!" O'Connell then said that he had "no evidence to support my first statement, nor do I wish to bring up any. I should be exceedingly sorry to state anything here which I did not believe to be true, or which on being corrected by competent evidence I should not be ready to retract." His apology was followed by an absolving murmur of "hear, hear" from the assembled MPs.

But the greatest setback in the effort to use the now infamous case to spurn a closer examination of the landlord's behavior—and thus the actions of landlords throughout Ireland—was the intensifying focus on Father McDermott's alleged role in the conspiracy. It was perhaps inevitable in an atmosphere of long-standing denominational animosities that the behavior of such an "agent of disorder" would become paramount. The accusations against him played directly into the English polity's longtime, bipartisan suspicion of the destabilizing influence of Catholic priests upon the Irish poor. The issue was settled once and for all when Father McDermott issued his response to the charges against him. With his angry, evasive, impolitic, and unapologetic polemic, the priest ensured that discussion of the Strokestown affair would center around his actions, alleged to have led to a single death, rather than on Major Mahon's deeds, which were the cause of far more misfortune. Instead of providing stark, hard-to-refute testimony that might cause the British government to offer the kinds of protections for tenants threatened with eviction that the prime minister supported, Father McDermott offered up a call to arms that was bound to heighten the animosities of the debate.

His open letter, dated December 7, was apparently written before he had learned of Lord Farnham's presentation in the House of Lords on the previous day or heard the specific accusations that he had equated Major Mahon with Cromwell. Father McDermott attacked the "vague and unfounded assertions unaccompanied by a single circumstantial proof, except that which interested bigotry supplies" and challenged his accusers to attempt a prosecution. The priest was not merely offering a defense. He was proposing a fight. "If, as is gratuitously asserted, any Catholic clergyman has denounced any one of those obnoxious landlords from his altar previous to the fatal event in which he has fallen a victim to the wild justice of revenge, the legal process of rendering that clergyman amenable to the law, and responsible for his seditious preaching, is neither expensive nor difficult," he wrote. Father McDermott was denying a denunciation while issuing a denunciation—"obnoxious landlords"—and pleading his innocence while taunting his accusers.

Then he delivered a dark sneer at the landlord's survivors. "May I ask why such steps are not taken by the afflicted relatives, or by the more fortunate, but yet mourning inheritor of the property, which has devolved upon him from the hand of assassin?" he wondered. He answered his own question by commencing an attack on the "informer" within his parish who sold him out for monetary compensation, an oddly vehement sally from someone claiming innocence. "Oh! The informer will not come forward, his courage oozes through his fingers," he wrote. "He skulks into his lurking hole, and laughs at the credulity of those who employed him after he received his reward of turpitude." He said such an individual was a "hireling serf whose embarrassment [or poverty] tempts him to court the patronage of his landlord, and to offer his services as an officious whisperer, for the purpose of drawing a little grist to his mill." Perhaps the most troubling aspect of this passage was the priest's willingness to attack one of his parishioners by pointing to his destitution, using the word "serf" as an epithet. Unable to let go of the subject, Father McDermott then issued a veiled warning. He said that the informer "stands back because he knows his perfidy would be detected, and that he should then be held up to public scorn as a liar and calumniator." He was daring anyone in his own community to corroborate the charges against him, thereby joining the ranks of those who would "court the patronage of his landlord."

After baiting his English accusers, the aggrieved Mahon survivors, and the (lying) secret agent within his flock, he issued a formal denial:

I have now to assure the public, by the most solemn asservations a clergyman can utter, that the late Major Mahon was

never denounced, nor even his name mentioned, from any cha-
pel altar in Strokestown, or within 20 miles of Strokestown, in
any direction, on any Sunday before his death. I can under the
same sacred pledge, declare that a single sentence was never spo-
ken from the altar, which by misconstruction or otherwise, could
tend to stimulate the peasantry to the atrocious murder which
has been perpetrated.

The priest was not only denying the charge that he had employed inciting language—by uttering the lines about Cromwell or about the landlord finding his property "all safe"—but also seemed to be suggesting that Major Mahon and his behavior were never a topic of his sermons.

Finally, he issued a denunciation of Major Mahon's actions that was likely a milder version of what he had obviously been delivering from the pulpit all along. It is the most detailed description of the evictions on the Mahon estate that has survived, casting a much-needed spotlight on actions that continued to be countenanced by the laws of the nation. Tragically, much of what he said about the sufferings of his parishioners would be ignored in the ensuing debate.

He provided a description of the removal process that directly contradicted the landlord's supporters' statements about the benevolence of Major Mahon's clearances. "I saw no necessity for the idle display of a large force of military and police, carrying outside so many rounds of ball cartridge, and inside some substantial rounds of whiskey and baker's bread, surrounding the poor man's cabin, setting fire to the roof while the half-starved, half-naked children were hastening away from the flames with yells of despair, while the mother lay prostrate on the threshold writhing in agony, and the heart-broken father remained supplicating on his knees." This is a long way from Ross Mahon's November 8 comment that "in no case has there been any undue severity used in taking possession." The priest added that the sheriff's men and the crowbar brigade had reveled in "triumph and exultation" following their actions and that Mahon's bailiff had revisited the evictions sites to ensure that the "wretched outcasts" had not returned to their former places of residence.

"In my opinion these scenes, of which I can only draw a very inefficient portrait, had more to do with the murder of Major Mahon than all the thundering denunciations of the Vatican could effect had they been rolled on his head," he wrote. "I tell, therefore, the Orange press, and I tell Sir Benjamin Hall, that they have asserted a groundless and egregious falsehood, and that their fabricated charge of denunciation against the Catholic clergy is a monstrous, outrageous, and flagitious calumny." His evicted tenants, after all, had been "left to subsist on the precarious alms of their neighbors, roving about as houseless wanderers, without a friend to console, or a resting place whereon to lay their aching bones." This, he said, caused them to lose "all reasonable control" over the "bad passions" of their nature.

But the priest had not yet concluded. He finished by again singling out Sir Benjamin Hall for attack, showing his propensity to personalize disputes. He wondered if the MP would "exchange his comparatively high and exalted position for the downtrodden condition of those miserable outcasts." Perhaps he, too, might "turn upon his oppressor, and to seek revenge even at the hazard of an existence, which is only dragged on in wretchedness and destitution."

One reaches the conclusion of the letter to discover that Father McDermott had not issued a forthright and explicit condemnation of the *murder itself*.

From the moment of its publication, the first half of the letter was pulled apart by a wide spectrum of English commentators. When Lord Clarendon read the text in the December 10 edition of the *Freeman's Journal*, he took little notice of the "scenes of horror and conflagration." Instead he detected something irregular about Father McDermott's seemingly full-throated paragraph of denial.

In a letter to Lord John Russell, he wrote that "it struck him as odd" that the priest would say that Major Mahon's name was not mentioned on any *Sunday* before his death. "[O]n speaking to [Thomas] Redington [the Irish undersecretary and Catholic landlord] about it, he remembered that Mahon was murdered on the Tuesday and that the day before (Monday) was All Saints Day, which is a great festival of the Catholic Church, so the denunciation might have taken place then," he wrote. This point was soon made in public. An anonymous letter was published in the *Times*—likely written by the lord lieutenant or someone assigned by him—repeating Clarendon's theory as truth, and saying that "this fact is known in Dublin Castle."

The *Times*, a genuinely anti-Catholic publication, focused (among other things) on Father McDermott's gibe about the absence of charges lodged against him. "The legal process . . . is neither expensive nor difficult," the priest had written. The newspaper accused Father McDermott of knowing full well that no one in his parish would come forward to testify. "The stronghold of the priest is in their [parishioners'] abject and superstitious notions of his power over their future destiny," the paper wrote. "This it is which makes them pliant as wax in his hands, and enable him to laugh to scorn the provisions of the law and the indignation of his countrymen." Some honed in on Father McDermott's claim that Major Mahon's name was never "mentioned" from the altar. Why would he need to utter the name of a person known intimately to every worshipper? Others pointed to the priest's ugly phrase about "the more fortunate, but yet mourning inheritor" of the property. The *Morning Chronicle* saw it as an example of "unfeeling and brutal levity," which made it "really uphill work for us, defending the legitimate claims of the clerical order on public respect and confidence." The line even made Father McDermott's supporters uncomfortable. When the Repeal leader John O'Connell read the letter in the House of Commons, he edited it out of the text.

A principal argument of many was the fact that the letter itself seemed to confirm the charges made against him. A priest accused of speaking intemperately toward Major Mahon had defended himself by speaking intemperately of Major Mahon. To the *Daily News*, Father McDermott's "violent and unmeasured abuse of the murdered man" proved that even if he didn't mean to have the landlord killed, he "may have encouraged it by his previous sympathy and evidently habitual intemperance of language." The priest's chief accuser, Lord Farnham, wasn't willing to interpret the text as charitably. In the House of Lords, he said that he was so disgusted by the letter that he would not read to his fellow lordships. But he did say that "the whole tenor, tone, and language of it were calculated to arouse the worst passions of the misguided people, whose spiritual director he was, and to excite them to deeds of violence and blood." The *Times* concurred. "Could poor Major Mahon be called to life again, the explanatory letter of Mr. McDermott would be quite sufficient to consign him again to a bloody grave, without any second denunciation from the altar on 'Monday.'"

With the public mood turning so decisively against those speaking against landlord excesses, the first verdict of sorts was delivered in the Mahon case. On December 20 the Crime and Outrage Bill received royal assent after sailing through both houses of Parliament. In the House of Commons, the vote was 296–19, with Irish MPs in favor of it by a count of 91–14. A dispirited Lord John Russell, who didn't speak during the debates, was frustrated by the ease with which a coercion bill could be enacted while measures of permanent improvement for Ireland continued to encounter resistance. But he was not so dispirited to offer his resignation.

While the legislation didn't include a clause forbidding priestly denunciations, the government was moving closer to encouraging the pope to issue his own prohibition of the practice. On December 19 Lord Minto was granted another audience with Pio Nono to present the promised evidence about recalcitrant priests. In two memoranda and other accompanying documents, the earl outlined for His Holiness "the general character of the agitation in which the Roman Catholic clergy were engaged," which mostly included priests and bishops offering their support to one kind of Repeal campaign or another. In his mention of the centerpiece example, Lord Minto noted that "it appears that the denunciation in the particular case of Major Mahon has since been denied in a letter published by Archbishop MacHale." (Word of Father McDermott's defense had not yet arrived in Rome.) After glancing over the documents, the pope offered Lord Minto "the most unequivocal assurance of his desire to manifest as strongly as possible his disapprobation of the political activity of the clergy, and to do what might be in his power to check it in Ireland," wrote the earl. The pontiff, though, wasn't willing to act on Lord Minto's word. He handed the material over to his Sacra Congregatio de Propaganda Fide (Sacred Congregation for the Propagation of the Faith), which was responsible for regulating ecclesiastical affairs in Ireland. Three days later the congregation asserted that the evidence, based largely on newspaper reports, wasn't conclusive enough to serve as the basis for a papal pronouncement. The pope decided it was time to conduct his own investigation into the charges.

At the same time, the highest British officials were privately conceding that the legal case against Father McDermott was weak. Ross Mahon had told Redington "that the reports were so vague and various that he himself would not feel sure what the priest had said or whether he had denounced Major Mahon at all." In a letter to a *Times* journalist, Lord Clarendon wrote that while it had been proven beyond doubt that Father McDermott was "a vindictive illconsidered blackguard," there was not enough evidence to place him within the walls of the Roscommon jail.

CHAPTER II

Decided Measures

Already the minions of our absentee landlords are at work. The late Coercion Bill may justly be called "The Leveling Act." The landlords and agents have now a large military and police force to support them in carrying out their demon-like intentions. . . . Need we be surprised that the assassin is sheltered, and that the lives of the landlords are jeopardized? What people on the face of the habitable globe would endure half what the Irish this moment are enduring?
—*Roscommon Journal*, JANUARY 29, 1848

Irish Game Laws.
1st January. Landlord shooting begins.
31st December. Landlord shooting ends.
Certificates may be had from John Archbishop of Tuam, and Father McDermott.
—*Punch*, JANUARY 22, 1848

WHATEVER THE MOTIVATIONS OF those who carried out the assassination of Major Denis Mahon, the death of the landlord of Strokestown was another disaster for the starving paupers who remained on his estate and those who had already been removed from it.

For the tenants who still clung to the land, the killers had eliminated an individual who, though guilty of causing much suffering, had proven that he possessed a conscience. His several acts of consideration prior to May 1847—including his brief call for a halt in evictions in early 1847—indicated that he might have been swayed to adopt more generous policies. It was a slim hope, particularly since he had remained committed to a course of mass clearance during the six months prior to his death. But at least there was a chance he could be convinced to adopt a policy that addressed his tenants' distress. With an incensed Pakenham Mahon, who was safely ensconced in his Gloucester Place home in London, now controlling the property, all hope seemed to be gone.

To Ross Mahon, the murder, and the support it seemed to have among the people, confirmed what he had been saying all along. A full-scale rebellion against the estate's management had been in force since the blight descended on the potato crop in the fall of 1845 and even before. From the earliest days of his tenure, he had told an initially skeptical Major Mahon that the tenants who weren't paying rent deserved "no indulgence." Yet he placated his employer's desire for humane policies. He offered seed and reduced rents. He organized an assisted emigration scheme. But now, with his accusations about the degeneracy of the Mahon tenants spectacularly confirmed, Ross Mahon was able to proceed unimpeded with his plan to clear the property of a majority of its inhabitants. There would be no resuscitation of the talk about the "good and willing" and the "idle and bad." In fact, in the weeks after Major Mahon's death, the land agent began making plans to *increase* the rate of removals, delivering his own kind of verdict in the murder case. In a letter to Marcus McClausland, he called it "the decided measures I hope to pursue on the Strokestown property."

His gravest concern, as expressed in his letters, was for the safety of the individuals assigned to deliver documents of eviction. (The land agent was also understandably concerned for his own safety. He was now spending much time in Dublin, assigning tasks in and around Strokestown to his under agent, Thomas Roberts.)

"We have a number of decrees obtained against the tenants," he wrote to a colleague, "but are afraid of employing a bailiff to execute them fearing that he may be murdered." On December 20, the day the coercion bill became law, Ross Mahon wrote to Thomas Redington in Dublin Castle asking "for the protection of police for the persons serving notices of ejectment." He noted to the Irish undersecretary that he merely sought the force for *protection*. The actual job of expelling the tenants from the land would remain in the hands of the sheriff, he assured him. Ross Mahon was also thinking of shielding his local staff by sending Guinness Mahon employees from Dublin to Strokestown to serve the ejectment processes on the tenants. Unlike John Robinson, the longtime bailiff who had surely engendered hatred among the populace, the Dubliners would be less irksome figures of authority. In a letter to Roberts, Ross Mahon said such a course would only be followed if Robinson had any "apprehension" about completing his job. But apparently Robinson had no worries. On December 23 Ross Mahon wrote to Roberts about the good news he had received from Redington, who had additional troops at his disposal as a result of the coercion legislation inspired by Major Mahon's murder. "Mr. Redington informs us that directions have been given to afford you the protection of having two policemen when going through the country," Ross Mahon wrote from Dublin. "Robinson can have the same and further protection when serving the ejectments."

For the tenants who had already been removed from the land—and all those on the estate who held plots of less than a quarter acre—the death dealt a blow to the strained relief effort that provided them with a limited hope of survival. The local rates, which had already slowed to a trickle, started to dry up. The bulk of Roscommon landlords, the figures the government expected to rescue the starving poor, were fleeing the country en masse for the safety of England. Among this group was the most active member of the Roscommon Board of Guardians, Lord Crofton, whose disappearance left the vital organization without a compass. On

December 16 a government official complained of "the apathy and inactivity of the board." In Strokestown Dr. Terence Shanley noted that "almost all the resident gentry have left this neighborhood, and the remaining few, from the number of Maguireite notices they are in the daily habit of receiving, are afraid to leave their own homes, or take a part in public business."

Dr. Shanley made this comment in a letter he penned to the Central Board of Health on December 8, one day after Father McDermott wrote the notorious dispatch that would be scrutinized in the Apostolic Palace, on Downing Street, and in Dublin Castle. The Catholic physician likely would have been killed moments after Major Mahon if the second shooter's weapon had not misfired. Yet he appealed for landlords, government officials, and private entities not to rescind assistance from the suffering poor because of the murder, cautioning against punishing the many for the actions of the few. "A charitable donation of £10 was some time given by the chairman of the Board of Guardians of the Union, drawn in favor of Major Mahon, but in consequence of his sudden and barbarous assassination was forthwith returned," Dr. Shanley wrote. "All aid from England and other charitable societies is withdrawn, on the plea that they would 'no longer continue support to murderers.' This doctrine, if universally acted on, I make no doubt will have the effect of quartering at least the well disposed of the lower orders, while the assassins can walk abroad with the most perfect impunity, shooting and getting rid of the wealth and intelligence of the land, that they may have the country to themselves, which is avowedly their object." It is perhaps fruitless to wonder what would have happened if Dr. Shanley's message, with its direct and practical concern for the poor, had been given wide distribution in place of Father McDermott's, which mentioned nothing about the simple matter of providing food for the suffering. Could the debate have veered into an examination of the wisdom of allowing the Strokestown masses to be abandoned in the face of the heedless act and providing the secret society with the triumph it was so eager to claim for itself?

In a sense, the government took Dr. Shanley's advice. On December 27 the Roscommon Board of Guardians was officially dissolved for "default of duty"—as eventually were boards in all the twenty-two unions earlier declared "distressed" and an additional twenty unions—and replaced with paid vice-guardians assigned to take over the job of administering relief to the poor. In the more than three months since the eighteen soup kitchens in the Roscommon Union had closed, the workhouse had remained the sole avenue of government relief for the qualifying poor from the Mahon estate. But the indebted facility, which had long been filled over capacity, had so far been unable to distribute outdoor relief under the amended Poor Law. In making the decision to fire the guardians, the government had deemed that the officials had "no inclination . . . to attend to business," wrote Captain Henry Evans, the temporary inspector who sought the dissolution order. Mindful of the fate of Major Mahon, they were more worried about surviving the evening trip back to their residences. "The gentlemen who come in five, ten, and fifteen miles, are thinking more of returning home than anything else," wrote Captain Evans, who was appointed two weeks after Major Mahon's murder.

The task of the vice-guardians was to *force* the landlords to pay the rates necessary to fund the Poor Law—it was believed that they would be uninfluenced by local pressures—and to reform the operation of the workhouse to prevent any undue expenditure of funds. In its effect, the arrival of the vice-guardians represented the first hint of good news for the Roscommon poor in some time, at least for the small portion within the workhouse. Some improvements were immediate. An energetic effort was begun—more than ten women were appointed to the task—to clean the "disorderly and dirty" facility. "No attention has heretofore been paid to the cleanliness of the house," wrote Captain Evans. Deals were struck with the baker and milkman, both of whom were owed vast sums of money, to lower their fees. Clothing was ordered for scores of inmates who were "nearly naked." The rate collectors, provided with updated account books, were sent out into the field to "vigorously" pry money from reluctant landlords. More significantly, space was opened up to allow more paupers entry into the workhouse. With a loan of 300 pounds from the private British Relief Association—distributed by the Treasury to assist the vice-guardians until the new rates could be collected—auxiliary structures were soon prepared to lessen overcrowding.

When word spread among the poor about the possibility of gaining admittance, a huge throng arrived at the structure early one January morning, providing many observers with a chance to behold the true effects of the Famine. "From before eight o'clock in the morning the streets were full of more than half-starved creatures moving towards the workhouse, the sick generally brought on asses cars, the children packed together in turf kishes, while their parents were moving on assisted by holding these cars," wrote a visiting Quaker. "So early as seven o'clock our streets were studded with creatures almost dead or dying," wrote the *Roscommon Journal*. "Eight, nine, ten could be seen on carts and cars drawn by asses, or probably in a charitable neighbor's cart given for the purpose. Affected with contagious fever the young and old were huddling together. No man in the world could have imagined that any locality could have so much destitution."

Two hundred and twenty of the worst of this group—"most of whom were laboring under dysentery, etc.," wrote the vice-guardians—were permitted entry. "These were so far gone that one half of them would not survive a fortnight," the Quaker wrote. The rest were turned away. "When more than 900 were refused admission the scene was awful," he wrote. "These poor creatures returned to town and it would rend the most hardened heart to see death pictured in so many faces. Homes many of them have not. Land they have had in many cases, but it was of no use to them and they have given it up." "The inhabitants naturally became alarmed, and many of the shopkeepers closed their doors," wrote the *Journal*. "The wailing and dying moans of the unfortunates, as they were obliged to wend their way back to their respective localities, was truly heart-rending.... Several of them died before they left the town; and hundreds unable to quit the streets, are strolling about black with fever, spreading disease as they go."

This multitude of unfortunates—and the thousands unable to make the early morning trip—continued to be failed by the relief apparatus in the Roscommon Union. Without the ability or permission to distribute outdoor relief, the amended Poor Law was still not fully in effect. The landlords, who had little interest in aiding their potential assassins, had so far failed to deliver the funds necessary for the job. The vice-guardians were even unable to borrow the money. "The Union being already so deeply in debt," the vice-guardians wrote to Dublin on January 24, more than four months after the soup kitchens had closed, "we cannot obtain the necessary credit to enable us to administer any outdoor relief." And the government continued to be unwilling to do anything "which would tend to revive the mendicant spirit, and countenance a feeling of dependence upon the state instead of upon local exertion and contribution," wrote Trevelyan in response to a request for clothing and bedding for the workhouses.

But at least the prosecution of Father McDermott was gaining in momentum. In the wake of the wide publicity given to the priest's letter, a new figure emerged as the cleric's principal accuser: the most prominent Catholic laymen in England. John Talbot, the sixteenth Earl of Shrewsbury, hailed from a family that had managed to hold on to its land through generations of anti-Catholic oppressions, emerging as the predominant property holder in the Midlands. He now resided in his just-completed baronial seat, Alton Towers, one of England's great estates. A Whig, Lord Shrewsbury was a vociferous Church apologist who made it a habit of writing long statements on the Catholic issues of the day, often publishing them as pamphlets for the edification of the masses. His dedication to his faith led him to contribute vast sums of money for the construction and beautification of churches throughout England. He strongly opposed the Repeal movement, believing that the seditious activities of the Irish flock besmirched the Church's mission in the eyes of his English neighbors. Daniel O'Connell, who traded public letters with him, had called him a "pious fool," which became something of a nickname.

Incensed by Father McDermott's "objectionable" defense of himself, Lord Shrewsbury penned a private communication to Bishop George Browne, asking that the leader of the Diocese of Elphin conduct a "most searching investigation" into the charges against his priest. "All, indeed, will be astonished if no investigation take place by his ecclesiastical superior, and that immediately for all think that, for the honor of the church, such investigation should precede any criminal prosecution on the part of government if, unfortunately, there be evidence against Father McDermott sufficient to put him on his trial for the crime imputed to him." He asked the bishop to consider "the very great importance of the question; for there has seldom been an event before the public which has created so lively and so deep a sensation against the Irish clergy generally."

When Bishop Browne failed to immediately respond, Lord Shrewsbury took the matter higher up the ladder to Archbishop John MacHale, a one-time mentor to the Elphin bishop. In a several-thousand-word public letter—published in the newspapers alongside the unanswered letter to Bishop Browne—he castigated the Lion of Tuam for his failure to more forthrightly condemn the actions of Father McDermott. The nobleman assailed the archbishop for making it difficult for Catholic Englishmen to persuade their countrymen that "the excesses of some who profess Catholicity in Ireland ... are neither the natural nor usual results of the teaching of the ancient and universal church." The letter included a wide-ranging assault on the archbishop—for failing to support national elementary education, for refusing to allow Father Theobald Mathew, the temperance priest, to preach within his archdiocese, for collecting the Repeal "rent" while communities lacked worship facilities. It was especially energetic in countering Mac-Hale's attacks on the "the apathy and neglect" of Whig relief policies. Lord Shrewsbury defended the government's exertions as "an effort such as no nation has perhaps ever yet made," and cautioned against "visiting the sins of a hundred successive ministers on the head of one, who has now to work against the accumulated evil of ages."

The blame for any relief failures, he wrote, should be directed at other sources. "If that effort were not altogether successful; if it still fell short of the necessities of the case; the defect at least was not in the intention, but may, with far more justice and propriety, I venture to submit, be imputed to the unerring, though inscrutable designs of God, who so blinded the understanding of our rulers that His visitation might not be averted by any human ingenuity." In other words, God had prevented the Whigs from initiating a success-ful relief program because He *intended* for the Famine to be devas-tatingly severe. Lord Shrewsbury then went further, in what he obscenely described as a "subject for reflection." God had *worsened* the Famine, he wrote, because He was angered by the ingratitude of the Irish people in the face of what Shrewsbury admitted was a faltering relief effort. "I would even suggest it as a subject for reflec-tion whether that visitation were not aggravated—whether it be not very grievously aggravated at this particular moment; because, my lord, sufficient expression of gratitude has been withheld both from the government and the people of England, for the very gen-erous sacrifices which in their charity, as in their duty, they were pleased to make last year in favor of their suffering brethren in Ire-land; but which this year have been arrested by the scantiness of her thanks, the bitterness of her reproaches, the crimes of too many of her people, the unrestrained violence of some few of her pastors, the apathy of still fewer, as we hope, of her prelates."

The letter, destined to be published as a pamphlet, was a smash-ing success in many quarters of England. No longer was a Tory Orangeman like Lord Farnham leading the fight against Father

McDermott in particular and insurrectionist Catholic clergy in general. Now a titled Catholic and loyal Whig was sallying forth, lending his considerable prestige to grave allegations that couldn't be dismissed as the products of mere bigotry. Lord John Russell felt that his words of censure would "shame the Irish clergy into a less barbarous behavior." The *Times*, which hated Archbishop MacHale with a passion that almost equaled its loathing of the late Daniel O'Connell, called his letter "the best antidote to Archbishop MacHale's poison." The *Morning Chronicle*, which, as Shrewsbury's ideological home, was the first to publish his letter, wrote, "A man in Earl Shrewsbury's position can say, with the best effect, what others could not say without the certainty of their motives being misconstrued and their meaning perverted. . . . A distinguished Roman Catholic layman, anxiously soliciting the means of vindicating Roman Catholic prelates against the charge of connivance at a sacrilegious profanation of priestly functions, cannot decently or safely be put off with subterfuges."

Even Lord Clarendon, who had privately admitted two weeks earlier that he could find no evidence that Father McDermott denounced Major Mahon, was eager to apply pressure on the Roscommon clerics. In a private letter to Bishop Browne on January 5, he asked for a fuller explanation of the priest's behavior. He wrote that he believed that the priest "excited the people against that unfortunate gentleman," which resulted in his death. The lord lieutenant said that it would "be a sincere pleasure to me if this painful impression is removed from my mind."

Bishop George Browne wasted little time in issuing his response to Shrewsbury's now-public challenge. Among the many replies delivered by Catholics in Ireland and England to the layman's galling reprimand of two senior ecclesiastics, the Dove of Elphin's was the most even-tempered and courteous. "For your lordship's high character I have the most profound respect," he wrote in one section. He also spoke of how the peer had done "me the great honor of addressing me." The letter was "beautiful and dignified," commented a correspondent for an Irish newspaper based in New York. "Brief, mild, and modest," said the *Boston Pilot*. Even the *Morning Chronicle* was disarmed, calling it "honest and touching," a welcome relief from the fury of "John Tuam."

He countered Shrewsbury's suggestion that members of the hierarchy had been derelict in their duty to inveigh against murderous acts by noting his long history of speaking out against secret societies. He even described preaching in the chapel of Strokestown "three or four weeks previous to the horrid murder of Major Mahon," where he "portrayed the dreadful and awful consequences of murder and of seeking private revenge. I have declared to them that all vengeance pertained to God. I preached patience, resignation to the Divine will, etc." This was an utterly believable claim. It was integral to the bishop's liturgical language—sometimes to the exclusion of all other matters—to scold "those who would seek to connect you with secret societies or secret obligations," as he wrote in his Lenten letter of 1846.

He then turned to Father McDermott. The bishop said he had already examined the charges against him and found them wanting. "The result of my inquires and investigation has been, that he has not on Sunday, Monday, ferial, or holy day, nor at any time nor in any place, directly or indirectly, denounced Major Mahon, or encouraged any species of harm or injury to him," he wrote. In Bishop Browne's reckoning, Father McDermott neither denounced the landlord nor used inciting language against him, a distinction he seemed to grasp. Bishop Browne was ready with proof to back up his assertion. Included with his letter was a statement signed by twenty-eight of Father McDermott's "respectable" male parishioners—grocers, farmers, woolen drapers, wine and spirits merchants, bakers, publicans, innkeepers, victuallers—who pledged to defend their "beloved and revered pastor" against "the facts which are falsely and malignantly put forth as the foundation of these calumnies." They said that Father McDermott "did not open his lips to address one word to his flock" on Monday, November 1, and that they never heard him "denounce the late Major Mahon, or to express the words attributed to him in the reported speech of Lord Farnham, or any SUCH words, or any words of SIMILAR IMPORT or MEANING."

Like their bishop, the parishioners swore that Father McDermott *never* denounced the late Major Mahon. Ever. "Surely this will silence the Thugs of the English press and settle the Strokestown calumny for ever," said the *Freeman's Journal*. But surely this was unnecessarily definitive. Father McDermott's heated expressions against Major Mahon were on record. Even while he denied denunciations, he denounced. And why shouldn't he? wondered the *Tablet*, the influential London-based Catholic weekly. "Where laws stop short; where tyrannical power and will are all but omnipotent; where the arrangements of society afford no protection to the weak; where iniquitous force cannot be resisted by any legal method; and where the oppressed and injured are held of too little account by those who wield the fiery sword which God has entrusted to the magistrates of every society—there, positively the wrong must be made known by outcry, by indignant exposure, by some sort of denunciation, to shame and move the tyrant who has thrown off the fear of God and a great part of the fear of man."

Bishop Browne concluded his letter by cautioning Lord Shrewsbury against giving "too much credit to the malignant slanders of our enemies," but also politely noted that he believed him to be "solely actuated by the purest zeal for the credit and defense of our holy religion." Archbishop MacHale would not be so kind. After a few-week delay, His Grace delivered what an ally called a "cannon roar from Tuam's impregnable fortress." His interminable riposte was more than double the length of Lord Shrewsbury's original letter, forcing many newspapers to print only portions of it. The *Morning Chronicle* called it a "heap of words." The *Daily News* deemed it "one of the most prolix epistles we ever remember having read." *Punch* said it was "reeled off like twine from a roller." The *Times* devoted nearly an entire broadsheet page to printing every angry word.

Archbishop MacHale quickly dispensed with the issue of Father McDermott. Without mentioning him by name—"a very singular omission," said the *Daily News*—he wrote that the charge against the priest was a "scandalous assertion [based] on calumnies which not only have not been proven, but have been fully refuted." He then went into a lengthy point-by-point rebuttal of the statements made by the "alien calumniator" and "peripatetic intriguer," who "grossly insulted and calumniated the Catholic hierarchy of Ireland" and "wished to court the ghastly smiles of some of the Protestant peers of England." Of the collection of Repeal rent, he said the practice continued because it would eventually result in "sound legislation which will secure the fruits of industry and avert the recurrence of famine, brought on not by scarcity alone, but produced and aggravated by cruel and unequal laws." Of national schools, he said he was against them because their purpose was to "surreptitiously" teach "the Protestant catechism . . . to Catholic children." He argued that that the young of his archdiocese were going unschooled because landlord "bigots" wouldn't provide the land needed for Catholic schools. Of his refusal to allow Father Theobald Mathew to preach on temperance within his jurisdiction, he lamely offered that "we claimed, as we should always do, the right of regulating the means best calculated to give fixity and permanence to the dominion of this noble virtue." In fact, the "apostle of temperance" was banned because he was seen as too closely allied with heretical Protestants.

MacHale challenged the claim that the Irish people hadn't been sufficiently appreciative of private assistance—making no comment on God's role in punishing them—but mocked Shrewsbury's suggestion that they hadn't been thankful enough of the government. "How ungrateful of the Catholics of Ireland not to pour forth canticles of thanksgiving to the Ministers, who had promised none of them should perish, and who then suffered well nigh a million to starve!" To Shrewsbury's comment that the government had "resources on hand to relieve the people when all their local efforts shall be exhausted," he bellowed: "They have resources on hand! Had they not those same resources on hand during the last season, while the people perished? For the only resources administered by the new Parliament was COERCION!"

Near the end of the letter, the Lion of Tuam joined in an attack that was being made by many Catholic commentators in Ireland and England. He charged that Lord Shrewsbury was assisting in the Whig government's effort to "enslave" the Irish Church through the ministrations of Lord Minto in Rome. (Shrewsbury was indeed involved with Lord Minto's efforts, writing long letters of advice and sending emissaries to speak with him.) "It is the representations of such an ambassador, said to be so hostile to the Holy Father, you have been strengthening by your calumnies on the Irish hierarchy," MacHale wrote. "And for this public scandal I now demand adequate reparation."

The letter inspired predictable revulsion from the England press—"five dreary columns of trash and twaddle," said the *Morning Chronicle*—and predictable acclamation from the Irish nationalist press, which regarded it as a "crushing reply," as the *Roscommon Journal* wrote. "The Earl of Alton is indeed laid low," wrote one layman to MacHale.

But what of Father McDermott? Where was his response? Perhaps under instructions from Bishop Browne, who was clearly seeking to end the controversy, the priest did not deliver another public defense to the newspapers. But it was utterly out of character for the "Hammer of the Heretics," as the memorial plaque in his church describes him, not to issue some kind of rejoinder, whether his opponent qualified as a heretic or not. And so he did. On January 15 he wrote a letter to the Nottingham Catholic Association, thanking its members for a statement of support they had sent to him following the attacks made on his reputation. In this semi-private missive, addressed to the "gentlemen" of the group, Father McDermott offered a taste of the kind of unrehearsed vitriol he reserved for the objects of his wrath. Even more than the revealing

December 7 letter, which was composed with the understanding that it would be widely distributed, this communication provided a faithful example of how Father McDermott truly expressed himself in the pulpit.

After relishing his "present persecuted and calumniated position before the British Empire," he accused Lord Shrewsbury of earning "unenviable notoriety" by joining "with the relentless enemies of my creed and my country," speaking sarcastically of the "incontrovertible evidence of a peer, who concealed his shame and his infamy under the guise of his anonymous signature." Soon he grew more unhinged. "Oh, this nameless, shameless, fameless peer! . . . —who sacrificed honor, integrity, and principle, for the political purpose of his party, and left upon record a crime the dishonor of which the waters of the Boyne can never wash away from his escutcheon!" With his mention of the 1690 battle that was a symbol of Protestant conquest and hegemony, the priest revealed his propensity to make use of the language of national grievance to attack his foes. Following the appearance of Shrewsbury's letter, Father McDermott continued, "the whole horde of my calumniators renewed the attack with increased virulence and vigor—they flung the filth of the Orange kennel upon me—the bloodhounds were let loose upon me—they tore my flesh, and lapped my blood—while those who should have been silent, or should have licked my sores, were louder in their yelping, and more ferocious in their ravening." In accusing his adversaries of pelting him with excrement and sending dogs to tear and devour at his flesh, the priest showed his penchant for employing bizarre overstatement. "I could almost weep to see" Lord Shrewsbury "falling down at the feet of the British minister, and licking his stingy hand with the fawning and cringing servility of a lap dog, while he offered the whole Irish Catholic Church as a holocaust to his caprice and his policy," he wrote. By calling his accuser a wicked, groveling beast intent on the annihilation of the Church in Ireland, the priest made clear that he saw him as something less than fully human.

On the evidence of both this letter and the earlier one, Father McDermott was fully capable of delivering a line that linked Major Mahon with Ireland's great Protestant antagonist and questioned why such a figure thus remained among the living. It is little wonder, then, that Bishop Browne now emerged as the public voice of the tenants of the Mahon estate.

And they were badly in need of defenders. Even while the public controversy swirled around the case, John Ross Mahon didn't hesitate to move forward with his plan for clearing vast tracts of the property. Assisted by the additional police forces the land agent had requested from Dublin Castle, the estate staff was able to safely deliver roughly three hundred ejectment processes—targeting some fifteen hundred people—in the first few weeks of January 1848. Included in the effort were one hundred families in the three townlands nearest to the murder site: Doorty (where "forty policemen attended the bailiffs"), Cornashina, and Leitrim. "We have had a peak number of ejectments served on the Strokestown estate," Ross Mahon wrote to Marcus McClausland on January 18, claiming that the action had been successful in convincing some to produce rent. He noted that no tenants had appeared in court to challenge ejectment processes. "In no case was any defense taken, which seems very extraordinary as it certainly does not arise from any good disposition," he wrote. With the approval of Henry Sandford Pakenham Mahon, Major Mahon's son-in-law and heir, Ross Mahon continued to remove tenants without resorting to formal evictions, now offering "1 pound or 30 shillings on giving up possession." As Ross Mahon told his under agent Thomas Roberts, "In all cases the walls of the house [must be] *completely leveled* before money is paid," and the cleared land must be monitored to prevent the return of "either persons who have surrendered or others from squatting."

But few were willing to leave. Scores of petitions and memorials were received in the estate office from tenants under ejectment. Likely written with the help of a local priest or teacher, the statements were composed in formal, respectful tones, promising that the memorialist would pay rent if just given a little more time and begging to be spared from a final visit from the eviction troops. With titles like "The Humble Petition of Widow Flanagan, Church Street," these impassioned calls for mercy were full of apocalyptic fears of being thrown "on the mercy of a . . . world of calamity and destitution in this inclement season of the year," in the words of George Carton's memorial. Of particular interest to an unmoved Ross Mahon were the pleas that came pouring in from Doorty, Cornashina, and Leitrim. In one, seven families from Cornashina expressed the fear that they were being punished for "the act of the cruel murderer that took away the life of their landlord." They swore that they were "innocent of the deed by act or knowledge," and beseeched "for the Lord's sake that the act of such savage wretches will not be the means of casting them and their large families to perish houseless by the ditch in a cold and severe winter."

Pakenham Mahon and Major Mahon's widow had already specifically approved the eviction of "all the tenants on Doorty and the lands adjoining"—in clear retaliation for the murder and the conspiracy that supported it. "They deserve no consideration," Ross Mahon affirmed. But after receiving the memorials, the land agent came up with another plan. He mailed several of them to the landlord and wondered whether he would "approve of the tenants who are anxious to stay being informed that they will be allowed to do so if the murderers are surrendered. I do not think it would have effect but it is possible it might." With the investigation into the crime stalled for months, Pakenham Mahon agreed to the idea. On February 7 Ross Mahon told Roberts that the landlord "is quite willing to retain them as tenants in the event of their coming forward and bringing the murderers to justice and actually convicting the perpetrators at the next assizes."

The results were immediate. By the middle of February, police and military forces were descending upon the Four Mile House area again, sweeping up several suspects, a few of whom had been caught up in earlier sweeps. According to Ross Mahon's business partner, Robert Guinness, the arrests were based on the testimony of a Doorty tenant he named as Enews Salt Galt. (The 1843 estate rent book listed an "Elias Salts" as holding property within Doorty.) It is likely that Galt/Salts's evidence corroborated what authorities had already been hearing from at least one other Mahon tenant. A herd named Patrick Flynn, who held four and a half acres in a townland other than Doorty, had been speaking to Four Mile House's constable, William O'Brien, from at least February 1, many days before the eviction threat was issued. Flynn had told police that he witnessed the fatal shot being fired.

With the help of these declarations, three men were arrested and marched before the authorities on February 17: James Commins, "a dead shot," said to be the assassin; Patrick Hasty, a carpenter who was "notorious for keeping a shebeen house, where every description of villainy was concocted"; and Patrick Doyle, a herd's son. On the following day, a number of alleged accessories to the crime were lodged in prison. Over the next few weeks, three of this group would reflect on their circumstances and turn on Hasty and Commins, becoming "approvers," the term for those who confess involvement in a felony and agree to give evidence against their accomplices. Patrick Rigney, the old soldier in horrible health who was earlier detained after a woman claimed he was one of the assassins, told police he had been recruited by Hasty to commit the crime but had failed to carry it out. A thirty-two-year-old man named John Brennan, a peripheral actor in the plot whom an official described as "dangerously ill of typhus fever," described conversations he had with Hasty and Commins about the murder. But Patrick Doyle, one of the accused, provided the most potentially damning evidence. When he offered to testify on behalf of the Crown, Robert Guinness exulted that "there is no doubt of a conviction." Yet Doyle, suffering gravely from fever, never appeared in court. He died in the Roscommon jail, after reputedly declaring that everyone he had implicated in the plot was innocent of all charges.

During their first weeks in confinement, Hasty and Commins gained an understanding of the path before them. On February 26 one of the assassins of Reverend John Lloyd, the landlord and Protestant parson killed three weeks after Major Mahon, was tried and convicted of discharging "a pistol loaded with ball" into the clergyman. Partially on the testimony of two eyewitnesses, including Reverend Lloyd's coachman, the killer was convicted and sentenced to death. No amount of special pleading—in a memorial to the lord lieutenant he argued that he merely was present during the murder—prevented Reverend Lloyd's killer from swinging from the gallows.

Into March, police continued to comb through the Four Mile House townlands looking for more conspirators to the Mahon shooting. A young man named Patrick Hunt, whose father possessed five acres in the Doorty rundale village, came forward to offer details corroborating aspects of eyewitness Patrick Flynn's story. Hunt said he had met Hasty and Commins near the murder scene on the night of November 2. But when he returned home after his talk with the authorities—who did not take a sworn "information"—his father packed up his belongings and sent him to Manchester, England, seemingly to avoid retaliation that the murder gang—not named in police documents as the Molly Maguires—was sure to mete out to informers. By the third week of the month, law enforcement was focusing its search on John Hester, Patrick Hasty's servant boy, and Michael Gardiner, alleged to be one of the central conspirators. John Ross Mahon even participated in the chase. "Mr. [M. B.] Bermingham [the Strokestown magistrate] and I were in pursuit of them with the military and police during the whole of Wednesday night till six o'clock in the morning but were not successful," he wrote to Pakenham Mahon. "The police of Four Mile House took them on Thursday." Hester was found hiding in a smith's forge; Gardiner was concealed in a home with a locked padlock on the outside of the door, which was broken down by Constable O'Brien.

In a significant boost to the case, Hester, who had earlier claimed to authorities that his employer was innocent, agreed to testify against the conspirators, consenting to describe meetings in Hasty's residence during which the gang discussed the crime. But Gardiner, who was "ill of typhus fever," according to a police report, refused to cooperate, making him the third defendant in the case. He was imprisoned (with the approvers Patrick Rigney and John Brennan) in the Strokestown bridewell, where Dr. Terence Shanley was assigned to supervise the restoration of his health. "Gardiner is ill or pretends to be so and has not told anything," wrote Ross Mahon to Pakenham Mahon. The land agent was hoping that Dr. Shanley, with his intimate access to a criminal dependent on his care, would provide the police with important additional information about the plot. But despite public statements abhorring the murder and praising Major Mahon's benevolence, the doctor was curiously reluctant to assist the prosecution. "We find we can put no confidence whatever in Shanley," wrote a frustrated Ross Mahon. "He either knows more than he will tell or else he pretends to know more than he does. He told Mr. Bermingham that Gardiner told him everything, but he refuses to tell what Gardiner said—nor would he even put us in the way of taking Gardiner [as a Crown witness], although we have reason to think he could have done so—altogether his conduct has been so extraordinary that we do not know what to make of him." As a result, the doctor seemed to fall out of favor with Major Mahon's defenders. When he requested the use of a local home for a new temporary fever hospital, Ross Mahon coldly responded that he could not "think of any house in our possession suitable . . . and therefore suppose the best thing to do is repair the old one although its situation is very objectionable. The rent I presume will be the same as was charged during the major's lifetime."

It was little noted in the wake of the arrests that the alleged conspirators and their accusers all hailed from the vicinity around Four Mile House, which meant that they were not resident within the boundaries of Father McDermott's parish and were thus immune from his Sunday (or Monday) perorations. Ross Mahon was not troubled by this development. Nor was he troubled by his failure to find any other evidence against the priest. He still hoped for what he called "a legal enquiry" to be conducted into the priest's behavior. As he told Pakenham Mahon, "If the fact was not proved in such a way to convict Mr. McDermott, no doubt enough would come out to shew reasonable persons that the denunciation did take place."

CHAPTER 12

Summum Jus, Summa Injuria

❧

BY THIS TIME, THE pope had weighed in. Or at least he seemed to.

On February 5, 1848, the *Dublin Evening Post* published an English translation of a leaked copy of a letter from Cardinal Giacomo F. Fransoni, prefect of Pope Pius IX's Propaganda Office, to three of the four Irish archbishops. Representing the first act in the pope's investigation, the Latin-language letter sought responses to "the reports which have reached us relative to the murders which we are informed are so frequent, and by reason of which the clergy have been stigmatised, and some of them charged with imprudence, and as giving indirect provocation from the pulpit—or, at least, extenuating the guilt of these murders." It was true that "some" clergymen were "charged with imprudence," but only one priest in Ireland was accused of "giving indirect provocation from the pulpit" resulting in a specific murder: Father McDermott. Cardinal Fransoni's letter noted that the Sacred Congregation "cannot bring itself to believe . . . that ecclesiastics have ceased to recollect that they are ministers of peace, dispensers of the mysteries of God—men who should not involve themselves in worldly concerns—in a word, men who should abhor blood and vengeance." Priests should not involve themselves in "worldly concerns"—oddly equated in this passage with "blood and vengeance"—during the height of a famine? The letter concluded by asking for "satisfactory and speedy information concerning all these matters" and admonishing the clergy to avoid any actions that might bring their holy mission "into disrepute."

Scholar James P. Flint asserts that the pope and Propaganda gave little credit to Lord Minto's representations and were merely endeavoring to gather some firm denials for the record. If this were the case, the Holy See had an odd way of showing its skepticism. The English newspapers interpreted the letter as the Vatican's final statement on the matter and an obvious affirmation by the Supreme Pontiff's watchdog agency that the charges against Father McDermott and a few others had merit. "All this may be furiously denied and denounced as Protestant Scandal when Lord Farnham is the accuser; or still more vindictively branded as servile and Saxon malignity when repeated by the Catholic Earl of Shrewsbury," wrote the *Daily News*. "But nonsense of this description will not do when the question comes from that ecclesiastical tribunal which never publicly impugns the conduct of dignitaries of its own church on light or casual suggestions." Lord Minto, who was irritated that the letter wasn't signed by the pope himself, was widely recognized for his success. In Ireland, Lord Clarendon penned a letter of congratulations, and John Mitchel, the militant Young Irelander, delivered his contempt, saying that Lord Minto was trying to turn the pope into the "head of the Constabulary department in Ireland." Even Lord Shrewsbury, whose letter to Archbishop MacHale was translated and given to the pope, garnered some credit in the newspapers, with the *Tablet* saying that "the praise or ill-fame of the achievement" belonged as much to Shrewsbury as to Minto.

The vast majority of Irish bishops and priests were outraged, and many wrote letters and drew up petitions pleading their case to the Vatican. "[T]he yellings of the poor, on the roads, in the streets of our towns, at all our houses . . . the heart-rending scenes in the houses of the poor, lying sick of fever, starvation, of inanition and want, are the daily prospects of our clergy," wrote an elderly bishop to Rome. "[A]nd alas if we dare describe these afflictions of our people and our own agonies at their heart-rending sufferings, we are stamped by our enemies of the English press and the leading Members of Parliament as surplissed ruffians and instigators of the murder of the landed gentry and the exterminators of the people!" The three archbishops to whom the letter was addressed sent lengthy responses seeking to dissuade the Vatican from going forward with its inquiry. In his fiery thirty-one-page official response, Archbishop Michael Slattery of Cashel, an ally of MacHale, wrote that the government was seeking to punish priests because they were "the only persons to stand forward against the oppression of the people." Even the two moderate pro-government archbishops—William Crolly of Armagh and Daniel Murray of Dublin—dismissed the allegations as overheated. Crolly told Rome that only a tiny few of the twenty-seven hundred priests in Ireland had been accused of impropriety. They had denied making the statements attributed to them and challenged their accusers to bring actions in court. Since no actions were pending, the charges were obviously unjust. While he noted it was *nimis verj* (too true) that many priests had unwisely mixed themselves up in political activities—a suggestion that outraged MacHale and his allies—Crolly said that landlord assassinations were attributable to "the harshness of the owners of the soil, and the vengeance of their evicted tenants."

Lord John Russell's government took quick advantage of the warm feelings in England toward Pope Pius IX to introduce a bill establishing diplomatic relations with the Holy See. With an amendment attached by the Earl of Eglintoun in the House of Lords forbidding the pope's envoy from being a priest—he was worried about the embassy becoming "a nucleus for Jesuits"—the legislation began to make its way through Parliament.

Overjoyed at the pope's entrance into his side of the debate, Lord Shrewsbury issued his second letter to Archbishop MacHale, a bitter essay taking the prelate to task for substituting "invective for argument, . . . reckless assertion for truth." The "pious fool" even equated himself to a persecuted Jesus Christ, comparing MacHale's dishonesty with that of Pontius Pilate, who by "false testimony" conspired "the ruin of an innocent man." Shrewsbury responded to MacHale's points at tedious length, reserving most of his anger for the archbishop's involvement in the Repeal Association, which he called "a political confederacy working incessantly against the best interests of the whole empire." Near the end of the letter, he turned to the archbishop's "severest" charge—that he had been "a scandalous calumniator of Father McDermott." Shrewsbury said he "never asserted anything against Father McDermott," but only asked for an examination into his behavior because "there was not a reasoning man in the three kingdoms who doubted of the formal denunciation of Major Mahon from the altar." Now after the publication of Bishop Browne's letter—"a letter which I rejoice to have been the means of producing"—and the declaration from the twenty-eight Strokestown parishioners, Shrewsbury was comfortable in delivering his verdict: "Father McDermott is fully acquitted of the charge," he wrote. Yet he wasn't ready to exonerate the priest of all wrongdoing. He was troubled by the clash at the August 28, 1847, relief committee meeting between the priest and Major Mahon. He taunted MacHale, "I wish it were as easy to obliterate the impression made by the scene at the relief committee. . . . But this has not yet been attempted."

Even this was too much for the Dove of Elphin, who responded to Lord Shrewsbury's baiting by delivering his first caustic, even militant, letter in the debate. He focused on the August 28 confrontation, noting that he had previously sent a private letter to Shrewsbury detailing "the insulting provocations offered to Father

McDermott by the late Major Mahon" during the relief committee meeting. Bishop Browne said that Major Mahon's language "should prevent in every disinterested mind the expression of any feeling of surprise at the tone and temper of Father McDermott's words or correspondence on the occasion referred to." But the bishop failed to describe the "insulting provocations." According to Major Mahon's account, the priest lost his temper when the landlord asked a seemingly innocuous question about the revision of the relief lists. The priest had interpreted these queries as a "side wind" attack.

But Bishop Browne gave another reason for Father McDermott's anger—which he wisely did not deny—at the relief committee meeting, as indeed Major Mahon did in his account: the evictions. "If any honest Englishman were cognizant of the awful circumstances in which the Rev. Mr. McDermott was at the period alluded to placed, he would, instead of censure for perhaps an unguarded word, deeply sympathise with him, and feel astonished, that under the aggravated insults offered to him, he exhibited such forbearance," he wrote of "the terrific scenes of desolation that were exhibited in the vicinity of Strokestown, the heart-rending evictions of the famished emaciated poor." Bishop Browne said that if any Catholic cleric condoned the murder of a landlord, he would "justly deserve the execration of all honest men." But if it was a crime to sympathize with the plight of the poor and "remind their oppressors of their sacred obligations, I for one plead guilty to the charge." He then asked, "Can we every day behold scenes that would disgrace a Nero or Caligula present themselves to our view without any endeavor to throw the sacred shield of the Gospel over the dying victims, and avert by every means that religion sanctions the deadly arrows that are daily and hourly aimed at the poor of God by inhuman and unfeeling oppressors?"

Instead of acting as a sectarian combatant on behalf of the people, like Father McDermott with his talk of the bloody waters of the Boyne, Bishop Browne saw himself as a shield-wielding *protector* of the poor, fending off assaults from a landlord whose crimes he equated with two *Roman* leaders. In fact, the bishop's hyperbolic choice of historical analogy sent a deliberate message to those who chose to decipher it. Both tyrants perished as a result of uprisings against their rule, their deaths caused by nothing other than their own cruelty, corruption, and depravity. Nero committed suicide before a plot could depose him. Caligula was assassinated in his imperial palace, stabbed to death by his own praetorian guards. To Bishop Browne's mind, Major Mahon was worse than Nero and Caligula, and *he* alone was responsible for his own demise.

While the bishop was defending the right of the local clergy to advocate for the poor of the Mahon estate, the vice-guardians of the Roscommon Union were finally able to offer relief to some of those who couldn't be admitted into the workhouse. In late January 1848, nearly six months after the closure of the soup kitchens, the government issued the sealed order permitting the distribution of outdoor relief to the non–able-bodied—that is, the aged, infirm, and widows with two or more legitimate children. The funds required to begin the task had been provided by two sources: the private British Relief Association, which offered another 300-pound grant that was distributed through the Treasury, and Captain Henry Evans, the temporary inspector responsible for overseeing workhouse activities, who provided 100 pounds and twenty tons of Indian meal. Of Captain Evans's contribution, the vice-guardians merely wrote that they had "received, through Captain Evans," the money and the food. It was likely that the government employee, who had been in residence in Roscommon for nearly three months, had given a personal donation, performing a quiet act of charity in violation of regulations, that surely saved lives.

In the week ending February 5, it was recorded that 2,092 non–able-bodied persons had been provided with uncooked Indian meal distributed from several locations throughout the union. At the same time, the vice-guardians succeeded in opening an auxiliary workhouse structure for girls, a project started by Captain Evans in late December with British Relief Association funds. The added space allowed the vice-guardians to permit 221 additional paupers to enter the workhouse, which now housed more than 1,400 people. But with outdoor relief now available to some applicants, a few of the inmates leaped over the wall, preferring the possibility of receiving Indian meal (perhaps from a family member) to the reality of life in the pestilential facility. "Those parties have been discovered and punished," wrote the vice-guardians. They began a project to build a higher outer barrier.

As capacity improved and more depots opened, the numbers receiving outdoor relief increased throughout the month of February and into March. By the week ending March 18, some 9,424 non–able-bodied people were receiving food, more than five times the amount receiving indoor relief in the workhouse. During the same week the government issued the order permitting the vice-guardians to begin offering outdoor relief to the able-bodied poor. Seven months after the closure of the soup kitchens, the amended Poor Law was finally in operation in the Roscommon Union. The directive, however, came with two instructions that sought to limit the distribution of such aid.

First, the vice-guardians were commanded to employ the able-bodied for eight hours a day on stone-breaking crews. The work was intended to be "as repulsive as possible consistent with humanity" so that the "paupers would rather do the work than 'starve,' but that they should rather employ themselves in doing any other kind of work elsewhere, and that it would not interfere with private enterprise or be a kind of work which otherwise would necessarily be performed by independent laborers." Second, the vice-guardians were told to discharge the non–able-bodied—or "impotent poor"—from the workhouse, placing them on the outdoor relief rolls. The plan was to open up as many as eight hundred spots to be reserved for the able-bodied. Since outdoor relief could not be legally offered if room remained available in the workhouse, these vacancies would allow the vice-guardians to subject able-bodied individuals to the "workhouse test." Their poverty would be gauged by testing whether they would submit to the horrors of the squalid facility or endeavor to scour the countryside for private employment.

In the first instance, Captain Evans balked at the idea of forcing the able-bodied to break stones all day. He begged the relief commissioners in Dublin to waive the requirement, arguing that "such a system would be ruinous to this Union, deeply involved in debt as it is." He noted that "in order to carry out the project of employing paupers in the manner alluded to, it would be necessary to have a large staff of overseers with high salaries to superintend the works. This would entail an increased expenditure on the resources of the Union, whilst the numbers who would flock to those works, in order to obtain the outdoor relief, would be enormous, and the expense of supporting which would finally swamp the funds of the Union."

The relief commissioners responded that they would "on no account omit from their order the condition requiring labor from the able-bodied." They added that "if such a system be properly organized and judiciously superintended, it will result in repelling and not attracting, as you anticipate, application for relief, and be a means of economizing the expenditure in outdoor relief." In other words, the paupers would find private employment if the work were really unsavory. Captain Evans responded by changing the nature of his objection. He said he opposed the work requirement because stone-breaking *would* attract paupers, causing them to neglect private employment, fostering indolence and "habits of dependence" on Poor Law largess. On March 22 the relief commissioners ended the discussion by declaring that they regarded observance of the labor requirement "to be a matter of utmost consequence wherever able-bodied persons are relieved out of the workhouse."

For unexplained reasons, Captain Evans, who was earlier described as "untiring" in his efforts by the vice-guardians, was now relieved of his duties, replaced by a new temporary inspector named Captain Henry Musters. On March 25 the new official wrote to the commissioners, "[T]he system of stone-breaking for the able-bodied will be at once adopted throughout the Union."

In the second instance the vice-guardians sought to comply with the order to begin expelling non–able-bodied poor out of the workhouse. On March 24 they wrote, "We have removed . . . all the aged capable of being removed, also all widows with children." In the same letter the vice-guardians spoke of the necessity of dismissing "all the boys and girls under 15 years," which they said would bring the workhouse "to a healthy state." But Captain Musters objected to the order that the workhouse be immediately opened to the able-bodied. He wanted to halt all new entries into the workhouse until the facility, which had again descended into filthiness, could be thoroughly cleaned. He blamed an increase in "fever and dysentery" on the recent admittance of several sick individuals and on a lack of clean clothing. "It appears that from want of clothing, there being none made at present, the paupers admitted into the house have been obliged to remain in their own clothes," he wrote. The relief commissioners approved a plan to close the workhouse to new entrants for a "short time" until the problems could be remedied.

The vice-guardians mentioned nothing to the relief commissioners during these months about that other limitation on the distribution of relief: the Quarter-Acre Clause forbidding all those holding plots that exceeded that size from receiving help. Reports from throughout Ireland described how many landlords were misinterpreting the law to clear their estates, often by telling their tenants that they were ineligible for aid without giving up all their land. But it didn't require a misinterpretation of the amended Poor Law to inspire landlords to resort to eviction. In the end, it was a more economical option than offering widespread employment (if not as economical as an assisted-emigration plan, which removed all present and future fiduciary responsibilities toward the removed tenants with one payment). A property cleared of its dying paupers could immediately increase its grain and cattle production (and its profits) while causing only a temporary increase in a landlord's rate bill: Outdoor relief was scheduled to continue only until the autumn harvest.

Public opinion in Ireland was outraged by increasing reports of mass evictions, and Lord John Russell again called for legislation protecting tenants from landlord cruelty. "The murders of poor cottier tenants are too horrible to bear, and if we put down assassins, we ought to put down the lynch law of the landlord," he wrote to Lord Clarendon in March. But Russell encountered the usual strong resistance from his cabinet. After all, wasn't the point of the government's relief policy to impel smallholders to give up their potato plots and become wage laborers requiring only a tiny parcel? Lord Palmerston told the cabinet in March that "it was useless to disguise the truth that any great improvement in the social system of Ireland must be founded upon an extensive change in the present state of agrarian occupation, and that this change necessarily implies a long continued and systematic ejectment of smallholders and of squatting cottiers." It wasn't surprising that the tenant-protection legislation that passed Parliament was pitifully weak. Adopted in May, its strongest component made it a misdemeanor for a landlord to commence destroying a cabin *while the family remained inside*.

With or without government restrictions, the number who received outdoor relief in such a desperate area as the Roscommon Union was bound to be high—it was reported by relief officials that evicted families from around Strokestown were "bivouacking in the hedges and ditches along the road between Longford and Roscommon in the most abject state of destitution and starvation." In the week ending April 15—by which time the stone-breaking jobs should have begun—8,846 non–able-bodied and 11,470 able-bodied paupers were served food outside of the workhouse, which, however, represented less than half of the 50,000 people who had been assisted in the Roscommon Union at the height of the Soup Kitchen Act. Captain Musters, for his part, urged the relieving officers assigned to distribute food to be as generous as the law allowed. He told them to offer "provisional" relief to anyone who didn't meet government qualifications—while "at the same [making] every inquiry to prevent imposition"—and pushed them to give the full supply to those who did. Shockingly, he discovered that some relieving officers were "in the habit of giving much less than the authorized allowance," he wrote.

But the vice-guardians were anxious about their ability to meet the costs of indoor and outdoor relief into the summer. While the rate collectors in the Roscommon Union were receiving more funds from the landlords than previously—518 pounds was collected over two weeks in March, more than five times the amount extracted in all of October 1847—the vice-guardians knew that it would be hard to maintain levels of distribution. In a letter to the relief commissioners, they worried that without additional grants and loans they would not be able to continue. The commissioners sternly responded by telling them that "your appointment . . . was not made for the purpose merely of reporting your difficulties, but of doing everything in your power to surmount them." They were told that "much may be accomplished . . . where energy and method are employed."

At least the potato harvest was expected to be healthy. A sound potato crop would allow outdoor relief to be phased out in the autumn as planned and usher in the final days of a horrible period in Irish history. On April 24, with the planting season nearly completed, Captain Musters reported, "From my own observation, as well as from inquires I have made from intelligent persons in different parts of this Union, I find that very great exertions are being used generally in putting down crops of all kinds, particularly potatoes." He predicted that if the harvest turned out well, "we may fairly presume . . . on nearly double the quantity of potatoes to last year's crop, should that root not be again attacked with disease, and the general opinion is that it will not."

While Lord Clarendon was worried that a strong harvest would maintain the "old system" of potato subsistence, he and many relief officials based in Ireland were growing more concerned about what would happen in the wake of another failure.

Bishop Browne's stirring February 11 letter, such an unexpected contribution from a churchman regularly described by contemporaries as "meek," was bound to inspire a swift response from the supporters of Major Mahon. But unlike the case against Father McDermott, the public attack launched against the bishop didn't focus on the sentiments he expressed or the way he expressed them. Instead he was singled out for the words he didn't write in his account of the "scenes that would disgrace a Nero or Caligula." It was a determined attempt to tarnish his moral authority and embarrass him into silence.

On February 18 Ross Mahon wrote a private letter to Henry Sandford Pakenham Mahon in London "about Bishop Browne's late letter in defense of Mr. McDermott and speaking harshly of the ejectments in the Strokestown estate." He told the young landlord how Bishop Browne's elderly father, Martin, and his brother, Patrick, middlemen on the Clonfad townland, had done exactly as Major Mahon had done: They had conducted mass evictions. They had done so after being spared from eviction themselves, he wrote. Patrick Browne "took advantage of my having the sheriff on the land and put every tenant out who had not paid up his rent—I do not find fault with him for doing this—but I mention it to shew that the bishop's brother adopted the same course we did . . . and that he was treated with greater leniency than he shewed his tenants." If Major Mahon was an "inhuman and unfeeling" oppressor, in Bishop Browne's words, so then were the Messrs. Browne.

And, implied Pakenham Mahon in a February 22 letter to the *Times*, if the Brownes weren't guilty of cruelty to their tenants— after all, they hadn't been attacked by the bishop—then neither was Major Mahon. He wrote that the bishop "alludes to what he is pleased to term 'the terrific scenes of desolation that were exhibited in the vicinity of Strokestown,' without again stating any of the circumstances regarding the late Major Mahon's property (which have lately been brought before the public in the statement of his agent, Mr. Ross Mahon)." Pakenham Mahon was referring to Ross Mahon's November 8 declaration about the intransigence of the tenants in the face of Major Mahon's many acts of generosity. Further, Patrick Browne "adopted the very same course that Major Mahon had been compelled to resort to in other cases." Yet Bishop Browne, who could "hardly ... have been ignorant of these facts," nonetheless "denounced the conduct of the late Major Mahon, for the exercise of his just rights, in terms of such unqualified harshness."

Patrick Browne, who remained on the property solely due to the charity of the new landlord, lent his support to Pakenham Mahon. In a letter published in the *Roscommon and Leitrim Gazette*, he denied nothing about his own behavior and praised Major Mahon in the most lavish of terms. He said that "up to the period of his death" the tenants in his parish of Aughrim "were neither *harassed, oppressed, or ejected*, although I know that the great majority of them owed from two to three years' rent, and some even more. I challenge *from any quarter* a contradiction to this statement." He said that "no person deserved more credit for his kindness or was less liable to aspersion" than Major Mahon. Surely fearing for the lives of himself and his family, Patrick Browne had forsaken his own brother, County Roscommon's senior-most Catholic, for a landlord who might still spare him and his elderly father (and other Mahon tenants) from eviction. In a subsequent private letter to Pakenham Mahon, Patrick Browne claimed that he had ejected only "a few insolvent squatters," who had since returned to their still-standing houses. He added, "I regret more than I can express that my brother Doctor Browne should have interfered."

Patrick Browne's public act of contrition—Ross Mahon called it "very satisfactory"—was followed by the inevitable bulletin from the sixteenth Earl of Shrewsbury. Employing evidence he had gathered from Ross Mahon and Pakenham Mahon—he was in regular contact with the latter—he delivered a pompous and belittling response to what he called Bishop Browne's "little teasing annoyance" of a letter. Even though he was "well assured that there was no venom in the sting" administered by the bishop, he decided to answer him "at the suggestion of others rather than for my own satisfaction." Regarding Strokestown's pastor, he questioned the bishop's judgment in "bringing Father McDermott again before the world, which I had hoped was beginning to forget him." Seeming to backtrack on his earlier claim that the priest had been "fully acquitted of the charge" of denunciation, he noted that some prominent Strokestown Catholics—including Dr. Shanley and his son and Mr. Bermingham, the magistrate—had failed to sign the parishioners' declaration. He then dismissed the bishop's allegation that Major Mahon had abused Father McDermott during the relief committee meeting as lacking evidence. "You *say* that Father McDermott was *insulted*, and therefore all but justified in this conduct, but you bring no witness to the fact." He lectured, "Remember, my lord, that it is no exculpation to listen to the unsupported evidence of the party accused, and then to sit down and write that you find him guiltless."

Of the scenes of desolation in Strokestown, Shrewsbury doubted that "your lordship has shown any greater discretion in your continued accusations of inhumanity against Major Mahon, for his 'heart-rending evictions of the famishing poor.'" He offered proof: the Roscommon magistrates' November 5 announcement that "no unnecessary harshness has been used" by the landlord, and Ross Mahon's November 8 statement that "in no case has there been any undue severity in taking possession." "[A]nd, thirdly, we have the evidence of Mr. Pakenham Mahon to show in what sense this expression of undue severity was to be interpreted; for it appears that Major Mahon had only acted towards some of his subtenants precisely in the same manner as your lordship's father and brother, joint tenants of a large farm on the Strokestown estate, had acted towards theirs, without subjecting them to any 'rebuke or admonition' either from your lordship or from Father McDermott."

Lord Shrewsbury then wondered whether it was "just or fair then to throw all manner of opprobrium on the memory of poor Major Mahon, for offenses which passed without remark when committed by Messrs. Browne?"

These passages reveal that the peer was serenely unconcerned about the "misery and difficulties" on the Mahon estate—the realities hidden behind the phrases "undue severity" and "unnecessary harshness"—since these matters were incidental to his argument. He was merely suggesting that the bishop and the priest deserved rebuke for selective denunciation, for targeting the landlord with a cynical precision that called their honesty into question. It was the logic of a debate tactician interested only in vanquishing his opponent before the newspaper-reading public.

Over the next several weeks, as Bishop Browne formulated his landmark reply, the public's attention veered away from the intricacies of the Strokestown saga and the perfidies of the Irish Catholic priesthood. Pope Pius IX, angered by the "unworthy use" of Cardinal Fransoni's letter by the jubilant English press, softened the admonition he had been preparing to send to his Irish archbishops and bishops. When the pope's letter, the result of his investigation into the controversy spurred by Father McDermott's alleged words, was released, it eschewed politics altogether and blandly called for the Irish clergy to remain faithful to their spiritual mission. It was largely ignored. The pope also ended debate over the British government's bill establishing diplomatic relations with the Holy See, which had passed through both houses of Parliament and received royal assent. Insulted by the prohibition against the Vatican's representative in London being an ecclesiastic, the Holy Father refused to bow before its dictates, making the legislation a dead letter. It would be another 66 years (1914) before formal diplomatic recognition was secured and 134 years (1982) before the Vatican sent an ambassador to the Court of St. James.

The public mind in Great Britain was instead focusing on a

series of revolts sweeping across Europe, deposing monarchs and proclaiming freedom. But it was the revolution in France—a largely bloodless overthrow of the king, resulting in the formation of a republic—that most resounded for nationalists of all persuasions in Ireland. Perhaps the time was ripe for the English monarch to loosen—or even release—her grip on the suffering island. But plans at unifying the Repeal Association and the Young Irelanders of the Irish Confederation over the issue were hampered by continuing divisions over the propriety of violence. On March 18 Timothy Francis Meagher, who famously said that he looked "upon the sword as a sacred weapon," wrote in the *Nation*, the Young Ireland organ, that "if the Government in Ireland insists upon being a government of dragoons and bombardiers, of detectives and light infantry—then up with the barricades and invoke the God of battles." In late March the government acted. In an attempt to decapitate the nascent revolutionary efforts, it arrested three Young Ireland leaders—Meagher "of the Sword"; William Smith O'Brien, a moderate who still hoped that a rebellion could be avoided; and the fiery John Mitchel, who was so impatient for an immediate rising that he had resigned from Young Ireland in disgust. It was the kind of state action that was bound to add fuel to the nationalist fire. By early April the government passed a new treason law—it called for the transportation of anyone who promoted "by open and advised speaking" the "intimidation of the Crown or of Parliament"—to further obstruct the insurrectionary effort.

On April 29, 1848, nearly two months after Lord Shrewsbury's letter and long enough for the empire's concentration to fixate on more truly revolutionary figures than Father McDermott, the *Freeman's Journal* published Bishop Browne's multipronged response to the Catholic peer. His presentation, which spread across large sections of two broadsheet pages, included three components. One was a list of 605 families from twenty-eight townlands, removed from the property or assisted to emigrate in the months prior to Major Mahon's death, obviously prepared with the assistance of Father

McDermott. The second was a sworn declaration from three members of the Strokestown Relief Committee stating that during the August 28 committee meeting Major Mahon "seemed" to suggest that Father McDermott had mismanaged relief funds. "From his observations and manner [Major Mahon] seemed to cast suspicion on the correctness of the accounts before him, and to impeach the character of the Very Rev. Michael McDermott," they wrote. Oddly, this was a direct contradiction of the description of the August 28 confrontation given by Major Mahon, who wrote that "we then proceeded to examine the accounts and look over the vouchers, etc., etc., and having found them correct, I expressed myself to that effect." Perhaps the relief committee members were conflating two separate episodes. In his November 17, 1847, letter to the prime minister, Lord Clarendon wrote that Major Mahon had "last year [that is, in 1846] discovered some irregularities in the management of the relief fund by the priest, who then vowed vengeance against him." Or perhaps the relief committee members' use of the word "seemed" indicated that Major Mahon had hinted at the improprieties so obliquely that he himself was not aware he had done so. The display concluded with the third component, a letter from Bishop Browne, the most morally serious statement yet delivered in the debate. If it had been published in place of Father McDermott's initial December 7 letter, the Mahon debate might have veered in a more favorable direction for those hoping to stem landlord cruelties.

The bishop, dropping the ferocious tone of his Nero and Caligula missive, began in a conciliatory, even obsequious manner, offering a series of self-consciously mild comments. He even apologized for the tone of his previous letter, saying that "in my zeal to defend an innocent and maligned priest against the imputations cast upon him by Lord Farnham, etc. (I do not wish, if I could help it, to classify a Shrewsbury with such anti-Catholic company), I may, in describing the scenes that occurred, have written too warmly or hastily if I compared them to those that occurred under a Nero or Caligula."

With his adversary softened up by his legendary meekness, Browne moved on to deliver a vigorous and precise denunciation of Major Mahon's Famine policies. First, he addressed the now principal defense of the landlord's actions: In conducting lawful evictions, he was simply exercising his property rights in a manner that was legal. "I never questioned the abstract or legal right of Major Mahon to evict or distrain his tenants if he thought proper," the bishop wrote. "That large and immense sums of rent and arrears of rent were due to him are undeniable facts; but the question is, what does the divine and natural law prescribe in a year of famine, pestilence, and desolation? If any landlord in such a period shall urge too strongly his legal claims, may we not say—*summum jus, summa injuria*?" The fullness of the law is the greatest injustice. In a truly Christ-like manner, Bishop Browne was demanding that the landlord's defenders recognize a greater controlling authority than the laws of the British state.

Next he addressed the clearances themselves. He conceded that some families on the Mahon estate—like those in the parish of Aughrim described by his brother's letter—had been spared and were justly able to speak warmly of the landlord. But many others had not been so fortunate. "If many on a large property are treated with great indulgence and lenity, whilst a very large portion are handed over to the tender mercy of bailiffs, agents, etc., may not such severities be exercised upon the latter as will account for the cruel and heartrending scenes of which I made mention in my former letter as having occurred in the vicinity of Strokestown?" he wrote. He then noted that he was sending along a catalogue of "605 families dispossessed of their lands and houses in the immediate vicinity of that town, including 84 widows, in all amounting to 3006 souls." He noted that "the names of all the heads of families are given. The townlands in which they resided, the number in family, and the exact number of souls dispossessed in each village."

But he didn't only denounce the eviction part of the Mahon campaign. His list of victims included those who had participated in the emigration plan, an aspect of Major Mahon's policies that had vanished from the debate. (Father McDermott's only mention of it was favorable—"It is not true that the exterminated tenants of the late Major Mahon have all been sent to America," he wrote in his December 7 letter.) Bishop Browne challenged not only the notion that the plan was charitable—as had been the widespread belief when the emigrants left Strokestown—but also the idea that the emigrants embarked on the journey freely and willingly. While it seems true that some paupers clamored for inclusion in the plan—Major Mahon mentioned the "numerous applications we have had for assistance on the score of emigration," in his April 14, 1847, letter—it is far less certain that they "went cheerfully," as Ross Mahon wrote in his November 8 statement.

"It may be said that many of the families specified [on the list] emigrated voluntarily to America; but there is, my lord, as you well know, a vast distinction between what is termed inhuman acts *voluntarium simpliciter et voluntarium secundum quid*," the bishop wrote.

> *A merchant in the perils of a storm reluctantly consents to consign his goods to the waves. Quere—If he had a free choice would he do so? A poor tenant in a year of famine and general dearth, finding it impossible, if passed, to pay his rent, or arrears of rent, with the fear of ejectment processes served upon him, listening to the menaces of bailiffs, agents, etc., consents, like the merchant in the storm, because he has no choice, to surrender his house, his home, and all, and abandon for ever the country of his affections. The landlord pays in such cases some small sum, merely sufficient for transporting to America the unfortunate individual and his family, who are thus thrown, if they escape the pestilential vapors of an emigrant ship, upon a foreign shore and penniless.*

But, yes, Bishop Browne was willing to concede that Major Mahon was a benevolent individual who intended the emigration plan altruistically. In fact, all this unpleasantness probably wasn't even his idea, he suggested, articulating what would eventually become the conventional wisdom of both the Strokestown community and the Mahon family. He wrote that "many, and even some of my own, clergy speak well of the goodness of heart of poor Major Mahon, and declare that if left to himself he would not proceed to, or perhaps have countenanced, the extreme measures of severity that were practiced in his name," Bishop Browne wrote, hinting that he knew of the prominence of Ross Mahon's role.

With his denunciation concluded, the bishop sought to dispense with Shrewsbury's most recent accusations. Of the evictions conducted by his brother on the Clonfad townland, he claimed that he was unaware of them since they had occurred in a townland far from the limits of his travels. Left unanswered was Shrewsbury's suggestion that Father McDermott knew about the Browne evictions, yet ignored them. Of the assertion that Dr. Shanley, the doctor's son, and Mr. Bermingham didn't sign the parishioners' declaration, the bishop wrote that the three "were not in the chapel on the days specified" and thus couldn't attest to the priest's behavior. Left unexplored was what Mr. Bermingham, a magistrate who was investigating the murder, and Dr. Shanley, a witness and a victim, believed about Father McDermott's alleged actions.

Then Bishop Browne presented Major Mahon's supporters with a challenge: Respond to the list of 605 families. "I adopt the fairest means by publishing the data, giving the names, etc., thus affording to Mr. Pakenham Mahon, and to all his friends, an opportunity of discussing the merits of each case, and for the sake of humanity will rejoice if any false statements have been made to me reflecting upon the deceased or his agents, the same may be corrected, and the truth elucidated." Bishop Browne hoped that "when the cloud and mist that obscured the truth from your lordship's view shall pass away," he would "make reparation to the wounded feelings of Father McDermott, and renounce all connexion and association with the hereditary defamers of our holy religion."

The *Freeman's Journal* would not wait for Pakenham Mahon's reply to pronounce its judgment. Its accompanying commentary, EXTERMINATION BY THOUSANDS! THE STROKESTOWN MASSACRE DEVELOPED, described Major Mahon as guilty of committing "legal assassinations" against a people who because of their "hereditary connection to the land" and "long-continued" occupancy "had a right to that consideration which the law of nature attaches to the settlement and growth of ancient tribes." Although the O'Connellite newspaper doesn't explicitly voice approval of the murder, it comes the closest of any other commentator during these months. "If three thousand or three hundred Englishmen were visited with such a scourge, because in a year of famine and desolation they were unable to pay their customary tribute, would not all the reason and intelligence, and humanity of England rise up in insurrection against such an enormity?"

CHAPTER 13

So Injudicious a Course

FIVE MONTHS AFTER ONE of the most infamous crimes in Irish history, three men were lodged in jail cells in Roscommon and Strokestown awaiting trial for their suspected roles in the murder of Major Denis Mahon: James Commins, who from the time of his arrest in February was alleged to have fired the fatal shot; Patrick Hasty, whose servant boy claimed his Four Mile House residence served as a sort of gang headquarters; and Michael Gardiner, a high-level plotter accused of being intimately involved in all aspects of the crime's execution. While the police continued to search for more conspirators, medical officials like Dr. Shanley fought to keep those in custody from dying. Both Hasty and Gardiner were reported as suffering from typhus fever, the condition that had already killed James Farrell (arrested in November 1847) and Patrick Doyle (arrested in February 1848). In Gardiner's case, he was "supplied with proper food and medicine and a nurse tender" in the Strokestown bridewell, making him among the best-cared-for victims of the Famine in the region. Indeed, the three were living a life of luxury compared with many of their neighbors.

The witnesses who had pledged to testify against them were also given special treatment. Three were placed in the Roscommon jail, another two in the Strokestown bridewell—it was widely understood in Ireland during the Famine that prison was more comfortable than the workhouse—where they were offered the same kind of intensive medical monitoring as the defendants. It appears that in the case of "Enews Salt Galt" (or "Elias Salts"), the Mahon tenant whose testimony led to the first arrests, attentive care in the Roscommon jail couldn't prevent him from succumbing. His name disappeared from the documentary record in April. But it wasn't only witnesses who were being attended to by the authorities. Their immediate family members, who were sure to face reprisals back in the townlands for their kinsmen's betrayals, were put in prison, too. In the Strokestown facility—"intended to accommodate only eight persons," wrote Ross Mahon—were the approvers Patrick Rigney (the old soldier) with four family members—wife, Mary (age sixty); sons Michael (seventeen) and John (fifteen); and daughter, Eleanor (twelve)—and John Brennan (the minor plotter) with five of his family—wife, Catherine, and four young children, ages two, five, seven, and nine. By early April, however, John Ross Mahon had grown concerned that the witnesses' testimonies were being influenced by their close proximity to the accused. On April 3 he wrote to Thomas Redington in Dublin Castle, warning that they "may have already been tampered with" and asked that they be moved to "Dublin or elsewhere, which I believe to be quite necessary for the ends of justice." Over the next few weeks, with the addition of another two witnesses (from the same family), thirty-one individuals from six families were transferred to Dublin's Ballybough prison to await a trial that was now scheduled for the summer assizes in July.

But the police had not yet given up on collecting evidence and making further arrests. "We have got a great deal of information in addition to what we had before respecting the murderers of Mahon," wrote Ross Mahon to Marcus McClausland. By the third week of the month, two more men had been taken into custody: Martin Brennan, who was alleged to have been present during the gang's deliberations, and John Cox, who was also reported to be a lesser participant. Like James Farrell and Patrick Doyle before him, John Cox appears to have perished from Famine-related maladies, prevented from cooperating with authorities or facing the judgment of a jury. Martin Brennan refused to speak with police, officially making him the fourth defendant in the case.

Perhaps the most vital testimony supplied by the approvers during these weeks—John Brennan gave a second statement on May 15—confirmed for police that Andrew Connor, the "well known character and leader" that they had been searching for from the beginning of the investigation, was a senior figure behind the murder conspiracy. But he continued to elude authorities. A stout forty-year-old with stooped head, round shoulders, "dark, rather sallow" complexion, and "dark inclined to gray" hair, he was said to be "very shrewd and cunning," able to read and write, "rather intelligent," with a "mild and easy" way of speaking. Measuring five feet, nine inches tall, he was known to wear a black frock, "generally" dark vests, cord breeches, and leggings. He most often wore a hat (that is, a head covering with a brim and crown), but sometimes donned a (flat, crown-less) cap. A native of the Graffoge townland in the Lisanuffy parish, which unlike the Four Mile House townlands had been subject to the Major Mahon's eviction and emigration plans prior to the landlord's death, Connor was indeed "well known" on the Mahon estate. He and his brothers were widely regarded as disruptive forces on the property, just as eager to target individuals of their class and background as those from the realm of the rich and pampered. In a piece of correspondence found in the Strokestown House archive by researcher Patrick Vesey, a tenant wrote to the landlord complaining about a group of men who attacked him and stole money he had earned from selling oats. Unable to identify his attackers, the man was certain that the Connor brothers, whose reputations clearly preceded them, were the organizers of the crime.

By the end of May the authorities were confident that they could at least prove that the four defendants in custody were members of a conspiracy to assassinate Major Mahon. Three approvers—Rigney, Hester, and Brennan—were prepared to provide firsthand testimony about gatherings during which the men plotted the act. But prosecutors were less assured of proving that any of the accused men had been present at the murder scene, which would enable them to the show the world that they had arrested the actual killers. Only one witness available to testify, the herd Patrick Flynn, claimed to have seen the fatal shot being fired (outside of the two survivors from the carriage, Dr. Shanley and Martin Flanagan, the coachman), and his testimony was anything but flawless. That meant it was imperative for police to secure the services of Patrick Hunt, the young resident of Doorty—described as living in the "next house to scene of murder"—who had been sent to England by his father after telling police about meeting Hasty and Commins near the murder site. Constable William O'Brien of Four Mile House, using his deep connections within the community, eventually succeeded in learning where the young man was hiding. On May 24 a magistrate asked Dublin Castle to pay for O'Brien—"a highly deserving and meritorious constable"—to travel to the English city of Manchester to try to secure "evidence of importance in this case, which is at present so deficient of it." In an almost pleading tone, the magistrate went on for eight pages about the grave importance of the case. O'Brien was permitted to make the journey to Manchester, and on June 2 he reported that he convinced Patrick Hunt to return to Ireland for the trial.

Still, the authorities lacked basic facts about the shooting, including one of the most basic: where it happened. In February, likely after the statements of "Enews Salt Galt" or "Elias Salts" and the eyewitness Patrick Flynn, police noted that "the informants state that the murder of Major Mahon took place on the townland of Leitrim and not on the townland of Doorty," as had been initially reported based on the statement of Dr. Shanley at the inquest. (Dr. Shanley had said the shot was fired when the carriage "nearly reached the bridge of Doorty," which, since the bridge was located at the boundary that marked the end of the Doorty townland, meant that the murder occurred in the Doorty townland.) Since Leitrim was the townland that followed Doorty on the road from Roscommon town toward Strokestown, the "informants" of O'Brien's statement had obviously stated that the shot was fired on the other side of the bridge. But the crack constable, who was repeatedly praised by his superiors in internal documents, wasn't willing to concede the point. On May 29 he swore before a magistrate that the landlord was murdered at "Doorty or Leitrim," in a telling example of how he was torn between the account of Dr. Shanley on one hand and his informants on the other. At the end of June, less than two weeks from the beginning of the trial, authorities were still scrambling to pinpoint the precise location. At the request of Ross Mahon, an unnamed Strokestown official wrote to Dublin Castle suggesting that someone from the capital "be sent down" to draw up a map of the scene. The official said that Ross Mahon requested "the Crown witnesses who are at present under protection in Dublin [be] brought down to the exact spot where any map may be taken to enable them to give accurate information at trial." From the surviving evidence, it isn't clear if the witnesses made the trip. In fact, it seems doubtful that the witnesses had their memories jogged.

With the defendants and their accusers now ready to appear in the courtroom, Ross Mahon communicated an air of confidence. "The evidence seems so clear that I think there can be no doubt of the murderers being convicted at the next assizes," he wrote to Marcus McClausland. D. H. Kelly, Major Mahon's cousin and a County Galway landlord, wasn't as assured of such a satisfying outcome. In a letter to Pakenham Mahon on June 11, he wrote that the "case will be botched as all the parties who are to conduct it (with the exception of the Attorney General) have not an ounce of sense amongst them." And even the attorney general would prove susceptible to the pernicious authority of the local Catholic dignitaries, Kelly alleged. He "is a thorough papist and will be privately influenced by the priests who through McDermott and the Bishop are all strong in favor of the assassins."

Unlike the other letters published during the controversy, Bishop George Browne's explosive presentation in the *Freeman's Journal* did not succeed in claiming the British public's attention, which was now fixated upon the rebellious activities of the Irish nationalists from the Young Ireland and Irish Confederation orbit. In the middle of May, William Smith O'Brien and Thomas Francis Meagher were tried for sedition on successive days—more than ten thousand men marching in formation escorted Smith O'Brien from his lodgings to the law courts—and released after the juries couldn't agree on verdicts. The government was determined that John Mitchel, who had been providing precise directions on how best to attack British soldiers in the pages of his *United Irishman*, should not get off so lightly. The Trinity College–educated ex-solicitor, the son of a Protestant minister, was eager for the same result. He hoped his sacrifice would inspire his countrymen into attacking the occupying power, resulting not in the Repeal of the Act of Union but in the creation of an Irish republic. "[F]or me, I abide my fate joyfully," he wrote from jail, one of the few Irishmen to be experiencing joy during these days, "for I know that whatever betide me my work is nearly done . . . the music my countrymen now love best to hear is the rattle of arms and the ring of the rifle." He was tried under the new Treason Felony Act, found guilty by a packed jury, and sentenced to fourteen years' transportation in Bermuda, a verdict he freely accepted. Lord Clarendon hoped that Mitchel's conviction would intimidate would-be revolutionaries into acquiescence.

Instead it outraged even moderates Repealers who found Mitchel's tactics and rhetoric unpalatable.

Indeed, the English press ignored the bishop's letter altogether. Even its explicit defense of Father McDermott didn't rouse the attention of the *Times*, which had devoted several commentaries to the priest's alleged actions and statements. (In its last, printed on February 8, the newspaper suggested that Father McDermott was the "author of" Major Mahon's "doom.") Nevertheless, Pakenham Mahon was preparing a response to what, after all, was a direct challenge from a distinguished County Roscommon personage. In asking the young landlord to discuss "the merits of each case" to correct "any false statements," Bishop Browne had presented Pakenham Mahon with a daunting task. Either he had to confirm the accuracy of the list, which would force him to argue that the removal (by whatever means) of 3,006 people from twenty-eight townlands during a multiyear food shortage did not constitute an act of "undue severity"; or he had to challenge it, which would require him to speak directly about particular families and their status, requiring him to touch upon the justice or injustice of the various ways of removal.

In the days after the publication of the letter, it appeared that Pakenham Mahon was preparing to follow the established pattern of responding to attacks from the Browne/McDermott axis. He would use technicalities and evasions to defend Major Mahon's policies while cataloguing the failings of the Catholic clerics with miss-no-trick specificity.

Ross Mahon was busy supplying Pakenham Mahon and Major Mahon's widow with evidence to make his case. Of the evictions, Ross Mahon asserted that everyone who had been expelled from the property received the benefit of the major's munificence. As he told Henrietta Mahon in a May 4 letter, "All those who have left the Strokestown estate have received gratuities." One problem with this statement is that Ross Mahon's own letters and documents indicate that only some tenants were recipients of gratuities, if by "gratuities" he meant the small sums that were distributed to those who left without a struggle. Another was the difficulty of suggesting that dislodging a starving family from its only shelter with a small sum of money—or a small quantity of crops—was anything like a humane act. Bishop Browne had already challenged this kind of reasoning when, in discussing the emigration plan, he wrote, "A merchant in the perils of a storm reluctantly consents to consign his goods to the waves. Quere—If he had a free choice would he do so? A poor tenant in a year of famine and general dearth . . . consents, like the merchant in the storm, because he has no choice."

Further, "by far the largest number of those named by the bishop have left the estate since it became Pakenham Mahons and we have their written applications entreating us to accept . . . surrender and to give them compensation for their houses," Ross Mahon told the widow. The most obvious problem here was that Ross Mahon's own documents contradict this statement. His 1847 letters are full of references to the townlands mentioned on the bishop's list. It even appears that he conducted pre–November 1847 clearances on several townlands that *weren't* included on the bishop's list. In his memorandum of the "lands on the Strokestown Estate . . . of which the late Major Mahon got possession" during the summer of 1847, he listed six townlands not singled out by the bishop. It also appears that the bishop may have underestimated the number of clearances on townlands that he did include on his list. For the townland of Cregga, Bishop Browne listed thirty-two families removed by emigration and eviction, accounting for a total of 155 "souls," including six widows (named Farrell, Casserly, Gannon, Beirne, Duffy, and Shaughnessy). Of the same townland, Ross Mahon recorded in his memo that fifteen families participated in the emigration plan (an estimated 75 people). The remaining twenty-one families (an estimated 105 people) were dislodged, making a total of thirty-six families, or 180 people, cleared from the property.

Still, it seems true that the bishop may have overstated the number of clearances on particular townlands in some instances.

A Protestant middleman, who was behind on his rent, wrote to Pakenham Mahon that "several persons who never held any land from the late Major Mahon or his predecessors" from two townlands nearest him were on the list.

Of the personal failings of Father McDermott and Bishop Browne, Ross Mahon also provided the landlord with fresh information. He sent Pakenham Mahon a copy of the April 29 *Freeman's Journal* with scrawled challenges to the bishop's assertions filling the margins. Next to the statement of the three relief committee members who claimed that Major Mahon had insulted Father McDermott by "seeming" to suggest that he had misused relief funds, he wrote, "No mention of the slightest ill-temper on Mr. McDermott's part." Next to the bishop's comment that he knew nothing about his brother's evictions because he was far from the area, he wrote, "The bishop was at Clonfad a few days before the *haberes* were executed—therefore must I think [he was] aware of a portion of the facts." (The bishop's list did not include the Brownes' townland of Clonfad.) Next to the bishop's assertion that the Shanleys and Mr. Bermingham failed to sign the parishioners' declaration because they weren't in the chapel during the priest's sermons, he wrote, "The sole cause of Mr. Bermingham not attending . . . is Mr. McDermott's violence." He added that "many" of those who signed the original declaration "were not in the chapel" and "some" were "afraid not . . . to sign it."

Ross Mahon had thus laid out how Pakenham Mahon's letter of response would be written. The landlord would defend the clearances by asserting that *every* targeted family had been given a gratuity, which would have meant that no formal evictions were conducted. He would debunk the list by pointing out a few mistaken names and wrongly included townlands. He would embarrass the bishop by suggesting that he was lying when he claimed to know nothing of his brother's evictions. And he would attack the priest by reasserting the prevalence of his "violence." The most potentially damaging counterattack might explore the newly aired charge

that Father McDermott had misused relief funds. Since three supporters of the priest were the first to raise the issue publicly—Lord
Clarendon's mention of the "irregularities" in the relief fund in his
November 17 letter did not migrate into the newspapers—it would
seem that they were confident the allegation was unfounded (or
at least could not be proven). In a May 6 letter to Thomas Roberts, Ross Mahon hinted that the charges had merit. "If all about
the subscriptions could be brought to light I am sure those would
be very extraordinary disclosures," he noted cryptically. Yet Ross
Mahon wasn't confident enough of the information, which he did
not repeat in other letters during this period, to press for its public
disclosure.

Pakenham Mahon's counterattack would be published at an
opportune time. With the killers' trial now approaching, he would
present a defense of Major Mahon before the murderers and their
defense counsels could besmirch his reputation in the courtroom.
His reasoned dismantling of the bishop would offer a stark contrast
to the pathetic pleadings of the conspirators who committed the
awful crime.

For his part, Lord Shrewsbury decided to end his stream of
letters, forgoing the bishop's invitation to "make reparation to the
wounded feelings of Father McDermott, and renounce all connexion and association with the hereditary defamers of our holy religion." He attempted to convince the young landlord to do likewise.
"I am very much disgusted with Bishop Browne's letter," Shrewsbury wrote, "and considered it so weak a case (remembering the
statement of Mr. Ross Mahon, which is before the public) that I
wrote to good Mr. Mahon to say that I did not think of carrying
on the controversy and that probably you would act likewise." He
continued, "I cannot conceive why it is that Bishop Browne should
persist in so injudicious a course. It only shews how illogical a mind
he has—I have ever heard him reputed as a very good, but a very
weak man, and I think he fully proves this opinion of him."

By the time Lord Shrewsbury sent this letter to the landlord,

Pakenham Mahon had already made his decision. He would allow the detailed condemnation of his father-in-law's actions—and powerful assault to his family's honor—to go unanswered. Lord Shrewsbury hailed the decision. "I really think you have judged right," he wrote in a subsequent letter, "seeing that the English papers have taken no notice of Bishop Browne's letter and the Irish are pretty well aware of what degree of authority his statements on this subject are entitled to." Whatever his reasoning, the young landlord's silence, so unusual in a controversy where all the combatants were eager to discourse at length, confirmed that Major Mahon's policies could no longer be reasonably defended. The eight-month battle of assertion and counter-assertion had ended with one side waving the white flag of surrender. Confronted with unmistakable evidence of the consequences of his family's actions, Pakenham Mahon chose to withdraw from the contest.

But the young landlord delivered another kind of response in the wake of the bishop's letter, one of much greater import. With his family's gestures of benevolence now condemned as cruelty, he decided to dispense with the final one. He announced to his land agent that he wanted to halt the practice of offering a pound or so to some tenants to induce them to surrender. It was clear that his motivation was more punitive than financial. Even though the family was cash-strapped—in April nearly all the furniture in Strokestown House was put up for auction—the ending of gratuities would not markedly lessen the cost of clearances. Instead of paying tenants for leaving, he would now be paying the sheriff for dislodging them. (The crowbar brigade responsible for "tumbling" the cabins would be compensated in either case.) At least one local dignitary was urging Pakenham Mahon to take such a step. The Protestant rector of Strokestown, Reverend Joseph Morton, had told him that the gratuities were "considered by the tenants as symptoms of weakness." The money encouraged them to make a "stronger stand against the payment of rent than ever" and cling "to their holdings with greater pertinacity than ever." Reverend Morton, whose name did not appear on the lists of Strokestown Relief Committee members sent to Dublin, was eager for the land to be cleared of Catholic paupers and "colonized" by Protestants from England and Scotland. Even though Ross Mahon had placed advertisements in English and Scottish newspapers seeking such colonizers—receiving little response—Reverend Morton complained to the landlord that the land agent hadn't taken up the effort "with sufficient warmth."

Ross Mahon, who had twice threatened to resign when Major Mahon resisted his clearance hopes, was placed in the unusual circumstance of opposing Pakenham Mahon's new policy. "I am sorry you cannot proceed further in giving gratuities to persons surrendering their holdings," he wrote on May 30. His reason was far from humanitarian: He believed that a plan composed solely of forcible evictions would cause "great annoyance" to the police, military, and estate forces required to complete it. Now many more outright evictions would be required "to make clearances of paupers to the effect necessary" to bring the estate to the order, he wrote. With more evictions set to be conducted over the next few months—Ross Mahon was securing *haberes* against those tenants who had been served ejectment processes in January—Pakenham Mahon's decision meant that the cruelties on the Mahon estate were about to grow even worse, if such a thing were possible.

CHAPTER 14

Conspire, Confederate, and Agree Together

AT 5:30 P.M. ON July 11, 1848, a grand jury filed into the court-room in Roscommon town and delivered true bills against Patrick Hasty, James Commins, Michael Gardiner, and Martin Brennan to the clerk.

Mr. Close, a Crown counsel, rose before the judge and asked that the prisoners be brought in for arraignment. The seventy-two-year-old judge, Baron Thomas Langlois Lefroy, called for the accused men to be retrieved from the jail.

In a short time the four were brought into the room and placed before the bar. All the newspaper correspondents agreed that they were *not* starving paupers. The *Dublin Evening Mail* said that they appeared "to be comfortable, decent-looking men." The *Freeman's Journal* said they apparently belonged to "the more comfortable class of peasantry." Hasty and Gardiner, it seemed, had recovered from typhus fever.

The indictment against them was then read. It charged that "they, devising and intending to kill and murder one Major Mahon, late of Strokestown House, on the 1st of October, in the eleventh year of the Queen's reign, at Strokestown, did amongst themselves and with others unknown, feloniously conspire, confederate, and agree together to murder the aforesaid Major Mahon." Included within the conspiracy charge were several overt acts committed following the October 1 agreement to further the group's aim of murdering Major Mahon. The four men were said to have solicited "large sums of money to be by them applied in and about the causing and procuring the said Denis Mahon to be killed." They attempted to persuade two people—the old solider Patrick Rigney and the servant boy John Hester—to commit the crime. Failing that, Michael Gardiner and Martin Brennan joined with two other men not in custody, named as Thomas Brennan and Andrew Connor, to "encourage and persuade" Hasty and Commins to make an attempt on the landlord's life. Offered "divers sums of money," Hasty and Commins agreed to commit the deed, accepting the funds (or promised funds) "as their hire, and reward." Commins, "being so encouraged, did feloniously kill and murder him." Patrick Hasty "was feloniously present and aiding."

The most significant aspect of the indictment was that it didn't explicitly charge anyone with murder. It instead alleged that a conspiracy was arranged for the purpose of killing Major Denis Mahon and that his death was just one of several actions of equal weight carried out in the name of that conspiracy. Indeed, British law didn't require the Crown to prove each of the overt acts; prosecutors merely had to show that an agreement had been reached among the gang members to commit the crime. It was a perfectly emblematic accusation to be made against tenants of Major Mahon, who had been accused of conspiring against the landlord since the arrival of the blight and even before. The landlord himself had believed that "many" of his tenants were involved in an organized scheme to subvert his administration of the property. The other noteworthy aspect of the indictment was its failure to mention Father McDermott, whom both Pakenham Mahon and Ross Mahon hoped to implicate in formal proceedings. Two days before the trial opened, D. H. Kelly had told the young landlord that mention of the priest would be avoided because of fears it would "impair" the prosecution. "Roscommon jurors are odd people," he wrote. In the end, the grave charge that Father McDermott had a hand in the murder—in the House of Lords, Lord Stanley had said he believed the priest was "legally . . . guilty of the blood of the murdered Major Mahon"— would go unexamined by a judicial tribunal.

In a "firm voice," all the newspapers noted, the four men pleaded "not guilty."

The trial was scheduled for the following morning. The prisoners were then removed.

At 9:30 A.M. on July 12, Baron Lefroy took his seat on the bench. Descended from a Flemish Protestant family from County Longford, Lefroy was one of the most respected jurists in Ireland. He had just served as one of two judges presiding over the trial of John Mitchel, who spent a portion of his docket speech decrying "packed" juries, "partisan" judges, and "perjured" sheriffs. Within five years, he would be elevated to the post of Lord Chief Justice of Ireland. But by the far the greatest achievement of his life had nothing to do with his legal career. As a twenty-year-old preparing to study law in England, "Tom" Lefroy had a brief flirtation with Jane Austen, who called him her "Irish friend." Smitten with his high spirits and sharp intelligence, Austen hoped the relationship would grow. "I rather expect to receive an offer from my friend in the course of the evening" of the next ball, she wrote to an acquaintance. But Lefroy's affluent family would not allow him to wed the daughter of a modest clergyman, and the most significant romance of the never-married novelist's life ended abruptly. "It is apparent that the episode multiplied itself again and again in her novels, embedded in the theme of thwarted love and loss of nerve," wrote one of her biographers. Lefroy, following the completion of his studies, mar-

ried an heiress, produced a large family, and became "something of
a pious bore," asserted the biographer.

The four prisoners were brought in the courtroom and placed
before the bar. Peter McKeogh, the attorney general, asked if they
wished to be tried together. Mr. Skelton, the accused men's lead
counsel, replied that they did not. "Then put forward Hasty, and let
the others stand by for the present," McKeogh said.

Hasty, a man of "about 47 years of age" who had received a sizable dowry of 200 to 300 pounds at his marriage, stood alone before
the court. A carpenter, "he kept, near the scene of the murder, a kind
of *sheebeen* house," one of the newspapers wrote, repeating a comment that had been made in the papers when he was first arrested
in February. He would be the first to be tried.

A "respectable" jury of eleven Catholics and one Protestant was
selected—Hasty's counsel challenged twenty potential jurors; the
Crown had issue with only two. McKeogh then addressed the body
"for a half an hour, setting forth and commenting on the different
counts in the indictment and substance of the evidence he proposed
producing," wrote the *Roscommon Journal*. None of the newspapers
recorded his comments.

He then called his first witness. Patrick Rigney, a sixty-year-
old veteran of the Twenty-first Regiment, had first been arrested
a few days after the murder, accused by a local woman of being
one of the two assassins. The story was deemed unreliable, and a
"feeble and emaciated" Rigney was released for lack of evidence.
Soon after he was rearrested in February, the fever-afflicted Rigney
agreed to cooperate with authorities. He spent seventy-three days
in the Strokestown bridewell—where Dr. Terence Shanley treated
him—before being transported with his fellow witnesses to Dublin's Ballybough prison in April.

He began his testimony by describing meeting Patrick Hasty
on Friday, October 1, 1847, a market day during which the
Strokestown town center would have been full of people. Hasty was
a longtime friend of his from the Four Mile House area; they knew

each well enough to have visited each other's homes. It was about noon when Hasty escorted Rigney into the upper room of a public house, "where there was a great number of people drinking in different companies." Hasty asked him within the hearing of "all the others present" if he would shoot Major Mahon. Rigney told the court that he agreed to commit the crime because he was "afraid."

A man from the group asked if he had any weapons. Rigney said he did not. The man said he would send a "case of pistols to Hasty's house in the morning."

On the following morning, Saturday, Rigney arrived at Hasty's home before breakfast. He was soon followed into the residence by two men—"a boy named Cox" and "a man named Gardiner" from the Doorty townland. Although Rigney said he did not "know his Christian name," he identified the prisoner Michael Gardiner when he was put forward in the courtroom. The boy named Cox handed two loaded horse pistols to Hasty, who then handed them to Rigney. Hasty instructed him "to go meet the major" on the nearby road upon which his carriage would soon be traveling. For reasons that he didn't explain to the court, Rigney didn't leave Hasty's home immediately. Instead he remained in the house for another half hour, during which time Major Mahon's carriage passed on the way to Roscommon town.

Blamed for missing his chance, Rigney was told by Hasty and Cox to follow the landlord to Roscommon and shoot him there. The old man put the horse pistols in his jacket, went home, and quit the conspiracy.

On the following morning, Sunday, Michael Gardiner arrived at Rigney's home and expressed disappointment with his failure of nerve. But Rigney refused to rescind his decision, leading Gardiner to suggest that he "would get plenty to do it" without his assistance. Rigney then offered the pistols to Gardiner, who told him to give them to Hasty. Rigney then went to Hasty's house, where he, too, refused to accept the weapons. Rigney returned home, and a half hour later, John Hester, "a boy that lived with Hasty," arrived to retrieve the pistols. Rigney said he told the servant boy that "his master was a great fool."

Thus ended Rigney's involvement in the plot.

The attorney general asked Rigney if he was offered money to shoot Major Mahon.

He said he wasn't.

He was asked if he knew James Commins.

Rigney said he didn't.

He was asked about Martin Brennan.

Rigney said he knew him but did not see him at Hasty's or the public house.

After McKeogh finished his direct examination, Mr. Skelton rose to begin his cross-examination.

He asked Rigney about his living circumstances.

Rigney said that he had been "ejected" from his land on the Mahon estate following the murder of the landlord. His wife, however, was now living in the house, which she had been allowed to retain. (In April Ross Mahon noted that Mrs. Rigney was lodged with her husband in the Strokestown bridewell.) He said he now had no way of earning a living.

Skelton asked about his initial statements to police.

Rigney confirmed that he "did not tell them a word of what he tells today." He said he kept quiet because he didn't think they would believe the testimony of a "poor" man.

Skelton asked why he changed his mind after he was arrested in February.

Rigney said he "could not help it" after being "rammed in the black hole" for a second day. He said even Skelton himself would "tell it" if rammed into the black hole.

Rigney apparently averted his eyes as he made these statements. Skelton asked if he was afraid to look at the jury or at counsel.

He said he wasn't.

Skelton wondered if he was as poor the second time he was

rammed into the black hole as the first time, in a clear attempt to show the jury that Rigney's testimony was coerced.

Rigney repeated that he refrained from telling the story because he was afraid he wouldn't be believed. Apparently flummoxed, he then changed his story, saying he decided to talk because "there was another man" who could testify against him.

With Rigney stumbling, Skelton moved on. He asked the old soldier why he agreed to shoot Major Mahon in the public house on Friday.

Rigney said he was "afraid of these [men] as much as of the gallows." He said they were "all connected"—the first hint that Rigney was dealing with members of a secret society—and that he didn't know any of them but Hasty.

But he wasn't afraid to refuse Michael Gardiner's demand to kill the major on Sunday?

Rigney said he wasn't. "There were not so many present as were in the public house."

Wasn't there a market day on Friday in Strokestown?

Yes.

Were police and magistrates present in town?

Yes. But he was "afraid they would kill him if he refused to kill the major."

But he was not scared of Gardiner on Sunday?

No.

Skelton inquired how he had supported himself prior to his arrest.

He said he "was begging, as many other people had to beg." He said it would be no harm if he begged all his life.

Skelton asked if he had heard of the reward.

Rigney heard about it "before his first arrest." He said he didn't notice the poster because he could neither read nor write. He said he "never heeded the reward, nor does he expect it."

Would he take it if offered?

Rigney said he did not know.

After Skelton finished with his questioning, Baron Lefroy asked Rigney for the name of his landlord.

The major, he said.

In response to a juror's question, Rigney said had had lived for "33 or 34" years on the Mahon property.

A juror asked about the identity of the men in the public house.

"They were all from about Kilglass," Rigney said, referring to the parish that included the notoriously rebellious townland of Bally-kilcline. "There were six, twelve, or forty in the room," he said, but since they were "going in and out" of the room, he couldn't keep an account of them.

Another juror asked if he knew who Patrick Hasty's landlord was.

Rigney said he didn't know but "it is not on Major Mahon's land he lived." For the first time, it was revealed that one of the accused was not a tenant of the murdered landlord.

The Crown's second witness was John Hester, the servant boy of Patrick Hasty. Like Rigney, he had denied any knowledge of the plot upon first being questioned by the authorities in the crime's immediate aftermath. He had been in custody since March when he was captured in a smith's forge by Four Mile House's energetic constable, William O'Brien. Like Rigney, he had been lodged in Dublin's Ballybough prison for the last three months.

Hester said that on Friday, October 1, during the market day in Strokestown, Hasty asked him if he knew Patrick Rigney and Thomas Brennan. Hester said he did. Hasty then asked if he would go with Rigney and Brennan to murder Major Mahon. Hester declined, saying he was a bad shot. He had "never fired a shot" and would be "no good," he said, according to the *Roscommon Journal* account of his testimony. His statement differs from Rigney's in that the old soldier gave no indication that others were to join him in shooting the major.

On Saturday, "the day after the market in Strokestown," Hester said that he saw Patrick Rigney leave Hasty's house with a "bulk" under his shirt, corroborating Rigney's testimony. Hester did not mention that Rigney had just failed in his "attempt" to murder Major Mahon. The servant boy then described how his master expressed anger over the failure to murder Major Mahon. Hasty said that he would shoot the landlord himself because "the rest were only humbugging" and were "not worth a damn." Andrew Connor, who was present in the house with Martin Brennan and Michael Gardiner, said that it would be too much to ask him to do it. Hasty said he would do it anyway.

On the following day, "the Sunday before the fair"—the Ballinasloe cattle and horse fair, held every year during the first week of October in eastern Galway—Hasty sent Hester to retrieve the weapons from Rigney's home, corroborating that portion of Rigney's account. Hester said he left the old soldier's house with the horse pistols, traveling through the "bottoms and Mr. Taaffe's land," where he met Thomas Brennan, who took the pistols. He saw another man with a gun, but he "could not distinguish who it was."

The servant boy next described how Andrew Connor, who had remained all evening at Hasty's house, asked him to travel to Roscommon town to purchase glossed powder and mixed duck shot at Farrell McDonnell's. With funds given to him by Connor, Hester made the trip to Roscommon, buying the items at another shop, Mr. Murray's. Hester didn't explain why he needed to purchase shot and powder if the horse pistols that were being passed between conspirators hadn't yet been fired.

Did Connor say what the items were to be used for? the attorney general asked.

Hester said that Connor did not.

After returning to Hasty's house from his mission, Hester said he gave the ammunition to Andrew Connor in the presence of Hasty. Connor then suggested that they send for whiskey. Hasty countered that they shouldn't do so since they had failed in their mission to kill the landlord. No matter, said Connor. We have "plenty of money," another statement revealing that Connor was the possessor of the funds needed to pay for the job.

Then Hester described a meeting held in Hasty's house where James Commins and Michael Gardiner were present. He said he did "not wait to hear anything said by them."

Hester's story next leaped forward a few weeks to the evening of the murder, November 2, leaving a large gap in the story of the development of the murder plot. He said he saw Michael Gardiner, James Commins, and Patrick Hasty leave Hasty's house at half past five, roughly thirty minutes before Major Mahon was shot. Hasty and Commins went "towards the ball alley," a few hundred yards from the murder scene, while Gardiner went toward his own house in another direction. Later in the evening, following the assassination, Hasty returned home, but Hester didn't know exactly when he arrived. Hasty didn't have a gun.

McKeogh asked when he was hired by Hasty.

In August 1847, Hester replied.

McKeogh asked if Hester knew James Commins before he worked with Hasty.

Yes.

Hester then added that Commins had told him during the conversation that "three men were watching the major in Raftery's old house" near the road "on the day" the landlord returned to Strokestown "from the fair."

The story, then, was that Major Mahon passed through Four Mile House on Saturday, October 2, evidently on his way to the Ballinasloe fair in County Galway. Patrick Rigney, who had been assigned to kill him, failed to meet him on the road. After the conclusion of fair week, the landlord returned home along the same route, and three men were waiting in Raftery's house to shoot him. For reasons that Hester does not mention, no shots were fired.

The defense began its cross-examination by asking Hester about his living circumstances.

He said he worked on the public works before being hired by

Hasty. He said he was employed by Hasty for five months. He was dismissed after Christmas for his "honesty." Laughter filled the courtroom at this last comment.

Why was he dismissed by Hasty?

Hester said that no "charge of dishonesty" had been made against him. He was let go because Hasty "thought it too much to be paying him wages when he could get men to work for their support." If nothing else, this testimony shows that the accused Patrick Hasty, one of the few in his community able to employ a servant under any circumstance, was not pining for entry into the workhouse.

Hester was asked about the reward.

He said he did not tell the story "for the reward," but if he got it, "he would not leave it after him."

He was asked about his initial statements during which he vouched for Hasty's innocence.

Hester described how Hasty's wife brought him before a solicitor to swear an alibi for her husband at the last assizes, promising him 1 pound for his services. He told the solicitor, a Mr. Henry French, that he could prove that Hasty was in his house when Major Mahon was shot. So: Not only had Hester made a false statement to police—already a blow to his credibility—but he had also received payment to do so.

The Crown's third witness to the conspiracy was John Brennan—it is unclear whether he was related to the prisoner Martin Brennan or the at-large conspirator Thomas Brennan—who, since he wasn't asked to participate in the killing, had a less intimate connection to the plot than either Rigney or Hester. Like his predecessors to the stand, John Brennan had denied any role in the murder when first detained by the authorities. Following his second arrest in February, the thirty-two-year-old, then described as "dangerously" ill with typhus fever, agreed to cooperate with the prosecution. He was imprisoned in the Strokestown bridewell with his wife and four children before being transferred with them to the Ballybough facility with the other witnesses and their families in April.

Brennan picked up the story "a few days after the October Fair of Ballinasloe." or during the second week of October following the two failed "attempts" on Major Mahon. Brennan had a conversation with Patrick Hasty in "his own garden," wherein Hasty described his efforts to organize the murder. Hasty told him he had sent Thomas Brennan and John Hester, along with an unnamed man to "give the signal," to commit the crime. This seemed to conflict with servant boy Hester's statement that he had refused to be "sent" to kill the major, telling Hasty that he was a poor shot.

Hasty then allegedly told Brennan that "he intended to get Pat Rigney's to shoot him" because Rigney was "a good shot." This statement seemed to suggest that the old soldier had not yet been approached to perform the deed, which would have contradicted both Rigney's and Hester's testimonies, which put Rigney's entire involvement prior to the Ballinasloe fair. But while the *Roscommon Weekly Messenger* and the *Freeman's Journal* quoted Hasty's line as "intended to get Rigney," the *Roscommon Journal* rendered it as "had Rigney employed to shoot Major Mahon," indicating that Rigney had already been contacted.

Brennan then jumped forward several weeks to the period following Major Mahon's death. He said that James Commins, whom he identified in the courtroom, admitted to him that he shot Major Mahon, with Patrick Hasty and Michael Gardiner present. For the first time, it was suggested that three men were at the murder scene. (In the first days after the crime, the police released descriptions of two men lurking about the area of the crime; at the inquest two days after the murder, Dr. Shanley and the coachman Martin Flanagan described an assassin in a ditch on the right-hand side of the road and another shooter "in the fields" whose pistol misfired; in the indictment, the Crown named an assassin [Commins] and a single accomplice [Hasty].)

Commins told Brennan that he killed the landlord with Patrick Doyle's gun.

Brennan said he asked Commins why he didn't leave the country.

Commins responded that he hadn't yet been paid for shooting the landlord. This, the first explicit statement of motive made during the trial, indicated that the alleged assassin was not inspired to action solely by anger at the injustice and cruelty of Major Mahon's policies. Instead he was a contract killer looking to earn some money. Commins told Brennan that Hasty had "got" (all three newspapers used this word) 12 pounds for the deed and was "not dividing it fairly with him." Hasty, then, was a recipient of the money and a *distributor* of it—a middleman, for lack of a better description, who was superior to the assassin Commins and subordinate to the ringleader Connor.

Commins also told Brennan that he didn't abscond because it "would be too public."

Brennan next told of meeting Commins at a public house in Strokestown on December 24, Christmas Eve, at a time when the major's murder was being heatedly discussed throughout the kingdom. A "strange" man came into the room and asked Commins to come out. Commins gave Brennan a shilling to pay for the drinks and told Brennan to follow him to the Widow Smyth's establishment, where he said he would get money from Andrew Connor for killing Major Mahon. Brennan followed Commins to Smyth's, where the two met Connor, Hasty, and Gardiner. All but Connor and Commins then left the room, leaving the two to conduct their business, another instance of Connor's superiority over the other conspirators (including Hasty).

Brennan said he did not witness an exchange of money between the assassin and the ringleader.

Soon they all left the Widow Smyth's. Brennan "went into a smith's house to kindle his pipe," while the others commenced the journey back to the Four Mile House area.

During the cross-examination Brennan was asked why he didn't tell the authorities this story when he was first questioned in the days after the November 2 murder.

He said he "did not know as much about it that time as he does now." This ignores the fact that he said his conversation with Hasty in his garden occurred "a few days after the October Fair of Ballinasloe."

Why did he make a statement after being arrested in February?

After spending fourteen days in jail, he decided to provide one because he heard "there were informations swore before he swore his."

Why didn't he offer the statement after first being arrested?

Because he "did not wish to leave" his "little family."

Did he know the amount of the reward?

No.

The Crown next called the only witness to the conspiracy who was not entwined in the plot. James Donnelly described being approached on the road by Michael Gardiner on the evening after the public house discussion in Strokestown on Friday, October 1. Gardiner told him about a "great consultation" among the gang to determine whether Major Mahon or John Ross Mahon should receive the assassin's fire. "Major Mahon was the proper person to be shot," Gardiner said a Michael O'Beirne insisted at the meeting. "Ross Mahon was only a servant, and if he did not do his duty another would." It was the first time in the trial that the landlord's estate policies were asserted as a motive for the crime, indicating that an umbrella organization angered at the clearances set the plot in motion.

Upon further questioning, Donnelly admitted he couldn't say whether the conversation with Gardiner happened in late September or early October. With the prosecution alleging that the conspiracy was formed on Friday, October 1, in the public house, objections were raised about the admissibility of Donnelly's testimony. Conceding the point, the attorney general said "he would not press the evidence," and the witness was withdrawn.

Although Donnelly didn't make the statement before the court, he had earlier told Crown prosecutors that Gardiner, whom he said had been "appointed collector to receive the money to get the murder committed," had solicited half a crown from him to pay the assassins.

The Crown then turned exclusively to the events of the evening of Tuesday, November 2, 1847. The first witness to take the stand during this final portion of the trial was Patrick Flynn, the tenant of Major Mahon's who claimed to see the shot being fired. It was his statements—along with evidence given by "Enews Salt Galt" or "Elias Salts," who had disappeared from the scene—that had led to the arrests of Hasty, Commins, and the late Patrick Doyle in February. Flynn was the first witness to the stand who didn't admit knowledge of the plot prior to November 2.

Since the Crown was not explicitly charging anyone with murder, Flynn's testimony was less vital to the prospects of conviction than it might have been otherwise. He was merely providing evi-

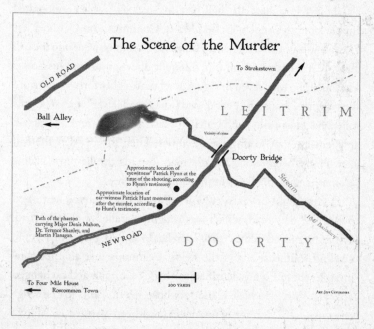

The Scene of the Murder

OLD ROAD

To Strokestown

Ball Alley

L E I T R I M

Vicinity of crime

Doorty Bridge

Stream

Approximate location of "eyewitness" Patrick Flynn at the time of the shooting, according to Flynn's testimony

Approximate location of ear-witness Patrick Hunt moments after the murder, according to Hunt's testimony

1841 Boundary

Path of the phaeton carrying Major Denis Mahon, Dr. Terence Shanley, and Martin Flanagan.

NEW ROAD

D O O R T Y

To Four Mile House
Roscommon Town

200 YARDS

ART: JEFF CUYUBAMBA

dence on just another event in an unfolding conspiracy that began in the public house in Strokestown on Friday, October 1. But it would be foolish to conclude that the prosecutors did not understand the vital importance of his account. (They had sent a policeman to Manchester to try to provide corroboration for portions of it.) Flynn alone could show the local community and the wider public that the true murderers had actually been caught. The integrity of any penalties meted out would largely rest on his reliability.

Flynn began by describing himself as a resident of Fortfield, which was located about a mile from the murder scene.

He was asked about the evening of November 2.

Flynn said he was "at a friend's home on the Elphin road" that night. He left to go "home to his father" when, after meeting his son on the road, he changed his course to "make up a rick of turf" that had become dislodged on a plot of his family's land in the Doorty townland.

On his way he spotted Commins and Hasty in the "ball alley" at "about five o'clock" or "half past five o'clock." This corroborated the servant boy's statement that Hasty, Commins, and Gardiner left Hasty's house at 5:30 P.M., and Hasty and Commins went into the ball alley while Gardiner went in a different direction toward his home. Flynn said he was "seven or eight" perches (roughly forty yards) from the two men. Apparently concealed from their view, Flynn saw Commins give Hasty a hat and watched Hasty hand Commins a cap, an apparent attempt to disguise identities. Then the two left the ball alley. Hasty "went along the old road towards Strokestown," while "Commins took the fields in the same direction."

Losing sight of Hasty, Flynn followed Commins as he turned toward the new road, which was roughly parallel to the old road. Commins moved across "forty perches" (or 220 yards) of terrain, traveling southeast across the fields. Commins met another conspirator, whom Flynn identified as Patrick Connor, and exchanged caps with him. (Patrick Connor, whose relationship to the ringleader Andrew Connor is unknown, had been arrested in March.

He, too, appears to have succumbed to Famine-related illness in the Roscommon jail.) Then Commins arrived at the "new road," crossed it, and "got inside a ditch very near where Major Mahon was shot" on the right side of the road.

The attorney general asked Flynn where he was concealed when he saw Commins go "inside" the ditch.

Flynn said that "when Commins got out on the road," he was "near the garden of Thady Hunt," according to the *Freeman's Journal*, on "the left hand side of the road." According to the *Roscommon Journal*, Flynn was "on the hill going in the direction of Doorty," close to the new road, "behind some sallies in Thady Hunt's garden." He had, then, traveled in a more southerly direction than Commins, arriving at a spot along the new road on a hill, looking onto a ditch at a lower elevation (a "hollow," he said) farther along the same road in the direction of Strokestown.

Flynn said he saw a second man "behind the wall where Commins went, but does not know who he was, but he had a hat on." Flynn did not explicitly identify the second man as Patrick Hasty or Michael Gardiner. But since Flynn said the man was wearing a hat, the implication was that it was Hasty, whom Flynn had just watched receive a hat from Commins in the ball alley.

He described the two men as positioned "beyond the second bridge, nearest to Strokestown," according to the *Freeman's Journal*. Contemporary historian Desmond Norton, who has studied the nineteenth-century ordnance maps and examined the topography of the vicinity, has written that there were two bridges along this stretch of the new road at the time of the crime. The first was located at the boundary of the townlands of Doorty and Leitrim. Dr. Shanley was speaking of this structure when he said at the inquest that the carriage had "nearly reached the bridge of Doorty" when the two assassins presented themselves. A second bridge was located more than four hundred yards farther up the road, "between the boundaries" of Leitrim and the next townland, Carrownalassan, Dr. Norton wrote. The scholar believes that Flynn was referring to this bridge in his testimony, which, since Flynn said the ditch was "beyond the second bridge," would have meant that the ditch was located within the boundaries of the Carrownalassan townland. Not only does this contradict Dr. Shanley's inquest testimony, it also contradicts Constable O'Brien's May 29 sworn declaration that the murder occurred at either "Doorty or Leitrim," a statement that the well-respected policeman surely did not make without careful consideration. For O'Brien, the question was whether Major Mahon was killed just before the Doorty Bridge in the Doorty townland or just after it in the Leitrim townland.

"In a short time," Flynn "saw a carriage come up with three persons none of whom he knew but Dr. Shanley." The vehicle passed near a settlement of homes in Doorty and "came in front" of Flynn in the sallows. The carriage then traveled down the hill and moved across a flat stretch toward the Doorty Bridge. Flynn said he "heard a shot from where the two men were behind the ditch."

Flynn's testimony, then, was that the two men at the scene were in the ditch when the murder was committed. He did not mention another shooter "in the fields" whose pistol misfired, which represented a conflict with the inquest testimony of Dr. Shanley. Further, he said he had *heard* a shot. Flynn was not claiming to have seen the shot being fired, nor was he explicitly identifying the assassin as James Commins.

Flynn said that Commins fled from the ditch and ran toward him, moving up the hill in his direction in Thady Hunt's garden, traveling along the section of the new road upon which Major Mahon's carriage had just passed. Commins "passed close by" him. He had "a pistol in his hand but no gun." After hiding his face for a brief moment, Flynn "looked up again" and "saw Commins going off through the fields."

He said the second man fled in a "different" direction.

Flynn was asked if he was able to view the actions of the men in the ditch prior to the carriage's arrival.

He responded that he "saw Commins and the man with him in the act of loading a gun." Again, he was stating that two men were in the ditch.

During cross-examination Flynn was asked how far he was from the murder scene.

Flynn said "there was a turn in the road in the place where he was hid." He said "he was two hundred yards from where the shot was fired, and still he knew Commins, because he saw him go into the place, and saw him run out of it after firing the shot, and he ran close by him." In other words, Flynn said he knew it was Commins because he was able to follow his movements before and after the shooting. This was less conclusive than his statements about seeing that the second man was wearing a hat and watching as a gun was being loaded.

But could Flynn witness *any* of the actions in and around the ditch from what he admitted was two hundred yards away? Would he have been able to see what the two men were doing? According to the evidence presented at the inquest, the answer is no, which created another conflict with the testimony from that proceeding. Both Dr. Shanley and coachman Flanagan said it was "dark" when Major Mahon was shot. By dark, they meant this: Both had trouble providing identifying characteristics of assassins who were *"not more than three or four yards"* (Flanagan) from the carriage. Dr. Shanley was only able to discern that the would-be shooter in the fields was wearing a cap—Flynn said that the second man in the ditch was wearing a hat—because the man's pistol had "burned priming," illuminating the area around his face and head. "It was dark," Dr. Shanley said, and he could not "accurately describe the size or description of the man." But from "the light caused by the flash of the pan," he saw "it was a cap the man had on," said Dr. Shanley. Flanagan said that he didn't think the assassin was wearing a cap—Flynn testified that Commins had just exchanged caps with Patrick Connor, although he didn't explicitly say whether Commins was wearing one—but he couldn't be sure because he "could not see distinctly" in the darkness.

Flynn was asked if it was a pistol or a gun that was fired at Major Mahon. (Flynn had said that he saw a "gun" being loaded by Commins and the unknown man in the ditch, but that Commins was carrying a "pistol" when he fled the scene. John Brennan had earlier testified that Commins told him he used Patrick Doyle's "gun" to kill the major. The old soldier Patrick Rigney had described receiving "horse pistols" to commit the deed.)

Flynn said he "saw by the light of the flash that it was a gun the shot was fired out of." It was a startling statement. Not only was Flynn stating for the first time during cross-examination that he had seen (as opposed to heard) the gunfire, he was also hinting that Commins, who he claimed wasn't carrying the murder weapon from the scene, hadn't been the assassin. Further, his statement about the flash represented another conflict with the inquest testimony. According to Dr. Shanley, there were two flashes—one caused by the fatal shot from the ditch and one caused by the misfire from the man "in the fields." According to Flynn, there was a single flash, and it came from the ditch.

Flynn was asked why he didn't provide information about the crime until February.

He said that it was "his priest who made him do so." Father Andrew Quinn of Kilbride parish told him he "was bound in conscience to reveal all he knew about the murder."

He was asked about the reward.

Flynn said he had heard of the reward from the poster on the police barrack. But he had heard of rewards for the last thirty years.

Did he covet the reward?

Flynn said "part of that would be a good thing to get, but he would not take any money under the name of reward."

How much land did he hold from Major Mahon?

Four and a half acres.

How much rent did he owe?

Two years.

Had he been turned out of his land?

No.

Had he ever been charged with "Whiteboyism"?

No.

Did he know Bernard Connor, a coworker of Flynn's? (Connor's relationship to the ringleader, Andrew Connor, is unknown.)

Yes. He had worked with him on the day of the murder.

Did he eat supper at Connor's house?

No.

Did he remain there that night?

No.

When did he quit work?

About dusk. His said he did not go more than halfway home when he went to "look at the turf."

A juror asked him to further explain his actions before he met Commins and Hasty in the ball alley.

Flynn said he was "going home from work" when he met his son on the road. He son told him that a "rick of turf of his was down," and so he started walking to Doorty, where his family held a tract of land, to investigate the matter.

Following Patrick Flynn to the stand was Patrick Hunt, the young man from Doorty who had been fetched from England to buttress Flynn's testimony. Like all the other residents from around the crime scene, Hunt had denied any knowledge of the crime when first questioned by the police. By March he voluntarily approached the authorities to tell them what he knew. Yet the magistrate who spoke with him, Mathew Browne, didn't ask him to make a sworn statement. As Browne explained in a May 24 letter to Dublin Castle, "I did not wish to reduce the intelligence to the form of an information lest it might clash with any former information taken and I could not at the time see them [the informations] as the clerk of the peace was about on [the] . . . assizes circuit, and by some neglect the key of the office could not be had." After his meeting with Browne, Hunt returned home to Doorty and told his father, a tenant of Major Mahon like all the others in the Doorty run-dale collective near the new road, what he was planning to do. His father, seemingly fearful of the wrath of the murder gang, sent him to Manchester, England, where he remained for three months until Constable William O'Brien convinced him to return to Ireland for the trial. In his letter, the magistrate told Dublin Castle that "at this

moment as regards the *murder* there is only the unsupported testimony of Patrick Flynn, and Patrick Hunt supports him in many
and important portions of his testimony." Without Hunt, prosecutors felt, Flynn's crime scene story meant little.

Hunt was asked if he remembered the night of Major Mahon's
murder.

Hunt said that he "was at Margaret O'Neill's house that night."
He testified that Ms. O'Neill, who would later be identified as his
aunt, lived in the townland of Leitrim. He left her home to return
to his father's house in Doorty, traveling "through the fields" in a
southwesterly direction roughly parallel to the new road. But before
reaching the townland of Doorty—again, its boundary began at the
location of the Doorty Bridge—he "met two men on the lands of
Leitrim." He said they were "ten yards" from the new road and thirty
or forty yards "above the bridge near Strokestown," according to the
Freeman's Journal. Since Hunt was approaching from the Strokestown
side of the Doorty Bridge, his statement meant that they were standing on the Strokestown side of the bridge. The *Roscommon Journal*
quoted him as saying that he saw them "near the bridge of Doorty,"
confirming it as the "first" bridge of Dr. Shanley's inquest testimony.

He said each man had a "gun."

Would he know the two men?

Hunt pointed out Commins and Hasty in the courtroom.

Commins and Hasty, who "were not doing anything,"
approached him and "swore him not to tell who he met, or that
he met any person." It was the closest any witness would come to
explicitly placing Patrick Hasty at the murder scene. James Commins "put him to his oath not to tell," a formal procedure that was
typical of secret societies.

Thus sworn, Hunt continued on his way, leaving them "on the
right hand side of the road"—the ditch side of the road. He walked
to his father's house, which he offered was "about" 250 yards from
where he had met the two. During cross-examination he said he
"went in through" the sallies in Thady Hunt's garden, where Pat-

rick Flynn said he was hiding 200 yards from the murder ditch. These few words confirm that Hunt and Flynn were positioned in roughly the same area within the settlement of Doorty: close to the new road, 200 to 250 yards from the vicinity surrounding the Doorty Bridge. Thus, Flynn would have been contradicting his own testimony if he were speaking of the bridge at the Leitrim and Carrnownalassan boundary when he said the murder occurred "beyond the second bridge," as the scholar Dr. Norton has argued. That bridge would have been more than 600 yards from his location near the cluster of homes of the Hunt clan in Doorty.

After he arrived in the house, Hunt heard the sound of gunfire. He said he "thought nothing about being sworn until he heard the shot."

He said he believed the shot was fired either from "about" or "above" the bridge of Doorty, depending on which newspaper you read. Since Hunt was not claiming to be an eyewitness—and would only have been speculating about the precise location—his testimony about the exact location should not be regarded as critically as the statements of eyewitnesses.

Hunt said he left his father's house and went out on the road near "the widow Hunt's door," presumably enabling him to look toward the section of road where the gunshot originated. He "saw two men crossing the road into the fields"—that is, both men fled from the ditch side of the road to the fields side of the road. Hunt mentioned nothing about one of the men dashing toward Patrick Flynn's hiding place in Doorty. He mentioned nothing about a would-be shooter in the fields.

Hunt identified one of the men crossing the road as James Commins. He said Commins was not carrying a weapon of any kind, contradicting Flynn's testimony that James Commins was carrying a pistol. Again we are confronted with the issue of darkness. How was Hunt able to discern that Commins had "nothing in his hand" from what he offered was a distance of about 250 yards?

Hunt added that he "did not know the second man." But the clear implication of his previous testimony—about meeting Commins and Hasty "ten yards" from the road—was that the second man was Patrick Hasty.

During cross-examination Mr. Skelton asked about his disappearance to England.

Hunt described how his "father send him off when he told him what he knew about the business." Hunt told the magistrate "what he knew on a Thursday, and he was sent to England on the following Wednesday."

Did he tell the authorities what he knew before he fled to England?

No.

Didn't he talk to the magistrate, Mathew Browne?

Yes. He "told" him "all about it."

Did he swear an information?

No, he "did not swear an information then as Mr. Browne did not ask him," which corresponds to what Browne said in his letter to Dublin Castle on May 24.

He was asked what time in the evening he saw the two men cross the road.

Hunt said he didn't know. But he confirmed "it was dark on that night when he met the two men."

Skelton asked if he was sure that it was James Commins who made him swear an oath of silence.

He said he was sure.

Skelton then read Hunt's June 23 statement to the authorities, in which he said he didn't know who "took out the book and swore him."

Hunt responded that he "did not know which of the men handed him the book, but he was sure it was Commins swore him," which didn't address the discrepancy.

He was asked how much land his father held from Major Mahon.

More than five acres.

How much rent did he owe?

Three years.

Did he still have possession?

Yes.

What were his family's living circumstances?

Hunt believed that "some of his family are getting relief meal."

The Crown then called its final witness: Dr. Terence Shanley.

The doctor added new details about the carriage ride from Roscommon town. He told how Major Mahon took out his watch and noted that it was ten minutes to six o'clock, likely around the time that vehicle was passing close to the homes of Patrick Hunt's father, the Widow Hunt, and Thady Hunt in Doorty. The landlord asked his friend if he thought they would make it home by half-past six. Dr. Shanley responded that he would need to "press on the horses" if he wanted to make it to Strokestown by then. This conversation had apparently followed Major Mahon's impassioned plea to the doctor about commencing a new effort to feed his poor—"Shanley, point out to me what is best to be done, and we shall be able to keep them from destitution," the landlord had said, according to the doctor's November 10 letter to the newspapers.

Within a few minutes—or a distance of either two hundred or four hundred yards, traveled at "four and a half miles per hour"— the fatal shot was fired. Confirming his earlier testimony at the inquest, Dr. Shanley said the crime was committed "a little below Doorty Bridge," which would have meant that the two-hundred-yard estimation in the *Roscommon Journal* was more accurate to his testimony than the four-hundred-yard estimation in the *Freeman's Journal*. Dr. Shanley was challenging Patrick Flynn's testimony that it happened "beyond the second bridge." To Dr. Shanley, the event occurred before a bridge. To Flynn, it happened after a bridge.

Major Mahon "instantly fell back on the cushion, and had scarcely time to articulate the words 'Oh! God.' He did not stir hand or foot after." At the inquest, Flanagan testified that "the deceased never spoke after he received the contents of the gun," which may not contradict Dr. Shanley's statement. Dr. Shanley said "his body was riddled with shot, and some grains passed through his heart. There were diamond-shaped slugs in the charge." In the *Roscommon Journal*, Dr. Shanley was quoted as saying that he himself got "one" ball lodged in his right arm.

Dr. Shanley said the assassin "jumped out of the ditch and ran by the carriage." The man wore a cap, he said. Dr. Shanley did not mention another man in the ditch.

Then he "saw a second man in the field who endeavored to discharge a second gun at them but it burned priming," repeating his inquest testimony.

Could he identify the killers?

Shanley said he "could not identify any one." It is curious that Dr. Shanley didn't say that he couldn't identify "the prisoners" or "the defendants." Instead he said he couldn't identify "any one," indicating that he believed it was impossible to identify the two men at the scene. It was another strike against the testimony of Flynn and Hunt, who, in key portions of their testimony, were describing individuals and actions from a few hundred yards away.

But Dr. Shanley's statement may have reflected a discomfort he had about the prosecution's case. Ross Mahon had earlier complained about Dr. Shanley's failure to share any information he was learning from Michael Gardiner, who was in his care in the Strokestown bridewell in the first months after the conspirator's arrest. "He told Mr. Bermingham that Gardiner told him everything. . . . Altogether his conduct has been so extraordinary that we do not know what to make of him," Ross Mahon had written to Pakenham Mahon. After all, why couldn't Dr. Shanley at least identify the would-be shooter in the fields? Just a few feet from the man, he was assisted by the illumination of the misfire. It was a vantage point Flynn and Hunt could only dream of.

After a few more questions and a brief cross-examination, Dr. Shanley was dismissed from the stand.

The Crown then closed its case against Patrick Hasty.

CHAPTER 15

It Has Been Indeed, Really Proved

The witnesses on both sides are such bad characters that it is impossible to say what credence the jury will give them.
> —JOHN ROSS MAHON TO HEN-
> RIETTA MAHON, JULY 13, 1848,
> MOMENTS BEFORE DELIBERATIONS
> BEGAN IN THE TRIAL OF PATRICK
> HASTY

No jury, having the least regard for their oaths, or who were impressed with the solemnity of the duty they had undertaken, could (without the commission of the awful crime of perjury) have acquitted you of a participation in that wicked conspiracy which deprived a respectable gentleman of this county of his life.
> —BARON LEFROY TO PATRICK
> HASTY, JULY 15, 1848

MR. SKELTON ROSE TO present the defense.

He was challenging what appeared on its face to be a decent case on the matter of the forty-seven-year-old carpenter's involvement in the conspiracy. Since two witnesses, Rigney and Hester, told corroborating stories, it was believable that Hasty would recruit Patrick Rigney, an old soldier begging on the streets who was reputedly a proficient marksman, to commit the murder. But would he draft him less than twenty-four hours before the shooting was to take place without offering him any money, as Rigney testified? A principal component of the indictment had alleged that the conspirators had collected money to pay off the killers. John Hester's tale also had the feel of some truth. In describing how he was sent to retrieve the pistols from Rigney under orders from Hasty (corroborating Rigney) and to purchase powder and shot from Roscommon town during a gang meeting at which Hasty was present, he was telling the kind of stories a servant boy would tell. But why would he mention nothing of the few weeks prior to the actual killing, during which time he remained an employee of Patrick Hasty? It would have been a time of considerable agitation and preparation. John Brennan's account of speaking with Hasty about his plans for the murder and visiting the Widow Smyth's on Christmas Eve (where Hasty was present) also seems plausible. But without any major corroboration or contradiction offered, the jury was left with no mechanism to determine the extent of the stories' reliability.

On the matter of Hasty's participation in the actual murder, the Crown seemed at first glance to be offering contradictory allegations. In the indictment, the prosecution alleged that Hasty was "feloniously present and aiding" when Commins fired the fatal shot. Since the eyewitness Patrick Flynn and the earwitness Patrick Hunt described two men near, at, and fleeing the murder scene, it would seem to follow that the prosecution believed that Patrick Hasty was the misfiring second shooter in the fields from Dr. Shanley's testimony. But this was neither what Flynn and Hunt claimed—both spoke of two men congregated on the right side of the road in (Flynn) or near (Hunt) the ditch—nor what the indictment alleged. The Crown did not charge anyone with pulling the trigger of a second weapon. So *was* Patrick Hasty "present and aiding" the assassin? The only evidence explicitly placing Hasty near the scene was Patrick Hunt's story about the oath-administration ceremony being held "ten yards" from the new road. (Flynn said he lost sight of Hasty after he left the ball alley, a few hundred yards from the scene.) Without corroboration, Hunt's story is hard to judge. But it wasn't necessarily a bad thing that the allegedly hawkeyed Flynn, who said he watched Commins from the time he left the ball alley until the moment he entered the ditch, mentioned nothing about a gathering of three people just off the road. It has already been shown that Flynn could not have seen more than a few feet in front of him in the sallies of Thady Hunt's garden.

Mr. Skelton's summation of the defense case appears not to have dealt with factual assertions of this sort, according to the newspapers. Instead he broadly challenged the credibility of the accusers. He didn't seem to have a difficult task. All the major figures in the trial had initially provided false statements to the police. The servant boy John Hester even offered to testify on behalf of his employer in exchange for 1 pound, which revealed how much it cost to purchase his testimony. Plus at least two of the Crown's witnesses—Patrick Flynn and Patrick Hunt (or his father)—were currently being allowed to retain properties on the Mahon estate, even though they were more than two years behind in rent. More significantly, all those who appeared on behalf of the Crown were being devotedly cared for. In addition to halting coercive treatment—Patrick Rigney was taken out of a "black hole" after he agreed to turn on the gang—the government provided the accusers and their families with the food and medical care necessary to survive. It was perhaps the most precious gift that could be given to a starving family in Famine-era County Roscommon. But such assistance, which the government had so signally failed to provide for the rest of the Irish population, called into question nearly every piece of evidence brought before court. It is one thing for John Brennan to provide information to save himself, but it is quite another for him to give the kind of testimony that would keep his four young children, ranging in age from two to nine, from perishing.

Even though he and his family were receiving the same care

and tending as the other witnesses, Patrick Hunt would seem to have more inherent credibility attached to his testimony than the others. He offered to testify on behalf of the Crown of his own volition in March. It was only after his father learned what he had done that Hunt was transformed into an unwilling witness, sent to England for three months to avoid speaking against the plotters. As the magistrate Mathew Browne said in his May 24 letter to Dublin Castle, "He is not a very reluctant witness by any means, but has been sent out of the way by his own friends."

But Mr. Skelton did not base his criticism of the accusers on false statements or special treatment. According to the *Roscommon Weekly Messenger*, Skelton asked the jury "to discredit the testimony of the several witnesses, who only appeared in the light of approvers." He was challenging the Crown's case by pointing to the simple fact that, since a conspiracy charge had been lodged, the entire matter rested on the reliability of informers. And what was the worth of a prosecution that relied so heavily on that most loathsome figure in Irish culture? In his famous December 7 letter, Father McDermott reserved some of his most overheated descriptions for the "hireling serf" within his own parish who spread the story about his denunciations. "He skulks into his lurking hole, and laughs at the credulity of those who employed him after he received his reward of turpitude," he wrote. It clear that those who testified on behalf of the government were aware of their pariah status even before Mr. Skelton made it clear to them. Why else, after all, would Patrick Hunt's father send him to England? And why else would the Crown go to such expense to maintain the family members of the witnesses? Ross Mahon confirmed that the "witnesses for the prosecution were hooted on the day of the trial by the mob and [Patrick] Hunt's father told me he was insulted wherever he went."

Yet Mr. Skelton's summation was most noteworthy for another of its omissions. The defense counsel did not speak of any inciting behavior that may have been committed by Major Mahon or his representatives. He neglected to do so despite the fact that Major

Mahon's estate polices were revealed to have been the inspiration for the crime, a fact that should not be lost in the thicket of evidence. Although John Brennan had testified that both James Commins and Patrick Hasty received money for the murder—Commins traveled to Strokestown on Christmas Eve to get it—James Donnelly told of a comment made during the public house meeting in Strokestown that pointed to the true, overarching motive. "Major Mahon was the proper person to be shot," said one of the participants during a debate over whether the landlord or the land agent deserved the assassin's bullet. "Ross Mahon was only a servant. If he did not do his duty, another would." Mr. Skelton declined to speak of Major Mahon's actions, which had just been highlighted with Bishop Browne's list in the moderate nationalist *Freeman's Journal*, even though the jury was composed of eleven respectable Catholics of the sort who would read that newspaper. Instead he made a point of praising Major Mahon, confirmation that polite society of both backgrounds was unwilling to view the landlord's murder as an act in any way justified by the behavior of a family that still wielded great power. "There was no attack made on your husband's memory," Ross Mahon wrote to Mrs. Mahon. "On the contrary, Mr. Skelton, the prisoner counsel, said from all he could learn he was a most humane man."

After he completed his speech—the *Freeman Journal* called it "very forcible," the *Roscommon Weekly Messenger* characterized it as "eloquent"—Skelton called his first witness, Henry French, a solicitor.

French confirmed that the servant boy John Hester had told him at the spring assizes that Hasty "was in his own house at the time Major Mahon's carriage passed on the evening he was murdered." He said Hester offered to become "a witness for the prisoner Hasty and others, then in custody." Not only had Hester offered his services to save Hasty but he was also looking to exonerate others, which may just mean that he had information to sell.

Skelton next called Bernard Connor, the coworker of the eyewitness Patrick Flynn.

Bernard Connor said he worked with Flynn "until duskish" on the night of the crime. After retiring, the two went into Connor's house for dinner, with Connor's brother-in-law joining them. (During his testimony, Flynn said that he left a "friend's house" on the Elphin road, met his son, and then turned toward Doorty to mend a rick of turf that had fallen. He also said he ended his workday with Connor "at dusk.")

Connor described how he departed the house to tend the sheep. As he was leaving, he told Flynn "to be with him early" the next day, which shows that Connor was an employer of some sort over Flynn.

Connor went outside and saw "a carriage pass, an open one he believed to be Mr. Mahon's."

Connor, then, was claiming that Patrick Flynn was in his home—not hiding in the sallies in Thady Hunt's garden near the road—when the fatal shot was fired. It was a serious charge that threatened the core of the prosecution's crime scene allegations.

Connor then said he returned to his house two or three hours later. Flynn was gone.

Did he see how many people were in the carriage?

Three.

Connor added that the bridge "where he was shot is more than a mile from where he saw the carriage pass."

Was he "positive" that Flynn was in his house at the time the carriage passed?

Connor said he was.

During cross-examination Peter McKeogh, the attorney general, asked Connor about the kind of work he was doing before he went in for dinner.

He said he was "turning out manure with his horse," with his brother-in-law leading the horse.

What did he have for dinner?

Stirabout. He said that he ate some cold stirabout after he returned to the house after his three-hour absence.

Did he often eat his dinner at nine o'clock at night?

Yes.

Where did he spend the three hours after he left Flynn?

Connor said he spent "part of the three hours smoking in the police barrack." He said he "very often before went to the police barrack."

When did he hear of the murder?

The next day.

The attorney general then asked if he knew Patrick Connor, a herd, in a clear attempt to show that Bernard Connor was sympathetic to the murder gang. During his testimony, Flynn had identified Patrick Connor as the man in the fields who exchanged caps with Commins just before the murder.

Bernard Connor said that Patrick Connor was his brother.

McKeogh then asked if he was once arrested "for further examination" when a servant boy of his was transported for firing a shot at Mr. Kenny, additional proof that Connor was close to a secret society.

Yes.

The defense then called its final witness, Thomas Dockery, Connor's brother-in-law.

Dockery corroborated Bernard Connor's story that Patrick Flynn remained at Connor's home "for two hours after nightfall."

Whatever Bernard Connor's familial relationship to an alleged conspirator, more people (Connor and Dockery) were now explicitly placing the eyewitness Patrick Flynn far from the area around the Doorty Bridge than were explicitly placing Patrick Hasty close to the area around the Doorty Bridge (Hunt).

The newspapers did not note whether the attorney general challenged any of the statements of Connor's brother-in-law.

The defense then closed.

As the attorney general offered his final words to the jury, Ross Mahon scribbled a note to Major Mahon's widow. "The attorney general is now speaking," he wrote. "When he has finished the case will be closed." He then offered a pessimistic assessment of the prospects for conviction. "The witnesses on both sides are such bad characters that it is impossible to say what credence the jury will give them," he wrote. "I have not time to add more as the post is just going out." It sounds as though Ross Mahon was himself having trouble sorting out a narrative that was as intricate as the distribution of land within the rundale collective where the Doorty witnesses all lived.

After the attorney general concluded, the judge offered his instructions to the jury, which then retired to deliberate. After just a few minutes, the twelve men returned with a verdict. Patrick Hasty was guilty of conspiracy to murder Major Mahon. Clearly, the jurors were convinced that the carpenter had been a member of the gang. But without any explicit statement by the jurors, it is impossible to determine what they actually believed about Hasty's actions around the murder scene. After all, they could have returned a guilty conspiracy verdict no matter how they felt about his actual role in the killing.

"The prisoner slightly changed color on the announcement, but remained otherwise firm," said the *Freeman's Journal*.

The court was adjourned.

On the following day, Thursday, July 13, the same cast of characters arrived in the same courtroom to repeat the same performance with James Commins in the dock. To Ross Mahon, this almost guaranteed the same outcome. He assumed that because "none of the witnesses failed in the least degree [in the Hasty trial], we may therefore reasonably expect that the jury of today will return a similar verdict to that of yesterday," he wrote to Mrs. Mahon. But there were two major differences in the trial: First, it was James Commins, not Patrick Hasty, who was being prosecuted. Second, the jury had an entirely different sectarian composition. According to the *Roscommon Journal*, the prosecutor "forced" many Protestants to serve, rejecting "many highly respectable Roman Catholics."

Instead of the eleven Catholics and one Protestant of the Hasty trial, it appears that the jury had eight or nine Protestants and three or four Catholics.

A wig-clad Baron Lefroy took his seat and ordered Commins to be placed at the bar. Little was known about the accused killer's personal background or characteristics. Upon his arrest in February, Commins was merely described in the newspapers as a "dead shot." It wasn't even noted whether he was a tenant of Major Mahon's. The indictment was read. It alleged that Commins was both a participant in the conspiracy to murder Major Denis Mahon and the man who "did feloniously kill and murder him." The attorney general then rose to begin the case. Since the newspapers transcribed only the portions of Commins's trial that differed from Hasty's—and since he had only a day to prepare—it is safe to assume that Peter McKeogh laid out the same argument as he did on the previous day.

On the matter of Commins's involvement in the plot prior to the night of November 2, the Crown offered far less evidence against Commins than it did against Hasty. Since the old soldier Patrick Rigney did not mention Commins in his testimony—when asked if he knew Commins he said "no"—he was not asked to testify, forcing one of the prosecution's stronger witnesses to sit out the proceedings. Next came the servant boy John Hester, who had focused most of his testimony during the last trial on his employer, Patrick Hasty. He placed Commins at a gang meeting in Hasty's home—he didn't hear anything because he was "going in and out of the house"—and described how Commins told him about "three men" who were waiting to ambush Major Mahon when he returned from the Ballinasloe fair in early October. Neither story—the second was offered almost as an afterthought during Hasty's trial—was corroborated.

During his cross-examination of Hester, the defense counsel asked the servant boy about his claim during the first trial that he was "dismissed for his honesty" from the service of Patrick Hasty. The line had inspired laughter from the courtroom.

Hester admitted that he had not exactly been truthful. He said he was fired for stealing a "cleave of turnips" from Hasty, which was one of the most prevalent crimes of the day. But he qualified the act by saying that he took the vegetables at the suggestion of Hasty's wife "and for her use."

Then John Brennan took the stand. He repeated his testimony about Commins admitting to him that he killed Major Mahon with Patrick Doyle's gun (with Hasty and Gardiner present) and complaining about not being paid for the murder. He then told the story about traveling with Commins to the Widow Smyth's, where he was hoping to receive his money from Andrew Connor, on Christmas Eve 1847. As in the Hasty trial, no corroboration was offered for Brennan's conversations with James Commins. But for the story about the meeting at Smyth's, the prosecution provided partial corroboration. Ann Smyth, the daughter of the Widow Smyth, was called to the stand.

Smyth said that "at one period" during the evening Andrew Connor, Michael Gardiner, and two others "were by themselves in a private room." She went into the room and "saw a heap of silver, amounting to £4 or £5 on the table before Andy Connor," apparently Commins's payment for the murder. (It was enough for a single ticket to America. Prices at this point in the Famine hovered around 4 pounds.) But that was the end of Smyth's testimony. She neither identified James Commins as one of the "two others" in the room nor described him as receiving Andrew Connor's heap of silver. She merely confirmed the fact that a gang meeting occurred in the Widow Smyth's, which was not insignificant.

The Crown next called the crime-scene witnesses, who were central to the prosecution's case against Commins. Indeed, Patrick Flynn's testimony focused almost entirely on Commins's actions. Flynn first spotted Commins in the ball alley from roughly forty yards away at about 5 or 5:30 P.M. Since Flynn was corroborating the servant boy's testimony about Commins traveling to the ball alley from Hasty's house, this aspect of his story is believable.

Flynn then said he watched the alleged killer leave the ball alley, cross the fields to the new road, and duck into a ditch on the right side of the road. From a position on the left side of the new road in Thady Hunt's garden, Flynn observed from two hundred yards away as Commins and an unknown man in a hat loaded a gun in a ditch "beyond the second bridge." After Major Mahon's carriage passed by and "the light of the flash" of a gun emanated from the ditch—Flynn did not identify Commins as pulling the trigger—Flynn watched Commins dash up the hill with a pistol in his hand and then turn off through the fields.

Patrick Flynn's son, John, was called to corroborate a tiny portion his father's story.

John said that he met his father on the Elphin road (prior to the ball alley sighting) as his father had testified. But he added nothing more.

Then came Patrick Hunt, the young man from Doorty who had been returned from England at the personal intervention of Constable William O'Brien.

He told his story about meeting Hasty and Commins ten yards from the new road, on the right side of the thoroughfare, and about being sworn by Commins not to tell anyone what he saw. Then he described walking to his father's house in Doorty, traveling through the sallies in Thady Hunt's garden to get there. After he heard the sound of gunfire, he went out on the new road near the Widow Hunt's door and watched from 250 yards away as an unarmed Commins and unknown man crossed the road and fled through the fields. Unlike Flynn, he didn't say that Commins ran toward Doorty. Unlike Flynn, he didn't say Commins was carrying a pistol.

In making the charge that Commins was the assassin, the Crown seemed to be offering the testimony of Flynn, who placed Commins in the ditch, as corroboration for John Brennan's story about Commins admitting to him that he was killer. Hunt's story about the oath-administration ceremony, then, corroborated Flynn's story about Commins's presence near the murder scene. Hunt further corroborated Flynn by testifying that he also saw Commins flee the scene. But a principal omission remained. No one had actually seen James Commins pull the trigger.

Following the appearance of Flynn and Hunt, the Crown called one other crime scene witness to the stand, an individual who hadn't appeared during the Hasty trial. Catherine Donnelly, another resident of the Doorty settlement, had been under police protection with her father (who vouched for her story) for at least two months.

She was asked about the night of the murder.

Donnelly testified that she heard a gunshot and went out on the booreen. She "saw Michael Gardiner coming through the fields as if from the place of murder, and he having a gun in his hand."

It is obvious that the prosecution was offering Donnelly's testimony as corroboration for John Brennan, the witness who claimed that Commins told him he shot Major Mahon with Patrick Hasty and Michael Gardiner present. But Donnelly's testimony did much more than that. In claiming that Gardiner ran "through the fields" with a gun in his hand, she was suggesting that Gardiner was the misfiring second shooter "in the fields" whose identity had not been discussed at all during the trials. But even further, she had given the first credible identification of anyone fleeing the murder site with what might be the murder weapon. The stories of Flynn and Hunt merely confused what actually happened just before, during, and just after the commission of the crime. And neither mentioned Commins carrying a gun. Could Donnelly have been identifying the actual assassin? Could it be Michael Gardiner, a man who was allegedly involved in nearly every facet of the conspiracy? According to court testimony, he was present at the public house meeting, at the gathering at Hasty's when the old soldier received the horse pistols, and at the Christmas Eve session at the Widow Smyth's. He had gone to retrieve the horse pistols from Rigney, he had sought funds from James Donnelly, and he had left Hasty's house with Commins and Hasty on the night of the murder.

After Donnelly concluded her testimony, the Crown closed its case.

Mr. Skelton then rose to defend James Commins. Since the newspapers didn't explicitly characterize what he said during his summation, it can only be assumed that he didn't veer from his Hasty text about the entire case resting solely on informers.

After he completed his speech, he called the solicitor Henry French, who described how Hester had offered to provide an alibi for Hasty.

Then he called the two men who claimed that Patrick Flynn was eating dinner at Bernard Connor's house when the major's carriage passed.

Finally he called three witnesses who spoke on behalf of Commins's good character. Two were "gentleman named Sands," including someone the *Roscommon Journal* identified as William Sands. It is apparent that this was William Sandys, a prominent Catholic middleman (on an estate other than Major Mahon's), who was one of the pillars of Four Mile House society and who himself had been the target of agrarian outrages prior to the Famine. He had donated the land upon which the Kilbride church stood and had served on the relief committee established after the arrival of the first blight in the fall of 1845. The endorsement of such a figure surely made an impression on the minds of the few Catholic members of the jury.

Then a third character witness was called: He was *a member of the jury* named George Clarke.

With the testimony of Clarke revealing that Commins had an ally on the panel, it is hard to imagine that court observers were expecting anything other than an acquittal or a hung jury.

After the attorney general delivered his concluding remarks—again, he merely had to prove that Commins was a part of the conspiracy, not that he was killer necessarily—Baron Lefroy charged the jury "at great length, making particular comments on the evidence as he proceeded," said the *Dublin Evening Mail*. The jury then retired to the deliberation room. But a swift judgment was not forthcoming. At 7 P.M. Baron Lefroy ordered the jury to be "locked up" for the night.

On the following morning, Friday, July 14, Baron Lefroy arrived in court at 10 A.M. and asked the jury to be brought into court.

"Gentlemen, have you agreed to your verdict?" the clerk asked.

"No," said the foreman, Oliver Irwin. "There is not the least chance of agreeing."

He did not give a reason.

Baron Lefroy responded that they "should return to their room, as he had no power to discharge them."

Irwin countered that "some of the jury had suffered very much from the cold of the night, in consequence of the sheriff not allowing their coats to be brought in and he did not think they would be able to stand any longer without refreshments." This would seem a clear attempt to influence the jury's verdict.

The attorney general argued that before the jury could be dismissed, a medical inspection would need to be conducted on any ill jurors.

Baron Lefroy agreed, and he asked Dr. Shanley to determine whether further confinement would "endanger the life and health of any of the jurors."

Dr. Shanley conducted the examination and "on his report the jury were discharged" without reaching a verdict.

The *Roscommon Journal* claimed that the jury "remained locked up all night sooner than find a verdict of guilty." According to the *Dublin Evening Mail*, the jury was divided eight for conviction and four for acquittal, which would seem to fall roughly along sectarian lines. In a letter to Mrs. Mahon, Major Mahon's brother said that "nine or less of the jury were for convicting, and the others would not agree being friends of his, it is supposed." He said the prosecution had blamed the failure on a "very defective" jury list.

But Michael Gardiner, who had been identified as fleeing

from the scene with a gun in his hand, wasn't comforted by the jury's failure. He was now ready to do what he could to avoid a harsh sentence. He offered to testify on behalf of the Crown. But Peter McKeogh refused his proposal to turn Queen's evidence. "The attorney general would not take him as such, he thought the evidence so clear," wrote Major Mahon's brother to Mrs. Mahon.

It was announced that the cases of Commins, Gardiner, and Martin Brennan, who had been barely mentioned during the two trials, would be put off until the winter assizes.

That left Patrick Hasty alone to face his punishment.

On the next morning, Saturday, July 15, he was brought before Baron Lefroy.

The clerk asked Hasty "why the sentence of death and execution should not be pronounced against him."

After some hesitation, Hasty said he was innocent of the charge and asked the judge to spare his life.

According to the *Roscommon Journal*, Baron Lefroy "appeared quite unmoved."

He then addressed the conspirator.

"You have been convicted of a conspiracy to murder the late Major Mahon; in the course of the trial it has been indeed, really proved that you have been guilty of more than a conspiracy. You appear to have been one of the guilty perpetrators; at least, it has appeared that you were present when the shot that deprived the unfortunate gentleman of life was fired. Although such a crime in any man is utterly inconceivable, it is more so, as far as you are concerned. You have not even a pretence of a grievance respecting yourself, that in any manner could account for your acting so—not even account—for nothing could justify—you have not even a pretence that could account for your entering a conspiracy."

Hasty responded by attacking the credibility of John Hester, who had provided such damning evidence about the gatherings at Hasty's home. He said that "his own servant boy could account for it all if he wished; that he attended at the last assizes to prove that he had nothing to do with the business at all; but that he had since turned him out of his employment, as he found him to be of bad character and heard of him having robbed some of the neighbors. Having put him away on that account, he turned against him, and swore all he did."

"It did not depend on your servant boy; for witnesses who could not be suspected of ill-will towards you, have sworn to the part you took in this transaction, so as to leave no doubt of your guilt," Lefroy responded. "No jury, having the least regard for their oaths, or who were impressed with the solemnity of the duty they had undertaken, could (without the commission of the awful crime of perjury) have acquitted you of a participation in that wicked conspiracy which deprived a respectable gentleman of this county of his life. The evidence was most conclusive. Take that of the servant boy entirely out of the case, and still there is sufficient evidence, which could not by any ingenuity be perverted, so as to make you appear an innocent."

Then Hasty responded to another portion of the evidence against him. He said, "Brennan was well known to have gone to Rigney to get them to do it." In other words, he didn't recruit the old soldier to shoot Major Mahon, as had been alleged by the old soldier himself. Instead the Crown witness John Brennan (or possibly the at-large conspirator Thomas Brennan or fellow defendant Martin Brennan) was the one who went "to Rigney to get them to do it." Hasty was admitting that he had foreknowledge of the plot, but he was also suggesting that such information was "well known."

Hasty went on to attack the credibility of all but one of his accusers by stating that they were poor and dishonest. "It is well known to everyone" that all the witnesses who swore against him were "begging about the country, and that for some time before, with the exception of [James] Donnelly, not one of them had the price of a stone of meal, or a bit but what they took from honest people," he said.

Baron Lefroy responded by acknowledging Hasty's admission that he had prior knowledge of the conspiracy. "There is now no doubt of the issue of that conspiracy—there can be no expectation but you must suffer for the crime you have been convicted of. It is worse than murder, for not alone life has been sacrificed, but society has been demoralized—a principle through which men are got to unite together to bring about the murder of their fellow man. Conspiracy has all the malignity of murder, while it is more extensive in its consequences."

Hasty responded that "he was never a tenant to Major Mahon, and had no object or benefit; had nothing to expect by his death, or to induce him to commit murder—he could live without it; he held land, and always paid his rent."

"That is what makes your case the more grievous and culpable," Baron Lefroy said. "It appears you had no cause or reason of ill-will towards the gentleman against whom you have headed a conspiracy to deprive him of life; he was a kind and indulgent landlord through life. It appeared on the trial that some of his tenantry owed over three years rent; he not alone offered to forgive them that, if they gave him his property, but had actually made arrangements, and offered them money to send them to America."

Hasty followed the lead of his defense attorney and praised Major Mahon, further evidence that speaking harshly of Major Mahon would do nothing to strengthen the case. He said "he knew him to be a good landlord; he did not know anything bad of him, and owed him no ill will."

"You have been engaged in a conspiracy to deprive that great man of life and . . ."

"I will leave that to God," said Hasty.

"I am sure I earnestly hope you may stand acquitted in His sight, but no human judgment can acquit you upon the evidence brought forward to prove your guilt of an offense involving the peace of the country, setting an example, which if allowed to proceed, would destroy all order and society," said Baron Lefroy. "Really at that time no man could feel safe in this country, for both life and property were in danger from the widespread conspiracy that existed and with which it appears you have been concerned, and took a heading part; that conspiracy, happily has been checked, and I hope that from that result and the example made, that the people will learn how vain, it is to enter into a conspiracy, however well contrived. That no league formed to commit crime, no combination of men formed for wicked purposes, can long continue united, but will break asunder and, as in this case, will betray one another."

Hasty said that "if he was about to do it he would not have a policeman in the house with him all that day, for whom he was making a boot jack," which wasn't a denial of his presence at the murder scene. He didn't attempt to challenge the strongest crime scene evidence against him: the oath-swearing ceremony described by Patrick Hunt.

"It is strange if such is the case, you neglected bringing forward such a material witness on your behalf," said Baron Lefroy. "You had able counsel and advice and if such was the case they would not fail to give you the benefit of such testimony."

Hasty said he didn't know the policeman's name, identifying him as "the second [to] last man who came to the station" or the second newest member of the local force. Hasty added that "the people said he would be of no use when he did not see the major's carriage pass." If the policeman wasn't in Hasty's house at the time of the murder, then it was true that he was "of no use" in providing an alibi for Hasty.

"I am sorry that under all the circumstances it is my painful duty to pass upon you the awful sentence of the law," said Baron Lefroy. "That is, that you be taken from the place you now stand to the place from whence you came, and from thence on a day to be hereafter named, to the place of public execution, there to be hanged by the neck until you are dead, and may the Lord have mercy upon your soul."

Hasty responded, "May the Lord judge that—May God forgive them all who swore, for I forgive them."

He was then removed.

CHAPTER 16

This Melancholy Exhibition of Human Suffering

The leveling of the houses has been done most effectually.
—JOHN ROSS MAHON TO HENRY
SANDFORD PAKENHAM MAHON,
SEPTEMBER 26, 1848

IT IS HARD TO imagine that the trials were much on the minds of the poor in the days after the proceedings. The starving masses of the Roscommon Union understood that they stood on the edge of another precipice. If the harvest that was about to be culled in the coming weeks withstood the revival of the blight, they had a chance for survival; if it didn't, they were doomed to rely on the limited charity of others. On August 15 the government was planning to end outdoor relief, which was feeding more than twenty thousand able-bodied and non–able-bodied people each week in the eighteen electoral divisions of the union. For those who were lucky or determined enough to cling to plots of more than a quarter acre, the government had already withdrawn its support. Encouraged by the partial recovery of the potato in 1847, these vulnerable figures had seeded their land in the spring and were now waiting for the earth to offer them a chance to continue their existence.

The forecast was mixed. Since early July reports had been circulating throughout western Ireland that the blight had reappeared in a form that was as virulent as in 1846. On July 15, in the same edition that reported Patrick Hasty's sentence of death, the *Roscommon Journal* dismissed such stories, which it blamed on speculators. "So far as this country is concerned, there was never a better prospect of a healthy and abundant harvest," the paper wrote. By the third week in July, with hopes still running high for a sound crop, the attention of the British government and public became preoccupied with what was widely interpreted as the ultimate act of ingratitude for the British government's efforts at saving Ireland: rebellion.

Talk of revolution had been intensifying among the political classes since the transportation of John Mitchel to Bermuda in June. British ministers were receiving reports about increased membership in the Confederation Clubs that had been formed to cultivate insurrectionary impulses. Randolph Routh believed fifty thousand men were "preparing and drilling" for the inevitable event. Even the limping Repeal Association attempted to harness the spirit by mending its fences with the Irish Confederation, and the two joined together to form the Irish League, a short-lived proposition. By late July Lord Clarendon convinced his government to suspend the Habeas Corpus Act—an action he first sought in the aftermath of Major Mahon's murder—allowing government forces to arrest and detain anyone suspected of being part of a revolutionary movement. Such a measure was bound to force the hand of the proud leaders of any potential insurgency. Faced with the option of surrendering to the authorities or attempting to provoke a peasant rebellion, William Smith O'Brien decided that the only option was to fight.

He led a small, poorly armed force around County Tipperary for a few days, failing to inspire much of a rebellious spirit within the dying population. The people would come out to hear his eloquent words, but would wander away when they learned that bread wasn't being distributed, often at the urging of priests opposed to violent action. On July 30 a confrontation was finally found. A few dozen Irish policemen marched toward Ballingarry where Smith O'Brien's two hundred rebels, fewer than fifty armed, were congregated. The rebels threw up a barricade and resolved to stand firm against any enemy incursion of the town. Hearing a rumor that the insurgents ahead numbered some three thousand, the police fell out of line and dashed to a house a mile away, owned by Widow McCormack. They barricaded themselves, along with Mrs. McCormack's several young children, inside the two-story structure and prepared for battle. The rebels descended on the house and began lighting hay to smoke out the police.

At this point, Widow McCormack returned home. She flew into hysterics when she learned that her small children were about to be sacrificed for the greater glory of the nation. The police responded by opening up negotiations with the rebels. With everyone's finger on the trigger, Smith O'Brien approached the house, positioned himself on a windowsill, and grasped hands with a constable. It was "not their lives but their guns we wanted," Smith O'Brien said. Suddenly a few rocks were thrown from the rebel line. In response, the police unleashed two volleys of gunfire, killing at least one person and injuring several and causing the ragged band to melt back into the hills. Smith O'Brien escaped the scene, only to be later apprehended by a railway guard effecting a citizen's arrest. Although the rising of 1848 would be added to the list of Irish rebellions, it is hard to see how it represented the most pressing desire of the people. Ireland needed food before she could think about picking up the sword.

On August 8, with the failure close to the thoughts of everyone in a position of authority, a large crowd descended on the square in front of the Roscommon jail to witness the hanging of Patrick Hasty. Two weeks earlier, Lord Clarendon had responded to a plea from Patrick Hasty's wife, Anne—who begged for the sake of her seven children "in a very deplorable state" that Hasty be spared—by writing in the margin of her letter: "Let the law take its course." By noon more than five hundred soldiers and police officers—members of the Scots' Greys from Athlone, the Thirty-first Regiment, and various constabulary units—had arrived to patrol the perimeter. They were joined by "a vast concourse of the peasantry, male and female, dressed in their holiday clothes, flocked in eager anxiety to get a sight of this melancholy exhibition of human suffering," wrote the *Roscommon Weekly Messenger*. With everyone in place, the hangman appeared upon the platform with "his face enveloped in black crape."

Hasty and another man—Owen Beirne, one of conspirators found guilty in the murder of Reverend John Lloyd—were then brought forward with their arms "closely pinioned."

"They seemed immersed in solemn meditation, and several times fervently struck their breasts as if in mental prayer," wrote the *Messenger*. The two were accompanied by a throng of Catholic clergyman, including the chaplain of the jail, his curates, and several other priests. The newspaper did not mention whether Father McDermott was present. Father Madden, the pastor of Roscommon parish, read aloud from the ritual while the other clerics joined together in their responses, providing this grim event with its soundtrack. Then the "vast crowd, who at a distance were anxiously awaiting the awful moment, uncovered their heads."

The newspaper said that the people "seemed to be forcibly struck by the scene before them."

Hasty and Beirne were fitted with their nooses.

At the hangman's motion, Hasty was the first to drop.

"Beirne appeared unmoved by the shock he must have felt from the fall of the trap so near him; he shortly followed." The newspaper commented that "in a few minutes eternity opened on them both, where, we hope, the expiation they have offered in this world to the outraged laws of society, will be received as some atonement to their offenses."

This "expiation" was represented by the written declarations signed by the two and released for public consumption. Clearly composed by one of the clergymen—or a committee of all of them—Hasty admitted his role in the murder for the first time. "I acknowledge the justice of my sentence for conspiring against the life of the late Major Mahon, which I now heartily regret and for which I expect pardon and mercy through the merits and suffering of my Redeemer." He said his "neglect of, and indifference to the duties prescribed by the Church of God, and so often enforced and recommended by her Pastors, have brought me into a knowledge and participation of that accursed system of Molly Maguireism, and I hope in God that all who hear or read this, my last declaration, will be directed by the advice of their pastors, and at once quit every communication with this and every other illegal association." Bishop Browne, who had written in his Lenten letter two years earlier of the "accursed and illegal system of Molly Maguireism, equally condemned by the law of God and the law of the land," couldn't have drafted it any better.

The bodies of Hasty and Beirne were taken down and "given to their friends," who conveyed them to burial spots. The *Messenger* reported that a "large number of decent well-dressed peasantry" made up the funeral corteges. The paper remarked on "the avidity with which the men seized on the coffins, to contribute their portion of the labor in carrying the remains, and which we know is always done as a mark of respect to the deceased." The writer characterized this behavior as a tribute to a fellow Irishman who had been wronged by an unjust system, noting that "the sympathy of our peasantry is ever extended to the fallen; generous to an extreme, they overlook the faults that have produced the fall, and think only of the wrongs he has suffered," the paper wrote. In this interpretation, Patrick Hasty had suffered a wrong and the attendees were showing affinity for a representative figure in their struggle against the oppressor. Ross Mahon saw the large display of fellowship in a similar light: It was an example that the revolt against the estate administration had not been quelled by the execution of one of its chief lieutenants. "There was a large attendance at Hasty's funeral which clearly shows the feeling of the people to be as bad as ever," he wrote to Pakenham Mahon.

The execution of Patrick Hasty represented one of the final acts of what might be called the pre-post-Famine era in Strokestown.

As he was being interred, word was spreading that the blight had reappeared. On the previous day, August 7, Ross Mahon wrote to Thomas Roberts, with whom he was in almost daily contact: "We presume the potatoes are still safe about Strokestown as you did not mention them." Sometime over the next three days, the land agent heard the news. On August 10 he wrote to Strokestown's Protestant minister, the noxious Reverend Joseph Morton, who had earlier complained about tenants being offered small gratuities to surrender their properties. "We are very sorry to hear that the potato crop about Strokestown is blighted—if it is lost we know not what will become of the country," Ross Mahon wrote mechanically. On August 13 a Poor Law official who had just completed a tour of the Roscommon Union wrote, "I regret to state that I observed a very great appearance of the potato blight, and that in places where last week a trace of it was hardly observable."

The poor were now reliant on a relief structure that was in the process of contracting. Even though the government did issue an order permitting outdoor relief to continue in the wake of blight reports, it wasn't willing to offer any significant money for the task. The Treasury was only prepared to give small grants to the worst of the unions. And with stories of the Young Ireland rebellion filling the newspapers, the British government was loath to do much more. Hurriedly drawn-up proposals from the genuinely alarmed Lord John Russell and Lord Clarendon (who feared that the people would now "die in swarms") that made loans available for public works and assisted-emigration programs failed to garner any support in the cabinet or Parliament. Private charity was not prepared to make up the deficit. The British Relief Association, which had provided vital funding for the Roscommon Union back in February and March, was winding down its Irish outreach with all of its money spent. Even the justly celebrated Society of Friends had largely left the country, citing its workers' exhaustion. It was doing little more than distributing seed in some areas.

The vice-guardians of the Roscommon Union had no choice but to begin slashing the number of people receiving outdoor relief. In the week ending August 5—just prior to the news about the blighted crop—some 20,362 able-bodied and non–able-bodied were in receipt of such aid, which hovered near the highest number who had been served since outdoor relief under the amended Poor Law was first permitted in the Union in February 1848. By the week ending September 2, the vice-guardians had cut that figure in half, mostly by pushing able-bodied paupers from the rolls. Some 9,125 people were in receipt of relief meal during that week, meaning that 11,237 had been cast out to depend on their own meager resources.

The only hope for the Strokestown poor was the landlord. But Henry Sandford Pakenham Mahon, the young, accidental inheritor of the Strokestown estate, wasn't prepared to do anything exceptional for them. Indeed, he decided that the evictions would go forward in the face of a crop failure that turned the Famine into a seismic event, one of the great social catastrophes of history. The area around the murder site would be first on the list of townlands targeted, which proved that the February promise that the tenants would be allowed to remain if they produced the assassins was a gross lie.

On August 5, a few days before the blight appeared, Ross Mahon had written to the landlord wondering about his "wishes about the *haberes* at Doorty and the lands adjoining—perhaps it would be well to eject them during the fine weather." On August 10, a few days after it was detected, Ross Mahon informed Thomas Roberts, his under agent in Strokestown, of Pakenham Mahon's decision. Writing from the Guinness Mahon offices at 26 South Frederick Street in Dublin, Ross Mahon told Roberts that "Mr.

Pakenham Mahon has determined on having the *haberes* executed at Doorty, Cornashina and Leitrim immediately—will you be good enough to have the tenants warned of this—of course if they go before the sheriff arrives we will not prevent them taking the roofs of their houses." It was clear that anyone who was evicted from Doorty, Cornashina, and Leitrim would have nothing but the tatters on their back. Ross Mahon said that tenants from other townlands "had better also be warned to the same effect." But the land agent revealed a slightly softer policy in regard to the nonmurder townlands. "If there are any who can pay up the rent they owe either to the executrix of Major Mahon or to the middleman (if there was such) we will retain them upon their doing so," he wrote. He concluded the note by asking Roberts, "Can you say about how many houses will have to be thrown down by the sheriff—the number of tenants served with ejectments will shew."

On August 12 Ross Mahon told Roberts to go ahead and conduct evictions on the townland of Clonfad, which, prior to the Famine, was the largest piece of land held by a single leaseholder on the Mahon estate. The land agent said that Patrick Browne, the lessee of the property and brother of Bishop George Browne, should be allowed to retain "his house and some land," obviously in recognition for the help he had provided during the public controversy with his brother. All the other cabins on Clonfad would be destroyed. "You may take Pat Browne's tenants out of his hands," Ross Mahon wrote to Roberts. The land agent's correspondence also indicated that other big farmers were unable to pay their rent. "It is unfortunate that even the largest tenants on the Strokestown estate are nearly as much reduced in their circumstances as the smaller—Mr. Robert Devenish, Mr. John Devenish, Mr. Morton of Castlenode, Mr. Pat Browne and Mr. Digan are all in bad circumstances," he wrote to Mrs. Mahon.

On the same day that the land agent set the Clonfad evictions in motion, Ross Mahon sent Pakenham Mahon a petition from "some of the Cornashina tenants" from near the murder site who were again pleading to be allowed to remain. "Possibly they are worth some consideration though it is scarcely probable that they were not in some measure privy to what was going on," he wrote. He also informed the landlord that the evictions on the three murder townlands would remove "one hundred families" or roughly five hundred people from the Mahon estate. On August 17 Ross Mahon made one last effort to convince Pakenham Mahon to distribute small sums of gratuities to threatened tenants. "If you give £200 toward removing those persons against who we have *haberes*, it shall be distributed with great caution and I have no doubt will be very useful," he wrote. It appears that the landlord approved offering the money to some tenants, but not to those who resided on the murder townlands.

At this point in the middle of August, everything was set. Ross Mahon wrote to the sheriff and asked him to set a date for the evictions on Doorty, Leitrim, and Cornashina.

As the last views of old Ireland were being glimpsed, there were growing indications of what the new post-Famine era would look like. From September 5 to 12, while Ross Mahon still waited for word from the sheriff, Bishop Browne and "fifty-three of his patriotic clergy" attended a spiritual retreat in Strokestown conducted by "the Very Rev. Doctor Haly, the truly eloquent Rector of Clongowes Wood College," a gathering likely much like the one Major Mahon had condemned as "feasting and stuffing and praying" in August 1846. Then, on September 13 and 14, Bishop George Browne presided over confirmation services for 535 men and women, ushering the young Catholics into the adulthood of their faith, in "the new magnificent Church of Kiltrustan, situated about two miles northeast of Strokestown," one of two principal worship facilities within Father McDermott's Strokestown parish.

The new edifice replaced a church that the writer John O'Donovan had described a decade earlier as "very ancient." "A great portion is stilling standing," he wrote in his 1837 account of the antiquities of County Roscommon, noting that it was "a church of considerable extent and beauty . . . in its day." O'Donovan passed along a story that claimed that the Kiltrustan church was founded by St. Patrick himself. During his fifth-century travels, the saint arrived in the area and met a local pagan named Trostan who agreed to be converted. The saint began the baptism ceremony by raising his pastoral staff high in the air. Intending to plunge the stick into the ground, he instead "thrust the spike of it into Trostan's foot in which it remained firmly fixed," O'Donovan wrote. As the baptism continued, poor Trostan bore his burden patiently, believing that it was part of the stranger's rite. "When the ceremony was over St. Patrick discovered his blunder and expressed his admiration of Trostan's patience and religious fortitude, and on the spot where such an instance of Christian patience occurred, he thought it should bode well to the future prosperity of the Faith to erect a sacred edifice which he thought prudent to name Kill-Trosdian from the name of the convert," wrote O'Donovan.

The new church, which would have been in construction throughout a period of mass death and mass departure, was the subject of the following gushing description in the *Roscommon Journal*: "This grand temple is 110 feet long, 60 feet broad, and 35 feet high, its style of architecture Gothic; between the nave and the aisles there are two rows of beautiful cut pillars, connected at top by acute arches, which support the center roof over the nave, besides there is a roof over each aisle. At one end of the spacious building stands the grand altar in the sanctuary, equi-distant from both sides with a small chapel to the right and another to the left—and lighted by two grand Gothic windows of stained glass. There are besides distributed all over the building eleven Gothic widows of very large dimensions, and two entrance doors into the Church, at the entrance and opposite the sanctuary."

The paper continued:

This august temple which (with the exception of the Tuam Cathedral) is the largest church in Connaught, was erected

*through the super-human efforts of the much respected par-
ish priest of Strokestown and Kiltrustan, the Very Rev. Dr.
McDermott, vicar-general of the diocese whose indefatigable
exertions (in these years of famine and pestilence) in raising, to
the honor and glory of God, so noble an edifice are only equalled
by his exemplary piety and untiring zeal in behalf of his suffering poor flock. After making the great sacrifices he has already
made, it will be impossible for him to complete this splendid
monument of religion if not assisted by the wealthy and charitable, particularly in a parish where (like its neighbor Kilglass)
destitution prevails to an alarming extent.*

This paragraph provides a powerful testament to Father McDermott's essential nature: He was a determined soldier, recently promoted to vicar-general, in the effort to guarantee a strong Catholic
foundation for those who survived in the tragedy. Even "in these
years of famine and pestilence," he was willing to employ "indefatigable exertions" to build a "monument of religion." In this, Father
McDermott's behavior mirrored that of Archbishop John MacHale,
the Lion of the Fold of Judah, who had written so witheringly
of the crimes being committed against his people. Following the
controversy over Cardinal Fransoni's letter of admonition to the
Irish clergy in early 1848, John of Tuam left Ireland and traveled
to Vatican City, where he spent seven months working to shore up
curial support for his interpretation of Irish Catholicism.

The *Roscommon Journal* noted that at the conclusion of the
confirmation celebrations each day, "his lordship and the clergy
were splendidly entertained at the hospitable home of the excellent
parish priest of Strokestown."

Two weeks after the christening of the new church, Ross Mahon
heard from the sheriff about the eviction schedule. "The sheriff
has fixed Tuesday next for commencing to execute the *haberes*," he
wrote to Roberts on September 15. He instructed his underagent

that "a good supply of crowbars will be necessary and some saws to cut the rafters into short pieces would be useful." He continued, "Mr. Pakenham Mahon wishes the walls left without one stone on another—very likely the best way would be divide the laborers into groups of 4 or 5 men and pay so much for each house leveled satisfactorily . . . say 8 shillings/12 shillings a house and give them a drink of porter when they come and a supply of bread during the day. By doing the business quickly even at apparently some additional expense, money will be saved as the longer the sheriff occupies the more money we must pay him."

Three days later Ross Mahon wrote a letter to a subsheriff, John Hackett, and made some final requests. "Mr. Pakenham Mahon is very anxious that the houses thrown down should be completely leveled so as that the ruins should be as little seen as possible," he wrote. "I have given the necessary directions but would be obliged by your having a look. Mr. Natty, a gentleman in our [Guinness Mahon] office [in Dublin], will attend you when [you obtain] possession of the lands against which we have *haberes*." He added, "I think it would be well if one of the houses we get possession on Doorty or the adjoining land was kept standing as I intend applying for a police party to be stationed on the lands."

On the following day, September 24, 1848, the destruction crew arrived at the three townlands: Mr. Natty, the sheriff and his men, and Roberts's liquored-up crowbar brigade.

According to a letter Ross Mahon mailed the following day after hearing from Mr. Natty, everything went "satisfactorily." Ross Mahon reminded Roberts in this note that the "greatest care must be taken that no huts are to be erected—[John] Robinson [the bailiff] should visit them frequently."

Ross Mahon also wrote a thank-you letter to the subsheriff. "Thanks for the trouble you took at Strokestown—it is pleasant that the business was done so satisfactorily." On the same day he penned a letter to his employer, filling in some of the details of eviction day: "I am happy to say that the *haberes* have been executed without any accident or disturbance," he told Pakenham Mahon. "The leveling of the houses has been done most effectually. There is not a wall standing and the stones are removed from the foundations—there was no case of fever or sickness which I consider very fortunate. It was thought advisable by Mr. Blakeney the subinspector of police that the houses belonging to Michael Gardiner who is now in gaol and John McNamara, both of Doorty, should be left standing—it is possible that both these persons may help in giving information."

In this letter to the young landlord, Ross Mahon established two facts of pertinence to our story, one concerning Strokestown's past, the other about its future. First, Michael Gardiner, the only conspirator who had been identified as fleeing the murder scene with a gun in his hand, was a resident of Doorty, thus a tenant of Major Mahon, and therefore a man with a motive. Second, the eighty-four-acre rundale community near the new road—the complex scattering of plots 200 to 250 yards southwest of the Doorty Bridge that had been leased by "James Hunt and Co." since 1808—was no more. The settlement of Doorty had ceased to exist.

Epilogue

THE PROCESS WOULD CONTINUE over the next few years. During the autumn and winter of 1848, the vice-guardians of the Roscommon Union struggled to maintain the same levels of outdoor and indoor relief—complaining in January 1849 that "the resources of all classes of ratepayers are now very considerably exhausted"—while the landlord and land agent kept up the campaign of clearances. By February 1849 the government was finally able to free some additional funds for the relief effort. With Lord John Russell threatening to resign over the matter, Parliament (which had approved nearly 8 million pounds in Famine spending since 1845, half of which had been earmarked to be paid back) reluctantly permitted an immediate 50,000-pound grant to the most distressed unions. The small outlay, wrote the *Times*, "has almost broken the back of English benevolence." The money was approved with the understanding that any subsequent relief expenditure would come from a "rate-in-aid" scheme then being debated. Its objective was to transfer rates from the less hard-hit unions in the north and east of Ireland to the more Famine-ravaged ones in the west, a controversial plan to force Irish property from better-off areas to pay for Irish poverty in worse-off areas.

To the chief Poor Law commissioner in Dublin, who had been pleading with Trevelyan to increase Treasury contributions for months, this measure represented a gross abdication of the government's responsibility to the Irish people. Edward Twisleton saw it as nothing less than an act of extermination, which was the precise word that Lord Clarendon used to characterize his colleague's position. "He thinks," Clarendon wrote to Lord John Russell, "that the destitution here [in Ireland] is so horrible, and the indifference of the House of Commons to be so manifest, that he is an unfit agent of a policy which must be one of extermination." It should be noted that the *British* official responsible for overseeing relief in Ireland following the introduction of the amended Poor Law used this provocative word to describe the state's behavior in the wake of the failure of the 1848 potato crop. "Twisleton feels that as Chief Commissioner he is placed in a position . . . which no man of honor can endure," wrote Lord Clarendon in the letter to the prime minister. Instead, he resigned in March. Later, before a parliamentary committee, Twisleton said that people were dying from lack of sufficient food in the worst areas because the government was even unwilling to advance a few hundred pounds to each of the distressed unions, "say a small part of the expense of the Coffre War." He was speaking of the Kaffir War, which pitted British troops and colonists against the Xhosa people of the Eastern Cape, South Africa. The seventh Kaffir War had concluded in May 1847; the eighth would commence in 1850. Again, these were the statements of a British official in loyal service to the Crown, not a rabid Irish revolutionary intent on the violent overthrow of British rule in Ireland. In his testimony, Twisleton also rebuked the conventional view espoused by the political economists that Famine sufferers should be left to the natural forces of the free market. He said "that it is part of the system of nature that we should have feelings of compassion for those people, and that it is a most narrow-minded view of the system of nature to think that those people should be left to die; that because the material elements do not produce sufficient food for them at the time, they are to perish, and their brothers in the rest of the empire are to look on and let them die. . . . I believe it is part of the system of nature that we should feel compassion for them and assist them." His statement revealed a view of famine relief that was tragically missing from the government's policy: The people must be fed because it was a God-ordained duty to *simply feed them.*

But at least the rate-in-aid legislation was something. For a segment of the poor, it was even something substantial. In late April, with only 6,000 pounds remaining from the 50,000-pound grant issued in February, Parliament approved an advance of 100,000 pounds to the most distressed unions, an outlay to be paid back with money collected through the rate-in-aid. And when the rate-in-aid legislation was formally adopted in late May, it included a provision that allowed another 100,000-pound advance for the hardest-hit areas. In practical terms, this money enabled the Roscommon Union to increase the number of people receiving outdoor relief—from 7,775 in January 1849 to 9,845 in March (after the issuance of the 50,000-pound grant), and to 16,378 in June 1849 (following the approval of the two 100,000-pound advances). Like so many of the government's relief initiatives, it was too late for many and too little for others. But the delivery of these funds showed that the British government was not willing to *fully* abandon the poor, which goes a long way toward proving that its explicit objective was not to commit mass murder on the Irish people. Instead the government's crime, which deserves to blacken its name forever, must be characterized differently. From the time of the adoption of the Poor Law Amendment Act in late 1847, the British state showed that the effort to regenerate Ireland—furthered by the landlord-engineered replacement of tillage plots with grazing lands, a primary aim of government policy since the passage of the Irish Poor Law in 1838—took precedence over the obligation to provide food and protection for its starving citizens. It is little wonder that this policy looked to many people like genocide, to use the modern description.

In the early months of 1849 the judicial system resolved the matter of the assassination to its satisfaction. In late February James Commins was put on trial for the second time. Although the court testimony was largely the same, a few differences stood out. Patrick Flynn now claimed that he did in fact witness James Commins fire a gun at Major Mahon. In the first trial he claimed to see only the "flash" from the ditch where Commins was hiding, and he claimed to see it only during cross-examination. But now he said he "watched the carriage until Commins fired at it," according to the *Roscommon Journal*. Further, he said he "heard a moan after the shot was fired." The only way he could have heard anything from Major Mahon's mouth was if the landlord screamed upon being struck. The earwitness Patrick Hunt also shored up his testimony against Commins. He now said that the alleged assassin did indeed flee from the murder scene in the direction of Doorty before crossing into the fields, finally corroborating Flynn's account. He said Commins "was coming up towards them"—that is, he was coming up the hill toward Doorty—before he turned away from the new road into the fields.

The prosecution offered one surprise witness: Thomas Brennan, who had been named in the indictment as one of the conspirators who convinced Commins and Hasty to commit the crime. Apprehended in England earlier in the month, he agreed upon his return to Ireland to testify on behalf of the Crown. He largely corroborated the stories about the pre-murder conspiracy, seeming to confirm that Patrick Hasty, James Commins, and Michael Gardiner were indeed members of the gang. He filled in details on the second failed "attempt" on Major Mahon, describing how he, Commins, and "another man" equipped with a case of pistols and a gun waited near the road for the landlord's carriage to pass on his way home from the Ballinasloe fair at the end of the first week of October. Assigned to fire the fatal shot, Brennan said he became "afraid" and convinced the others to abandon their positions. But his testimony about the post-murder conspiracy had noticeable problems. In describing the Christmas Eve gathering at the Widow Smyth's, he mentioned nothing about James Commins being present to receive his payment, which was the reason the story was told in the first trial. Instead he claimed Hasty, Gardiner, and Andrew Connor talked "about collecting money for those who shot Major Mahon." Was Thomas Brennan suggesting that neither Hasty nor Gardiner was among "those who shot Major Mahon"?

Of the murder itself, he said that Commins told him that Michael Gardiner bore much of the responsibility for the success of the shooting. Commins told him that Major Mahon would not have been killed but for the actions of Michael Gardiner, who behaved admirably during the crime.

Asked if he knew who fired the fatal shot, Brennan responded that Commins "did not say who fired the gun." So Commins wasn't the shooter, either?

In the end, it is hard to accurately discern Commins's role in the crime. Plenty of circumstantial evidence pointed to Commins as the assassin—it appears that the community had come to the collective decision that he committed the crime. But there was no concrete evidence to prove that he and he alone pulled the fatal trigger, and plenty of confusing and inconsistent testimony that discredited the witnesses who suggested he did.

Some testimony pointed toward Michael Gardiner, who, if he wasn't the assassin or the misfiring second shooter, was clearly the most active member of the gang.

Catherine Donnelly again identified Gardiner as fleeing the murder scene with what might have been the murder weapon (because it was a "gun" not a "pistol") in his hand. She said that she was in her aunt's house "near the bridge of Doorty" when she heard the sound of gunfire. A few minutes later she left the house and was "going home by a booreen up to her father's" in Doorty—she was walking toward the hill that led to the Doorty settlement. She said she "heard a great noise coming up through the pasture—noise of a person's feet running." She saw "Michael Gardiner running with a gun in his hand," and watched as he approached "his own house" in Doorty and entered it. During cross-examination she admitted that her family had been feuding with Gardiner, who had accused her uncle of "sticking his mare"—or putting pins into his horse. The charge apparently had some merit. Donnelly admitted that her uncle's son had been put in jail for the crime.

The jury returned its verdict "without almost any delay," wrote Ross Mahon to Mrs. Mahon: James Commins was guilty.

Michael Gardiner and Martin Brennan (the conspirator was shown only to have attended a single gang meeting) both responded to the verdict by pleading guilty. They were given sentences of death, which were soon commuted to transportation for life.

On the morning of March 21, 1849, James Commins was hanged in the square in front of the jail before a crowd of only one hundred people. His final statement released for public perusal had none of the instructive flavor or emotive repentance of Patrick Hasty's. "As I, James Commins, am now to appear before a just and merciful God, I am anxious to make this my last Declaration hoping through the merits of my Savior suffering for me, that all my sins may be forgiven. I admit before God and man the Justice of my sentence, and as I expect forgiveness and pardon from a merciful Redeemer, I forgive from my heart all my Prosecutors and the whole world."

But the case was in no way settled. As the months passed, stray facts about the crime trickled in. On April 17 a shoemaker named Luke Lyons told police that James Commins had used Martin Mulligan's gun—not Patrick Doyle's, as was alleged at trial—to kill

Major Mahon. In his sworn information, Lyons also noted something that had not been mentioned at trial: The murderers were believed by the community to be Molly Maguires. He quoted Martin Mulligan as saying that "it was a pity that there was not six or seven more of them shot and damned the Mollys for not doing so as it would do much good in the country."

By the summer of 1849 the police learned that the ringleader, the money-distributing Andrew Connor, the only conspirator who didn't reside in the Four Mile House townlands near the crime scene, had apparently reached America like so many of his countrymen. On August 10 a superintendent of police at Welland Canal, located just across the Canadian-American border from the city of Buffalo, New York, wrote Irish officials that "Andrew Connor, a laborer at this place, answering the name and description handed me by Copeland a few days ago, left Port Robinson about six week since. It is supposed he is now in the neighborhood of New York. . . . I shall keep a sharp lookout in case of his return."

In the fall of 1849 the Crown rewarded its cooperating witnesses. The servant boy John Hester and the approver Thomas Brennan were given free passage to New Orleans and a few pounds to purchase new clothes. The earwitness Patrick Hunt and Catherine Donnelly were also provided with transport to the United States. A few of the others refused the offer to leave the country. The eyewitness Patrick Flynn was among those who requested to be sent to another part of Ireland.

Of the convicted men, the barely mentioned conspirator Martin Brennan sailed to Québec aboard the *Agnes* with his wife and seven children on June 7, 1850, never to be heard from again. At the same time, the other surviving defendant, Michael Gardiner, was lodged in Philipstown prison to serve a twelve-year prison term in lieu of being transported out of the country.

In reviewing all the statements that emerged from the court proceedings, it is apparent that the prosecutors had succeeded only in proving one thing, if hazily: that a conspiracy, composed of a collection of people on and near the Mahon estate, had banded together to kill Major Mahon. Unsurprisingly, the local folklore has always expressed doubts about the integrity of the convictions, with one correspondent noting that "common opinion held that the murderers were never convincingly identified." But this is to suggest not that the community believed the wrong men were prosecuted, merely that they were never *convincingly* proven guilty.

In the autumn of 1849, the potato crop in County Roscommon was healthy, although far below pre-Famine levels. In September, with the number of people on outdoor relief reduced to 1,112, the paid vice-guardians of the Roscommon Union were dismissed and an elected board of guardians was reinstated. That same month the first race day in three years was held at a Roscommon horse track, a signal event for a horse-loving people. And in the spring of 1850 Pakenham Mahon was confident enough of his safety to be named deputy lieutenant for County Roscommon, revealing that the family's power had not been diminished in the least during the crisis. By April outdoor relief was being offered to just a handful of recipients, which showed that the Famine in Roscommon was now largely judged to be over. (In some sections of western Ireland, however, outdoor relief continued until 1852.)

In the summer of 1850 the brother of the famous political economist Nassau Senior made a visit to the Mahon estate, and in a subsequent book, the economist transcribed his brother's description of its state of affairs. He noted that "the diminution of numbers, and distrust of the potato, had diminished the competition for land" on the Mahon property. "The petty tenements are now consolidated into farms of about thirty acres each," he said. "The new tenants are not injured, and some rent, perhaps half the old rent, is paid."

In recounting the murder of Major Mahon, Senior's brother blamed the death on local anger over the disastrous emigration plan, repeating the rumor that one of the ships drowned. He also said it was committed after Father McDermott commenced his pulpit denunciations. According to Senior, the priest was angered not by the clearances but by Major Mahon's accusation that he "embezzled £100, which been placed in his hands for the poor." For the first time it was explicitly stated that Father McDermott had stolen from the destitute—Lord Clarendon had told the prime minister of "irregularities" in the relief fund; Ross Mahon had hinted at unspecified problems with the subscriptions that "would be very extraordinary disclosures" if made public; the three relief committee members had noted that Major Mahon "seemed" to accuse Father McDermott of financial impropriety during the August 28, 1847, relief committee meeting. (Of course, Major Mahon did not quote himself as accusing Father McDermott of malfeasance. The landlord wrote that the priest's anger flashed when he asked about a revision of the relief lists.) The money would have been less than a fifth of the £558 raised by his relief committee for the soup kitchen during the first three months of 1847. It was enough to buy a significant quantity of Indian meal (which sold for less than 20 pounds a ton throughout the Famine) or send a few dozen people to America. But Senior isn't necessarily to be trusted. He also claimed that the clearances on the Mahon estate and the nearby Marcus McClausland property (which was once part of it) had reduced the numbers on both by a total of only one thousand people. Someone had provided him with incorrect information.

Senior's account makes clear that Pakenham Mahon had sought revenge against the *entire* community for the murder of his father-in-law. He "thought himself justified in treating with little forbearance a peasantry whom he considered accomplices to the assassin. He ejected them in great numbers, and left them to what was in fact nothing—their own resources."

Senior told of visiting John Ross Mahon at his residence.

We found our host, the agent, inhabiting a large house in Strokestown, with a garrison of eight policemen. After dinner we went into a vacant room to smoke our cigars. The shutters were instantly closed. It would be the height of imprudence, they said, to sit with lights and unprotected windows. Every aperture through which anyone on the outside could see that there were persons in the room within, was carefully closed before the candles were lighted.

The next day we went out in a car, with the agent, to examine the estate. He used never to leave home without policemen; but as we were four, and all well-armed, as our visit was unexpected, and our route could not be foreseen, we thought that we could do without them.

We drove about for four days, and were never attacked or treated uncivilly. . . . I was glad, however, when the visit was over, and I could take my double-barreled pistols out of my pocket.

These final passages made evident that the landed establishment wasn't yet convinced that the anger of the Irish people had been snuffed out. In this regard, they would be proven correct.

When the 1851 census was released, the transformation wrought by nature and man was made clear. In the ten years since the last census in 1841, the population of the country had fallen from 8,175,124 to 6,552,385. Census officials calculated that a normal rate of growth would have put the population at 9 million. It has been estimated that a million people perished during the Famine and that another million and a half left the country for new lands, mostly America. In the province of Conaught, 28.6 percent of the population, many of them speakers of the Irish Gaelic language, was gone. On the Mahon estate, the percentage was higher. In the Bumlin portion of Father McDermott's Strokestown parish, the population decreased from 5,257 to 2,605, a decline of 50.4 percent; in the Kiltrustan portion, the numbers went from 3,938 to 2,325, a reduction of 40.9 percent. The story was the same in other parishes populated by

Mahon tenants. In Father Boyd's Lisanuffy parish, the population dropped from 4,832 to 2,977, a loss of 38.3 percent. In the Kilbride parish that contained the murder townlands, the population went from 8,578 to 4,719, a decrease of 44.9 percent. In Father Brennan's Kilglass parish the drop was from 10,053 to 4,202, a decline of a stunning 58.2 percent. An entire segment of the rural society had disappeared: In 1841 there were 445,750 holdings of land under five acres in Ireland, which represented 53.7 percent of the whole; in 1851 there were 125,811 holders of plots less than five acres, 20.7 percent of the whole. By 1901 just 10 percent of the population would hold plots in this size category. The victors were the Catholic middle-class farmers and graziers who had warred with the restive poor in the years before the Famine. In 1841 just 48,625 people out of 8.1 million held property of more than fifty acres, 5.9 percent of the whole. In 1851, however, 149,090 out of 6.5 million held a plot of such a size, 24.5 percent of the whole. These individuals would take their place in the center of Irish civil society in the period after the Famine, serving as the class who would lay the foundation of the eventual Irish state.

In the years after the tragedy the Mahon estate appeared to return to health, as Ross Mahon had predicted it would in his letters to Major Mahon in 1846 and 1847. In the 1850s Henry Sandford Pakenham Mahon and his agent inaugurated a period of improvement on the now consolidated lands, commencing the second golden age in the family's administration of the property. After introducing a number of schemes to "improve the condition and trade of Strokestown," including the construction of a new fair green and an extensive effort to upgrade area infrastructure, Pakenham Mahon was pronounced to be "alive to his duties" as landlord by the *Roscommon Journal* in 1857, ten years after the murder of Major Mahon. Unlike some Irish landlords who had gone bankrupt during the Famine, he was not forced to sell all or part of his estate in the years following it. Indeed, with his inheritance from his own family, he more than doubled the size of his holdings. In 1881 Pakenham Mahon was listed as holding 26,980 acres, far more than the roughly 11,000 acres that Major Mahon had bequeathed to him in 1847. By now the grasslands and sheepwalks that were made possible by the absence of landless laborers, cottiers, and small farmers were regarded as the richest in the province of Connaught, according to Susan Hood, the Mahon family chronicler. In the 1880s "the sheep sold at the Strokestown fairs were reputedly the best in Ireland, and recognized as a distinct class by being awarded special prizes by the Royal Agricultural Society of Ireland," she wrote.

In 1861 Michael Gardiner was released from prison. According to documents in his convict reference file, he returned to his hometown upon being set free. According to legend, he came back to "desecrate the Mahon tomb," wrote local historian Billie Donlon, but was chased off by police before he could complete the task. In fact, Ross Mahon was so alarmed by his presence around Strokestown that he fired off a letter to Dublin Castle, demanding to know why he had been discharged. Gardiner is "now at large residing just outside Strokestown *demesne*," he wrote in anger and fear on April 18, 1861. Somehow the matter reached the House of Lords. Rising before that body, the Earl of Donoughmore claimed that Gardiner "was allowed back to the scene of his crime, and, so to speak, to walk over the grave of his victim." The authorities in Dublin investigated and responded that Gardiner's transportation-for-life sentence had been commuted to twelve years in prison in keeping with all applicable laws. They also noted that the convict had registered with the constable after arriving Strokestown, as required by the conditions of his release, before moving to "Manchester in England to join his wife and family who reside there." He gave their address as 140 London Road, Manchester. If the folklore is correct and Gardiner returned to Strokestown to vandalize the landlord's grave, this singular figure in the Mahon story also serves as a representative of all the Famine survivors who fled the country with anger in their hearts.

There are other representative figures in the Mahon story. The two Quinn boys from the Lisanuffy parish who lost their parents aboard the *Naomi* grew into adults who would be prime forces in efforts to build communities in the New World, helping to establish a North America that would emerge as the world's richest and powerful region by the twentieth century. Both the orphan Quinns, who were raised on the grounds of a seminary by a maintenance employee, joined the priesthood and tended to fledgling French-Canadian towns in rural Québec. Patrick, the older of the two, became a revered figure in Richmond, where he served as pastor of Paroisse Sainte-Bibiane for more than fifty years, building the parish from the ground up. According to a local history, he was a "broad-minded Catholic" who "never levied a church tax upon his flock, but . . . accomplished much by means of voluntary contributions." Perhaps he never forgot that Catholic priests in Ireland had once extracted dues to perform sacraments and collected "rent" to support the Repeal Association. A current church official described Quinn as "very kind and open-minded about mixed marriage with Protestants, getting the dispensations for them, baptizing their children even if the couple had married in another Church, etc." When he died in 1915 his obituary listed three survivors in Strokestown, two in Québec, and three in Cleveland, Ohio.

The younger Thomas served in communities closer to the St. Lawrence River, not far from the island where he landed as a small child in the summer of 1847. When he gave a speech in 1912 before the First Congress of the French Language, held June 24–30, the seventy-one-year-old showed himself to be as proud of his new country as he was of his former one. Indeed, he seemed to be more passionate about French Canada than Ireland, for which he nonetheless retained a deep and abiding pride. Noting that he was an "adopted" child of the French family, he said that his adoption was now "complete, and I claim my own seat at the family table. The French language is mine, just as it is yours," he said, before he offered his voice on behalf of *French-Canadian* demands from Great Britain.

He continued his speech by noting that he spoke as a person who had himself experienced "suffering and oppression."

"Which people have borne this weight more than Ireland?" he asked, speaking in French.

It is not my intention or occasion here to mention those pages of tears and blood that make up, as it were, its only history.

You shall permit me, however, ladies and gentlemen, to extract one incident that enters through one side into my subject here, an event in which I myself was actor and victim.

It happened in 1847. A famine more terrible than the previous one threatened to totally exterminate the Irish people. The most surprising spectacle was not seeing people die, but seeing them live, as great as the distress was.

During a three-year period, more than four million of these unfortunate souls miraculously escaped death and took to the road of exile. Walking ghosts, they left in tears, asking for hospitality from more fortunate countries.

After traveling by sea for two months, divine Providence wished us to be thrown onto the coast of Grosse Île, Québec.

A sickness that science has not mentioned anywhere else, famine fever, added its terrible torments to so much other pain.

Canada, however, saw these unfortunate souls coming, and welcomed them as brothers. Filled with compassion and braving the epidemic, French-Canadian priests ignored their glory in going to aid them.

French-Canadian clergy, may you be eternally blessed for your heroism! More than others, you, who fell victim to your own devotion, glorious martyrs of charity, bask in the glory of your justly deserved reward!

Thanks to your tireless charity, my unfortunate parents were able to attain their final sleep in peace with God, pardoning their enemies, carrying away their ineffable consolation of leaving their children under the protection of the French-Canadian priest.

I still remember one of these admirable clergymen who led us to the bedside of my dying father. As he saw us, my father with his failing voice repeated that old Irish adage, "Remember your soul and your liberty."

Quinn noted that sixty years had passed since those days, but "my soul has retained its thanks to the French-Canadian people, and my spirit remains jealous of its rights and liberties." It was a simple statement of loyalty for a place that was not initially pleased to see him—as a sickly six-year-old, Thomas Quinn was the last in a group of twenty-five orphans to be adopted—and that had now grown into his home. Famine emigrants to America and Australia were also initially unwelcome in those countries, "thrown onto the coast" of vast lands that regarded them with suspicion and contempt. But both populations had succeeded over the hard-working generations to shape the culture in such a way that they became an integral part of it. This is as much a part of the Famine story as any other.

John Ross Mahon would remain a hated figure in the countryside, a symbol of the tensions that continued to fester in rural Irish communities over the next several decades. He continued to work as the Guinness Mahon land agent for Pakenham Mahon and other Roscommon and Galway landlords, prying rents from poor tenants and evicting those who failed to come up with the money. He also remained a target of agrarian agitators. Although the Molly Maguires disappeared in the years after the Famine—a secret organization of Irish Americans bearing that name soon popped up in the anthracite coalfields of eastern Pennsylvania, killing sixteen mining officials during the 1860s and 1870s—other groups emerged to foment violence against a landed elite that was slow to release its grip on the populace. In 1882 members of the Land League made an attempt on his life by placing dynamite on the drawing-room windowsill of his County Galway home. The ensuing explosion broke a few windows, but Ross Mahon wasn't at home at the time. He died of natural causes a few years later on June 5, 1886. The land and banking business that he cofounded and under whose name he cleared the Mahon estate would far outlast him. It continues to exist today under new ownership, having experienced financial scandal, foreign merger, and multinational expansion over the last few decades.

In keeping with his nature, Father McDermott spent the final years of his life building another church, this one in the Bumlin portion of his parish. Completed in 1863, the impressive structure, which still towers over Elphin Street near the center of Strokestown, would remain his legacy, his final blow for his faith. In its November 3, 1866, edition—published nineteen years and one day after the murder of Major Mahon—the *Roscommon Journal* reported that had the priest "died suddenly, at Strokestown, on Tuesday morning last, at an advanced age, very sincerely regretted by his parishioners and numerous friends, Dean McDermott, PP—RIP." Both Father McDermott and Bishop George Browne, who died in 1858, passed from the scene having known that they helped usher in a so-called devotional revolution that made the Catholic Church a bedrock institution in Irish society, a force that would influence nearly every aspect of its life until widespread scandal and increasing secularism ended its monopoly in the 1990s.

Upon the death of Henry Sandford Pakenham Mahon in 1893, the estate went into a long period of decline. The family grew less involved in the day-to-day operation, and there were several efforts to sell the land and house, which remained standing through the violent upheavals that precipitated and accompanied the granting of partial Irish statehood in the early twentieth century. During the War of Independence, British troops were stationed within its walls and Irish Republican Army suspects were questioned in the demesne, a clear indication of Pakenham Mahon loyalties. Even after the establishment of an Irish state extinguished the last traces of the influence of the old Protestant Ascendancy, the house remained in the family's hands, an increasingly anachronistic symbol of a bygone era. By the 1970s an elderly great granddaughter of Major

Mahon, Olive Hales Pakenham Mahon, was the only relative who spent much time in the tottering, mice-filled house staffed by a few ancient employees. An eccentric woman who would eagerly recall the balls she attended as a young woman at Buckingham Palace, she struck up an unlikely friendship with a local businessman named James Callery, with whom she had once quarreled in a property dispute. Eventually she sold him the property and embarked for the English nursing home where she would die. Lord John Russell's Famine-era hopes of having prosperous Irish Catholic business-men buy up the estates of insolvent Protestant landlords had finally come to pass in Strokestown.

Sifting through the papers that had been left behind by the fam-ily, Callery found a written plea from starving tenants who lived in the townland where he was raised. It inspired him to turn the old sta-bles into an impressive Famine Museum and renovate the house and gardens for tours. In 1994 Irish president Mary Robinson arrived to officially open the museum. A human-rights lawyer with both rebels and loyalists in her lineage, Robinson was the perfect figure to inau-gurate a new era in Famine memory, a representative of a new way of looking at an old story. Describing herself as committed to an honest remembrance of Ireland's past, she called upon her listeners to extend a hand toward those who continue to suffer from famine conditions in unhappy regions of Africa. It is not hard to see in Robinson's state-ment a quiet gesture of forgiveness toward those who had wronged the Irish poor, delivered as it was by a symbolic leader of the Irish people at home and abroad. The battles of the past are now over, she was saying. We are a prosperous and contented people. Now it is time to channel our anger away from the former enemy and direct loving attention to those who had not yet been freed from their trials—trials that the Irish people are able to recall deep within their essence.

Notes

PROLOGUE

xi *Even 160 years after its occurrence:* Many modern histories of the Famine explore the varying interpretations of the Famine in folkloric memory and historical scholarship. James Donnelly Jr., *The Great Irish Potato Famine* (2001), 1–40, 209–245. Christine Kinealy, *The Great Irish Famine: Impact, Ideology and Rebellion* (2002), 1–30. The populist, nationalist interpretation—in which the British government is judged to be guilty of deliberate murder—is proffered mostly famously in John Mitchel's 1861 jeremiad, *The Last Conquest of Ireland (Perhaps)*. In his book, Mitchel delivered the single most memorable line in all of Famine literature: "The Almighty, indeed, sent the potato blight, but the English created the Famine." The academic, revisionist interpretation—in which the British government is exonerated of such foul intent—is put forward most prominently in R. Dudley Edwards and T. Desmond Williams, eds., *The Great Famine: Studies in Irish History, 1845–52* (1956). In its foreword, the editors wrote, "There was no conspiracy to destroy the Irish nation. The scale of the actual outlay to meet the famine and the expansion of the public relief system are in themselves impressive evidence that the state was by no means always indifferent to Irish needs."

xi   *In recent years a consensus:* Among modern scholars of the Famine who reject the charge of genocide while delivering severe judgments against aspects of the British government's policies are Donnelly, Kinealy, Peter Gray, and Cormac Ó Gráda.

xi   *Yet no expert on the Famine:* In her song "Famine," which appears on the 1994 album *Universal Mother*, Sinéad O'Connor challenged the use of the word *famine* to describe the Irish tragedy, suggesting that sufficient food existed in the country to feed the starving. "There was no famine," she sings. In an October 9, 1996, press release, Governor George Pataki of New York stated, "History teaches us the Great Irish Hunger was not the result of a massive failure of the Irish potato crop but rather was the result of a deliberate campaign by the British to deny the Irish people the food they needed to survive."

xii   *Indeed, it is usually* Irish *writers:* For evidence that it is the native Irish who are most passionate in their denunciation of those who would make extreme charges, see novelist Colm Tóibín's powerful, scolding essay on the Famine. Colm Tóibín, Diarmaid Ferriter, *The Irish Famine: A Documentary* (2002). In her essay "Revisionism and Irish History: The Great Famine," Irish historian Mary Daly wrote that the popular success of a fictional Famine diary that was passed off as nonfiction suggested "a strong desire to wallow in its emotional horrors, perhaps at the cost of a wider understanding." D. G. Boyce, Alan O'Day, eds., *The Making of Modern Irish History: Revisionism and the Revisionist Controversy* (1996), 71, 85.

xii   *A prominent scholar of Ireland's past:* Edwards and Williams, eds., *Great Famine*, 476.

xii   *While some regard Major Mahon:* Of the folkloric memory of Major Mahon, local historian Billie Donlon wrote, "Major Mahon . . . is usually remembered as a fair and reasonable landlord." John Ross Mahon, he wrote, "acquired an infamous reputation in the folk history of the area on account of his harsh treatment of the tenantry." Billie Donlon, "The Mahon Murder Trials," *Roscommon Historical and Archaeological Society Journal*, vol. 1 (1986), 31–32. Local storyteller Bernard Cunningham wrote, "Major Mahon . . . did his best to alleviate the sufferings of his tenants for whom he was truly sorry." He added that "no reason for the dastardly crime was every discovered." Bernard Cunningham, "Some Traditional History of the Parish of Strokestown from the Days of St. Patrick to the Famine," Schools Manuscript Collection, vol. 253, Department of Irish Folklore, University College, Dublin, 329. Cunningham's statement was collected sometime between November 4, 1937, and December 16, 1938. In her popular history of the Famine, Cecil Woodham-Smith described Major Mahon as "handsome, amiable, and well-intended." She repeated an unconfirmed story that on the morning of his death he addressed a gathering of his poor tenants, who responded by breaking into applause. "The legend in the west of Ireland is that 'coffin ships' were chartered, when one foundered, and all aboard were lost, Major Mahon was shot by the lover of a girl who had been drowned," which would have meant that the landlord was killed for a crime he actually didn't commit. Cecil Woodham-Smith, *The Great Hunger* (1962), 324–325. A project completed by local Strokestown students concluded, "According to tradition, Strokestown didn't fare too badly—the landlord and his family did tremendous work in relieving the hungry, and the assassination of Major Mahon in 1847 was frowned upon by many of his tenants. . . . The older people still living in the locality believe the bullet that killed the major was really intended for his ruthless cousin and agent Mr. Ross Mahon." "A Century and a Half of Strokestown: A Project by Students of the Diploma in Social Action," undated, the collection of the Roscommon Library, 25. An exhibit in the Famine Museum, Strokestown Park, quotes a local citizen from February 24, 1952. Dan Kelly said the murder was a case of mistaken identity: "Nobody would harm a hair on his head, as he was much beloved of the people, especially his tenants." Kelly identifies the killers' true target as the land agent, whom he incorrectly names as Thomas Conry. Of the Mahon family's posthumous view of Major Mahon, author Ann Morrow wrote, "The Pakenham Mahons still smart over the implication that Denis Mahon was assassinated by some of Strokestown's destitute tenants inflamed as they watched grain being sent to England while they were hungry. . . . [The family] believes they really had planned to kill the overzealous Strokestown agent, responsible for 6,000 tenant evictions, and not Denis Mahon." Ann Morrow, *Eccentric Lives of the Anglo-Irish* (1989), 13–26. In 1954 an Irish magazine wrote that Major Mahon was believed by the family to be a "kindly man," who was "deeply interested in the welfare of his tenants. . . . The murderers were never convincingly identified, and common opinion held that it was a case of mistaken identity." "Strokestown Park, Co. Roscommon: Residence of Major Hales Pakenham Mahon and Mrs. Hales Pakenham Mahon," *Irish Tatler and Sketch*, January 1954, 8–13. In a 1991 letter Nicholas Pakenham Mahon, the great-great grandson of Major Mahon, wrote, "Denis Mahon, like the men, women and children who died in Roscommon or at sea, was the victim of circumstances beyond his control." Exhibit, Famine Museum, Strokestown Park. Pakenham Mahon wrote that the landlord was in an "unenviable" position when he inherited the indebted estate at the onset of the Famine. In an interview with Ann Morrow, he pinned the ultimate blame on the government. "The wretched Denis was expected to pay for everyone," Pakenham Mahon said. "Take the Sudan; governments step in and help." Morrow, *Eccentric Lives of the Anglo-Irish*, 24.

xii *A related tale in the folklore:* Of Father McDermott's culpability in the murder, a local citizen who would have been born in the 1880s said that Major Mahon and Father McDermott had a dispute over a chapel that the priest was in the process of building. Claiming that the construction was halting traffic, the landlord arranged for the priest to be issued a summons. "He is able to summon," the priest said, "but he will not be able to prosecute." A supernatural force rose up to exact revenge on behalf of the priest. "When the court day came the landlord drove his carriage and near Gannon's corner, his horses took flight and he was thrown out of his carriage and killed and the next time he passed the new building he was dead and going to be buried," according to John Shaughnessy. "Landlords," Schools Manuscript Collection, vol. 253, 280–281.

xii *The other predominant analysis:* Of the charge that the Molly Maguires were the guilty party, Anne Coleman wrote, "Major Mahon was unlucky in that bitterness had been building up for years on such an extensive, subdivided and populous estate, that there was such high mortality among those 'emigrated' at his expense, and that he fell foul of the Mollies who were serious terrorists." Anne Coleman, *Riotous Roscommon: Social Unrest in the 1840s* (1999), 49. Kevin Kenny called the murder of Major Mahon "the most celebrated case of Molly Maguire activity in County Roscommon." Kevin Kenny, *Making Sense of the Molly Maguires* (1998), 30. Stephen J. Campbell is more cautious. "It appears it

[the murder] was the result of a conspiracy which targeted landlords as enemies of the people and which was confident of popular
support." Stephen J. Campbell, *The Great Irish Famine: Words and
Images from the Famine Museum, Strokestown Park, Co. Roscommon*
(1994), 49. Of the local view of the murderers, Paula Mullooly
repeats a tale about a woman in a local inn who heard a conversation between two men who were plotting the death of Major
Mahon. "She was in the next room and did not see the men only
heard their conversation and it was on her evidence alone that sent
James Commins to the gallows. The woman was brought to and
from the Courthouse under armed guard and after the trial she was
given passage to Australia." Paula Mullooly, "A Brief History of
the Pakenham Mahons and Strokestown," undated, in the collection of the Roscommon library. This story appears to be referring
to Ann Smyth, daughter of the Widow Smyth, who testified about
a gang meeting at her mother's establishment on Christmas Eve,
1847. But her testimony did not mention Commins by name and
did not appear to be decisive in his conviction.

CHAPTER ONE: THE CONSENT OF THINGS

1 *Legend tells us:* Walter A. Jones, "Historical Sketches," *Strokestown
   Democrat*, July 7 and 14, 1917.

4 *The environs of County Roscommon:* James Scott Wheeler, *Cromwell
   in Ireland* (1999), 171.

5 *Scholar Susan Hood, who has studied:* Susan Hood, *The Landlord-
   Planned Nexus at Strokestown, County Roscommon: Case Study of an
   Irish Estate Town, c. 1660–c. 1925* (1994), 45.

5 *In a declaration written:* Gerald Hanley, "Nicholas Mahon and
   17th Century Roscommon," *Irish Genealogist*, vol. 3, no. 6 (1963),
   228–235.

6 *Costello's war ended:* Hood, *Landlord-Planned Nexus*, 47.

6 *He received his land grant:* Interview with Olive Hales Pakenham
   Mahon, "Looking West," a production of RTÉ radio, presented by
   Jim Fahy, September 24, 1982.

6 *It seemed to offer:* Redcliffe Salaman, *The History and Social Influence of the Potato* (1949), 243.

7 *Over the final decade:* Hood, *Landlord-Planned Nexus*, 55–60.

8 *But local people:* Cunningham, "Some Traditional History," 316–
   317.

8 *By age twenty-three:* Edith Mary Johnston-Liik, *The History of the*

Irish Parliament, 1692–1800: Commons, Constituencies, and Statutes (2002), vol. 5, 178.

9   *He proved himself:* Ibid., 178.

10 *In 1709 the bishop:* Francis Beirne, *The Diocese of Elphin: People, Places and Pilgrimage* (2000), 86–87.

11 *Two years later:* Ibid., 92–93.

11 *Only thirty-three priests:* Marcus Tanner, *Ireland's Holy Wars: The Struggle for a Nation's Soul, 1500–2000* (2001), 164.

11 *A stone on which:* "Strokestown Park, Co. Roscommon," *Irish Tatler and Sketch*, 8–13.

12 *For Thomas would evolve:* Hood, *Landlord-Planned Nexus*, 64–77.

13 *Thomas Mahon, the writer commented:* Susan Hood, "Through the Gates: Power and Profit in an Irish Estate Town," *Power, Profit and Urban Land: Landownership in Medieval and Early Modern Northern European Towns* (1996), 244–269.

14 *"There were six teams":* Hood, *Landlord-Planned Nexus*, 77.

15 *Indeed, when Arthur Young:* Arthur Young, *A Tour of Ireland; With General Observations on the Present State of That Kingdom, Made in the Years 1776, 1777, and 1778 and Brought Down to the End of 1779* (1780), 297–305.

17 *Young recorded how some:* Robert Scally, *The End of the Hidden Ireland: Rebellion, Famine, and Emigration* (1995), 18.

19 *The Parliamentary List:* Johnston-Liik, *History of the Irish Parliament*, vol. 5, 182.

20 *In April 1795 the priest wrote:* Raymond Browne, "Part of Original Documentation Re Transfer of Land as Site for New Church in Strokestown," *Roscommon Historical and Archaeological Society Journal*, vol. 7 (1998), 130–131.

21 *During a meeting in Roscommon town:* Coleman, *Riotous Roscommon*, 14–15.

22 *On the evening of May 24:* Major E. W. Sheppard, *The Ninth Queen's Royal Lancers, 1715–1936* (1939), 38–41.

23 *So he nominated his war-hero son:* Johnston-Liik, *History of the Irish Parliament*, vol. 5, 182–183.

CHAPTER TWO: UNTIL DECISIVE STEPS ARE TAKEN

25 *The population had risen:* For discussion of pre-Famine rural society, see Michael Beames, *Peasants and Power: The Whiteboy Movements and Their Control in Pre-Famine Ireland* (1983), 1–21; Kerby

Miller, *Emigrants and Exiles: Ireland and the Irish Exodus to North America* (1985), 41–60.

29 *In June of that year:* E. G. Wakefield, *An Account of Ireland Statistical and Political* (1812), vol. 1, 274–275.

30 *In an 1808 letter:* Michael James Huggins, "A Secret Ireland: Agrarian Conflict in Pre-Famine County Roscommon" (2000).

31 *The secret society's profile:* Hood, *Landlord-Planned Nexus*, 197.

31 *The Protestant bishop in Elphin:* Reverend Joseph D'Arcy Sirr, D.D., *A Memoir of the Honorable and Most Reverend Power Le Poer Trench, Last Archbishop of Tuam* (1845), 55.

32 *Incidents of this sort:* Hood, *Landlord-Planned Nexus*, 196–203.

33 *He voted for several:* Johnston-Liik, *History of the Irish Parliament*, vol. 5, 181.

33 *But perhaps the moment:* Sirr, *Memoir of the Honorable*, 53–55.

34 *While the elderly Lord Hartland:* Hood, *Landlord-Planned Nexus*, 162.

34 *A local physician:* Sirr, *Memoir of the Honorable*, 46.

35 *The short campaign ended:* Sheppard, *Ninth Queen's Royal Lancers*, 49–64.

35 *Looking over the ledgers:* Susan Hood, "The Famine in the Strokestown Park House Archive," *Irish Review* (Winter 1995), 110–111.

37 *After six years during which he purchased:* Major H. Everard, *History of Thos Farrington's Regiment, Subsequently Designated the 29th (Worcestershire) Foot, 1694 to 1891* (1891), 335–352. See also the record of service for Denis Mahon, the Worcestershire Regiment Museum Trust, Norton Barracks, Worcester.

37 *Lord Bishop Henry Bathurst, then seventy-eight:* Mrs. Thistlethwayte, *Memoirs and Correspondence of Dr. Henry Bathurst, Lord Bishop of Norwich by His Daughter, Mrs. Thistlethwayte* (1853), 255, 348, 428, 429–430, 476. Also see Charles Linnell, *Some East Anglian Clergy* (1961), 130–156.

40 *The* Times of London *commented:* Times of London, August 10, 1830.

41 *Isaac Weld, a Dublin Quaker:* Isaac Weld, *Statistical Survey of Roscommon* (1832), 319–337.

42 *His wife and her daughter:* Scally, *The End of Hidden Ireland*, 241–242.

42 *"We shall make it":* Exhibit, Famine Museum, Strokestown Park.

42   *"Denis will not only":* Mrs. Thistlethwayte, *Memoirs and Correspondence,* 429–430.

43   *In March 1836 Father McDermott: Hansard's Parliamentary Debates,* vol. 95, series 3, December 6, 1847, 680–681.

44   *As Lord Grenville said: Times of London,* December 14, 1803.

44   *The provision of welfare assistance:* Christine Kinealy, *This Great Calamity: The Irish Famine,* 1845–1852 (1995), 8.

45   *Once inside, every able-bodied individual:* Edwards and Williams, eds., *Great Famine,* 52.

45   *The idea was to "awaken":* Ibid.

46   *Those "who have property":* Ibid., 17.

46   *George Nicholls, who devised:* George Nicholls, *A History of the Irish Poor Law: In Connexion with the Condition of the People* (1856), 166.

47   *In late August 1843 O'Connell arrived: Times of London,* August 23, 1843.

48   *It happened on September 20, 1843, at around 11 A.M.: Times of London,* September 25, 1843, September 28, 1843, and October 5, 1843.

51   *On Monday, July 22, 1844, John Mahon: Evidence Taken Before Her Majesty's Commissioner of Inquiry into the State of the Law and Practice in Respect to the Occupation of Land in Ireland* (1845), vol. 3, 355–357.

55   *A Catholic farmer named John Balfe:* Coleman, *Riotous Roscommon,* 44–45.

56   *"The [perpetrators] deliberately": Dublin Evening Mail,* February 3, 1844.

56   *A Catholic farmer named Peter Nolan:* Coleman, *Riotous Roscommon,* 22–25.

56   *a senior Repeal official: Roscommon Journal,* March 29, 1845.

56   *The rural clergymen, often collectors: Athlone Sentinel,* January 23, 1846.

56   *The Repeal officials would rather: Roscommon Journal,* March 29, 1845.

57   *On a day in early 1845:* Huggins, "Secret Ireland."

57   *Indeed, one of the last major crimes: Times of London,* April 11, 1845, reprint of *Dublin Evening Mail* report.

CHAPTER THREE: IN THE NAME OF GOD DO SOMETHING FOR US

59   *It may have reached:* Henry Hobhouse, *Seeds of Change: Five Plants That Transformed Mankind* (1985), 210.

59 *In late June 1845:* Austin Bourke, *The Visitation of God? The Potato and the Great Irish Famine* (1993), 140–141.

59 *Out of a population of 8.5 million:* Donnelly, *Great Irish Potato Famine*, 1.

59 *"We stop the press":* Salaman, *History and Social Influence of the Potato*, 292.

59 *On September 26:* Raymond Browne, *The Destitution Survey: Reflections on the Famine in the Diocese of Elphin* (1997), 11–15.

59 *In the middle of November: Roscommon Journal*, November 15, 1845.

61 *But Peel had come to believe:* Peter Gray, *Famine, Land and Politics: British Government and Irish Society, 1843–1850* (1999), 99, 109.

61 *His decision violated strict laissez-faire injunctions:* Stanley Ayling, *Edmund Burke: His Life and Opinions*, 107–109.

62 *A meeting of magistrates:* Coleman, *Riotous Roscommon*, 27.

63 *"The people begin to show":* Edward Lengel, *The Irish Through British Eyes: Perceptions of Ireland in the Famine Era* (2002), 64–65.

63 *One figure in County Roscommon:* Martin Coen, "George Joseph Plunkett Browne," *Old Athlone Society Journal*, vol. 2, no. 5 (1978), 26–32.

63 *Daniel O'Connell himself: Times of London*, August 14, 1840.

64 *Even after the pope: Times of London*, September 12, 1836; Ambrose Macaulay, *William Crolly: Archbishop of Armagh, 1835–49* (1994), 274; Oliver MacDonagh, *The Emancipist* (1989), 264.

65 *In his sermons: Roscommon Journal*, July 26, 1845.

65 *During a celebration: Roscommon Journal*, July 25, 1846.

65 *But Bishop Browne's Lenten address: Roscommon Journal*, March 7, 1846.

67 *On June 5 Father Michael McDermott:* National Archives of Ireland [hereinafter NAI], RLFC 3/1/2977.

67 *These bodies, which were vital:* Browne, *Destitution Survey*, 63.

68 *In his response to Father McDermott:* NAI, RLFC 3/1/2977, draft reply.

69 *But in its letter to the Relief Commission:* NAI, RLFC 3/1/2936.

69 *For within six days:* NAI, RLFC 3/1/3168

70 *In his first letter to the Relief Commission:* NAI, RLFC 3/2/25/57.

70 *The major's robust involvement:* Major Denis Mahon [hereinafter MDM] to Thomas Conry, June 28, 1846, National Library of Ireland, Pakenham Mahon Papers [hereinafter NLI, PM Papers], 10,101 (5).

71 *The arguments were convincing:* MDM to T. Conry, July 10, 1846, NLI, PM Papers, 10,101 (5).

71 *In a subsequent letter to the Relief Commission:* NAI, RLFC 3/1/5166

72 *"The combination not to pay rents":* MDM to T. Conry, June 28, 1846, NLI, PM Papers, 10,101 (5).

CHAPTER FOUR: GOOD AND WILLING; IDLE AND BAD

73 *In a widely cited letter:* Woodham-Smith, *Great Hunger,* 91.

74 *While the poor of Ireland:* Gray, *Famine, Land and Politics,* 228.

74 *He even suggested in the House:* T. P. O'Connor, *The Parnell Movement with a Sketch of Irish Politics for 1843* (1887), 105.

75 *When wages were lowered:* British Parliamentary Papers [hereinafter BPP], *Correspondence Relating to the Measures Adopted for the Relief of Distress in Ireland,* Famine, vol. 6, 113–114.

76 *An anonymous letter to a newspaper: Roscommon Journal,* August 19, 1846.

76 *But a written protest lodged:* Strokestown Park archive, uncatalogued.

77 *Like others in elite society:* Gray, *Famine, Land and Politics,* 232–233, 251–255.

77 *Although he was on record:* Cormac Ó Gráda, *Black '47 and Beyond: The Great Irish Famine in History, Economy, and Memory* (1999), 78. "Even Trevelyan accepted the need for minimal relief; otherwise 'the deaths would shock the world and be an eternal blot on the nation, and the government will be blamed,'" Ó Gráda wrote, quoting Trevelyan. Bourke, *Visitation of God?,* 173. Bourke quotes from a Trevelyan letter from April 29, 1846: "'Our measures must proceed with as little disturbance as possible of the ordinary course of private trade, which must ever be the chief resource for the subsistence of the people, but, *coûte que coûte,* the people must not, under any circumstances, be allowed to starve."

77 *It was a position he held:* Gray, *Famine, Land and Politics,* 255. Jennifer Hart wrote, "Trevelyan believed the Irish famine was the judgment of God on an indolent and unself-reliant people, and as God had sent the calamity to teach the Irish a lesson, that calamity must not be too much mitigated: the selfish and the indolent must learn their lesson so that a new and improved state of affairs would arise." Jennifer Hart, "Sir Charles Trevelyan at the Treasury," *The English Historical Review,* vol. 75, no. 294, January 1960,

99. Trevelyan believed that the lesson was well learned. "Unless we are much deceived, posterity will trace up to that famine the commencement of a salutary revolution in the habits of a nation long singularly unfortunate, and will acknowledge that on this, as on many other occasions, Supreme Wisdom has educed permanent good out of transient evil." Charles Trevelyan, "The Irish Crisis," *Edinburgh Review* (January 1848), 229–230.

79 *In his study in London, Lord John Russell:* John Prest, *Lord John Russell* (1972), 236. Paul Scherer, *Lord John Russell: A Biography* (1999), 159.

79 *The priest, as was his wont:* NAI, RLFC 3/2/25/58.

80 *"The depots in Strokestown and Roscommon":* NAI, RLFC 3/2/25/60.

81 *By the second week of October:* House of Commons, Parliamentary Papers, 1847, *Correspondence Relating to Measures for Relief of Distress in Ireland (Commissariat Series),* July 1846–January 1847, 200, 222.

81 *Randolph Routh responded to a request:* NAI, RLFC 3/2/25/58.

81 *The* Roscommon Journal *called it:* Roscommon Journal, October 17, 1846.

81 *The* Roscommon and Leitrim Gazette *described how:* Roscommon and Leitrim Gazette, October 24, 1846.

81 *Trevelyan believed such a "shortsighted":* Peter Gray, "Famine Relief Policy in Comparative Perspective: Ireland, Scotland, and Northwestern Europe, 1845–1849, *Éire-Ireland,* vol. 32, no. 1, 97.

82 *As Cormac Ó Gráda:* Cormac Ó Gráda, *Black '47 and Beyond: The Great Irish Famine in History, Economy, and Memory* (1999), 125.

82 *The potato accounted for such a large portion:* Donnelly, *The Great Irish Potato Famine,* 214–215.

82 *The repeal of the Corn Laws:* Edwards and Williams, *The Great Famine,* 225.

83 *"The country is still, thank God":* Roscommon Journal, November 28, 1846.

83 *In a September letter:* Roscommon Journal, September 26, 1846.

83 *In his second public statement:* Roscommon Journal, November 28, 1846.

84 *Susan Hood seconded this assertion:* Hood, *Landlord-Planned Nexus,* 187.

84 *Just thirty-two years old, he had cofounded:* Ivy Frances Jones, *The Rise of a Merchant Bank: A Short History of Guinness Mahon* (1974),

8–16; Michele Guinness, *The Guinness Spirit: Brewers, Bankers, Ministers, and Missionaries* (1999), 123.

84–85 *In Strokestown he would be forever:* Schools Manuscript Collection, vol. 253, 392.

85 *Ross Mahon was hired:* John Ross Mahon [hereinafter JRM] to MDM, September 18, 1846, NLI, PM Papers 10,102 (2); BPP, *First, Second, and Third Reports from the Select Committee on Colonisation from Ireland,* Emigration (1848), vol. 5, 203.

85 *Thirty-three years later: Report of Her Majesty's Commissioners of Inquiry into Working of the Landlord and Tenant (Ireland) Act, 1870, and the Acts Amending the Same* (1881), 655–658.

86 *In a November 21 letter:* MDM to JRM, November 21, 1846, NLI, PM Papers, 10,102 (1).

86 *"There are many parts":* MDM to JRM, January 3, 1847, NLI, PM Papers, 10,102 (2).

87 *Even the revolutionary nationalist:* John Mitchel, *The Last Conquest of Ireland (Perhaps)* (1861), 92–94.

87 *But Major Mahon wasn't yet: Roscommon Journal,* December 5, 1846.

87 *"There are many on the estate":* MDM to JRM, December 27, 1846, NLI, PM Papers, 10,104 (1).

87 *Charles Greville, the Whig diarist:* Scherer, *Lord John Russell,* 158.

88 *The townland of Ballykilcline:* For further study of this fascinating case, see Robert Scally, *The End of the Hidden Ireland: Rebellion, Famine, and Emigration* (1995), and Mary Lee Dunn, *Ballykilcline Rising: From Famine Ireland to Immigrant America* (forthcoming from University of Massachusetts Press).

88 *The Crown's land agent:* BPP, *First, Second and Third Reports,* Emigration, vol. 5, 199.

88 *In a mid-1847 letter he said a few:* Ibid., 203.

89 *He began delivering the three levels:* W. E. Vaughan, *Landlords and Tenants in Mid-Victorian Ireland* (1994), 20–23; Alexander Richey, *The Irish Land Laws* (1880), 34–46.

CHAPTER FIVE: THE SUPERNUMERARY PORTION OF THE INHABITANTS

92 *On January 9, 1847, a notice was posted:* Browne, *Destitution Survey,* 45.

92 *A priest from a town near Strokestown:* NAI, RLFC 3/2/25/60.

92 *A Limerick Relief Committee member:* Aubrey De Vere, *The Bard*

of Curragh Chase: A Portrait of His Life and Writing (1997), 41–42.

92 *A Board of Works engineer characterized:* BPP, *Correspondence Relating to the Measures,* Famine, vol. 7, 126.

92 *While the government continued:* Prest, *Lord John Russell,* 246.

93 *"We entered a cabin":* Transactions of the Central Relief Committee of the Society of Friends, in 1846 and 1847 (1852), 163.

94 *In England the response was:* Kinealy, *Great Irish Famine,* 66–82.

96 *On January 9 Father McDermott:* NAI, RLFC 3/2/25/58.

96 *In a letter to John Ross Mahon:* MDM to JRM, January 23, 1847, NLI, PM Papers 10,104 (2).

97 *One accused the body:* BPP, *Correspondence Relating to the Measures,* Famine, vol. 7, 166.

97 *Another official complained:* Ibid., 126.

97 *The same official wrote:* Ibid., 289.

97 *In his 1874 history:* Canon John O'Rourke, *The Great Irish Famine* (new edition, 1989), 210–211.

98 *By March 31 the committee reported:* NAI, RLFC 3/2/25/58.

98 *From England, Major Mahon:* MDM to JRM, February 26, 1847, PM Papers, 10,102 (3). MDM to JRM, March 2, 1847, 10,102 (4). MDM to JRM, March 7, 1847, 10,102 (2).

98 *Despite the accusations of lassitude:* House of Commons, PP, 1847, *Correspondence Relating to Measures for Relief of Distress in Ireland* (Commissariat Series), January–March 1847, 58, 145, and 157.

99 *The abrupt stoppage resulted:* R. F. Foster, *Modern Ireland: 1600– 1972* (1988), 326.

99 *As a Board of Works official:* BPP, *Correspondence Relating to the Measures,* Famine, vol. 7, 176.

99 *The government was expecting:* Woodham-Smith, *Great Hunger,* 172.

99 *"Five hundred destitute starving families":* NAI, CSORP/Distress Papers D4906.

100 *On March 26 Father McDermott:* NAI, RLFC 3/2/25/58.

101 *The club's most newsworthy event:* Major-General Sir Louis Charles Jackson, *History of the United Service Club* (1937), 44–47.

101 *"I have had a letter":* MDM to JRM, February 26, 1847, NLI, PM Papers, 10,102 (2).

101 *With words from Father Boyd:* MDM to JRM, February 23, 1847, NLI, PM Papers, 10,104 (2).

101 *according to a new survey conducted by Ross Mahon:* Census of the

Strokestown property, March 21, 1847, Strokestown Park archive, uncatalogued.

102   *On March 2 he repeated:* MDM to JRM, March 2, 1847, NLI, PM Papers 10,104 (1).

102   *In a February letter to the landlord:* JRM to MDM, February 27, 1847, NLI, PM Papers 10,102 (2).

102   *In a statement written after Major Mahon's death:* BPP, *First, Second and Third Reports,* Emigration, vol. 5, 203.

103   *After receiving the landlord's:* JRM to MDM, February 27, 1847, NLI, PM Papers, 10,102 (2).

103   *Major Mahon responded on March 7:* MDM to JRM, March 7, 1847, NLI, PM Papers, 10,102 (2).

105   *The Irish landlords were aghast:* Gray, *Famine, Land and Politics,* 279–283.

107   *Major Mahon responded to the prospect:* MDM to JRM, March 30, 1847, NLI, PM Papers 10,102 (2). Agreeing that a plan to purchase seed for his poor tenants "would not answer," Major Mahon wrote, "I am therefore willing, if you but undertake to carry out a plan of emigration, to provide funds to be at your command."

107   According to Sections 11, 12 of the amended Poor Law: Nicholls, *History of the Irish Poor Law,* 330–333.

107   *No less a representative of the people than Father Henry Brennan:* Roscommon Journal, March 27, 1847.

107   *The landlord made it clear:* MDM to JRM, April 14, 1847, NLI, PM Papers 10,102 (2).

CHAPTER SIX: QUIET AND PEACEABLE POSSESSION

109   *By early 1847 the movement of refugees:* Oliver MacDonagh, "Irish Emigration to the United States of America and the British Colonies During the Famine," *The Great Famine: Studies in Irish History* (1956), 319–324.

110   *"Ireland is pouring into the cities":* Times of London, April 2, 1847.

110   *"I have been considering over":* MDM to JRM, April 14, 1847, NLI, PM Papers, 10,102 (2).

111   *The scholar Oliver MacDonagh has chronicled:* Oliver MacDonagh, *A Pattern of Government Growth 1800–60: The Passenger Acts and Their Enforcement* (1961), 94–95, 99, 110, 203.

111   *On May 11 he sent a letter:* MDM to JRM, May 11, 1847, NLI, PM Papers, 10,102 (3).

112 *"They expressed themselves":* BPP, *First, Second, and Third Reports,* Emigration, vol. 5, 203.

112 *"[I] often heard them express":* Mr. Morton to Henry Sandford Pakenham Mahon, May 9, 1848, NLI, PM Papers, 10,103 (1).

112 *Of the other travelers who hadn't been served:* BPP, *First, Second, and Third Reports,* Emigration, vol. 5, 201.

112 *The tenants endured the entire voyage:* Donnelly, *Great Irish Potato Famine,* photo caption.

113 *A young Herman Melville:* Peter Aughton, *Liverpool: A People's History* (1990), 143.

113 *One local newspaper saw Famine refugees:* John Belcher, "Whiteness and the Liverpool Irish," *Journal of British Studies* (January 2005), 149.

113 *If the travelers were not already sick: Times of London,* March 8, 1847.

114 *"The passengers . . . were, generally speaking":* BPP, *Correspondence and Other Papers Relating to Canada and to Immigration in the Provinces* (1847–1848), Colonies, Canada, vol. 17, 388.

114 *Since the port officials:* Woodham-Smith, *Great Hunger,* 223.

114 *A Scottish doctor, looking over a group: Times of London,* September 17, 1847.

114 *Under the power of a moderate north-northwest wind: Times of London,* May 31, 1847.

114 *In addition, the tenants were in possession:* BPP, *First, Second and Third Reports,* Emigration, vol. 5, 388, 203.

115 *According to an investigation:* Woodham-Smith, *Great Hunger,* 222.

115 *In all, Major Mahon paid for the passage:* In the first batch, 467 statute adults traveled aboard the *Virginius* and *Erin's Queen* at a rate of 3 pounds, 2 shillings, and 6 pence for each adult. See Noel Kissane, *The Irish Famine: A Documentary History* (1995), 160. In the second batch, 405½ statute adults traveled aboard the *Naomi* (which carried 350½ statute adults) and the *John Munn* (which carried 55) at a rate of 3 pounds, 13 shillings for each adult. See MDM to JRM, June 15, 1847, NLI, PM Papers, 10,102 (3).

116 *On April 2 Major Mahon wrote:* MDM to JRM, April 2, 1847, NLI, PM Papers, 10,102 (1).

116 *"The inhabitants are more like":* Raymond Browne, "The Great Irish Famine in Co. Roscommon," *Co. Roscommon Remembers An Gorta Mór: The Great Famine in Co. Roscommon* (1999), 15.

117 *In response to a plea:* Browne, *Destitution Survey*, 15.

118 *On the Strokestown kitchen's busiest day:* BPP, *Correspondence Relating to the Measures*, Famine, vol. 8, 349.

119 *In the words of a proprietor:* Gray, *Famine, Land and Politics*, 180.

120 *On June 5, with the passengers:* MDM to JRM, June 5, 1847, NLI, PM Papers, 10,102 (2).

120 *According to Ross Mahon's calculations:* BPP, *First, Second, and Third Reports*, Emigration, vol. 5, 201.

120 *In suggesting this common tactic:* JRM to MDM, June 8, 1847, NLI, PM Papers 10,102 (2).

121 *On June 11 Major Mahon instructed:* MDM to JRM, June 11, 1847, NLI, PM Papers 10,102 (1).

121 *In his memorandum the land agent noted:* BPP, *First, Second, and Third Reports*, Emigration, vol. 5, 201.

122 *By his accounting, 191 families:* Ibid.

122 *With this in mind, the land agent wrote:* Ibid., 202.

CHAPTER SEVEN: WRETCHED, SICKLY, MISERABLE

123 *An early June letter from the archbishop:* *Québec Gazette*, August 11, 1847.

124 *They were "packed inside of the hold":* "Childhood Memories of Thomas Quinn," *Métaire St.-Joseph, Nicolet (Chronicles) 1895–1935*, vol. 1, 58–60.

124 *A secondhand account of the* Naomi's *passage:* Marianna O'Gallagher, "The Orphans of Grosse Ile: Canada and the Adoption of Irish Famine Orphans, 1847–48," *The Meaning of the Famine* (1997), vol. 6, ed. Patrick O'Sullivan.

125 *"Before the emigrant has been":* Woodham Smith, *Great Hunger*, 226.

125 *Several of De Vere's suggestions:* MacDonagh, *Pattern of Government* Growth, 195–196. Of De Vere's letter, MacDonagh wrote, "The letter made a profound impression on the commissioners. It is scarcely too much to regard it as the basis of most of their future legislation for ship life."

125 *In late July, partially inspired:* *Times of London*, September 17, 1847.

126 *Unlike the Dr. Combe and De Vere:* Robert Whyte, *Robert Whyte's 1847 Famine Ship Diary: The Journey of an Irish Coffin Ship* (1994), 22, 24, 30, 37, 40, 43, 54, 63, 66, 70.

128 *On the following day Dr. George Mellis Douglas:* BPP, *Correspondence*

and Other Papers Relating to Canada), Colonies, Canada, vol. 17, 385.

129 *"Upon my mentioning the subject to J. and W. Robinson":* Ibid., 388.

129 *Since Famine ships began arriving:* André Charbonneau and André Sevigny, *1847 Grosse Ile: A Record of Daily Events* (1997), 1–17.

130 *"New hospitals were started":* Marianna O'Gallagher and Rose Masson Dompierre, *Eyewitness Grosse Ile, 1847* (1995), 325.

131 *After six days the captain fled: Québec Gazette,* July 19, 1847.

131 *If the emigrant's departure from Ireland:* Whyte, *Robert Whyte's 1847 Famine Ship Diary,* 70.

131 *A total of seventy-one of the* Queen's *quarantine patients:* All death figures come from the following book: André Charbonneau, Doris Drolet-Dube with the collaboration of Robert Grace and Sylvie Tremblay, *A Register of Deceased Persons at Sea and on Grosse Ile in 1847* (1997).

133 *In his summation of the unprecedented:* BPP, *Correspondence and Other Papers Relating to Canada,* Colonies, Canada, vol. 17, 535–539.

133 *Research by Grosse Île scholar:* Marianna O'Gallagher, *Grosse Île: Gateway to Canada, 1832–1847* (1984), 118–137.

134 *Thomas would later recall:* "Childhood Memories of Thomas Quinn," 59–60.

134 *When his twelve-year-old:* The overcoat remains in the possession of the Diocese of Nicolet, Québec, archives.

134 *The Charitable Ladies of Québec City:* O'Gallagher, *Grosse Ile,* 134.

135 *In February 1848 her brother:* Ruth-Ann M. Harris and B. E. O'Keefe, *The Search for Missing Friends: Irish Immigrant Advertisements Placed in the Boston Pilot,* 1831–1920 (1989), vol. 1, 263.

135 *A few years later, an ad in the same newspaper:* Ibid., vol. 2, 363.

135 *In 1851, four years after his arrival:* Ibid., 79.

CHAPTER EIGHT: UPON THEIR DEVOTED HEADS LET THE
RESULT LYE

136 *On July 6 he wrote to Ross Mahon:* MDM to JRM, July 6, 1847, NLI, PM Papers, 10,102 (2).

136 *By the time he reached Strokestown: Roscommon Journal,* July 3, 1847.

137 *On August 12 he penned a note:* MDM to JRM, August 12, 1847, NLI, PM Papers, 10,102 (1).

138 *Then, on August 28, he made an appearance: Hansard's,* vol. 95, series 3, December 16, 1847, 1199–1201.

139 *Earlier in the month:* House of Commons, PP, 1847–1848, *Fifth, Sixth, Seventh Reports from the Relief Commissioners*, 15.

143 *The government had advanced a total:* BPP, *Correspondence Relating to the Measures*, Famine, vol. 8, 349.

144 *"The breadth of land sown this year":* Browne, *Destitution Survey*, 43.

145 *On September 14 Major Mahon wrote:* MDM to JRM, September 14, 1847, NLI, PM Papers, 10,102 (1).

145 *On September 21 he wrote of a tenant:* MDM to JRM, September 21, 1847, NLI, PM Papers, 10,104 (1).

146 *When the possibility of retaking:* MDM to JRM, June 11, 1847, NLI, PM Papers, 10,102 (1).

146 *According to an eviction list: Freeman's Journal*, April 29, 1848.

146 *"Mr. Hague forgets":* MDM to JRM, March 4, 1847, NLI, PM Papers, 10,102 (3).

146 *The evidence suggests that the farmer: Freeman's Journal*, April 29, 1848.

146 *The most prominent eviction proceeding: Times of London*, February 23, 1848, letter of Henry Sandford Pakenham Mahon. JRM to Henry Sandford Pakenham Mahon, February 18, 1848, Strokestown Park archive, uncatalogued.

147 *"My heart sickens at the sight":* Browne, *Destitution Survey*, 75.

147 *(Indeed, imports of cheap grain far surpassed):* Austin Bourke, *The Visitation of God? The Potato and the Great Irish Famine* (1993), 168; Cormac Ó Gráda, *The Great Irish Famine* (1989), 54. Christine Kinealy has noted that Tory leader George Bentinck challenged the government's export figures. While the Russell administration conceded some inflation, it argued that the numbers were "generally correct." Christine Kinealy, *The Great Irish Famine: Impact, Ideology and Rebellion* (2002), 106.

148 *"I see that almost all the Irish elections":* G. P. Gooch, *The Later Correspondence of Lord John Russell, 1840–1878* (1925), 172–173.

148 *Instead two Irish Whigs: Times of London*, August 11, 1847. "There is reason to believe that the Roman Catholic Bishop of Elphin refused to support any opponent to the late representative, Mr. French," wrote the *Times*.

149 *While it is true that violent acts:* S. H. Palmer, *Police and Protest in England and Ireland, 1780–1850* (1988), 473.

149 *Father Boyd argued that few:* John Boyd statement, January 10, 1848, NAI, Outrage Papers, County Roscommon, 1848.

CHAPTER NINE: THAT FLAME WHICH NOW RAGES

152 *"'Shanley, point out to me'":* Morning Chronicle, November 10, 1847.

153 *When the vehicle had "nearly reached":* Roscommon and Leitrim Gazette, November 6, 1847.

154 *By that afternoon a party of military:* Police reports, NAI, contained with the Outrage Papers, County Roscommon, 1848.

154 *According to the estate's rent books:* 1824 and 1843 Mahon rental book, portions of which were provided to the author by the Ballykilcline Society.

154 *"From . . . their uniform denial":* Hansard's, vol. 95, series 3, November 29, 1847, 283–285.

155 *On November 8 John Ross Mahon:* BPP, *First, Second, and Third Reports,* Emigration, vol. 5, 203

156 *The* Roscommon and Leitrim Gazette *wrote:* Roscommon and Leitrim Gazette, November 6, 1847.

156 *Blakeney concluded his November 4 report:* Thomas Blakeney's November 4 report, NAI, Outrage Papers, County Roscommon, 1848.

156 *A Board of Works engineer:* Woodham-Smith, *Great Hunger,* 325.

157 *The chief mourners at his private service:* Illustrated London News, November 13, 1847.

157 *The* Freeman's Journal, *the Dublin-based:* Freeman's Journal, November 3, 1847.

157 *The* Morning Chronicle, *the most prominent:* Morning Chronicle, November 6, 1847.

158 *The* Dublin Evening Mail, *the Ascendancy mouthpiece:* Dublin Evening Mail, November 5, 1847; November 12, 1847.

158 *The* Times, *the unaffiliated but Tory-leaning newspaper:* Times of London, November 6, 1847.

159 *In her diary entry on that Friday:* Royal Archives VIC/QVJ/1847:5 November.

159 *The* Daily News, *the London paper:* Daily News, November 11, 1847.

160 *(A week after the killing):* Robin Haines, *Charles Trevelyan and the Great Irish Famine,* 381.

160 *"I am sorry to say intelligence":* Lord Clarendon to Lord John Russell, November 3, 1847, Bodleian Library, Oxford, Clarendon Deposit Irish, Irish Letterbook 1.

160 *"There never was so open":* Sir Herbert Maxwell, *The Life and Let-*

ters of George William Frederick, Fourth Earl of Clarendon (1913), 1, 285.

161 *"It is quite true that landlords":* Ibid., 282–283.

161 *"If I do not see any reasonable ground":* Ibid., 284–285.

162 *He soon discovered that his ministry:* Gray, *Famine, Land and Politics*, 182–183. Prest, *Lord John Russell*, 272–275.

162 *According to Charles Greville:* Charles Cavendish Fulke Greville, *The Greville Memoirs (Second Part): A Journal of the Reign of Queen Victoria, from 1837 to 1852,* ed. H. Reeve, 3 vols. (1885), 466.

162 *the* Times *slashed and hacked: Times of London*, November 11, 1847.

163 *The* Morning Chronicle *threw its support: Morning Chronicle*, November 18, 1847.

163 *The* Daily News, *safely positioned: Daily News*, November 11, 1847.

163 *The pro-landlord* Dublin Evening Mail: *Dublin Evening Mail*, November 12, 1847.

CHAPTER TEN: GUILTY OF THE BLOOD OF THE MURDERED
MAJOR MAHON

164 *"The lower orders exult in the murder":* Coleman, *Riotous Roscommon*, 49.

164 *"His death was instantaneous": Morning Chronicle*, November 15, 1847.

165 *"He is down now not like the last time":* Thomas Blakeney statement, November 26, 1847, NAI, Outrage Papers, County Roscommon, 1848.

165 *Investigators also combed through several townlands:* Police reports, NAI, Outrage Papers, County Roscommon, 1848.

166 *"As the son of Major Mahon was going": Times of London*, December 4, 1847.

166 *A cousin of Major Mahon and his wife both: Hansard's*, vol. 95, series 3, November 29, 1847, 295–296.

167 *An Anglo-Irish diarist wrote:* Elizabeth Smith, *The Irish Journals of Elizabeth Smith, 1840–1850* (1980), ed. David Thomson with Moyra McGusty, 163–164.

167 *"Molly Maguire wishes to let you know":* Liam Swords, *In Their Own Words: The Famine in North Connacht, 1845–1849* (1999), 243.

167 *On Sunday, November 28, the gravity of the threats:* Patrick Vesey, "'I

Flatter Myself We Have Strangled the Evil in the Bud,'" *Hanging Crimes: When Ireland Used the Gallows* (2005), 22–47.

168   *Palmerston wanted Lord Minto to ask:* Lord Palmerston to Lord Minto, December 3, 1847, *Gran Bretagna e Italia nei Documenti: Della Missione Minto* (1970), ed. Federico Curato, vol. 2, 240–241.

169   *"Two Sundays before Major Mahon was murdered":* Maxwell, *Life and Letters*, 283–284.

170   *By the time Parliament reconvened:* *Hansard's*, vol. 95, series 3, November 23, 1847, 76–82, 122.

170   *One man who was prepared to respond:* Reverend Bernard O'Reilly, *John MacHale, Archbishop of Tuam: His Life, Times, and Correspondence* (1890), vol. 2, 55–70.

171   *Seán O'Faoláin wrote of his "stubborn, tight mouth":* Seán O'Faoláin, *King of the Beggars: A Life of Daniel O'Connell* (1938), 87–88, 269–270.

172   *The* Dublin Evening Mail *felt the legislation:* *Daily News*, December 6, 1847. The London paper reprinted the *Evening Mail* report.

172   *(It boasted 428 converts):* Marianne Elliot, *The Catholics of Ulster: A History* (2000), 273.

172   *On December 6 in the House of Lords:* *Hansard's*, vol 95, series 3, December 6, 1847, 675–696.

174   *During the November 30 meeting, Lord Minto:* Lord Minto to Lord Palmerston, December 1, 1847, *Gran Bretagna*, vol. 2, 238.

174   *D. H. Kelly published a letter:* *Dublin Evening Mail*, November 29, 1847.

175   *After reading Kelly's statement:* JRM to Editor of the *Times*, November 29, 1847, NLI, Guinness Mahon Letterbooks [hereinafter GML], 32,019, 541. JRM to D. H. Kelly, December 4, 1847, NLI, GML, 32,019, 600. Ross Mahon also wrote to Kelly, "Your letter to Henry Grattan was a capital one."

175   *When O'Connell failed to do so:* *Morning Chronicle*, December 10, 1847.

176   *His open letter, dated December 7:* *Freeman's Journal*, December 10, 1847.

180   *In a letter to Lord John Russell:* Lord Clarendon to Lord John Russell, December 10, 1847, Clarendon Deposit Irish, Irish Letterbook 2.

180   *The* Times, *a genuinely anti-Catholic publication:* *Times of London*, December 16, 1847.

180   *The* Morning Chronicle *saw it as an example:* *Morning Chronicle*, December 21, 1847.

180 *When the Repeal leader John O'Connell: Hansard's*, vol. 95, series 3, December 13, 1847, 974–975.

181 *To the* Daily News, *Father McDermott's: Daily News*, December 15, 1847.

181 *In the House of Lords, he said: Hansard's*, vol. 95, series 3, December 16, 1847, 1197–1198.

181 *The* Times *concurred: Times of London*, December 16, 1847.

181 *In two memoranda and other accompanying documents:* Two memoranda provided to Pope Pius IX, December 19, 1847, *Gran Bretagna*, vol. 2, 274–277. Lord Minto diary entry, December 19, 1847, *Gran Bretagna*, vol. 1, 242–245. James P. Flint, *Great Britain and the Holy See: The Diplomatic Relations Question, 1846–1852* (2003), 86.

182 *At the same time, the highest British officials:* Lord Clarendon to Lord John Russell, December 10, 1847, Clarendon Deposit Irish, Irish Letterbook 2.

182 *In a letter to a* Times *journalist:* Lord Clarendon to Reeve of the *Times*, December 20, 1847, Clarendon Deposit Irish, Irish Letterbook 2, c. 534. For further discussion of the McDermott controversy see Donal A. Kerr, *A Nation of Beggars? Priests, People, and Politics in Famine Ireland, 1846–1852* (1994), 88–99. Also Donal A. Kerr, *The Catholic Church and the Famine* (1996), 51–69, and Donal A. Kerr, "Priests, Pikes and Patriots," *Piety and Power in Ireland, 1760–1960: Essays in Honour of Emmet Larkin*, 28–29. In the final essay, Kerr writes, "No proof could be found for the accusation against McDermott, which was almost certainly unfounded." This pointed is echoed by James Donnelly: "Father McDermott produced credible evidence that he never publicly denounced Major Mahon at any time." Donnelly, *Great Irish Potato Famine*, 143.

Chapter Eleven: Decided Measures

184 *In a letter to Marcus McClausland:* JRM to Marcus McClausland, December 8, 1847, NLI, GML, 32,019, 602–603.

185 *"We have a number of decrees obtained":* JRM to unspecified, December 8, 1847, NLI, GML, 32,019, 664.

185 *On December 20, the day:* JRM to Thomas Redington, December 20, 1847, NLI, GML, 32,019, 714.

185 *In a letter to Roberts, Ross Mahon:* JRM to Roberts, December 23, 1847, NLI, GML, 32,019, 854–855.

185 *On December 23 Ross Mahon wrote to Roberts:* JRM to Roberts, December 23, 1847, NLI, GML, 32,020, 9.

186 *In Strokestown Dr. Terence Shanley:* BPP, *Correspondence Relating to the Measures,* Famine, vol. 2, 528.

187 *On December 27 the Roscommon Board of Guardians:* Ibid., 528–532, which includes all the correspondence from union through January.

188 *When word spread among the poor:* Browne, "Great Irish Famine in Co. Roscommon," 17–18.

189 *And the government continued to be unwilling:* Gray, *Famine, Land and Politics,* 293.

190 *Incensed by Father McDermott's: Freeman's Journal,* January 8, 1848.

192 *The* Times, *which hated Archbishop MacHale: Times of London,* January 5, 1848.

192 *The* Morning Chronicle, *which, as Shrewsbury's ideological home: Morning Chronicle,* January 4, 1848.

192 *Even Lord Clarendon, who had privately admitted:* Lord Clarendon to Bishop George Browne, January 5, 1848, Clarendon Deposit Irish, Irish Letterbook 2, fols. 62v.–63v. [3x FPA 3].

192 *Bishop George Browne wasted little time: Freeman's Journal,* February 10, 1848.

193 *"Brief, mild, and modest": Boston Pilot,* March 4, 1848.

193 *Even the* Morning Chronicle: *Morning Chronicle,* January 13, 1848.

194 *After a few-week delay, His Grace:* O'Reilly, *John MacHale,* vol. 2, 73–88.

194 *The* Morning Chronicle *called it: Morning Chronicle,* January 25, 1848.

194 *The* Daily News *deemed it: Daily News,* January 25, 1848.

194 Punch *said it was "reeled off": Punch,* February 28, 1848.

196 *In this semiprivate missive: Daily News,* January 22, 1848.

198 *"We have had a peak number":* JRM to Marcus McClausland, January 18, 1848, NLI, GML, 32,020, 316–317.

198 *As Ross Mahon told his under agent:* JRM to Thomas Roberts, January 20, 1848, NLI, GML, 32,020, 399.

199 *With titles like "The Humble Petition of Widow Flanagan":* Thomas Carton memorial, NLI, PM Papers, 10,101 (5).

199 *In one, seven families from Cornashina:* Cornashina memorial, Strokestown Park archive, uncatalogued.

199 *"They deserve no consideration":* JRM to Mrs. Mahon, January 24, 1848, NLI, GML, 32,020, 433.

199 *On February 7 Ross Mahon told Roberts:* JRM to Thomas Roberts, February 7, 1848, NLI, GML, 32,020, 931.

200 *According to Ross Mahon's business partner:* Robert Guinness to Henry Sandford Pakenham Mahon, February 21, 1848, NLI, GML, 32,021, 4.

200 *With the help of these declarations: Times of London,* February 22, 1848.

200 *Over the next few weeks:* Various enclosures, NAI, Outrage Papers, County Roscommon, 1848.

201 *Into March, police continued:* Ibid.

201 *John Ross Mahon even participated:* JRM to Henry Sandford Pakenham Mahon, May 17, 1848, Strokestown Park archive, uncatalogued.

202 *In a significant boost:* Various enclosures, NAI, Outrage Papers, County Roscommon, 1848.

202 *"We find we can put no confidence":* JRM to Henry Sandford Pakenham Mahon, May 17, 1848, Strokestown Park archive, uncatalogued.

202 *When he requested the use of a local home:* JRM to Terence Shanley, April 14, 1848, NLI, GML, 32,021, 501.

203 *As he told Pakenham Mahon:* JRM to Henry Sandford Pakenham Mahon, January 6, 1848, NLI, GML, 32,020, 226.

CHAPTER TWELVE: *SUMMUM JUS, SUMMA INJURIA*

204 *On February 5, 1848, the* Dublin Evening Post: *Daily News,* February 7, 1848. The London paper reprinted the *Evening Post* item.

205 *Scholar James P. Flint asserts that the pope:* Flint, *Great Britain and the Holy See,* 87–88.

205 *"All this may be furiously denied":* Daily News, February 8, 1848.

206 *"[T]he yellings of the poor":* Kerr, *Catholic Church and the Famine,* 62.

206 *Even the two moderate pro-government archbishops:* Macauley, *William Crolly,* 342–343.

207 *Overjoyed at the pope's entrance: Freeman's Journal,* February 12, 1848.

207 *Even this was too much: Times of London,* February 15, 1848.

209 *While the bishop was defending the right:* BPP, *Correspondence Relating to the Measures,* Famine, vol. 2, 400–411. Includes all the correspondence from the Roscommon Board of Guardians through March.

209 *In the week ending February 5:* BPP, *Correspondence Relating to the Measures,* Famine, vol. 3, 1035. Includes outdoor relief numbers for the period up to mid-April. Since the government had asked that depots be located in the center of each electoral division, it is probable that the Strokestown depot established in June 1846 was used for this purpose.

210 *The work was intended to be "as repulsive":* Kinealy, *This Great Calamity,* 200.

213 *"The murders of poor cottier tenants":* Donnelly, *Great Irish Potato Famine,* 115.

213 *it was reported by relief officials that evicted families:* Haines, *Charles Trevelyan and the Great Irish Famine,* 434.

213 *In the week ending April 15:* BPP, *Correspondence Relating to the Measures,* Famine, vol. 4, 244. Includes outdoor relief numbers for the period up to mid-July.

215 *On February 18 Ross Mahon wrote a private letter:* JRM to Henry Sandford Pakenham Mahon, February 18, 1848, Strokestown Park archive, uncatalogued.

216 *In a letter published in the* Roscommon and Leitrim Gazette: *Roscommon and Leitrim Gazette,* March 18, 1848.

216 *In a subsequent private letter to Pakenham Mahon:* Patrick Browne to Henry Sandford Pakenham Mahon, undated, Strokestown Park archive, uncatalogued.

216 *Employing evidence he had gathered: Freeman's Journal,* March 6, 1848.

219 *On April 29, 1848, nearly two months after Lord Shrewsbury's letter: Freeman's Journal,* April 29, 1848.

Chapter Thirteen: So Injudicious a Course

225 *Five months after one of the most infamous crimes:* Various enclosures, NAI, Outrage Papers, County Roscommon, 1848.

227 *"We have got a great deal of information":* JRM to Marcus McClausland, March 24, 1848, NLI, GML, 32,021, 313.

227 *By the third week of the month:* Various enclosures, NAI, Outrage Papers, County Roscommon, 1849.

227 *In a piece of correspondence found in the Strokestown House archive:* Patrick Vesey, "The Murder of Major Mahon," Thesis for the Degree of M.A., Department of Modern History, National University of Ireland, Maynooth, November 2002, 47–48.

228 *By the end of May:* Various enclosures, NAI, Outrage Papers, County Roscommon, 1848.

229 *"The evidence seems so clear":* JRM to Marcus McClausland, March 24, 1848, NLI, GML, 32,021, 313.

230 *In a letter to Pakenham Mahon on June 11:* D. H. Kelly to Henry Sandford Pakenham Mahon, June 11, 1848, NLI, PM Papers, 10,103 (1).

230 *"[F]or me, I abide my fate joyfully":* Woodham-Smith, *Great Hunger,* 344.

231 *As he told Henrietta Mahon:* JRM to Mrs. Mahon, May 4, 1848, NLI, GML, 32,022, 49–50.

232 *In his memorandum of the "lands on the Strokestown Estate":* BPP, *First, Second and Third Reports,* Emigration, vol. 5, 201.

233 *A Protestant middleman, who was behind on his rent:* Thomas Morton to Henry Sandford Pakenham Mahon, May 9, 1848, NLI, PM Papers, 10,103 (1).

233 *He sent Pakenham Mahon a copy of the April 29:* Exhibit, Famine Museum, Strokestown Park.

234 *"If all about the subscriptions":* JRM to Thomas Roberts, May 6, 1848, NLI, GML, 32,022, 78.

234 *"I am very much disgusted":* Lord Shrewsbury to Henry Sandford Pakenham Mahon, May 6, 1848, Strokestown Park archive, uncatalogued.

235 *"I really think you have judged right":* Lord Shrewsbury to Henry Sandford Pakenham Mahon, May 7, 1848, Strokestown Park archive, uncatalogued.

235 *The Protestant rector of Strokestown:* JRM to Henry Sandford Pakenham Mahon, January 20, 1848, NLI, GML, 32,020, 401–402.

236 *"I am sorry you cannot proceed further":* JRM to Henry Sandford Pakenham Mahon, May 30, 1848, NLI, PM Papers, 10,103 (3).

CHAPTER FOURTEEN: CONSPIRE, CONFEDERATE, AND AGREE TOGETHER

237 *In a short time the four were brought into the room:* The testimony from Hasty's trial comes from *Dublin Evening Mail,* July 14, 17, and 21, 1847; *Freeman's Journal,* July 14 and 15, 1847; *Roscommon Journal,* July 15, 1847; and *Roscommon Weekly Messenger,* July 19, 1848.

239 *Two days before the trial opened:* D. H. Kelly to Henry Sandford Pakenham Mahon, July 10, 1848, NLI, PM Papers, 10,103 (4).

239 *Descended from a Flemish Protestant family:* Thomas Lefroy, *Memoir of Chief Justice Lefroy by His Son, Thomas Lefroy* (1871), 6–15.

239 *As a twenty-year-old preparing to study law:* Carol Shields, *Jane Austen* (2001), 49–52.

253 *Contemporary historian Desmond Norton:* Desmond Norton, "Where Was Major Mahon Shot?" Centre for Economic Research Working Paper Series, University College, Dublin (2001). Dr. Norton notes that today there are *three* bridges along the road as it runs from the townland of Doorty, through the townland of Leitrim, and into the townland of Carrownalassan. The bridge that didn't exist in 1847 is positioned in the townland of Leitrim between the Doorty Bridge on one side and the Leitrim/Carrownalassan Bridge on the other. This bridge is often misidentified as the site of the murder, he writes.

259 *Thus, Flynn would have been contradicting his own testimony:* In his article, Desmond Norton writes, "We can be certain that the shooting took place either on Leitrim townland or within about 200 yards beyond the boundary of that townland on the Strokestown side—on the townland of Carrownalassan. In fact we can be virtually certain that a point near the eastern boundary on the townland of Carrownalassan was the location of the murder." He based this contention on eyewitness Patrick Flynn's statement that the landlord was shot "beyond the second bridge"—the first bridge being the Doorty Bridge, the only other one that existed in 1847 along this stretch of road. He seconded this assertion by pointing to the testimony of a local man, Martin Gerald Flanagan, who was seventy-four years old when Norton spoke to him in 1998. Flanagan, who would have been born more than seventy-five years after the murder, told Norton he was "relying on statements made by elderly people during his youth" in saying that the murder occurred near the bridge at the border of Leitrim and Carrownalassan. As I point out in the text, Dr. Norton's assertions about the murder occurring anywhere other than just before or just after the Doorty Bridge are contradicted by every piece of crime scene evidence provided in police documents, inquest findings, and court testimony. Only Patrick Flynn's reference to a "second" bridge hints that the eyewitness wasn't referring to the Doorty Bridge. But, as I show in the text, Flynn would have been contradicting his own testimony if he were speaking of any bridge other than the Doorty Bridge. Dr. Norton repeated his contention in his new book. Desmond Norton, *Landlords, Tenants, Famine: The Business of an Irish Land Agency in the 1840s* (2006), 68, 204.

Chapter Fifteen: It Has Been Indeed, Really Proved

266 *Ross Mahon confirmed that the "witnesses for the prosecution":* JRM to Henry Sandford Pakenham Mahon, July 15, 1848, NLI, PM Papers, 10,103 (4).

267 *"There was no attack made on your husband's memory":* JRM to Mrs. Mahon, July 12, 1848, Strokestown Park archive, uncatalogued.

269 *"The attorney general is now speaking":* Ibid.

270 *On the following day, Thursday, July 13:* The testimony from Commins's trial comes from *Roscommon Journal*, July 15, 1848; *Roscommon Weekly Messenger*, July 19, 1848; and *Dublin Evening Mail*, July 17, 1848.

275 *It is apparent that this was William Sandys:* Desmond Norton, "On the Crichton Properties Near Strokestown," *The Bonfire: Newsletter of the Ballykilcline Society* (Fall 2005), 6–14.

276 *In a letter to Mrs. Mahon, Major Mahon's brother:* John Mahon to Mrs. Mahon, July 15, 1848, Strokestown Park archive, uncatalogued.

Chapter Sixteen: This Melancholy Exhibition of Human Suffering

283 *He led a small, poorly armed force:* Woodham-Smith, *Great Hunger*, 348–360. Thomas Keneally, *The Great Shame and the Triumph of the Irish in the English-Speaking World* (1998), 156–165.

284 *Two weeks earlier, Lord Clarendon had responded:* Petition of Anne Hasty to the Lord Lieutenant, July 24, 1848, NAI, Convict Reference File 1857/57. This reference file includes documents relating to all the defendants.

284–285 *By noon more than five hundred soldiers and police officers:* Roscommon Weekly Messenger, August 9, 1848.

286 *"There was a large attendance":* JRM to Henry Sandford Pakenham Mahon, August 12, 1848, NLI, PM Papers, 10,103 (5).

287 *On the previous day, August 7:* JRM to Thomas Roberts, August 7, 1848, NLI, GML, 32,023, 260–261.

287 *On August 10 he wrote to Strokestown's Protestant minister:* JRM to Reverend Thomas Morton, August 10, 1848, NLI, GML, 32,023, 311.

287 *On August 13 a Poor Law official:* BPP, *Correspondence Relating to the Measures*, Famine, vol. 4, 16.

288 *The vice-guardians of the Roscommon Union:* BPP, *Correspondence Relating to the Measures*, Famine, vol. 4, 594. Includes all the outdoor relief figures until the end of 1848.

288 *On August 5, a few days before:* JRM to Henry Sandford Pakenham Mahon, August 5, 1848, NLI, GML, 32,023, 299.

288 *On August 10, a few days after it:* JRM to Henry Sandford Pakenham Mahon, August 10, 1848, NLI, GML, 32,023, 316–318.

289 *On August 12 Ross Mahon told Roberts:* JRM to Thomas Roberts, August 12, 1848, NLI, GML, 32,023, 333.

289 *The land agent's correspondence also indicated:* JRM to Mrs. Mahon, September 28, 1848, NLI, GML, 32,028, 108–109.

289 *On the same day that the land agent:* JRM to Henry Sandford Pakenham Mahon, August 12, 1848, NLI, GML, 32,023, 338.

290 *On August 17 Ross Mahon made one last effort:* JRM to Henry Sandford Pakenham Mahon, August 17, 1848, NLI, GML, 32,023, 399.

290 *The new edifice replaced a church:* John O'Donovan, *Letters Containing Information Relative to the Antiquities of the County of Roscommon* (1837), 33.

291 *The new church, which would have been in construction: Roscommon Journal,* September 23, 1848. Francis Beirne's *Diocese of Elphin* doesn't mention the opening of the new church in 1848. In the book's history of the Strokestown parish, the text reads, "The present [Kiltrustan] church of St. Patrick was originally erected around 1840 as a barn chapel but was extensively remodeled in 1871," which contradicts O'Donovan's account of an old church "a great portion of which is still standing" in 1837 and doesn't account for the *Roscommon Journal's* description of a new church opening in the autumn of 1848.

292 *"The sheriff has fixed Tuesday next":* JRM to Thomas Roberts, September 15, 1848, NLI, GML, 32,023, 731.

293 *"Mr. Pakenham Mahon is very anxious":* JRM to John Hackett, September 18, 1848, NLI, GML, 32,023, 778–779.

293 *According to a letter Ross Mahon mailed:* JRM to Thomas Roberts, September 25, 1848, NLI, GML, 32,028, 19–21.

293 *Ross Mahon also wrote a thank-you letter:* JRM to Thomas Hackett, September 25, 1848, NLI, GML, 32,028, 34.

293 *On the same day he penned a letter to his employer:* JRM to Henry Sandford Pakenham Mahon, September 25, 1848, NLI, PM Papers, 10,103 (6).

Epilogue

296 *"He thinks," Clarendon wrote to Lord John Russell:* Woodham-Smith, *Great Hunger,* 380.

296   *Later, before a parliamentary committee:* Gray, *Famine, Land and Politics*, 314–315.

297   *In late April:* Sir Spencer Walpole, *A History of England from the Conclusion of the Great War in 1815* (1912), vol. 5, 212.

297   *And when the rate-in-aid legislation: Times of London*, March 31, 1849.

297   *In practical terms, this money:* House of Commons, PP, 1850, *Statistical Statement for Each Poor Law Union in Ireland*, 1848–1849, 16.

298   *In late February James Commins was put on trial: Roscommon Journal*, March 3, 1849. *Roscommon Weekly Messenger*, March 7, 1849.

300   *But the case was in no way settled:* Various enclosures, NAI, Outrage Papers, County Roscommon, 1849 and 1850.

302   *Unsurprisingly, the local folklore:* Paula Mullooly, "A Brief History of the Pakenham Mahons," undated.

302   *In the summer of 1850 the brother of the famous:* Nassau Senior, *Journals, Conversations and Essays Relating to Ireland* (1868), vol. 2, 40–43.

304   *When the 1851 census was released:* The parish populations come from Browne, "Great Irish Famine in Co. Roscommon," 23.

306   *By now the grasslands and sheepwalks:* Hood, *Landlord-Planned Nexus*, 215–216.

306   *According to documents in his convict reference file:* NAI, Convict Reference File 1857/57.

306   *According to legend, he came back:* Donlon, "Mahon Murder Trials," 32.

306   *Somehow the matter reached: Hansard's*, vol. 158, series 3, June 13, 1861, 991–994.

307   *According to a local history, he was:* Richmond County Historical Society, *The Tread of Pioneers: Annals of Richmond County and Vicinity* (1968), vol. 2, 39.

307   *When he died in 1915: Sherbrooke Daily Record*, March 12, 1915.

307   *When he gave a speech in 1912:* Father Thomas Quinn, "A Voice from Ireland," a lecture at the First Congress of the French Language in Canada, Québec, June 24–30, 1912. In the possession of the archives of the Diocese of Nicolet.

309   *In 1882 members of the Land League: Times of London*, March 28, 1882; September 19, 1882; and July 10, 1883.

311   *Sifting through the papers:* Author's interview with James Callery, June 11, 2005.

Acknowledgments

MANY INDIVIDUALS AND INSTITUTIONS aided in the completion of this book. The National Library of Ireland, National Archives of Ireland, Diocese of Elphin archives, Diocese of Galway archives, New York Public Library, Department of Irish Folklore at University College Dublin, Bobst Library of New York University, Library of Congress, Roscommon Library, Yale University Library, Union Theological Seminary Library. Special thanks are due to James Callery and John O'Driscoll of Strokestown Park for offering me access to the Famine Museum's archives. Mary Lee Dunn of the Ballykilcline Society provided invaluable advice, encouragement, and assistance throughout the project, as did other members of the Ballykilcline group. Marianna O'Gallagher, the world's foremost expert on Irish emigration to Canada, gave considerable help during my visit to Québec, directing me to Abbé Denis Fréchette of the Diocese of Nicolet, Québec, who patiently guided me through the French-language files on the Quinn orphans. Valuable help was provided by Nicole Blake of Paroisse Sainte-Bibiane, Richmond, Québec. Thanks also to Rev. Raymond Browne of the Kilbride parish in County Roscommon; Diane Yeadon of the Norfolk Heritage Center of Norfolk, England; Lt. Col. (Retired) C. P. Love of the Worcestershire Regiment Museum Trust, Worcester, England; Roger Hull of the Liverpool Record Office; Pamela Clark of the Royal Archives, Windsor Castle; Robert Pitler of Brooklyn Law School. Karen Melham offered valuable research assistance at the Bodleian Library of Oxford University. I am quoting from Queen Victoria's journal with the permission of Her Majesty Queen Elizabeth II and from the papers of the fourth Earl of Clarendon with the permission of the current Lord Clarendon. Praise also to Alan Goldberg, Dennis Heaphy, Janon Fisher, Andrew Page, Mark Stamey, Charles Solomon, David Goldman, Michele Iuliano, Giuseppe Castellano, Carlos Garcia, Jon Hart, Barney Schecter, Leo Jakobson, Jeff Cuyubamba, Noel Kennedy, Corey Kilgannon, Ran Graff, Joe Fodor, Patrick Weaver, Eric Heidt, Johnny Driscoll, and Norman Seaman. This project would have languished without the spirited advocacy of my agent, Mary Evans, and her deputy, Devin McIntyre, and the professional direction of my editor, Tim Duggan, and his deputy, Allison Lorentzen. And it would have meant nothing without the love and support of my wife, Laura, and daughter, Eleanor.

Index

Act of Union, 23, 39
  Repeal movement, 46–48, 51, 55,
    56, 64, 65, 75, 76, 83, 106, 157,
    190, 191, 219, 230
Agnes (ship), 301
"American wake," 131
Anglican Church of Ireland, 7
Austen, Jane, 239
Australia
  famine immigrants, 309
  transportation to penal colonies, 63

Balfe, John, 55, 56
Ballingarry, 284
Ballykilcline, 88, 97, 102, 166, 244
Ballynamully, 1, 5
  Castle, 7, 40
Barbados, 94
Bathurst, Lord Bishop Henry, 37–39

Battle of the Boyne, 8–9, 197
bawn, 7
Beirne, Owen, 285
Bennett, William, 93
Bentinck, Lord George, 124,
  330n
Bermingham, M. B., 201, 202,
  217, 223, 262
Bessborough, fourth Earl of, 77
Blakeney, Thomas, 154, 156, 165,
  294
Boston Pilot, 193
Bourque, George, 134
Boyce, D. G., 314n
Boyd, Father John, 101, 112, 135,
  147, 149
  parish, population loss, 305
Brennan, Father Henry, 107, 168
  parish, population loss, 305

Brennan, John, 200, 202, 227, 244, 245
  Patrick Hasty response to, 278
  as witness for the prosecution, 247–50, 255–56, 264, 265–66, 267, 272, 273, 274
Brennan, Martin, 227, 228, 247, 278
  arraignment of, 237–38
  disappears to North America, 301
  guilty plea and sentence, 300
  John Hester's testimony about, 245
Brennan, Thomas, 238, 247, 248, 278, 298–99
  free passage to America, 301
Briggs, Right Reverend Dr., 98
British Association of the Relief of Extreme Distress, 94
British government. *See also* Peel, Robert; Russell, Lord John
  attempt to regenerate Ireland, 68, 213, 297–99 (*see also* England, laissez-faire economics)
  Catholic MPs, 40
  charges by Irish nationalists, 81
  decisions on Irish famine, x
  diplomatic ties with Pius IX, 206–7, 218
  famine or coffin ships and, 123–24
  famine relief measures, 67–72, 74, 78–84, 99, 104, 105–6, 116–17, 191, 195–96, 287, 295–98, 313n
  fear of Irish uprising, 74, 82, 283–84
  40-shilling freeholders, 21, 40
  Irish coercion bills, 62–63, 74, 149, 162–63, 168, 175, 181, 185, 196
  Irish MPs, 95, 170, 175, 180
  Irish reform measures under Peel, 51
  Irish rule and, 24, 39, 40
  "justice to Ireland" (Whig slogan), 79

new treason law, 219
persecution of Father Michael McDermott, 170–82
policy change, famine relief, 92–93
Poor Law, 44–46, 62, 67–68, 104–6
proposed emigration assistance, 136
rate-in-aid legislation, 296, 297
Repealers/Repeal Association seats, 106, 148
seeks to end fiduciary role in Famine relief, 104
tenant-protection legislation, 161, 213
Tory party, 46, 60, 78, 124, 173
Whig party, xi, 37–38, 40, 44, 74, 78, 81, 93, 136, 148, 149, 174, 189, 191
Whiteboy acts, 30
British Relief Association, 98, 101, 144, 188, 209, 210, 287–88
Browne, Bishop George J. P., 63–67, 72, 80, 83, 98, 140–41, 145, 149, 190, 196, 207, 286, 310
  blames Major Denis Mahon for provoking his murder, 209, 267
  building of post-famine Catholic Ireland, 290–92
  denunciation of Major Denis Mahon's clearances, 221–23
  as Dove of Elphin, 64
  family evicted, 146–47
  Lenten address, 65, 76
  reply to Earl of Shrewsbury, 192–94
  Ross Mahon attacks through family pressure, 215–16
  second reply to Earl of Shrewsbury, 207–8, 215
  third reply to Earl of Shrewsbury, 219–24, 230, 231, 234
  as voice of tenants of Mahon estate, 198, 208–9

Browne, Martin, 66–67, 147, 215–16
Browne, Mathew, 257, 260, 266
Browne, Patrick, 67, 147, 223, 289
  evictions of tenants, 289
  public act of contrition, 215–17
Burke, Edmund, 45
Burleigh, Lord, 34
Byrne, Mary, 135
Byrne, Michael, 135

Caligula, emperor of Rome, 208–9, 220
Callery, James, 311
Campbell, Stephen J., 316–17n
Canada
  account of Robert Whyte, 127–29
  disease epidemic from famine travelers, 130
  fate of Patrick and Thomas Quinn, 307–9
  Irish emigration to, 111, 113, 115, 122, 129–34
  life of French Canadians, 128
  orphan adoptions, 134, 307
  quarantine station at Grosse Île, 123, 128–29, 130–31, 133, 135
Carlow, battle of, 22, 35
Carrownalassan, 253–54, 259, 339n
Carton town, 15
Castle, Richard, 14
Castlenode townland, 146, 289
Castle Rackrent (Edgeworth), 27
Catholic Association, 39
Catholic Church. See also Browne, Bishop George J. P.; MacHale, Archbishop John; McDermott, Father Michael
  anti-revolutionary position, 83
  Archbishop of Tuam, John MacHale, 170–71
  charges of gorging during famine, 72, 140–41
  clergy attending to the sick and dying, 97

in England, 190, 205
  famine relief measures, 72, 79–80
  papal letter that priests not involve themselves in "worldly concerns," 204–5
  response to papal letter, 206
Catholic rent, 39
Catholics, 63–67
  anti-Catholic laws, 9–10, 18, 20, 26
  building of post-famine Catholic Ireland, 290–92, 310
  emancipation of, 39, 46
  Gaelic and Old English and, 3
  growth of middle class, 9, 305
  Irish rebels, 5–6
  landowning by, 21, 28
  loss of right to vote, 9, 19
  in Mahon family, 8
  militia, 21
  MPs, 40
  nationalism, 95
  nonviolent movement for emancipation, 39
  oath of "renunciation" imposed, 10–11
  Peel's reforms and, 51
  Penal Laws and, 9, 18, 26, 37, 39
  political machine of, 39
  relief (pre-Famine, 19, 32–33, 39
  squireens and, 26–27
  in Strokestown, 20–21
  targeted by secret societies, 30
  voting rights, 20, 21, 40
Charles I, king of England, 3, 5
Charles II, king of England, 5
Choctaw Indians, 94
Church of England, 37
Church of Ireland, 13–14, 18, 35
Clarendon, fourth Earl of
  conviction of John Mitchel and, 230–31
  Draconian measures called for, 160–61, 162, 168, 171–72

Clarendon, fourth Earl of (*cont.*)
eviction protection and, 213
famine relief measures, 287
Father McDermott and, 179–80, 182, 192, 205, 220
government inaction as act of extermination, 296
leaks to press by, 169
murder of Major Denis Mahon and, 149
rejection of plea of mercy for Hasty, 284
suspension of Habeas Corpus and, 283
Clarke, George, 275
Clonfad townland, 147
evictions, 289
Close, Mr., 237
coffin ships, xi, 123–35, 315n. *See also* emigration
Coleman, Anne, 316n
Colulombe, François, 134
Combe, Andrew, 125–26
Commins, James, 200, 201, 225, 228, 264
arraignment of, 237–38
case against, 270–75, 317n
character witnesses for, 275
death sentence, 300
defense of, 275
Enews Salt Galt's evidence against, 251
guilty verdict, 300
hanging of, 300
indictment, 271
John Brennan's testimony about, 248–49, 267
John Hester's testimony about, 246
murder trial of, 270–77
Patrick Flynn's testimony about, 252–53, 254–56
Patrick Hunt's testimony about, 258, 259–60

Patrick Rigney's testimony about, 242
second trial and conviction, 298–300
conacre
auction, 28
movement, 54, 56, 57, 62, 82–83
Confederation Clubs, 283
Connacht, kings of, 1
Connor, Andrew, 165–66, 227, 228, 238, 272, 299
escape to America, 301
John Brennan's testimony about, 249
John Hester's testimony about, 245
Patrick Flynn's testimony about, 252
Patrick Flynn's testimony about, 256–57
Connor, Bernard, 256
as witness for the defense, 267–69, 275
Connor, Patrick, 252, 255, 269
Conry, Thomas, 70, 315n
Coote, Sir Charles, 4–5
Corcoran, John, 135
Cornashina townland, 198, 199
evictions, 289–90
Corn Laws, 60–61
repeal, 60–61, 63, 74, 78, 82, 147–48
Costello, Charles, 139
Costello, Dualtagh (Dudley), 5–6, 48
cottiers, 28
cottier tenure, 28
County Clare, 2, 40
County Cork, 93–94
County Kilkenny, 24
County Londonderry, 42
County Louth, 136
County Roscommon and Roscommon town, ix, 23–24, 97

Bishop George J. P. Browne and, 63–67

Catholic Church, suppression of, 11

Catholic office holders, 40

end of Famine, 302

English confiscation of land, 5

escalating violence in, 54–57

hanging of James Commins, 300

hanging of Patrick Hasty, 284–86

Indian maize imports, 209–10

leading families of, 29

local relief committees (*see below,* Roscommon Union)

Mahon history in, 5–15

Mahon land in, 6

map, *49*

martial law proposed, 62

mounting Famine privations in, 116–17

murder investigation of Mahon case, 164–82

murder of Major Denis Mahon and, 229

murder of Rev. John Lloyd, 167–68

new church at Kiltrustan, 290–92

number of food recipients in Roscommon Union, 209, 213, 288, 297, 337n, 340n

O'Connell speaking in, 47–48

pacification of, 4

paid guardians assigned to relief effort, 187, 209, 210–12, 213–14

population loss, 304–5

potato crop failure, 1845, 60

potato crop failure, 1846, 73–84

potato crop failure, 1848, 282–83, 287

public works projects, 99

public works projects protest, 75–76

relief failure, 288

relief failure, 1848, 287–88

Repeal candidate, 148–49

Roscommon Union, 96–97, 117, 138, 139, 144, 189, 209, 210, 213–14, 282–83, 287, 297, 337n, 340n

secret societies in, 64–66

soup kitchens in, 117, 138, 187, 209, 282–83, 288

threats against landlords, 166

workhouse, 69, 71, 91–92, 139, 144, 145, 151, 155, 209–10

County Sligo, 97, 107

threats against landlords, 164, 167

County Tipperary, 173

rising of 1848, 283–84

Cox, John, 227

Cox family, 165–66, 241

Cregga townland, 120–21, 232

crime

attacks on landlords, 48–50, 54–57

exaggerated in England, 149

murder of Major Denis Mahon and, 158

theft of food, 82–83, 149

violence during the famine, 149

Crime and Outrage (Ireland) Bill, 171, 181

Crofton, Lord, 185–86

Crolly, Archbishop William, 206

Cromwell, Oliver, 3–4, 5, 40

Cullagh townland, 165

Cunningham, Bernard, 314–15n

Daily News (London)

on coercion bill, 163

on McDermott letter, 180

murder of Major Denis Mahon and, 159–60

response by to MacHale's defense, 194, 195

Davidson, J., 131

Dempsey, John and Martin, 135
Devenish, John, 289
Devenish, Robert, 289
De Vere, Stephen, 124–25, 328n
Dickens, Charles, 159
Digan, Mr., 289
Dignan, John, 57
disease
  death of clergy, 97
  diarrhea, 118
  dysentery, 188, 212
  1817 to 1818, outbreaks of pesti-
    lence, 35
  on emigration ships, 109–10,
    111–12, 123–35
  famine fever, 110, 120, 188–89
  fever sheds, 117
  from improperly prepared Indian
    maize, 71
  medical care for paupers, 117
  scurvy, 118
  ship fever, 125–26
  smallpox, 12
  typhus, 124, 200, 202, 225, 237,
    247
  in workhouses, 212
Dockery, Thomas
  as witness for the defense, 269
Dolan, Father William, 33, 43
Donlon, Billie, 306, 314n
Donnelly, Catherine
  free passage to America, 301
  as witness for the prosecution,
    274–75, 299–300
Donnelly, James, 274
  as witness for the prosecution,
    250–51, 267, 279
Donnelly, James, Jr., 313n, 314n
Donoughmore, Earl of, 306
Doorty townland, 153, 154, 198,
    199, 200, 201, 229, 253, 254, 257,
    258, 259, 261, 274, 300, 339n
  evictions and leveling of, 288–90,
    293–94

Douglas, George Mellis, 128,
    129–31, 133
Doyle, Patrick, 200, 225, 227, 272,
    300
  murder of Major Denis Mahon
    and, 249, 251, 255–56
Drummond, Thomas, 137
Dublin
  Ballybough prison, 226, 244, 248,
    265–66
  as departure port, 126
  Parliament House, 14–15 (see
    also Irish government [Dublin
    Castle])
Dublin Evening Mail, 56, 57, 158,
    159, 172
  on coercion bill, 163
  coverage of Mahon murder trial,
    237, 275, 276
Dublin Evening Post, 204
Dunnigan, Matthew, 165

Eccentric Lives of the Anglo-Irish,
    The (Morrow), 315n, 316n
Edgeworth, Maria, 27
education
  four queen's colleges proposed, 51
  "hedge" school, 16
  Major Denis Mahon and school
    construction, 87
  Maynooth, 51
  national schools, 195
  nondenominational elementary
    schools, 51
  Peel's reforms and, 51
Edwards, R. Dudley, 313n
Eglingtoun, Earl of, 206–7
Elphin, Ireland, 49, 49–50. See also
    Browne, Bishop George J. P
  Diocese of, 97
  soup kitchen, 97
emigration, 109–16
  accounts of journey, 124–29,
    328n

to America, xi, 112–16, 125, 134–35, 309

"American wake," 131

assisted (by landlords or government), x, 44, 53, 85, 106–8, 124–25, 136, 287

cheapest destinations, 111

cost of, 113, 115, 122, 272, 327n

defrauding of passengers, 111

epidemic disease and, 109–10, 111–12, 113

impact on Ireland, xi, 304–5

in-passage mortality, 128, 131, 132

Liverpool departure port, 109, 112–13, 116, 125

from Mahon estate, 109–16, 120, 145, 162, 175, 307–9

Major Denis Mahon and, 107–8, 110, 110–16, 120, 122, 143–44, 155, 162, 184, 219, 222–23, 232, 302–3, 326n, 327n

medical inspection, 111–12, 113, 114, 116, 128

number of emigrants, 1847, 109

Passenger Act, 114, 125, 328n

passenger agents, 110, 116

shipboard conditions, 114–15, 123–35

Strokestown orphans, 133–34, 307–9

typical journey, 112–16

waterfront cellars, 114, 116, 128

England. See also British government; Russell, Lord John

accusations of Irish genocide by, xi–xii, 81, 295–98, 313n, 314n

British troops sent to Ireland, 1790s, 21–23

Catholics allowed to occupy public office, 40

concerns about European revolts, 219

confiscation of Irish land, 4–5, 6

crime in Ireland exaggerated, 149

Cromwell campaign in Ireland, 3–4

famine refugees, 148

fear of Irish uprising, 32, 40, 160–63

ideas about social welfare programs, 44–45

Irish emancipation and, 40

Irish resistance to, 5

Jacobean, 8

laissez-faire economics and Irish suffering, 44, 77, 78, 81, 82, 92, 297, 322n

murder of Major Denis Mahon and suspicion of Father McDermott, 168–82

premature judgment the famine is over, 147–48

public response to famine, 94, 98, 188

Restoration, 5, 7

waning support for famine victims, 148

wars of, 37

English Civil War, 3

Enniskillen, Earl of, 123–24

Erin's Queen (ship), 116, 131, 327n

Evans, Henry, 187, 209, 211

evictions, xi

Browne family evictions, 146–47

as cause of crime, 74

cost of, 107

cottages destroyed, 121–22, 198, 235, 289

Cregga, 120–22

Doorty townland, 288–90, 292–94

early nineteenth century, 35

ejectment decree (*habere*), 89, 102, 103, 120, 147, 236, 290, 292

ejectment processes, 89, 112

evictions (*cont.*)
  fate of those evicted, 213
  Father McDermott's description, 178–79
  40-shilling freeholders, 40
  Lord Russell on, 161
  Mahon estate, x, 52, 86, 91, 101–4, 118–22, 136–37, 145–47, 154, 155, 198–99, 288–94, 302–4
  Molly Maguires and revenge for, 55–57
  notices to quit, 89, 119
  Pakenham Mahon and, 235–36, 288–94, 302–3
  petitions and memorials (appeals), 198–99, 289–90
  in retaliation for murder of Major Denis Mahon, 199, 288–94, 302–3
  Ross Mahon and, 85, 89–90, 102–4, 118–22, 145–47, 155–56, 178–79, 184–85, 198–200
  tenant-protection legislation, 161, 213

"Famine" (song), 314n
Famine Museum, xii, 311, 316n
famine ships. *See* coffin ships
Farnham, seventh Baron (Henry Maxwell), 172–73, 180, 191–92, 194, 205, 220
Farrell, James, 164–65, 225, 227
Ferriter, Diarmaid, 314n
Flanagan, Martin, ix, 151–52, 153, 154, 228
  testimony on the murder of Major Denis Mahon, 248, 255, 261
Flanagan, Martin Gerald, 339n
Flint, James P., 205
Flynn, John, 273
Flynn, Patrick, 200, 201, 228, 229
  Bernard Connor's testimony about, 267–69, 275

relocation of, 301
as witness for the prosecution, 251–57, 258–59, 261, 262, 264, 265, 272–73, 298, 339n
Fortfield, 252
Foster, R. F., 99
Four Mile House, 48, 150, 151, 153, 199, 200, 201, 202–3, 225, 227, 228, 240, 244, 246, 249, 275, 301
  map, *49*
France
  Irish allies, 22
  republic formed, 219
  war with England, 34
Fransoni, Cardinal Giacomo F., 204–5, 218
Freeman's Journal, 157, 179, 194
  Bishop Browne's letter in, 219, 230, 232, 267
  comes close to approving of Major Denis Mahon's murder, 224
  coverage of Mahon murder trial, 237, 248, 253, 258
Freemasons of India, 94
French, Fitzstephen, 149
French, Henry, 247
  as witness for the defense, 267, 275
Froste, T., 115

Gaelic Irish, 1–3, 304
  language, 1
Galt, Enews Salt (Elias Salt), 200, 226, 228–29, 251
Galway
  Ballinasloe cattle and horse fair, 245, 248, 250, 299
  Bishop George J. P. Browne and, 64–65
  English victory at, 4
  Gardiner, Michael, 201, 202, 225–26
  arraignment of, 237–38

attempt to vandalize landlord's grave, 306–7

Catherine Donnelly's testimony about, 274

Dr. Shanley's care of, 262

feud with Donnelly's, 300

guilty plea and sentence, 300

house of, 294

James Donnelly's testimony about, 250–51

John Brennan's testimony about, 248, 272

John Hester's testimony about, 246

offer to testify for the state, 276–77

Patrick Flynn's testimony about, 253

release from prison, 306

relocation of to Manchester, 306

as resident of Doorty, 294

sentence served in Philipstown prison, 301

Thomas Brennan's testimony about, 298–99

witness testimony against, 241, 243

Genesis 41:30, 57

genocide, xi–xii, 81, 295–98, 313n, 314n

George (ship), 127–29

Gill, John and Patrick, 135

gombeenmen, 81

Grace, Oliver D. J., 149, 175

Graffoge townland, 165, 227

Grattan, Henry, 18

Grattan, Henry, Jr., 170, 174–75

Gray, Peter, 74, 314n

Great Famine, The (Edwards and Williams), 313n

Great Hunger, The (Woodham-Smith), 315n

Great Irish Famine, x, 109–16. *See also* emigration

account of Stephen De Vere, 125

arrival of blight in Ireland, 58–59

blight seen as opportunity for reform, 44, 68, 77, 213, 297–99

British government and (see British government)

called pretext to avoid rents, 62–63, 87–88, 102

cessation of aid after murder, 186–87

deaths, x–xi, 81, 91, 93, 118, 145, 195, 296

disease and (*see* disease)

as Divine Will, 77, 78, 191, 322n

end of, 302

failure of relief efforts, 80–81, 91, 92, 97, 189, 287–88

failure to provoke uprising, 83–84

Famine Museum, xii, 311

famine relief efforts (*see* British government, famine relief measures; Relief Commission)

first national disaster to attract international sympathy, 94

first signs of food shortage, 67

grain exports during, xi, 81–82, 330n

illustrations of, 93

Indian maize imports, 61–62, 67, 71, 77, 92

Irish groups providing relief, 95

lasting controversy of, xi, 313n

long-term effects begin, 73–74

mounting privations, 116–17

paid guardians assigned to relief effort, 187, 189, 209

poor blamed, 77

population loss, 304–5

population reduced to destitution, 145

potato crop failure, 1845, 59–62

potato crop failure, 1846, 73–84

potato crop failure, 1848, 282–83, 287, 296

Great Irish Famine (*cont.*)
  protests by tenants and peasantry,
    67, 75–77
  public works projects, 67, 68,
    70–71, 77
  removal of tenants from land, x
  rising of 1848 and, 283–84
  soup kitchens, 92–93
  sources of food/food substitutes,
    70
  suffering and hardships, 1848,
    282–83
  violence during, 149
  world response to, 93–94
Great Irish Famine, The (Campbell), 316–17n
Great Irish Famine, The (Kinealy),
  313n
Great Irish Potato Famine, The
  (Donnelly), 313n
Grenville, Lord, 44
Greville, Charles, 87, 162
Grey, Earl, 125
Grey, Sir George, 171, 175
Guinness, Robert, 84, 200
Guinness Mahon land and banking agency, 84, 185, 200, 288,
  309

Habeas Corpus Act, 160, 171–72,
  283
Hackett, John, 293
Hall, Sir Benjamin, 170, 179
Hartland, First Baron Lord
  (Maurice Mahon), 19–21,
  23–24, 32, 33
  alliance with Catholic clergy,
    32–33
  death of, 35
  financial woes, 34–35
  impoverished state of tenants, 29
  land buys, 34
  mismanagement of estate, 34
  peerage, 24, 25, 29

Hartland, Second Baron Lord
  (Thomas Mahon), 22, 23–24,
  35–36
  death of, 42
  debts of, 44
  London residence of, 36, 42
  succession problem, 41–42
Hartland, third Baron Lord (Maurice Mahon), 42–43, 51, 60
Hasty, Anne, 284
Hasty, Patrick, 200, 201, 202, 225,
  228
  arraignment of, 237–38
  case against, 240–62, 298–99
  defense of, 263–70
  Enews Salt Galt's evidence
    against, 251
  expiation, statement of, 285–86
  hanging of, 284–86
  James Commins, case against
    and, 274
  James Donnelly, witness for the
    prosecution, 250–51
  John Brennan, witness for the
    prosecution, 247–50
  John Hester, witness for the
    prosecution, 244–47
  Patrick Flynn, witness for the
    prosecution, 251–57
  Patrick Rigney, witness for the
    prosecution, 240–44
  statement to the judge and death
    sentence of, 277–81, 283
Henry (emigration ship), 111
Hester, John, 201, 202, 228
  Brennan's testimony and, 248
  free passage to America, 301
  Henry French's testimony about,
    267, 275
  Patrick Hasty response to, 277–78
  Rigney's testimony and, 241–42
  as witness for the prosecution,
    238, 244–47, 263–64, 265, 271
Hood, Susan, 5, 14, 15, 84

Howard, Major, 138, 142
Hunt, James, 154
Hunt, Patrick, 201, 228, 261
  free passage to America, 301
  as witness for the prosecution,
    262, 264–65, 266, 273–74, 280,
    298
Hunt, Thady, 253, 258–59, 261,
    265, 268, 273
Hunt, Widow, 261

Illustrated London News, 157
Indian maize imports, 61–62, 67,
    69–70, 71, 92
  in County Roscommon, 209–10
  halting of, 77
  as "Peel's Brimstone," 71
  in Strokestown, 80–81, 152
Ireland
  agriculture in, xi, 16, 25–29, 30,
    34, 56, 78, 105, 297–98
  Anglo-Irish aristocracy, 12
  anti-Catholic laws, 9–10, 18, 20,
    32–33, 37
  architecture, 14–15
  arrests of Young Irelanders for
    sedition, 219
  Big Houses in, 15
  British troops in, 1790s, 21–23
  building of post-famine Catholic
    Ireland, 290–92, 310
  Catholic Church, suppression of,
    10–11
  Catholic nationalism, 95
  Catholics, 3, 8, 9
  conflict, 1790s, 21–23
  consequences of the murder of
    Major Denis Mahon, 160–61,
    183–84
  Costello's war, 5–6
  Cromwell campaign in, 3–4
  division of nationalists in, 75
  economic depression, 1815-22,
    34–35

education, 16
effect of Great Irish Famine on
  peasant society, xi
English confiscation of land, 4–5
English rule, xi, 2, 4–5, 9, 31, 32,
  39, 40, 44–46, 51, 54 (*see also*
  Act of Union; British Government)
escalating violence, 1844 to 1845,
  54
fears of peasant rebellion, 32, 40,
  63, 160–63
French alliance, 22
Gaelic population, 3
grain and food exports during
  famine, xi, 81–82, 330n
grain imports, 147–48
growth of Catholic middle class,
  305
independence, 18, 19, 21, 22, 33,
  40
Irish rebels, 5–6
Jacobites versus Williamites in,
  8–9
landscape as "bleak country," 16
legislative independence from
  England, 19
Mahon family as prominent in,
  18
map, *4*
nationalism, 219, 230–31,
  283–84 (*see also* Appeal Association; O'Connell, Daniel;
  Young Ireland)
New English in, 3
O'Connell and political agitation,
  46–48, 50–51
Old English in, 3
peasants of, 6, 17, 25–26, 27–28,
  30, 39
population increase, nineteenth
  century, 25
population loss, Famine numbers,
  304–5

Indian maize imports (*cont.*)
　post-famine era, 290
　potato crop, dependence on and
　　social ills, 6, 16, 25–26, 46, 54,
　　61, 68, 74, 77, 78
　poverty in, xi, 25, 26, 27, 28,
　　29–32, 34, 44–46, 52, 53,
　　61–62, 67, 74
　pre-Famine dependence on
　　potato, 59
　Protestant rule (Ascendancy),
　　7–8, 15, 18, 21, 23, 72, 158,
　　310
　Protestant-Catholic strife, 31–32
　rebellion of 1798, 23
　rising of 1848, 283–84
　scheme to change peasantry into
　　wage laborers, 68, 78–79, 213,
　　297–99
　secret societies (see Molly Magu-
　　ires; secret societies)
　social inequity in, xi
　symbolism of the murder of Ma-
　　jor Denis Mahon, 157–58
　trial of Young Irelanders for sedi-
　　tion, 230
　Ulster uprising of 1641, 3
　unemployment, 148
　War of Independence, 310
Irish Confederation, 95, 148, 219,
　230, 283
Irish Famine, The (Tóibín and Fer-
　riter), 314n
Irish government (Dublin Castle),
　9, 11–12, 19, 31, 32, 46, 48, 54,
　180. *See also* Clarendon, fourth
　Earl of
　coercion bill, 62, 160, 183, 185
　fear of class warfare, 160–63,
　　283–84
　Mahon murder investigation,
　　226, 257, 258
　repeal of Habeas Corpus, 283
　Thomas Mahon in, 18–19

Irwin, Oliver, 276
Irwin, Richard, 48–50, 54, 151

James II, King of England, 8
John Munn (ship), 115, 120, 132,
　327n
Jones, H. N., 113
Jones, Walter, 1

Kaffir War, 296
Kelly, Dan, 315n
Kelly, Denis H., 47, 154, 157,
　174–75, 229, 239
Kelly, Father James, 20, 32–33
Kelly, John, 11
Kenny, Kevin, 316n
Kenny, Martin, 150
Kilgrass parish, 107, 244, 304
Kiltrustan, church at, 290–92,
　341n
Kinealy, Christine, 94, 313n, 314n,
　330n
Knox, George, 88, 97, 98

Ladies Relief Association, Brook-
　lyn, NY, 94
Land League, 309
landlords
　absentee, 55, 183, 184
　ambiguous status of tenants and,
　　26
　blame on tenants for troubles, 52
　clearance campaigns, x, 15, 35,
　　137, 295 (*see also* evictions)
　destruction of cottages, 121–22,
　　198, 213
　effort to use Mahon murder to in-
　　vestigate abuses by, 175–76, 181
　emigration assistance, x, 53,
　　85, 124–25 (see also Mahon,
　　Major Denis)
　escalating violence against, 54–57
　evictions, x, xi, 35, 52, 119, 137,
　　161, 212–13 (*see also* Mahon,

Major Denis; Pakenham Mahon, Henry Sandford)
  evictions, 40-shilling freeholders, 40
  famine relief provided by, x, 67, 70–72, 78, 81, 87, 93, 104, 122, 148, 288
  fiscal troubles, early nineteenth century, 35
  40-shilling freeholders, 21, 40, 52
  generous individuals, 153
  greed blamed for Ireland's problems, 74
  insolvency because of relief policies, 79
  land allocation and, 17
  life of peasants and, 16
  Mahon family (ancestors) as, 13, 26, 29, 36
  Major Denis Mahon as (see Mahon, Major Denis)
  middlemen or squireens and, 26–27, 112, 146, 215–16, 275, 305
  militia formed by, 21
  murder of, xi, 206
  murder of Major Denis Mahon and, 157, 160
  murder of Rev. John Lloyd, 167–68
  Poor Law and, 44–46
  poor rates (tax), 45, 93, 107, 122, 144, 151, 185, 187–88, 189, 214, 295
  Quarter Acre Clause used to clear estates, 212
  shooting of Richard Irwin, 48–50, 54, 151
  subtenants of, 26, 27
  threats against, 164, 166, 285–86
  as Tories, 47
Langrishe, Sir Hercules, 24
Lansdowne, Marquess of, 173
Last Conquest of Ireland (Perhaps),

The (Mitchel), 313n
Lefroy, Thomas Langlois, 237, 239–40, 263, 275–76, 277–81
Leitrim townland, 198, 199, 229, 253, 258, 259, 339n
  evictions, 289, 290
Limerick Relief Committee, 92
Lisanuffy parish, 101, 112, 118, 135
Liverpool
  as departure port, 109, 112–13, 116, 125
  disease in, 110, 113, 128
  passenger agents, 110, 116
Lloyd, Rev. John, 167–68, 201
Longford, Baron, 119
Lyons, Luke, 300–301

MacDermott, Bishop Ambrose, 10
MacDonagh, Oliver, xii, 111
MacHale, Archbishop John, 170–71, 182, 183, 190, 193
  fight for Irish Catholicism, 292
  response to Shrewsbury, 194–96, 205
Madden, Father, 285
Maguire, King of Fermanagh, 2
Maguire, Patrick, 88
Mahon, Major Denis, 23–24
  alliance with Father Michael McDermott, 43
  appearance, 42
  arrests in murder case, 164–65
    (see also Mahon murder investigation; Mahon murder trial)
  Bathurst family and, 37–39
  Bawn House, White House, Strokestown House (family home), 11, 14–16, 19–20, 30, 41, 120, 227 (archive)
  belief tenants avoided rent payment, 88–90
  Browne family evictions, 146–47
  as chair of local famine relief committee, 70–72, 79–80

Mahon, Major Denis (*cont.*)
  clearance policies (and volun-
    tary surrender), 120-21, 122,
    145-47, 155-56, 326n
  conacre movement and, 57
  conditional charity of, 87
  conflict with Father McDer-
    mott, 72, 79-80, 95-98, 136,
    138-43
  consequences of murder, 160-61,
    183-86
  conspirators among tenants, 90,
    102, 122, 147, 155, 301-2
  demand for rents during famine,
    72
  denounced by McDermott
    (1847), 140-43, 169-70, 173,
    174, 179 (*see also* McDermott,
    Father Michael)
  emigration assistance, x, 107-8,
    110-16, 122, 126, 133, 143-44,
    155, 219, 222-23, 232, 302-3,
    326n, 327n
  estate in Strokestown, x, 6, 7, 21,
    157, 183-84
  evictions, x, 52, 86, 89-90, 91,
    101-2, 103, 118-22, 136-37,
    141, 145-47, 154, 155, 178-79,
    184, 208, 217, 219, 221-23
  evictions at Cregga, 120-22
  family alliances with Catholic
    clergy, 32-33
  family history, 5-15, 18-24, 32-36
  famine relief measures by, 69,
    101, 137-39, 143-44, 152
  financial woes, 119
  folkloric memory, xii, 314-16n
  funeral and burial, 157
  as high sheriff of Roscommon,
    48
  home as Famine Museum, xii,
    311, 316n
  inherits estate and title, 42, 60
  inquest into murder of, 153
  instructions for handling of fam-
    ine crisis, 86-87
  investigation of landlord shoot-
    ing, 1843, 48-50, *49*
  keeping of public order and,
    48-50
  killing of, ix, 151-54
  lack of male heir, 119
  as landlord, x, 43-44, 48,
    51-54, 60, 71-72, 87, 104, 261,
    266-67, 279
  letters to land agent (Ross
    Mahon), 90, 91, 96, 98, 101,
    103-4, 110, 111-12, 116, 120,
    137
  line of Mahon family succession
    and, 36-37, 42
  living standards of tenants, 53
  marriage of, 37
  Martin Browne as largest single
    tenant, 66-67
  military career, 36-37
  motives for killing of, xii, 154-55,
    157, 162, 179, 249, 250,
    266-67, 302-3
  number of people on his land,
    52, 60
  obtains pistol, 137
  plot against, 150-51, 154-55,
    156, 184
  rent strike on estate of, 87, 88,
    155, 156, 184
  reward offered to find murderer,
    164-65
  school construction, 87
  standard of living during famine,
    100-101, 141
  symbolism of the murder, 157-58
  as Tory, 38
  turns control over to land agent,
    84 (*see also* Ross Mahon, John)
Mahon, Henrietta Bathurst, 37,
  152, 199, 231, 267, 269, 270,
  276, 289

Mahon, John, 8–9, 10, 11–12

Mahon, John (brother of Major Denis Mahon), 25, 66, 157, 276

Peel's commission on landlord-tenant relations, 51–54

Mahon, John Ross. *See* Ross Mahon, John

Mahon, Magdalene French, 8, 11

Mahon, Maurice. *See* Hartland, First Baron Lord (Maurice Mahon)

Mahon, Maurice (the younger). *See* Hartland, third Baron Lord (Maurice Mahon)

Mahon, Nicholas, 5, 6, 25, 40, 48

community founded by, 7

Mahon, Nicholas (the younger), 12

Mahon, Stephen, 24, 32–33, 39, 41

Mahon, Thomas, 12, 18

Mahon family motto, 1

Mahon murder investigation, xii, 164–82, 199–203, 225–30

informants and "approvers," 200, 202, 226, 228, 298–99

map for, 229

post-trial information received, 300–301

suspects, 165–66, 199–200, 201–2, 227, 228, 238

suspects never heard McDermott's preaching, 202–3

Mahon murder trial, 234, 237–81

Ann Symth, witness for the prosecution, 272, 317n

Attorney General Peter McKeogh, 240, 246, 268–70, 271, 275, 277

Bernard Connor, witness for the defense, 267–69

British law on conspiracy, 238–39

Catherine Donnelly, witness for the prosecution, 274–75, 299–300

charge of conspiracy, 237–38

defendants indicted, 237–39

defense counsel Mr. Skelton, 240

Father McDermott omitted from, 239

Henry French, witness for the defense, 267, 275

James Commins, case against, 237–38, 270–77

James Commins, death sentence, 300

James Commins, defense of, 275

James Commins, guilty verdict, 300

James Commins, jury for, 270–71, 275–76

James Commins, lack of verdict, 276–77

James Commins, second trial and conviction, 298–300

James Donnelly, witness for the prosecution, 250–51, 267, 279

John Brennan, witness for the prosecution, 247–50, 255–56, 264, 265–66, 267, 272, 273, 274, 278

John Flynn, witness for the prosecution, 273

John Hester, witness for the prosecution, 241–42, 263–64, 265, 271–72, 277–78

John Ross Mahon as target of assassination, 250

Judge Thomas Langlois Lefroy, 237, 239–40, 263, 270, 271, 275–76, 277–81

Martin Brennan, case against, 237–38

Martin Brennan, guilty plea and sentence, 300

Michael Gardiner, case against, 237–38, 298–99

Michael Gardiner, guilty plea and sentence, 300

Mahon murder trial (*cont.*)
motives for killing, 249, 250, 266–67
Patrick Flynn, witness for the prosecution, 251–57, 258, 261, 262, 264, 265, 272–73, 298, 339n
Patrick Hasty, case against, 237–38, 240–62
Patrick Hasty, death sentence, 277–81
Patrick Hasty, defense of, 263–70
Patrick Hasty, guilty verdict, 269
Patrick Hasty, jury for, 240, 269
Patrick Hasty, sentencing of, 263
Patrick Hunt, witness for the prosecution, 257–61, 262, 264–65, 266, 273–74, 280, 298
Patrick Rigney, witness for the prosecution, 238, 240–44, 256, 263–64, 265, 271, 278
reliance on informants, 266, 275
rewards for informants, 301
scene of the murder, map, *251*
secret society implicated in, 243, 269, 301
Skelton cross-examination of Brennan, 250
Skelton cross-examination of Hester, 246–47
Skelton cross-examination of Hunt, 258–61
Skelton cross-examination of Rigney, 242–44
Terence Shanley, witness for the prosecution, 261–62, 264
Thomas Brennan, witness for the prosecution, 298–99
Thomas Dockery, witness for the defense, 269
weapons implicated in, 241–42, 245, 246, 248, 249, 254, 255–56, 258, 259, 262, 264, 272, 273, 274, 298, 299–301

witnesses held in Ballybough prison with their families, 226, 247–48, 265–66
Mahony, James, 93
Making of Modern Irish History, The (Boyce and O'Day, eds.), 314n
Making Sense of the Molly Maguires (Kenny), 316n
Malthus, Thomas, 44
Manners, Lord John, 124
Mathew, Father Theobald, 73, 190–91, 195
McClausland, Marcus, 42, 60, 98, 166–67, 184, 198, 227, 229, 303
McCormack, Widow, 284
McDermott, Father Michael, xii, 43, 68–69, 72, 77, 151
alliance with Major Denis Mahon, 43
building of post-famine Catholic Ireland, 292
on burning of cottages, 121–22
charges of mismanagement of funds, 139–40, 219–20, 233, 234, 303
conflict with Major Denis Mahon, 72, 79–80, 95–98, 136, 138–43
death of, 310
defense by Archbishop MacHale, 170–71, 182, 194–96
denunciation of Major Denis Mahon, 140–43, 169–70, 173, 174, 179, 192, 193–94, 207, 223, 266, 303, 334n
description of evictions, 178–79
emigrations and, 112
as "Hammer of the Heretics," 196
letters, miscellaneous, 196–98
local relief committee work, 118, 139–43

manner of expression, 196–98
new church at Kiltrustan, 290
on new potato crop, 144–45
not indicted, 239
papal inquiry into, 174, 181–82,
    204–5
parish, population loss, 304–5
parish boundaries, 203
prosecution of, 170–82, 189–98
public verbal attack on Major
    Denis Mahon, 80
second church built by, 310, 341n
soup kitchen and, 100, 101, 116,
    117, 138–39, 152
suspected role in the killing of
    Major Denis Mahon, xii,
    168–82, 183, 316n, 334n
written response to accusations,
    176–78, 186, 190
McDonnell, Farrell, 245
McGann, John, 166
McGreal, Father Thady, 11
McKeogh, Peter, 240, 268–70,
    271, 275, 277
McNamara, John, 294
Meagher, Timothy Francis, 219,
    230
Melville, Herman, 113
Minto, Lord, 168, 174, 181, 196,
    205
Mitchel, John, 87, 205, 219, 230,
    283, 313n
Mitchell or Mulmitchell, Maol,
    1–2
Molly Maguires, xii–xiii, xii,
    55–57, 62, 65, 66, 82, 83, 164,
    167, 186, 201, 286, 301, 309,
    316n
in America, 309
Monteagle, Lord, 124–25, 136
Morning Chronicle, 157–58, 159, 180
on Browne reply to Shrewsbury,
    193
on coercion bill, 163

response by to MacHale's de-
    fense, 194, 196
on Shrewsbury letter, 192
Morrow, Ann, 315n, 316n
Morton, Mr., 289
Morton, Reverend Joseph, 235-
    236, 287
Morton, Thomas, 112, 235–36
Mulligan, Martin, 300
Mullooly, Paula, 317n
Murray, Archbishop Daniel, 206
Musters, Henry, 211–12, 213–14

Naomi (ship), 115, 120, 132, 133,
    134–35
National Library of Ireland, 120
Nation newspaper, 47, 157, 219
Nero, Emperor of Rome, 208–9,
    220
Newtown townland, 146
Nicholls, George, 46
Nolan, Peter, 56
Norton, Desmond, 253–54, 259,
    339n
Nottingham Catholic Association,
    196

O'Beirne, Michael, 250
O'Brien, William, 200, 228, 229,
    244, 257
sworn statement on site of mur-
    der, 254
Ocean Plague, The (Whyte), 126–29
O'Connell, Daniel, 39–40, 46–47,
    63, 64, 65, 66, 171
alliance with landlord class, 95
arrest and trial, 50
death of, 148
last speech in Parliament, 106
Peel's reforms and, 51
public meetings suppressed, 50
Repealers/Repeal Association,
    47–48, 55, 75, 95, 141, 148
Russell government and, 75

O'Connell, Daniel (*cont.*)
Shrewsbury and, 190
speech in Roscommon Town,
47–48
split with Young Ireland, 75
O'Connell, John, 148, 180
O'Connell, Maurice, 170, 175–76
O'Connor, Sinéad, xii, 314n
O'Conor clan, 1–2, 40
poem on battle by, 2–3
O'Day, Alan, 314n
O'Donovan, John, 290–91
O'Faoláin, Seán, 171
O'Gallagher, Marianna, 133–34
Ó Gráda, Cormac, 82, 314n, 330n
O'Neill, Margaret, 258
O'Rourke, Canon John, 97

Pakenham, Dean, 157
Pakenham Mahon, Grace Catherine, 119, 157
Pakenham Mahon, Henry Sandford, 119, 157, 199, 217
attack on Bishop Browne, 215–16
challenged by Bishop Browne to
answer charges of clearances,
223, 231–36
death of, 310
descendants of, 311, 315n, 316n
desire to colonize land with Protestants, 236
ends gratuities to tenants who
surrender, 235
eviction policies, 199, 235–36,
288–94
implication of Father McDermott in murder, 239
as landlord of Mahon estate, 184,
198, 201, 202, 203, 235–36,
262, 288–94
prosecution of murder suspects
and, 230
prosperity post-Famine, 302–4,
305–6

Pakenham Mahon, Nicholas, 316n
Pakenham Mahon, Olive, 311
Palladio, Andrea, 14
Palmerston, Lord, 107, 148, 162,
168, 174, 213
Passenger Act (Imperial Passenger
Act) 114, 125, 328n
Pataki, George, xii, 314n
Patrick, Saint, 9
Patrick Rigney, witness for the
prosecution
John Hester, witness for the
prosecution, 244–47
Patriot movement, 18, 19
peat, 27
Peel, Robert, 40, 46, 48, 50, 51, 82
coercion bill, 171
commission on landlord-tenant
relations, 51–54, 66
commission on potato famine, 60
famine relief measures, 60–62,
75, 77, 80
importation of Indian maize, 61–62
repeal of Corn Laws, 60–61, 74
Penal Laws, 9, 18, 26, 37, 39
Physiology of Digestion, The
(Combe), 125
Pius IX, Pope, xii, 94, 168, 174,
181–82, 204–25, 292
refuses terms of English recognition, 218
Polk, James, 94
Poor Law, 44–46, 122, 287
agricultural reform and, 56, 297–98
Amendment Act, 105–6, 107,
122, 138–39, 144, 149, 152,
163, 187, 189, 282–83, 296,
297–98
commissioner Twistleton, 296–98
English, 45–46, 148
Irish, 45–46, 62, 67–68, 104–5,
298
Quarter Acre (or Gregory)
Clause, 106, 212, 282

rules and restrictions for the poor, 92, 210–11

poor rates (tax), 45, 93, 107, 122, 144, 151, 185, 187–88, 189, 214, 295

Pope, Alexander, 64

potato crop, x
blight of, x, 17, 58–59, 73–74, 99
blight reappears, 1848, 282–83, 287
conacre auction, 28
conacre movement, 54, 56, 57, 62, 82–83
dependence on and social ills, 26, 46, 54, 61, 68, 74, 77, 78
failure, 1845, 59–62
failure, 1846, 73–84, 109
failure, 1848, 296
as food of peasantry, x, 6, 16, 25–26, 54, 59
healthy, post-blight, 144, 214–15, 302
inadequate amount to feed peasants, 144–45
poteen (alcoholic drink), 27
taken as tithe by Protestant clergy, 30

Powerscourt, County Wicklow, 15

Prospect House, Dundalk, 136

Protection of Life Bill, 63

Protestants, 3
Ascendancy, 7–8, 15, 18, 21, 23, 72, 158, 310
converts by offering famine relief, 168
dissenters, 9
militia, 21
Nicolas Mahon as, 7–8
Orangemen, 21, 22, 31–32
rule over Ireland, 9
squireens and, 26–27
targeted by secret societies, 30, 31–32
view Irish peasant as irredeemable, 158

public works projects, 70–71, 77, 81, 91, 148, 287
cessation of and "famine roads," 99–100
mob protest in Country Roscommon, 75–76
written protest, Strokestown, 76

Punch magazine, 94, 183, 194

Quakers (Society of Friends), 92–93, 116, 288
publicizing famine suffering, 93–94, 188

Quakers' Central Relief Committee of Dublin, 98

Quarter Acre (or Gregory) Clause, 106, 212, 282

Quinn, Father Andrew, 256

Quinn, James and Margaret, 134

Quinn, Joseph, 124, 134

Quinn, Patrick, 124, 134, 307

Quinn, Thomas, 124, 134, 307–9

Redington, Thomas, 180, 182, 185, 226

Relief Commission, x, 67–72.
See also County Roscommon and Roscommon town; Strokestown
failure of, 91, 92, 97, 189, 287–88
guidelines, 67–68, 69, 79, 210–11
Indian maize imports, 61–62, 67, 69–70
local relief committees, 67–68, 79, 92, 118, 139–43
Major Denis Mahon and, 70
matching funds from England, 67, 70, 78, 92
poor rates (tax) as funding for, 45, 93, 107, 122, 144, 151, 185, 187–88, 189, 214, 295
rate-in-aid legislation and, 296, 297
relief ended, 1848, 282–83

Relief Fund, Birmingham, England, 98
relief lists, 138, 140
rent strikes, 87–88, 102, 155, 156, 184
Repealers/Repeal Association, 47–48, 55, 75, 83, 95, 148, 207, 219, 231, 283, 307
Repeal rent, 83, 195, 307
Richard III (Shakespeare), 150
Rigney, Patrick, 165, 200, 202, 226, 228
  John Brennan's testimony and, 248
  John Hester's testimony about, 244–45, 246, 263–64
  as witness for the prosecution, 238, 240–44, 256, 263–64, 265, 271, 274, 278
Riotous Roscommon (Coleman), 316n
Rising of 1848, 283–84
Roberts, Thomas, 184, 198, 234, 288–89
Robinson, John, 90, 112, 185, 293
Robinson, Mary, xii
Robinson, William and James (J. & W.), 110–11, 113, 115–16, 129
Rory, Father Terence, 11
Roscommon and Leitrim Gazette, 81, 97, 156, 216
Roscommon Board of Guardians, 151, 185–86
Roscommon Journal, 73–74, 75, 81, 83, 87, 90, 116, 144, 183, 188, 258, 270–71
  attacks on Major Denis Mahon's eviction policy, 136–37
  church built by Father McDermott, 310
  coverage of Mahon murder trial, 240, 244, 248, 253, 261, 262, 275, 276, 277, 283, 298
  new church at Kiltrustan, 291–92

report of blight, 1848, 283
response by to MacHale's defense, 196
Roscommon Weekly Messenger, 267
  coverage of Mahon murder trial, 266
  hanging of Patrick Hasty, 285, 286
Ross Mahon, John, x, 98, 169
  actions after the murder, 184–85
  advertises for Protestant tenants, 236
  attack on Bishop Browne, 215–16
  attempt to kill, 309
  belief tenants avoided rent payment, 88–90
  blight used to reform land use, 89
  chase after suspects, 201
  conspiracy against, 122
  death of, 309–10
  emigration scheme, 85, 106–8, 110–16, 122, 133, 175, 223
  evictions pursued by, 102–4, 118–22, 145–47, 155–56, 178–79, 184–85, 198–200, 231, 236, 288–94
  evidence for Pakenham Mahon to refute Browne, 231–34
  famine relief measures, 152
  fear of Irish uprising, 286–87, 303–4
  fever sheds and, 117
  food for emigrating tenants and, 115–16
  Gardiner's release from prison and, 306
  as hated figure, xii, 309, 314n, 315n
  implication of Father McDermott in murder, 239
  as intended target, xii, 267
  as land agent, 84–87
  letters to Major Denis Mahon, 91, 103–4

letter to the *Times*, 175
on McDermott charges, 182
on murder of Major Denis Mahon, 155
on murder trial, 262, 263, 266, 267, 269–70
prosecution of murder suspects and, 202, 203, 226, 227, 229–30
removal of tenants without eviction, 198
on Rigney ejection, 242
strong-arm tactics, 89
testimony on clearances, 155–56
threats against, 166–67
told to spare poorest tenants from evictions, 101–3
visit by Nassau Senior, 303–4
Routh, Randolph, 68, 69, 71, 81, 82, 96, 160, 283
rundale system, 17, 26, 27, 28, 52–53, 154
Russell, Lord John, xi–xii, 74, 75, 86, 99, 105, 107, 148, 168, 192
blames landlord troubles on themselves, 161
coercion bill and, 171–72
on evictions, 161, 213
famine relief measures, 79, 92, 95, 287, 295, 296, 330n
hopes for Ireland, 311
on Major Denis Mahon, 162

Salaman, Redcliffe, 6
Sandys, William, 275
Scally, Robert, 16–17
scalpeens, 121
secret societies, 29–32, 39, 55–57, 64, 87, 186. *See also* Molly Maguires
bonfires and, 31, 156–57
murder of Major Denis Mahon and, xii, 165, 201, 243, 269, 301, 316n
Senior, Nassau, 302–3

Shakers of New Lebanon, Pennsylvania, 94
Shakespeare, William, 150
Shanley, Terence, ix, 49, 117–18, 140, 142, 172, 186, 202, 217, 223, 240
examination of jury in murder trial of Commins, 276
murder of Major Denis Mahon and, 151–54, 225, 228, 229
testimony on the murder of Major Denis Mahon, 248, 253–54, 255, 256, 261–62, 264
Shannon River, 13
shebeen (illegal tavern), 55, 200, 240
Shrewsbury, John Talbot, Earl of, 189–90, 196, 197, 205
acquits McDermott, 207, 217
Alton Towers, 189
ends letter-writing, 234
letter against McDermott, 190–92, 197
response by Archbishop MacHale, 194–96
response by Bishop Browne, 192–94
response to Bishop Browne's second letter, 216–18
second letter, 207
Signay, Archbishop Joseph, 123
Skelton, Mr., 240
Skibbereen, 93–94
Slattery, Archbishop Michael, 206
Sligo, Marquess of, 119
Smith, Elizabeth, 167
Smith O'Brien, William, 148, 219, 230, 283–84
Smyth, Ann, 317n
as witness for the prosecution, 272
Smyth, Widow, 249, 274, 299
"snug" farmers, 145–46
Society of the United Irishmen, 21, 22

soupers, 168

Soup Kitchen Act, 92–93, 95, 99, 104, 105, 116
  expiration of, 144, 147
  number of recipients in Roscommon Union, 213

soup kitchens, 92–93, 95–96, 98, 100, 101, 102, 116–17, 119, 137–39, 148, 187, 189
  lack of nutrients, 118
  stirabout, 117
  shutting of, 144, 209, 282–83, 288

spalpeens, 28

Spectator magazine, 169

squireens, 26–27

Stanley, Lord, 173–74, 239

Statistical Survey of Roscommon, The (Weld), 41

stirabout, 117, 268

Strokestown
  alliance of comfortable classes in, 30–31, 32
  attack on John Dignan and, 57
  building and improvements by Thomas Mahon, 13–14
  Catholic parish of, 32–33, 35, 43
  Catholics in, 20–21
  cessation of aid after murder, 186
  church built by Father McDermott, 310, 341n
  conacre movement and, 57
  Defenders, 21
  economic depression, 1815–1822, 34
  economic depression, 1830s, 41
  emigration from (Mahon tenants), 109, 110, 112–16, 124, 126, 131–35, 145
  emigrating from (Mahon tenants) number of, 115
  ethnic tensions in, 41
  evictions, number of tenants, 137, 147, 221, 231, 290 (*see also* Mahon, Major Denis, evictions)

famine deaths, 145

famine relief committee (Strokestown Relief Committee), 68–69, 70–72, 79–80, 95–98, 137, 139–40, 143, 220

famine relief committee, failure of, 97, 98

famine relief measures, 68–69, 116

fate of Mahon estate, 310–11

fate of those evicted, 213

fever hospital, 117–18, 140, 151, 155, 202

food distribution, 91–92, 98

Hartland estate (Mahon lands), x, 6, 21, 27, 29, 44, 51–54

history, 1–3

improvements by Pakenham Mahon, 305

Indian maize imports, 69–70, 71, 80–81, 98, 152, 303

industry, 13, 34, 41

Mahon family in (history), 5–15, 18–21

map, *49*

Maurice Mahon's improvements, 20–21, 34

new church at Kiltrustan, 290–92

Peel's commission on landlord-tenant relations, 51–54

poor of, 29–32, 52

population loss, 304–5

potato crop failure, 1845, 59–60

potato crop failure, 1848, 287

public works projects, 91

reaction to killing of Major Denis Mahon, 156–57

rundale system in, 17, 27, 52–53, 154

secret societies in, 29–32

soup kitchen, 95, 98, 100, 101, 102, 116, 117, 118, 119, 137–39, 143–44, 187, 303

spalpeens in, 28

starvation and deaths in, 91–92, 208

support for Molly Maguires in,
56–57
tenant protest on public works
failure, 76
Threshers, 30–32
vista of, 18
Sultan of Turkey, 94

Tablet, 194, 205
Tamerlane (ship), 126
Temporary Relief Destitute Persons
Act, 93
Threshers, 30–32
Tighe, Catherine, 134
Tighe, Daniel, 124, 134
Times of London, 47, 48
accusations against Father
McDermott, 180, 181, 231
on coercion bill, 162–63
famine relief measures, 295
famine ship accounts, 126
hatred of MacHale and
O'Connell, 192
letter against McDermott, 168–69
letter by Pakenham Mahon, 215–16
murder of Major Denis Mahon
and, 158–59
response by to MacHale's de-
fense, 194
Virginius emigration horror, 133
Tóibín, Colm, 314n
Toronto Globe, 133
townlands, 16–17, 27, 120,
145–46, 147. *See also* Doorty
townland; *specific townlands*
Treason Felony Act, 230–31
Treaty of Ghent, 37
Treaty of Limerick, 9
Trevelyan, Charles, 67, 73, 77–78,
82, 189, 322–23n
Twistleton, Edward, 296–98
Tye, Leo, 124

Ulster uprising of 1641, 3

United Service Club, 101
United States
emigration to, xi, 112–16, 125,
134–35, 309
famine relief sent from, 94
Irish political machine in, 39
potato blight in, 58–59
Ross Mahon's emigration plan
and, 107–8
Uprising of 1798, 22, 35

Vesey, Patrick, 227
Victoria, queen of England, 94,
100, 148
"they are a terrible people," 159
Virginius (ship), 113, 116, 126,
128–29, 132–33, 327n

Wakefield, Edward, 29, 34, 35,
85
Wallace, Sir John, 101
Washington, James, 135
Weld, Isaac, 41
Wellington, Duke of, 40, 101, 119,
159
Whiteboys, 30, 31, 39, 256
Whyte, Robert, 126–29
William of Orange (William III),
King of England, 8, 9
Williams, T. Desmond, 313n
Wilson, Thomas, 132
Wolfe Tone, Theobald, 21
Wood, Charles, 106
Woodham-Smith, Cecil, 315n
workhouses, 45, 62, 68, 69, 71,
78, 91–92, 104–5, 139, 151,
155, 210–12. *See also* County
Roscommon and Roscommon
Town
auxiliary for girls, 209–10
as principal engine for relief, 144,
145, 187, 188
Quarter Acre (or Gregory)
Clause and, 212

workhouses (*cont.*)
   rules and restrictions for the poor,
      92, 210–11
   "workhouse test," 210–11

Young, Arthur, 15, 16, 17–18,
   19–20, 29
Young Ireland, 47, 51, 83, 148,
   157, 205, 230

arrests for sedition, 219
Catholic and Protestant Repealers, 65, 75
famine-relief measures, 95
rising of 1848, 283–84, 287
use of violence and, 219

BOOKS BY PETER DUFFY

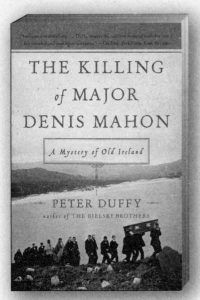

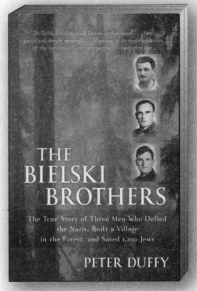

THE KILLING OF MAJOR DENIS MAHON
A Mystery of Old Ireland

ISBN 978-0-06-084051-8 (paperback)

Peter Duffy tells the story of Mahon's assassination and its connection to the cataclysm that would forever change Ireland and America. With full access to historical records, including Mahon's private papers, government documents, and extensive court and police files, Duffy tries to uncover the truth about Mahon's murder and the role he did—or did not—play in the sufferings of his tenants.

"A splendid example of the new writing of Irish history."
                                    —Pete Hamill

THE BIELSKI BROTHERS
The True Story of Three Men Who Defied the Nazis, Built a Village in the Forest, and Saved 1,200 Jews

ISBN 978-0-06-093553-5 (paperback)

In 1941, three brothers witnessed their parents and two other siblings being led away to their eventual murders. It was a grim scene that would, of course, be repeated endlessly throughout the war. Instead of running or giving in to despair, these brothers fought back, waging a guerrilla war of wits against the Nazis.

"Fast-paced and deeply moving . . . inspiring in its representation of the heroism of ordinary people."
                                    —*Washington Post*